The Death of Politics

The Death of Politics

FRANCE UNDER MITTERRAND

John Laughland

MICHAEL JOSEPH
LONDON

MICHAEL JOSEPH

Published by the Penguin Group
27 Wrights Lane, London w8 5tz
Viking Penguin Inc., 375 Hudson Street, New York, New York 10014, USA
Penguin Books Australia Ltd, Ringwood, Victoria, Australia
Penguin Books Canada Ltd, 10 Alcorn Avenue, Toronto, Ontario, Canada m4v 3b2
Penguin Books (NZ) Ltd, 182–190 Wairau Road, Auckland 10, New Zealand

Penguin Books Ltd, Registered Offices: Harmondsworth, Middlesex, England

First published in Great Britain 1994

Copyright © John Laughland 1994

Printed in England by Clays Ltd, St Ives plc

ISBN 0 7181 0028 x

All, all of a piece throughout:
Thy Chase had a Beast in View;
Thy Wars brought nothing about;
Thy Lovers were all untrue.
'Tis well an Old Age is out.
And time to begin a New.

– John Dryden (1631–1700)

In memory of Alexandra Tuttle

Contents

Acknowledgements

This book has a very censorious tone, but I love France. I have been especially touched by the extraordinary openness and warmth which I have encountered during four very happy years in France: it is, indeed, a mystery to me why the French (or the Parisians) are so often thought unfriendly. On the contrary, they are among the most civilised people in the world.

In particular, I have profited from my attachment to two magnificent institutions. One is Sciences-Po, the Institute of Political Science in Paris, where I have taught philosophy and politics since 1991, and where I have always felt very much at home. The other is the Angelina Club, an informal group of friends which meets every week to discuss politics, philosophy, economics and religion, or just to pass the afternoon. Its organiser, Bernard Cherlonneix, deserves the warmest praise and gratitude.

I am also very grateful to my editor, Alexander Stilwell, who suggested this book in the first place, and whose advice has been indispensable.

Introduction: The Wizard of Oz

François Mitterrand's career in politics spans over half a century. As President, he has outlasted all his Western colleagues, enjoying huge, almost unchecked power. He has never had any other career or interest than politics, and knows no other environment than the political world. He has been a candidate for election to the National Assembly ten times; he has fought four presidential elections; he stood once for the Senate, six times at Cantonal elections, and six times again at municipal elections. Elected to the presidency in 1981, he has served as French Head of State for longer than anyone since Napoleon III.

During this long political career Mitterrand has betrayed almost no ideological or political consistency whatever. He entered politics in 1942 at the age of twenty-six, when he worked for the Vichy government; he made contact with de Gaulle at the end of 1943 and offered his services to the Resistance; he was a minister in de Gaulle's provisional government after the war, and the first government of the Fourth Republic in 1946. He had ten other ministerial portfolios between 1946 and 1958, as the leader of a centre-right party, after which he spent twenty-three years as the leader of the left-wing opposition. While President, he has presided over hard-left, centre-left, free-market liberal, and centrist governments, and has ministers who have been Communist and Thatcherite. If General de Gaulle is the archetype of a hero, Mitterrand is the quintessence of a politician.[1]

When de Gaulle set up the Fifth Republic in 1958, his strong personal charisma, his frequent recourse to referenda, and his masterly and innovative use of television to communicate directly with the French people, provided a genuine sense of communion between the President and the electorate, which had seldom been seen before in French history. The General succeeded in invigorating the political life of the country, which, under the Third and Fourth Republics (1875–1958), resembled that of Italy after the

Second World War. Since Georges Pompidou and Valéry Giscard d'Estaing, however, the presidency has declined from the semi-divine status given to it by de Gaulle. Presidents have increasingly become mere politicians and mere managers of the economy. Their sense of attachment to the 'Republic' – which in French denotes not just the opposite of a kingdom, but that public space in which participatory democracy may flourish – has been weak. The practice of citizenship has declined with it, as the political world has ceased to offer real choices, and in direct proportion to the accretion of power to the President, which has reached its apogee under Mitterrand.

During Mitterrand's long reign, the presidency has not motivated the French, but paralysed them. Government and society are disorientated, and the public spirit is degraded. With a stalling economy, with educational and social security systems in disarray, and with a notoriously corrupt political class, Mitterrand's appeal has been soporific. In 1981, when elected to power, the Socialists had promised to 'change life': Mitterrand, however was already preparing to allow that 'change' to haemorrhage into stagnation. His personal slogan, 'The tranquil force', was an oxymoron whose intention was to soothe the French into believing that no hard choices would have to be made. Moreover, because all power resides in the Elysée Palace, the whole of France is encouraged to expect everything to come from the top, and so no one takes responsibility for anything.

While Mitterrand devoted his efforts to vain politicking, France drifted. During his fourteen years in office, French industry stood still. The rise in unemployment and poverty has been matched only by the multiplication of the favours and privileges accorded to Mitterrand's personal friends; he has preferred to govern through his private clan rather than through the public institutions of the state, and he pursues power for no other purpose than itself. If 'Thatcherism' denotes an invigorating economic creed and a style of government which has left a significant legacy, 'Mitterrandism' denotes opportunism, favouritism, corruption, and the substitution of illusions and talk for concrete action. If Margaret Thatcher's political personality was dynamic, determined and single-minded, Mitterrand, the candidate of the united Left, has effortlessly assumed the persona of an ageing monarch; 'cynical, calculating, regal in his manner and immensely vain'.[2]

Instead of creating any political institutions for posterity, Mitterrand has preferred to hollow out the old ones and pervert their logic. Instead of leading from the front, he has preferred to devote his energy to confusing and destroying his enemies. Instead of substantial decision-making, Mitterrand has preferred to evoke general moods or images about himself. His rhetoric, the political equivalent of lift music, is the key both to his personal success and to his policy failures. A Soviet-style *langue de bois*, it is strewn with slogans which are as meaningless as they are boring – 'the defence of our social achievements', 'Europe', 'the modern economy', 'France united', 'the fight against exclusion', 'the young'. He has a knack for bringing the discussion into an area where no discussion is possible.

Losing all relevance to reality, politics has become incomprehensible to the man in the street. But if 'democracy' involves the conservation of a public space in which genuine alternatives can be debated and genuine choices made, and if 'politics' connotes public commitment, civic virtue and responsible action, then Mitterrand has indeed presided over its death.

De Gaulle once famously asked in exasperation, 'How on earth does one govern a country which makes 265 kinds of cheese?' He did not mean to boast of France's culinary genius, but to bemoan her endemic tendency to fragmentation. France is a large, ethnically and culturally diverse country, and civil war has often disfigured her political life.

Centralism, *dirigisme*, and the building of large infrastructure networks have usually been the blunt instruments by which France's kings and presidents have sought to unify the state. The construction of canals under Colbert, Louis XIV's Minister of Finance, and the building of the TGV network under Mitterrand are different aspects of the same old French habit. When the Englishman Arthur Young travelled throughout France just before the Revolution, he was struck by the poverty of the population and the extremely high quality of the roads and bridges. Thus, ever since John Locke in the seventeenth century and Edmund Burke in the eighteenth, many British thinkers have associated France with absolutism.

The Revolution changed neither the perception, nor the substance of French political practice. Indeed, it probably aggravated it.

Instead of establishing a system of checks and balances against overweening executive power, as the American Founding Fathers had done, the French revolutionaries were more inspired by the positivist and unitarian doctrine of the 'general will'. Theorised by Rousseau, this supposedly democratic concept in fact encouraged abolutism, because it displaced the notion of an independent or transcendent source of justice in favour of the view that legislation should be the administration of the perceived immediate needs and interests of society.

Rousseau held that in a fully participatory democracy, positive law would inevitably conform to the public interest. He wrote, 'The sovereign, who is formed only of the individuals of which it is composed, cannot have any interest contrary to theirs. Consequently, the sovereign power has no need of a guarantee with respect to its subjects, because it is impossible for the body to wish to damage all its own members.'[3] Thus the revolutionaries implemented dictatorial and centralising measures with a ferocity of which even the kings of France would not have dreamed, such as abolishing the independence of the judiciary.[4] The Terror, in which thousands of people were summarily executed every month, was only the logical outcome of this.

Because of the confusion between law and administration, it has often been assumed that the more 'independent' the administrator, the wiser his decisions will be. To this day, enlightened despotism still gets a good press in France, and, as a result, there has been a reluctance to place political leaders under proper scrutiny. The belief also persists that for political power to be efficient it must be free from unwelcome interference by the public or parliament. Moreover, a common instinct has assumed that the simple transfer of political authority from the king to 'the people' meant that political power was so purified that it is inappropriate to call the motives of politicians into question. As one French critic remarks,

> Those things which disgust and outrage us in our modern politics are a direct result of our history. That is to say, of the history of a country where the first modern, strong and centralised state grew up. We have never since finished paying the price for this historical privilege ... Reason of State has been the unwritten rule for all politicians who have exercised

administrative and judicial powers over the last two centuries. Scores of thinkers have said it already – that France has never rid herself of the *Ancien Régime*, nor of an oligarchy founded on privileges and illegality.[5]

This has been aggravated by the curiously large role which philosophy has exerted on French politics during and after the Revolution. In preparation for it, France had turned massively towards an abstract philosophy of social and political order, which was all the more radical because it was nourished by a lack of widespread political experience on the part of nobles and bourgeois alike, itself a result of royal absolutism in the seventeenth century. Voltaire was to protest in vain that intellectuals were the worst rabble of them all, but France remains a country where philosophers enjoy an extraordinary role in public life, comparable perhaps to the didactic role in society once enjoyed by Catholic priests. Indeed, it has been argued that France retains the three old medieval social strata of those who command, those who pray (or think), and those who work.

Unlike Britain or America, therefore, French constitutionalists were more concerned to enunciate general and abstract principles than to think about the mechanics of government itself. Far from being 'a human contrivance to provide for human wants', in Edmund Burke's phrase,[6] they often thought of government and politics as the earthly manifestations of idealistic principles. To this day, French politics can have an abstract and theoretical air, which is often ungermane to more pragmatic British ears. As the Germans were to do so disastrously in the nineteenth and twentieth centuries, the French, 'deprived of true liberty, went straight to natural law; incapable of collective experience, without the means to feel the limitations of politics, they orientated themselves unconsciously towards the revolutionary utopia.'[7]

Moreover, the fatal conceit, shared by other countries, that society has one single common interest, and that it alone should dictate the laws of that society, has entrenched the view that 'individual interests' are of secondary importance. Rousseauist Republican theory assumes that citizens have a capacity for blending private interests with the public interest, or, rather, suppressing the former in favour of the latter. As a result, French political language still adheres to a simple and radical dichotomy between individual interests on the one hand, and general interest on the other. The former are always suspected of being a threat to the public good. It is hardly even necessary to specify its contents: it is usually sufficient for the competent authorities (whether political or administrative) to proclaim something to be the common good for it to be so.[8]

By contrast, the British and American political systems have individual interest as their driving force, for this is believed to be the only sure means by which to defend the common good. Rather than having a unitarian vision of society, they also assume that men will form into mutually hostile factions and interest groups. As Publius writes in the 10th Federalist paper,

> There are two methods of removing the causes of faction: the one, by destroying the liberty which is essential to its existence; the other by giving to every citizen the same opinions, the same passions, and the same interests.
>
> It could never be more truly said of the first remedy that it was worse than the disease. Liberty is to faction what air is to fire, an aliment without which it instantly expires. But it could not be less folly to abolish liberty, which is essential to animal life, because it imparts to fire its destructive agency . . .
>
> The regulation of these various and interfering interests forms the principal task of modern legislation, and involves the spirit of party and faction in the necessary and ordinary operations of the government . . . It is vain to say that enlightened statesmen will be able to adjust these clashing interests, and render them all subservient to the public good. Enlightened statesmen will not always be at the helm.[9]

Not only that: the British and American constitutions assume that bodies of men *must* form themselves into interest groups if the executive power is to be checked. Only if every administration's tenure was made to depend upon the support of a declared party could it be controlled. Edmund Burke wanted to see the essential and traditional role of the House of Commons – to keep the Crown and the administration in control by refusing to vote for the funds they wanted – to be strengthened by the creation of political parties, for he realised that only then could the tactics of the court cabal be defeated. Honest men, publicly committed to stand or fall together, could not be picked off one by one, by offers of place or office.

By contrast, French Jacobinism has traditionally been sceptical of political parties, as of all other secondary group interests. To this day, members of the French parliament (deputies) are not supposed to defend their constituent's particular interests, but rather to defend those of the entire nation. This scepticism has been aggravated by the fundamental French fear that too much conflict will lead to blood in the streets.

> It is indeed with reference to this criterion of unity, or more precisely to participation in the one single undertaking of unification, that our sovereigns, their ministers and our statesmen, are legendarily represented. The history of France tends to be presented as a constant struggle between two foci of contradictory forces, the beneficial forces of convergence, of *rassemblement* and of cohesion, and the wicked forces of dispersal, disintegration and dissociation. On the one hand, that which belongs to communal law and to the sovereignty of the state, everything which reduces opposites by integration and assimilation; on the other hand feudalisms, local particularities, the rivalries of interests, religious antagonisms.[10]

As such, the old invidious rupture has persisted in France between the Real Nation of ordinary people and the Legal Nation of the politico-administrative world in Paris. This gap has been the cause of France's multiple revolutions: a political class becomes increasingly distant from the real country, its structures and preoccupations rigid and narcissistic, until it is swept away or withers on the vine. In a country famous for its political turbulence, French citizens have very often been mere onlookers.

Perhaps it is a secret of Mitterrand's internal political success that, like de Gaulle, he has repeatedly made use of the theme of 'Unity' in his own propaganda. He is well known for his ferocious and hypocritical denunciation of the 'parties', 'factions', 'groups', 'clans', and 'bands' into whose hands France might supposedly fall. In 1965 and in 1988 he campaigned on the slogan of unity, the slogan in the latter campaign, *La France unie*, being intended to present him as the unifier of the country against the supposed factionalism of the Gaullists.

Throughout his career, and in defence of all possible decisions, the theme has returned: 'Everything tends to separate, but I want to try to bring everything together' (in justification of his building projects);[11] 'There cannot be a durable victory of one fraction of France against another ... it is essential with wisdom and with love to protect the unity of the nation';[12] 'It is not sane for one single party to govern. Other political families must take part in the government';[13] 'Maastricht is not the affair of one clan; it is an affair which touches all the French, its partisans as well as its adversaries. And it is of France that I am thinking.'[14] Anything which might disturb the rampant consensus, of that 'united France' whose real divisions have been redeemed by the illusions which the President conjurs up, must be banished. He exalts unity, rejects diversity, conflict, and fears all the unforeseen events which are normal in any institutional process.[15]

De Gaulle felt it imperative to help the French overcome their history: but he feared that they could never quite come up to what France demanded of them, and therefore invented the myth of a courageous France which had resisted the Germans. Whatever the validity of the myth, it was a powerful one which succeeded in giving French politics a coherence it lacked before and since. Unlike de Gaulle, Mitterrand was never to give the French a credible myth to underpin his own use of similar language.

Whereas de Gaulle showed commitment *par excellence* to certain concrete things in politics by speaking and acting, the fascination Mitterrand elicits is explained by the fact that everyone can find in him what they wish.[16] He decides only when the course of things have become irreversible. On countless matters – education, tax, social policy, municipal policy – successive Mitterrand governments have floated, torn themselves apart, contradicted themselves, betrayed their private and public ulterior motives, while the President has looked on, making little comments here and there, as if nothing in the whole charade concerned him. As one of his critics puts it, 'François Mitterrand is a consummate politician who is afraid of true politics because, if he ever engaged in it, he would be shown up not to have any. Worse, he cannot conceive of anyone else having any either.'[17]

The victory of the Socialists in 1981 was presented at the time as a serious attempt to give France a hope and a myth – as if it were a good thing that politics is often more about dreams than about realities. But by 1983, the pretence that the government would bring about a decisive break with capitalism had been abandoned. Indeed, the 'grand project' now became the harnessing of capitalist and technological forces for the greater modernisation of France. During the interregnum of 1986–8, when the right-wing was in power, Mitterrand evoked the myth of France's 'social achievements', a dubious claim considering that he was to preside over an explosion in unemployment and poverty. He succeeded in portraying the Socialists as the party of morality, and further distracted attention from internal political failure by concentrating on the new theme which was to preoccupy him throughout his second term, 'Europe'.

Moreover, personality has gradually assumed greater and greater importance in politics, for Mitterrand's power has become an end in itself. He has shown little care or respect for the judiciary, for the Parliament, or even for the Socialist Party. Through his network of friends, which plunges its roots deep into France, it is the House of Mitterrand which has governed France. Nowhere else in the democratic world has there been so much contamination and infection of the body politic with the private passions and humours of its head.

Indeed, perhaps the most striking thing about his 'image' is that it is so obviously false. His faithful acolyte and long-time adviser, Jacques Attali, describes him thus,

> What shall I say of him? If I had not thought he would be a statesman, I would not have accompanied him. If I had not admired his culture, his memory, his sense for the essential, his hatred of modernity and of filthy lucre, his passion for public service, I would not have put up with any of the disillusions which these last ten years have brought in other respects.
>
> His hallmark can be summarised in one word: he is above all a provincial. He likes the secrets of the provinces, the diversity of the countryside, different varieties of trees, evenings spent reading or telling stories, a soup for dinner, simple dishes like sauerkraut or sea-food, well-bound books, first

editions, the strength of traditions, the long course of genera-
tions, the solidity of friendships, money which one inherits,
the discreet exercise of power, the modesty of ambitions.

In Paris he hates the rush, the vanity of adventures, the
superficiality of relationships, money for which one works,
the power of offices, careers which are too conventional, lives
which are too public. The only things he likes in Paris are the
things which provincial people like: having dinner with actors,
chatting with booksellers, going to the airport to depart on a
long trip and see the world . . . He hates earning money, and
does not like spending it either, except on things which last –
old books, old farms, a lake, clothes which last.[18]

This retiring image fits ill with a man who has devoted fifty
years to the dogged pursuit of power; who lives and breathes
the political atmosphere of the capital; who has devoted his
presidency to the construction of hyper-modernist buildings; whose
presidential term has been notable for an explosion in financial
corruption, notably in the Socialist Party; and whose fascination
for the rich and famous is notorious. Inasmuch as his 'literary'
or 'intellectual' image is true, it is little more than a fig-leaf for
the fact that, unlike de Gaulle, Pompidou or Giscard, Mitterrand is
only an intellectual: unlike them, he has no other interest or
vocation than politics.

But the references to Catholicism, old books, the hatred of
money, the unchangeability of the countryside, and the importance
of lasting friendship are all deeply conservative, or even reactionary
qualities. Many hagiographers write of his keen sense of the past,[19]
and Attali and others dwell at length on his curious obsession with
death. Indeed, with the passage of time, Mitterrand's self-cultivated
image has become increasingly somnolent and paternalistic: his
nickname for years was simply *'Dieu'*, God.

In an important television interview in late 1993, on the eve of
his seventy-seventh birthday, the interviewer began – no doubt on
the President's own personal suggestion – by saying that 'many
French people now regard you as the father of the nation'.[20]
France, it was implied, could only benefit from such selfless dona-
tion of his age and experienced person, as if this charade were
anything else than an attempt to reaffirm his political weight after

the Socialists' crushing defeat, by grabbing for himself the role of constitutional monarch. The man who had spent his whole life attacking de Gaulle, and whose commitment to the Resistance came only after a period working for the Vichy government, finished his political career by resembling no one so much as de Gaulle's principal rival, the aged Marshal Pétain, who also played to perfection the entirely fictitious role of all-knowing, stable guardian of France in difficult circumstances. No wonder some say that there is a whiff of Vichy in the air.[21]

Mitterrand's final years were marked by an obsession with the 'European' project. Few projects could have better symbolised the increasing distance between the political projects cooked up in the rarefied political world of Paris and the real life of the French nation. As La Rochefoucauld said of the Cardinal of Retz, 'He distanced himself from the world which distanced itself from him.'[22]

It is within the context of this project that this book is written. For the last two hundred years or so, people have been saying that the British constitution is archaic and that it ought to be reformed along European, usually French lines. Usually such views go hand in hand with a desire for more administrative government, and a dislike for the apparent anarchy of parliamentarianism and democracy. Now that Britain faces the prospect of being governed by a French or Franco-German style European government, it is time to crawl inside the political system of France to see whether the grass is really so much greener on the other side of the Channel. As Edmund Burke wrote to the Gentleman in Paris in 1790,

> Formerly your affairs were your own concern only. We felt for them, as men; but we kept aloof from them, because we are not citizens of France. But when we see the model held up to ourselves, we must feel as Englishmen, and feeling, we must provide as Englishmen. Your affairs, in spite of us, are made a part of our interest.[23]

1. The Amazing
Technocratic Turncoat

I have often found it to be true that to manage a mistake well
is better than certain kinds of success. The game of chess
teaches us this, for its art consists in exploiting one's mistakes
to one's own advantage: they throw your opponent into
greater confusion than they lead you astray. In other words, I
believe in the virtues of improvisation, provided that one
realizes that improvisation is a long exercise.

François Mitterrand[1]

That monument to conceit and sycophancy, Jacques Attali's memoirs, begins with a summary of the author's experiences at Mitterrand's side as his special adviser from 1981–6. In tones reminiscent
of the Book of Genesis, he intones, 'Everything begins in May
1981 with a hope, an ambiguity, a man.'[2] The 'hope' is Socialism.
After a breezy eight-line survey of 2,000 years of political philosophy, Attali defines the political creed to which he adheres, in the
most vapid terms, as 'justice, liberty and tolerance'. Such banalities
hardly constitute a programme for government, and they are not
obviously Socialist. The 'ambiguity' is that he is a Socialist and that
Eastern Europe is under a dictatorship which also calls itself
Socialist: this is dealt with in five lines.

It need hardly be said who the 'man' is. Indeed, Mitterrand is
not actually mentioned by name. Rather, his semi-divine presence
inhabits the chapter in the form of a disembodied 'He': nearly
three pages are devoted to him. There can be few more striking
illustrations of the relative importance to Mitterrand of ideology
and personal power than this introduction by his most faithful
acolyte.

The victory of 1981 was that of a man and not that of an
ideology or a project, even if the arrival to power of the first left-

wing President in the history of the Fifth Republic was greeted
with much euphoria on the Left and much foreboding on the
Right. Both wings of the political spectrum were to be proved
wrong in their own way. For far from fulfilling their grandiose
promises to 'change life' in 1981, the Socialist Party under Mitterrand became the chief culprit for France's somnolent conservatism
throughout the 1980s.

It is indeed a paradox of French politics that it assumes a very
ideological mantle, whereas in fact it is almost entirely about
personalities. No doubt the flowering of political ideology, and
the role of 'intellectuals' in politics, for which France is famous,
is in direct proportion to the degree of irresponsibility of the
purveyors of ideology. While this is an old French tradition – the
lively but unaccountable parliamentary regimes of the Third and
Fourth Republics were positive incubators for political extremism
– the effect of the Fifth Republic has been mainly to squash all
other contenders for power, and the result is ideological
stagnancy.

Indeed, if there is one consistent theme in Mitterrand's own
political career (and by extension, in that of the Socialist Party he
created), it is that of ideological opportunism. During the Fourth
Republic, when he was a minister eleven times, in coalitions of
all imaginable political hues, he belonged to a centrist political
party of his own creation. In the 1970s, he was the founder of
the radical left-wing union between the Socialists and the Communists. In 1983, he was the instigator of the definitive abandonment
of the policies of that union, and the chief protagonist of a drive
for economic and technological modernization. The twilight years
of his presidency were marked by the near-total destruction of
the Socialist Party, and with it, of the whole French Left.

Thus, whereas hardly a decade ago, the French Socialist Party
was lecturing its European counterparts, who had all long since
followed the example of the German Social Democrats' conversion
to the market, about the need for a 'definitive break with capitalism'
and for 'self-managed Socialism', the French Socialist Party is now
widely regarded as reactionary and capitalist by its Socialist brethren. Within a decade, the party has gone from the extreme left of
the International Socialist to its extreme right. While French Socialism may not have the same distinguished ideological pedigree as

that of other countries,[3] in no other comparable country would the conversion of a major political party be explicable solely in terms of the career, personality and choices of one man.

The personalization of politics is reflected in the traditional weakness of French political parties, which lack the history, cohesion and established ethic of the great British parties. They typically have a weak capacity for mobilizing the electorate. Modern French parties may now have more developed structures than in the past, but the rate of party membership and activism remains chronically low. Such weakly organized parties tend to follow perceived trends in the electorate, failing to give leadership or to generate political ideas. This explains why the French have not lost their proclivity to *descendre dans la rue*.[4] Indeed, with the single exception of the Communist Party, all French parties are recent creations. The Socialist Party was founded by François Mitterrand in 1971. The present Gaullist party, the RPR (Rassemblement pour la République) was founded by Jacques Chirac in 1976 after he resigned from Giscard's government, in which he had been Prime Minister.[5] Giscard d'Estaing's Union pour la Démocratie Française (UDF) was founded in 1978, and its name is taken from a book by Giscard, *Démocratie Française*, published in 1976. It is thus very much Giscard's private party, which explains why its fortunes wax and wane in direct proportion to those of its leader.

French political parties on both Left and Right are thus ephemeral organizations, designed mainly to advance the political career of their founder. This personalization is due to the enormous power which the Fifth Republic puts into the hands of one man. The focal point of the whole system is the leader, who fashions the party to suit himself, and thus it is less the party which selects its members and its militants, than the strong man at local or national level who recruits his men, places them and destroys or promotes them. Activists are less important than the entourages of the powerful, and the party attracts people less by the ideas which it supposedly represents, than by the interests which it can protect and guarantee. Party structures are thus little more than a system of old-boy networks.[6]

This distinguishes French from British political parties. For the latter, the leader is the tool they use to win elections, and who can be unceremoniously dumped if he (or she!) fails to deliver. That this is not so in France is clear from the extraordinary longevity of French political leaders, of which Mitterrand is only the most striking example. Jacques Chirac has already been Prime Minister twice (1974–6; 1986–8); he still entertains ambitions of becoming President on his third try in 1995. Valéry Giscard d'Estaing was the party leader of the Independent Republicans in 1962, a grouping he created after the overwhelming victory of General de Gaulle's UNR in the general election that year. He was Finance Minister before becoming President, and still thinks that he can be elected President again in 1995, having been President once already (1974–81). Indeed, it is amusing to find old copies from the 1970s of a standard paperback textbook on *Political Parties in France Today* which has been updated and reissued five times since it was first published in 1973. On the front cover, there are the four familiar faces, unchanged except for their haircuts, of Chirac, Giscard, Mitterrand and Georges Marchais![7]

The Socialist Party is thus typical for France. While it may once have been the largest party in France, it was always significantly weaker even than the Labour Party of Britain or the German Social Democratic Party. It has never had more than 200,000 members, even after the Left's victory in 1981. When there are 8.5 million Socialist voters (as there were in the legislative elections in 1986), this makes forty-two voters per member, a ratio which is far lower than that of comparable European Socialist parties.[8] Moreover, its activists are overwhelmingly not of working-class background or profession. In 1951, only 33 per cent were working-class; by 1973 that proportion had fallen to under 19 per cent. Instead, the dominant professions are executives and teachers, the latter achieving almost caricature status in the 1981 parliament, given their unusually strong representation then. This weakness is due above all to the absence of links between the Socialist Party and civil society. Unlike the majority of other European Socialist parties, the PS does not have any direct links with the unions, since these latter, with the exception of the Communist ones, traditionally reject all alliances with political parties.[9]

On the contrary, the French Socialist Party is the party of a candidate for the presidential election. Fashioned by the logic of the Fifth Republic, it was constructed around François Mitterrand, the Socialist candidate for the Elysée. With the straitjacket of a majoritarian voting system and the predominance of the presidential system, the Fifth Republic transformed the PS into a large electoral formation. But the same institutional mechanism, a sort of elective monarchy, also progressively emptied the party of its political substance during the Mitterrand years.[10]

Mitterrand founded the Socialist Party at the seminal congress in Epinay in 1971. He managed to combine various smaller social-democratic groups with the Section Française de l'International Ouvrier, the French Section of the Workers' International which had been led by Guy Mollet from 1946 to 1969.[11] Indeed, it is partly because of the party's heteroclite origins that, to this day, it contains within it a series of more or less mutually antagonistic 'currents' ('*courants*') grouped around prominent personalities in the party – Fabius, Rocard, Jospin, Poperen, Mauroy, and so on. These currents have historic sources: Mauroy and Chevenement were in the SFIO, Rocard was from the hard-left Parti Socialiste Unifié, while Mitterrand himself came from the centrist Union Démocratique et Socialiste de la Résistance (UDSR). Being in the centre, Mitterrand's current was able to play the other two main ones off against one another.

In 1958, the SFIO had been favourable to the return to power of General de Gaulle. Faced with a choice between an alliance with the Communists and with the Right, it preferred to opt for the latter. Nonetheless, even though declaring itself to be in the 'avant-garde of the Fifth Republic' in 1959, it soon slipped into opposition. This began a long period of decline, and Mitterrand realized that only a union with the Communists could provide him with the necessary number of left-wing votes to bring him to the Elysée. He thus set about trying to form the union of the Left. The Christian Democratic Mouvement Républicain Populaire was initially hostile to the successive attempts at union with the Communists which took place from 1963 onwards. However, the turning point came in 1965 when Mitterrand challenged the apparently immovable General de Gaulle for the presidency, forcing him unexpectedly through to a second round, and winning a very respectable 45 per cent of the vote. His candidature in 1965, which was supported by the Communist Party and by the PSU, brought the Christian Democrats closer.

This election campaign, the first in French politics to have been conducted largely through the medium of television, did wonders for Mitterrand's standing, for until then he had had a reputation as an opportunistic and ambitious man – in short, as the ultimate schemer and political wheeler-dealer in the scheming and wheeler-dealing Fourth Republic. Whether through carelessness or genuine weakness, Mitterrand had contributed to the scandalmongering which handicapped him. The ridiculous Observatory affair, when he faked a gun attack on himself,[12] had made him unpopular with the more intellectual elements of the French Left. He was not lightly forgiven for having been a member of eleven ministries during the Fourth Republic, when as the leader of a small centrist formation, he had made himself indispensable to nearly all coalitions. He failed to convince many people that he actually had a political programme.[13] Indeed, he was regarded with such suspicion by large sections of the new left-wing anti-Gaullist and anti-colonialist current which was in the process of organizing itself after 1958, that when in 1959, before the Observatory affair, he tried to join a small breakaway party, the Parti Socialiste Autonome, they simply refused to let him in.

Like the blandly named Convention des Institutions Républicaines, which he was later to form, his UDSR party was a small formation which had neither history nor culture nor specific traditions. Neither party was ostensibly Socialist: they were both centre, even centre-right. (The future President of the Ivory Coast, Felix Houphouet-Boigny, who spent many years in the 1940s as a French deputy, was later to remark that the UDSR was the only place where he had ever seen white men eating one other.) Indeed, Mitterrand could have joined the Christian-Democratic MRP. According to one of his colleagues within the UDSR at the time, the only reason why he set that party up instead of joining the MRP was that 'he knew straight away that he could become its leader'.[14]

The 1965 campaign, however, changed his image substantially. The television campaign, and the novelty of 'the united Left' made him appear to be the only politician capable of dislodging the General. Here, indeed, was the secret of his success: the most famous opponent of the institutions of the Fifth Republic, Mitterrand had been the first to understand the absolute importance of using the very mechanisms he attacked in order to win power. He understood what the other leaders of the SFIO were never to grasp, that the key to power lay in the Elysée and that in order to get it, it was imperative to exploit the bipolarization of the electoral map. In this sense, he represented what in the contemporary Labour Party in Britain is known as a 'modernizer', in that he laid great emphasis on the paramount need to gain power. For him, the traditional distinction between the conquering and the exercise of power made no sense: a political movement had government as its principal objective. His own political past under the Fourth Republic bore ample testimony to this fundamental choice.[15]

In concrete terms, it was the necessity of rallying the whole Left around one candidate in the second round of voting that led Mitterrand to seek the union of the Left, and therefore all his efforts to unite the Left were devoted to ensuring that he would be that candidate.[16] As he was subsequently to declare in his autobiography, *Ma part de vérité*, 'Ever since 1962, that is to say ever since it was decided to elect the President by universal suffrage, I knew that I would be a candidate.'[17] Having founded the moderate Federation of the Democratic and Socialist Left (FGDS) on 9 December 1965, he organized electoral pacts with the Communists and the hard-left Parti Socialiste Autonome in 1966 and 1967. In February 1968, the Federation published a common programme with the Communists. This was the first text of its kind, and it opened the way for the united Left to take power. The Pompidou government was therefore entirely right to recognize the importance of the declaration by attacking it virulently.[18]

The events of 1968 put paid to these apparently encouraging developments, not least because of the behaviour of the Communists. Everyone was caught off guard by the student revolt – an indication of how out of touch all political parties usually are with the political realities of France – but the Communists' position was especially ludicrous. In a manner which perfectly epitomized that party's love–hate relationship with the Gaullists, it supported the government against the students, who were mainly under Trotskyite influence. The Stalinist French Communists rightly judged that the students' actions threatened their monopoly on revolution. But because the moderate left, including Mitterrand, supported the students, hoping that this would be their chance to unseat de Gaulle, the tentative union of the Left blew apart. The ensuing elections in June 1968 all but wiped out Mitterrand's FGDS, and

twenty years later, it was clear that Mitterrand still resented 1968 as
the major lost opportunity of his long struggle for power.[19] As so
often before and since, however, he was able to wriggle out of the
crisis. In the 1969 presidential elections which followed de Gaulle's
unexpected resignation, the SFIO candidate, Gaston Deferre, received a humiliating 5 per cent of the vote. While this destroyed
any possibility of the Left coming to power in the near future, it
also consolidated Mitterrand's personal position as the only politician capable of leading them to that eventual victory.

His determination to gain power required a two-pronged action:
the creation of a large and unified Socialist Party to counterbalance
the weight of the Communists, which he achieved at Epinay in
1971, followed a year later by a policy agreement with the Communists. The Communists were then the more powerful, having won
20 per cent of the vote in the 1968 legislative elections, against 17
per cent for the non-Communists left. Indeed, just as he had done
throughout the Fourth Republic, Mitterrand was able to make
himself indispensable even though his 'current' of support within
the Socialist Party was relatively small (16 per cent of the total
votes in the party). He did this by allying his group, the Convention
des Institutions Républicaines, with both the right and extreme left
wings of the party. His ability simultaneously to agree with people
of opposite political orientations was also to serve him in good
stead throughout his career as President.

Thus, Mitterrand differed from his predecessors, Guy Mollet
and, earlier, Jean Jaurès, in two ways. Unlike him, they had
preferred ideological purism to the grubby pursuit of power; they
also had an almost carnal attachment to their party. By contrast,
Mitterrand was not primarily a party man. Indeed, his manner
towards his party colleagues already bore the traces of that regal
hauteur for which he was to be known as President. He addressed
everybody as 'vous', and, as First Secretary, demanded that they do
the same to him. One historian remarks that,

> The apparent egalitarianism of relationships within the Social-
> ist Party never suited him. He entered the Socialist Party with
> the sole intention of becoming its leader, and in order to use it
> as an instrument for his own ends ... Little concerned with
> questions of doctrine, he hardly took any interest in the

congress discussions in this area. The party whose activists were the instrument for social transformation and the creation of the society of the future, was for him essentially an instrument for taking and exercising power, and he never made any bones about the fact.[20]

A common text for discussion with the Communist Party was published, called *Changer la vie*, and the common programme of the Left was published on 27 June 1972. The 'Epinay choice' has thus passed into French left-wing folklore as the seminal moment when the PS made a decisive lurch to the left by its alliance with the Communists, a step to which Guy Mollet had always been opposed. It was thus the opposite of Bad Godesberg, the conference of the German Social Democratic Party in 1959 which led to that party's acceptance of the market economy. Within two years, Mitterrand was once again the undisputed candidate of the Left, when he lost the 1974 presidential election to Giscard by a slender 1 per cent. The formal union with the Communists broke up in 1977, on the initiative of the Communists. It was subsequently to be re-established, on Mitterrand's initiative, four years later, when he gave the Communists four seats in the first Mauroy government.

In the 1970s and early 1980s, Mitterrand's desire to play to the extreme-left gallery led him to make a series of ludicrous declarations. The most grotesque of these were the attacks against Georges Pompidou, Valéry Giscard d'Estaing and Raymond Barre, in which he tried to equate them with nineteenth-century exploitation. In 1978, he thundered,

> How many years of fighting did it take before children under the age of 10 stopped working 14 hours a day? You know how long we had to fight before children had the right to education! How long we had to fight before a woman expecting a baby had the right to take three days off work? Yes, there is a class struggle, organised by the class which has exercised its dictatorship, the moneyed bourgeoisie![21]

It is impossible to take such delirious rantings seriously. Child labour or lack of maternity leave were far from being current issues then: Mitterrand was just evoking a mood. If the strategy worked in electoral terms, it was to lead to brutal and sudden disillusionment

among those who had believed that Mitterrand's Left would hail
some sort of change in French political life. The Socialists' political
plans had evolved over a very long period in opposition and this
was visible in the ideological baggage they were carrying with them
in 1981. Their victory then forced them to translate into actions
that which had only ever been a programme for opposition.

Most of this talk was pure sham. Mitterrand knew full well that
it was imperative for him to win the party from the left by
hardening his political language. But such virulently Marxist ideological declarations show that he was prepared to say more or less
anything to satisfy the political pressures of the moment, no doubt
believing (as his accusers under the Fourth Republic had always
maintained) that the mere announcement of a political programme
involved no obligation whatever. Curiously, he never really convinced anybody. Ten years on, the consensus was that he was
making it all up. A typical view is that, 'Mitterrand never truly
believed in the mission or the vocation of a working class charged
with erecting a classless society.'[22] Another historian comments on
the congress at Metz in April 1979, when there was one of many
showdowns with Mitterrand's great rival, the more moderate Michel
Rocard, 'Did Mitterrand really believe in his own speech at Metz
about the need for a "rupture with capitalism"? Probably not.'[23]
Even a large part of the electorate did not believe in the announced
programme of mass nationalisations.[24] Moreover, Mitterrand was
already back-pedalling on the hard-left programme in 1981 during
the presidential campaign, thus paving the way for the abandonment
of that programme after the Mauroy government's first eighteen
disastrous months in power. Indeed, the very slogan which brought
him to power then, 'The tranquil force' – significantly, a reference
to the personality of Mitterrand himself – was intended precisely to
show that no decisive breach with the previous order was intended.
As if in compensation for the promise to 'change life', the message
was a soothing and reassuring one. As one commentator has
remarked, 'Mitterrand is . . . an actor who believes that political
programmes never represent a commitment; that one pledge can
chase away another; that one can ally oneself simultaneously to
Chevenement and to Mauroy, to Brezhnev and to Reagan, to the
hawks and to the doves. Mitterrand believes that it is sufficient to
talk in order to convince, and to make people dream in order to

win.'[25] In the words of another, 'Mitterrand does not use a theory or a method. He does not pursue a project. He foments a belief in order to bring himself to power: but a belief depends neither on consistency nor on logic.'[26]

His relationship to Communism is especially revealing in this respect. For if Mitterrand has one striking achievement in internal political terms, it is that he has effectively reduced the once-powerful French Communist Party to political irrelevance, even though he seemed throughout the 1970s to be courting their support. At the legislative elections in the spring of 1993, they received a meagre 8 per cent, a far cry from the 1950s and 1960s when there was serious worry that France could easily elect a Communist President. The way he did this and his motives for doing it are some of the most revealing things about Mitterrand's political psychology.

His appointment of four Communist ministers to the first Mauroy government in 1981 shocked the world, since it came at the height of the Cold War, only a couple of years after the Soviet invasion of Afghanistan. It seemed to confirm long-standing fears that France was a political loose cannon in the Western camp. This fear was not unjustified: it is astonishing to reflect on the extremist nature of French politics. The French Communist Party at the time was not only the Communist Party with a strong representation in a Western government, it was also resolutely Stalinist. Since then, however, Mitterrand has enjoyed something of a reputation as an anti-Communist. This is in spite of having constantly consorted with convinced Communists of both Trotskyite and Stalinist persuasions, and despite the fact that the Socialist governments of 1988–93 survived successive opposition no-confidence motions only with the resolute support of the parliamentary Communist Party. In 1981, he tried to explain to George Bush, then Vice-President of the USA, that his desire to have Communists in the government was a purely political tactic, and not evidence of any real ideological affinity.

> Belonging to the Socialist Party has never signified for me a support for Marxism. It is merely the means by which the Left can achieve power, and also the means of bringing Communism down to its proper level ... To have the Communists in the government makes them lose their originality, because they are associated with all the Socialists' decisions. They

ought therefore to be less and less able to obtain any votes
other than those of true Communists.[27]

Bush apparently went away very impressed with this conversation:
it was, of course, a classic Mitterrand double-act to soothe the
Americans while wooing the pro-Moscow Communists. But it is
important to grasp what it reveals about Mitterrand's attitudes to
Communism. What worried Mitterrand was that he and the Communists *were hunting on the same electoral territory*. This had been confirmed at the Socialist Party congress in Metz in 1979, when
Mitterrand had a decisive disagreement with Michel Rocard. Then,
Rocard was convinced that the Socialists had to take up an attitude
of ideological opposition to the Communists in order to win the
confidence of the electorate and thereby to gain power. But, in the
words of one historian, 'The First Secretary (Mitterrand), on the
contrary, thought that *the Socialist Party had to situate itself on the same
political terrain, propagating the same illusions as the Communist Party*, in
order to marginalize it and thus to open up the path to victory.'[28]
In other words, for Mitterrand, the real problem about Communism
was not that it is totalitarian, but that it represented an electoral
threat to him. Only the propagation of similar illusions would
enable him to overcome that threat.

Mitterrand's long background of intellectual prevarication helps to
explain the ideological roller-coaster ride on which he took France
during the 1980s. His economic policies began with the hard-left
socialism of Pierre Mauroy in 1981, and finished with the virtuous
monetarism of Pierre Bérégovoy in 1992. They varied from protec-
tionism and nationalization in 1981, to support for Europe and the
'single market' five years later; from a policy designed to please the
Socialist and Communist parties, to one whose main praise seemed
to come from the *Financial Times*. By 1988, he was campaigning for
re-election with a *Letter to all the French* which did not even propose
a return to Socialist ideology after the privatizations and other free-
market reforms undertaken by the right-wing cohabitation government of 1986–8.

In the Mauroy government of 1981, and in the '110 propositions
for France' made by Mitterrand during his electoral campaign, the
policies had been close to those defended by the union of the
Socialists and the Communists. The theme was 'a clean break with

capitalism'. A dominant role was reserved for the state, the economy was to be planned, industry and banking were nationalized, for they were considered 'an essential instrument for redressing the country'. The Finance Minister, Jacques Delors, and his supporters thought a 51 per cent stake by the state would be sufficient: Mitterrand insisted that it be 100 per cent. France alone was to make her way out of recession by relaunching demand. Mitterrand's first government increased the minimum wage in order to relaunch consumption. He promised that unemployment would not increase above 2 million, and in a splendid piece of back-to-front socialist engineering, reduced the working week to thirty-nine hours: only Socialists, who have a Chinese model of the economy in their heads, and for whom the size of the economic cake is fixed, could have dreamed up such a counterproductive plan. A tax on 'large fortunes' was introduced. Retirement was introduced at sixty.

Between 11 and 15 May 1981, money flowed out of France at the rate of $3 billion (thousand million) a day; between the 16th and 18th between $700 million and $1 billion. And yet, as the newly installed President-king descended the Champs-Élysées in his limousine on 21 May 1981, with the new Prime Minister at his side, he turned to Mauroy and declared sovereignly, 'One does not devalue on a day like today.'[29] The franc was eventually devalued in October 1981, when things were already looking so grim that even Jacques Delors demanded a 'pause' in the pace of reform. Unemployment had risen to 1,849,000, and was increasing at the rate of 60,000 per month: 18 per cent of young people under twenty-five were out of work.[30]

By June 1982 another policy had to be introduced. Salaries and prices were frozen by government fiat. The franc was devalued by another 10 per cent against the Deutschmark. Pierre Mauroy had to announce these draconian reforms to stunned trades unionists at their conference in his home town of Lille. The Social Security Minister, Pierre Bérégovoy, had to cut his department's spending by 10 billion francs, which he did by taking 300,000 people off unemployment benefit. Thus, the number of people out of work who were not entitled to benefits rose from 29 per cent in December 1982 to 41 per cent at the end of October 1984.[31] By September 1982, the trade deficit had reached 11 billion francs a month, in October it was 7 billion, in November 7 billion, 6 billion in Decem-

ber, and 10 billion in January 1983. The franc came under repeated
attack on the foreign exchanges. The reserves of the Bank of
France were being depleted at the rate of about 9 billion francs a
month. $500 million were lost in the first week of September.[32]
France started to borrow heavily, and soon became the biggest
borrower on international markets. Pressure mounted on Mitterrand
– exerted by Jean-Pierre Chevènement, Pierre Bérégovoy, Michel
Rocard and Laurent Fabius among others – to take the franc out of
the Exchange Rate Mechanism.[33] Meanwhile, it was essential to
deceive the Germans into thinking that floating was possible in
order to ensure that the final decision simply to devalue was
feasible.[34]

The way Mitterrand dealt with this essential issue reveals his
indecisiveness. For weeks, he refused to come to a public decision,
faced as he was with contradictory evidence from his advisers and
ministers. Indeed, for about a fortnight, he was tempted to leave
the ERM.[35] As his indecision became more and more unbearable,
all that Mitterrand could say to his frantic ministers was, 'People
say I am hesitating. No, I am reflecting. France will be grateful to
me for that.'[36] But in addition to the hesitation over this, there was
also his indecision over whether to keep Mauroy or to appoint
Delors as Prime Minister. At one point he was hesitating between
Delors and Bérégovoy, having decided to get rid of Mauroy.[37] He
even told Mauroy that he was to be sacked, when he finally decided
in favour of Delors. But Delors insisted that he be given the
Finance Ministry as well as Matignon, for he knew that this was in
fact the most important ministry in France. In a scene of comic
grotesqueness, Mitterrand spent an afternoon lifting up various
telephones, changing his mind with every phone call, as Henry
Kissinger, who happened to be in Paris that day, walked in and out
of people's offices at the Elysée. Finally, Mitterrand decided in a
matter of hours to stick with Mauroy and the ERM after all.[38]
Thus – almost by chance – was Mitterrand's commitment to the
European project entrenched.

An austerity plan was introduced, and the franc was devalued for
a third time. From this point onwards, his political language
changed completely. Mitterrand started to emphasize that an overall
balance had to be maintained in the economy. His message became
even Thatcherite: 'One cannot spend more than one earns.' He

even addressed the CNPF (the French equivalent of the CBI) about the problem of 'excessive' social and fiscal charges on industry.[39] The state had to stop financing lame-duck industries, and the free market had to be embraced.

No one should underestimate the momentousness of this apparent Socialist conversion to the free market. Most senior Socialist policy-makers (and commentators) were former Marxists, many of them from the wilder shores of Trotskyism, and the membership list of the Socialist *haute société* reads like a roll-call from the class of 1968.[40] Many of them refused to accept that Communism inevitably meant concentration camps until the left-wing intellectual, André Glucksmann, told them it was politically correct so to do in 1986. Jacques Attali, the President's long-time special adviser, believed in Marxist economics and described his own desire to see monetary union in Europe as the wish to see a 'Euro-rouble'.[41]

Indeed, no one should underestimate the general hostility to free-market economics within the French political class as a whole.[42] One explanation for this curious anomaly is that France has never quite fully entered the modern age, despite her Revolution. She is the only country in Europe not to have accepted the Scottish Enlightenment, the 'birth certificate of modernity'.[43] Adam Smith's doctrine of the 'invisible hand' has never really caught on in France, and the pursuit of self-interest and service to the community are often thought to be incompatible. Similarly, the French word *libéral* has none of the connotations of easy tolerance and mutual fairness which attaches to its English equivalent: it merely indicates an adherence to free-market economics, and is frequently used by opponents with the prefix *'ultra'*, as if those striving to release people's lives from bureaucratic control were the proponents of some pitiless dogma.

This hostility to free trade unites elements on the Right and the Left, as the hysterical French reaction to the GATT talks during 1991–3 demonstrated. *Le Monde* has no compunctions about publishing inflammatory articles entitled 'The conspiracy of international commerce',[44] or 'The Gatt must die'.[45] France's only Nobel Prizewinner in economics, Maurice Allais, is known for his hysterical railings against 'the intolerable American diktat' and the GATT accord in general.[46] Even the supposedly right-wing Prime Minister Édouard Balladur once declared that, 'The market is the law of the

jungle, the law of nature. Civilization is the fight against nature.'[47]
When the Blair House accord was signed at the end of 1992,
numerous politicians, economists and businessmen proposed the
creation of 'great geographical zones of delimited and protected
commercial blocs'.[48] Most extraordinary of all was a report published in 1993 by the CNPF, which concluded that the protection-
ism of the 1930s, which most people think of as one of the factors
leading to the outbreak of the Second World War, 'brought about
an increase in growth within a framework of a managed
economy'![49]

Indeed, Mitterrand's own speeches and writings throughout the
1970s and early 1980s were notable for their virulent anti-capitalism:
'French socialism from 1947 to 1965 has collaborated in the defence
of capitalist society. Opportunism and treachery have gravely compromised reform';[50] 'Violent or peaceful, revolution is above all a
rupture. Anyone who does not accept the rupture with capitalist
society cannot, I say, be a member of the Socialist Party';[51] 'There
is no socialism without the collective appropriation of the great
means of production, exchange and research'.[52] He was to become
well known for his semi-hysterical rantings against the role of
money in society: 'Money which kills, money which buys, money
which ruins, which rots right through to the conscience of men'.[53]
It is striking that such views, which are particularly common on the
social-democratic Catholic Left, of which François Mitterrand and
Jacques Delors are the prime representatives, were also espoused
by the Vichy government during the war. In 1942, a left-wing
Vichyite, Francis Delaisi, in a book entitled *La Révolution européenne*,[54] also attacked the doctrines of liberalism and free trade as
being little more than instruments of Anglo-Saxon imperialism. He
too called for 'the world to be divided into autonomous vital
living spaces'.[55]

These attitudes provide the key to the curious link between
Mitterrand and the extreme right.[56] When in opposition, the Socialist Party had virulently attacked the 'internationalism' of Valéry
Giscard d'Estaing, whom they called 'the ideological alibi of multinational capitalism',[57] a phrase that would not have been out of place
in the mouth of the most raving anti-Semite. Just as Sir Oswald
Mosley left the Labour Party to found the British Union of Fascists,
in France both extreme Right and the centre Left deplore the so-

called corruption and destructiveness of commerce, the selfishness of 'individualism' and the ravages of party spirit. Before the war, they identified these vices with both Jewry and American capitalism; after the war, only with the latter.[58] Instead they yearn for the spiritual unity of the nation – or a wider union of peoples – marching in step.[59]

Because these ideas are so deeply rooted in various sections of French politics, it would be a mistake to regard the Socialist conversion to the free market as all that authentic. In particular, it was compensated by two other growing characteristics, both of them also reminiscent of Vichy: first, an increasing attachment to technocracy as the élite capable of 'managing' the economy, and, second, an emphasis on 'Europe' as the overarching structure in which free trade should similarly be directed. Both projects were fundamentally neo-Socialist in their appeal.

Mitterrand's change took place in stages. At first, he only adopted a half-way house, that of the so-called 'mixed economy'. It was curious that Pierre Mauroy himself had attacked this in 1981 as being the brainchild of the previous right-wing government, arguing that it merely allowed the private sector to cream off profits while the state and the tax-payer had to deal with the loss-making sections of the economy.[60] Preparing the U-turn, Mitterrand declared tartly in May 1983, 'I speak little of Socialism, because I speak in the name of all France.'[61] By 1985, he was rejecting as outrageous the idea that nationalized industries should or could escape from the general crisis and preserve jobs artificially. To be Socialist was now to get inflation down. Mitterrand's own language became indistinguishable from that of Raymond Barre, Valéry Giscard d'Estaing's Prime Minister: 'Unemployment cannot be solved without solving the other problems of our economy. This is what we have done in fighting against inflation, against our trade deficit, and in other areas.'[62] But gradually, his pronouncements on economics became progressively devoid of any political commitment whatever. He would make such eliptic pronouncements as 'I fight the theory and practice of economic liberalism, which is an illusion. I also refuse collectivism, a trap'.[63] Finally, from about 1988 onwards, his language was almost totally soporific. He became the partisan of doing nothing at all. The phrase '*ni-ni*' ('neither-nor'), meaning neither privatizations nor

nationalizations,[64] soon stuck to him. It was odd that he should
use a slogan which seemed almost deliberately reminiscent of the
French fascists' penchant for saying that their own Socialist policies were 'neither right nor left'.[65] Seldom can a politician have
so determinedly exploited a people's desire simply to be fed
illusions.

From the mid-1980s onwards, the message was also that Mitterrand and the Socialists would be the technocratic modernizers of
the French economy. During a visit to the United States in 1984, he
was impressed by the technological development in Silicon Valley.
For the first time in the President's mouth, the notions of profit
and success were used approvingly.[66] He declared, 'Either France
will be able to confront international competition, or she will fall
behind into decline . . . People talk of Silicon Valley in the United
States, but we have Silicon Valleys all over the place in France, in
Aquitaine, in Rhone-Alpes, in Brittany, in Alsace, everywhere the
country is undergoing a transformation.'[67] This was a long way
from 1981, when he had pursued total nationalization. Instead of
laying red roses on the tombs of Lamartine and Jean Jaurès in the
Pantheon as he had done in May 1981, Mitterrand began to
worship computers and greenbacks. His admiration of the success
of the United States economy, and his grudging surprise at the
success of the Thatcherite experiment in Britain,[68] were the polar
opposite of Jack Lang's 1981 declaration in Mexico that 'The true
danger for the Western world is American financial and cultural
imperialism'. (Incidentally, Lang also went to see the *Lider Massimo*,
Fidel Castro, when he had declared approvingly that 'The Cubans
have the right to choose the leader they wish'.[69])

But the desire for accelerated industrial modernization through
the development of technology is not new to Socialists. On the
contrary, Nikita Khrushchev had travelled to the United States in
the 1950s, when he had been impressed by the result of its mecha-
nized agriculture; after Mitterrand, the Stalinist Romanian apparatchik, Silviu Brucan, was to call in 1988 for a technological
revolution to save the Romanian economy under Ceauşescu.[70]
Similarly, in a phrase reminiscent of Lenin's slogan 'Socialism is
power to the Soviets plus electrification of the Soviet Union', the
Socialist minister, Jean-Pierre Chevenement, was fond of saying
that 'Socialism is self-management (*autogestion*) plus computers'.[71]

Indeed, during the election campaign in 1965, Mitterrand's posters had shown him in front of progressive electric pylons and smoke-stacks, with the slogan 'A young President for a modern France'.

As usual, though, Mitterrand continued to bet on several horses at once. In 1981, his campaign to modernize the economy through Socialism had been counterbalanced by an electoral poster which displayed his face next to a fairy-tale drawing of a picturesque French village snuggling around its little church. His unkinder critics asked whether the combination of the two kitsch themes – the dynamism of modern industry and the bucolic serenity of agriculture – was reminiscent of the propaganda of Marshal Pétain and Vichy, not to mention other fascist leaders of the 1930s and 1940s. He replied,

> I do not see anything wrong with it. Indeed, I even see several advantages in symbolizing a certain France which one might fear is losing ground: rural France. There are many towns-people who would like to be able to find that France again, and above all to find again that civilization of reflection, of medita-tion and of silence, a certain slowness of movement which is terribly thrown out of joint these days by a society which has not found its civilized standards.[72]

This notwithstanding, Mitterrand continued to play on his progres-sive image. This extended into other areas than economics, the most obvious being culture, where his long-serving Culture Minis-ter, Jack Lang, epitomized the obsession with trashy modernism. By the time Laurent Fabius replaced Pierre Mauroy as Prime Minister in 1984, the new, flashy Socialism was firmly in place. Fabius, the youngest Prime Minister in French history, whom, in Mitterrand's words, he had 'given to France', wanted computers everywhere, in schools, in offices, in people's homes. Fabius was even to declare to *Paris-Match* that 'the vote of 1981 never seemed to me to be evidence of a conversion to Socialism'.[73] Mitterrand's conversion to the market was always covered with a syrupy patina of do-goodery which was as well received as it was meaningless. 'I am certainly no enemy of profit, providing that it is justly distributed.'[74]

Despite the change, the instinct was still to copy from abroad rather than engage in original or even substantial policies. The new

slogan, dear to the heart of Pierre Bérégovoy, the long-serving
Finance Minister, was borrowed from the German Finance Minister
and architect of the economic miracle, Ludwig Erhard: that of the
'social market economy'. Playing on the perennial French fear of
free trade – indeed of freedom *tout court* – something called 'Rhenish
capitalism' was introduced, which seemed to offer the perfect left-
wing mixture of 'freedom' with 'social protection'. This is a good
formula for allowing people to enjoy the fruit of their endeavours if
there are any, but to blame the 'excesses of the market' if there are
not. On a similar theme, during the cohabitation of 1986–8, he
regularly intervened from on high to defend what he misleadingly
called France's 'social achievements', a phrase which had been dear
to the East German Communist dictator, Erich Honecker, and this
has since become one of his favourite slogans. Unfortunately, it was
based on a lie. While many Continental newspapers – some French,
many German – illustrate any article on Britain with a photo of a
tramp, there were over 200,000 homeless people in France by the
end of 1993 and 37.7 per cent of households living on less than the
minimum wage of 5,100 francs a month. Over 4.7 million people in
France earn less than 2,250 francs a month.[75] Criminality is also a
very serious problem: in 1983 there were five times more murders
in Paris than in London.[76]

Over the structural reforms needed for French industry, over the
social-security budget flying totally out of control, over the rising
number of homeless and unemployed, Mitterrand preferred to pass
in sovereign silence. This has meant that he has not only left France
unreformed, but also intellectually unprepared for reform, an emu-
like attitude in which Édouard Balladur has been only too happy to
persist. It has also meant that his erstwhile Socialist friends have
been severely disappointed with his hollowing-out of the Socialist
project. 'In contrast to the whole tradition of its organisation, the
party of debate which the Socialist Party used to be, has transformed
itself – like the RPR of the Republican Party – into a mere party of
spectacle.'[77]

These ideological girations soon led to the death of the French
Socialist Party. Just as the party had been little more than a vehicle
for François Mitterrand's conquest of power, so, once safely installed for a second term in 1988, he cast it aside like a now useless
ladder. His second term of office culminated in the humiliation of

the Socialists in March 1993, when they scored a mere 18 per cent of the vote at the general election. Riven by ideological dissent and corruption scandals, the party lost all semblance of being a serious political force, and disintegrated into little more than a shabby band of quarrelling political godfathers, presided over by the basilisk and baleful eye of the President, who had devoted the first two years of his second term in office to destroying and undermining his own Prime Minister, his long-term rival in the Socialist Party, Michel Rocard. Indeed, some even suspected that the only reason why he had appointed Rocard was to destroy him.

Above all, unemployment was the greatest failure of Mitterrand and the Socialists. Inasmuch as they can be believed, the official figure for the unemployed in France in 1993 is over 3 million, a figure it had reached by 1990; but there are an additional 2 million on social security, which brings the total number out of work to 5.3 million.[78] Of this horrendous figure, those for the young are particularly bad: 25 per cent of people aged under twenty-six are out of work, largely because the low-skilled and unskilled are priced out of the market by the minimum wage, which rose by 125 per cent from 1981 to 1984, during which time prices rose by only 75 per cent.[79] There is, indeed, a direct correlation over a twenty-year period from 1970 to the 1990s between the rising minimum wage and the rise in youth unemployment, the former being a direct cause of the latter.[80] Moreover, 44 per cent of the jobless in France are now long-term unemployed, as opposed to 22 per cent in the early 1970s.[81] Expensive social costs falling on businesses (which rose from 18.5 per cent to 20.6 per cent of wage costs between 1981 and 1992) were also a factor, and thus throughout the latter half of Mitterrand's reign, unemployment remained obstinately 3 per cent higher than the OECD average.

It was aggravated by the persistent refusal of successive Mitterrand governments even to begin root-and-branch economic reform, especially where the inflexibility of the labour market was concerned. In 1994, over a decade after the Thatcherite reforms of the British economy had begun, and some fifteen years after deregulation had started under Jimmy Carter in the United States, Mitterrand was supporting Édouard Balladur, his right-wing Prime Minister, in backing down over plans to reduce the minimum wage, notably for students beginning work. Rather than having the courage to deal with reality, he and the Prime Minister preferred to keep the electorate pumped up on illusions about what was economically feasible. Thus in early 1994, the OECD concluded, 'The French economy is still suffering from major structural problems, most notably labour market rigidities, which are reflected in a high rate of structural unemployment, and a fast rise in social expenditure.'[82]

But the single greatest factor in France's economic slump was the deflationary policy of the *franc fort*. This policy, which was decided upon in ten days in 1983, and which was later to become the totem of the pro-European French Socialists, produced similar effects to that during British membership of the ERM between 1990 and 1992, only it was longer and more protracted. Moreover, the centralized monetary squeeze was applied to an economy which, despite the propaganda, was fundamentally weaker than those of its competitors.

By 1994 the Thatcherite reforms were showing their true worth, as Britain's economy was the only one to be buoyant while the rest of Europe languished in recession. It is amusing to see that, just as many French people cling to the myth of a neo-Dickensian England without France's 'social protection', so they fondly cherish the belief that the 1980s were a period of disindustrialization in Britain and America. It is depressing to see English commentators supporting the same view, when their judgement of France is often based on little more than a few days or weeks spent holidaying with a bulging wallet in one of France's richer regions or in the centre of Paris. In fact, the Atlantic economies grew from two to three times faster than those on the Continent. Between 1982 and 1989, the industrial production of Britain and the USA had grown by 22 per cent and 30 per cent respectively, while that of France grew a feeble 11 per cent in the same period, and even Germany only 13 per cent.[83] These growth rates corresponded to falls in the unemployment rate and job creation in the UK and the US, phenomena which obstinately refused to occur in France during the same period.

France had observed a relentless increase in unemployment from the moment Mitterrand came to power in 1981, despite his promises that it would never rise above 2 million. The boom years of the mid-1980s had made it clear that France was structurally slower to soak up extra job capacity than Britain, where unemployment had sunk to just over 1.5 million before John Major so proudly took Britain into the ERM. By 1989, the world economy was slowing down, and the tendency in Japan and the USA was to cut interest rates. By 1992 they had fallen to around 4 per cent in both countries. Meanwhile the monetary union between East and West Germany in mid-1990 had caused German rates to rise. The Bundesbank tried to conduct a rather ham-fisted monetary mopping-up operation after the government's foolish agreement to convert useless Ostmarks into Deutschmarks at the rate of 1:1. The German currency thus rose in value, obliging the other ERM currencies to follow suit, and to push their interest rates up to unbearable levels in order to maintain exchange-rate parity. This meant that by early 1993, French interest rates were at a staggering 10 per cent in real terms, over twice what they were in real terms in Germany. The pound, lira and peseta were ejected from the ERM in the monetary crisis of September 1992, but France pressed on regardless. French short-term interest rates remained over 6 per cent in real terms until well into 1994.

It is striking that the same policy was pursued even by the new right-wing government which was elected in March 1993, despite its very deleterious effect on the economy and employment. On the day Mitterrand appointed Balladur, he insisted during his broadcast to the nation that the monetary link with Germany would have to be maintained. No one in the new government demurred, and thus it found itself an accomplice to the very same economic policy as that of its recently defeated predecessor. Indeed, when the new government appointed a new governor to the Bank of France, it chose none other than the theoretician of the doctrine of 'competitive disinflation' himself, Jean-Claude Trichet, the former Director of the Treasury; and instead of following the British example, it made the Bank of France independent, in an attempt to seal the *franc fort* policy in stone.

Perhaps the most remarkable thing about this sorry story, which ended in August 1993, not with a bang but a whimper, after the margins of fluctuation within the ERM were widened to a meaningless and ridiculous 30 per cent, was the lurid terms in which the debate was posed. Anyone who supported the devaluation of the franc was branded as being a foreign infiltrator. Indeed, the myth

of the international plot against France is alive and well in French
political and journalistic circles: in 1982, Jacques Delors, the then
Minister of Finance had declared that 'There is an international
conspiracy against France. They want to smash our experiment and
make us devalue a third time'.[84] Ten years later, in defence of a
policy which was diametrically opposed to that which Delors had
been defending, similar hatred was expressed towards those who
suggested any other policy than that approved by the government.
When the semi-Thatcherite future Industry Minister, Alain Madelin,
suggested that interest rates were too high, his colleague Valéry
Giscard d'Estaing accused him of belonging to the 'foreigners'
party'. Journalists and politicians alike heaped opprobrium on the
international speculators who eventually forced the ERM to its
knees, and one leading commentator and former Interior Minister,
Alain Peyrefitte, compared the financial speculators who brought
down the Exchange Rate Mechanism in August 1993, to terrorists,
saying that they should be treated in the same way as the United
Nations had treated Saddam Hussein.[85]

On the crucial indicator of unemployment – one which is supposed
to be especially dear to Socialist hearts – Mitterrand has thus been a
clear failure. Other economic and industrial signals were hardly more
encouraging. Early 1994 saw the eruption of the crisis at Air France:
despite losing £2 million per day in 1993, and a full decade after
British Airways had embarked on becoming one of the most
successful airlines in the world, the management was finding it almost
impossible to introduce reform packages.[86] Indeed, overall French
industrial production fell below that of Britain in 1992, and went into
absolute decline while Britain's grew: it has remained obstinately
below it since.[87] Continuing demands for import quotas from the
prominent industrialist, the head of Peugeot, Jacques Calvet,[88]
suggest that France is also mentally unprepared to compete in world
markets. Mitterrand's governments are directly responsible for this
kind of political sleepwalking, because the President has always
preferred it to realistic and courageous reform. France, after all, had
'thirty glorious years' (*'les trentes glorieuses'*) of continuous and buoyant
growth after the war, until the mid-1970s, during which period she
overtook a United Kingdom whose economy was faltering, and thus
she accumulated riches which it will take a long time to fritter away.
But the 1980s suggest that the balance of forces is being reversed.

Unlike his contemporary, Margaret Thatcher, Mitterrand's name will never be attached to any economic doctrine. Instead, it will merely connote the constant pursuit of power for its own sake. His political decisions – and therefore his successes or failures – cannot be understood with reference to the real world outside, or to the needs of the country, but rather to the exigencies of the political microcosm whose rarefied atmosphere he has lived and breathed all his life. It is to a consideration of that systemic context that we now turn.

2. The Republican Monarchy

> I love France; and I am glad I saw it when I was young. For if
> an Englishman has understood a Frenchman, he has under-
> stood the most foreign of foreigners.
>
> G. K. Chesterton, *Autobiography*, 1936

In May 1983, François Mitterrand undertook a state visit to China.
An indefatigable critic of the constitution of the Fifth Republic
while in opposition – he once called the Gaullist regime 'a dictatorship'[1] – even he must have been rather taken aback when the
General Secretary of the Chinese Communist Party expressed the
sanguine belief that his own country enjoyed a greater separation of
powers than in France. 'In France,' Hu Yaobang declared, 'there is
one Republic with one President. Here in China, by contrast, we
have collegiate government, with decisions taken by Deng Xiao-
Ping and others together.[2]

The powers enjoyed by the French President are unequalled by
those of any other politician in the Western world. The monarchical
character of the constitution of the Fifth Republic has been universally commented on, for it restored to France an institutional order
similar to that which she had enjoyed for the first eight centuries of
her history.[3] Often attacked as authoritarian, absolutist and dictatorial, the constitution has also been felt to conform well to the
political needs and reflexes of the French people. In July 1987,
France celebrated the 1,000th anniversary of the Capetian monarchy,
and in July 1989 she celebrated the 200th anniversary of Bastille
Day: both anniversaries have their immediacy.[4]

If every country gets the constitution it deserves, then it is an
unjust omission when discussing another country's politics to neglect it; but the neglect is doubtless encouraged by the perverse
modern tendency to reduce all politics to sociology or economics,
an approach which deliberately avoids questions of legitimacy,

accountability and authority. It also ignores history, and thereby commits another, even more fundamental error: to assume that politics in all countries is driven by the same impersonal forces. On the contrary, a country's constitution – that totality of political habits and practices which defines the rules for the exercise of political authority – is its soul, through which historical legacy and political character determine its political behaviour and preoccupations.

It is sobering, especially for readers used to the pleasant harmony of an Anglo-Saxon constitution, to dwell on the fact that France made constitutional history when the Socialists came to power under François Mitterrand on 10 May 1981. Never before in the history of France had political power changed hands according to the British or American parliamentary model, where two political groupings of roughly equal size both peacefully accepted the same rules of the game.[5] Then, some predicted that the 'war of the Republics' which had so bedevilled France was over,[6] and that France could now operate like a normal democratic country for once.

For ever since Julius Caesar conquered Gaul, when he observed that its inhabitants were a quarrelsome and fractious people, the French have seemed more gifted at fighting civil wars than at winning battles.[7] De Gaulle was similarly much preoccupied with 'our old Gallic propensity to division and quarrel'.[8] Moreover, since the shock of the Revolution, France's political pendulum has been swinging violently between extremes: between revolution and reaction, republicanism and monarchy, semi-anarchic parliamentarianism and gross dictatorship. Unlike in Britain, there has been no consensus about the form of government, let alone its content. Indeed, some have seen in the history of French political life and sensibility since 1789 an essential continuity of conflict between revolution and counter-revolution. As Chateaubriand noted, the 'justice of civil war' is always latent in the politics of modern France.[9]

So chronic was France's constitutional dissensus that a Victorian number of *Punch* published a cartoon showing a man going into a library and asking for a copy of the French constitution. 'I am sorry, sir,' replied the librarian, 'we do not stock periodicals.' It was hardly even a joke: France has had sixteen constitutions since

1789:[10] five republics, two empires, and three monarchies, as well as various provisional governments. A man now in his fifties has experienced five different kinds of regime: the Third Republic, Vichy, the Liberation government of 1945–6, the Fourth Republic, and now the Fifth Republic. Even the present constitution has already been frequently amended.[11] No wonder that one historian refers to 'the hexagonal fever'.[12] Indeed, even François Mitterrand once remarked, 'In France, political problems can only be resolved through crises.'[13] It is this traditional political stability which gives Frenchmen their faith in the power of bureaucracy, for the administration represents a continuity which the political order cannot provide.

The British have often been ready to have a laugh at France's expense on this issue. Edmund Burke made fun of the revolutionary Abbé Sieyès and his 'whole nests of pigeon-holes full of constitutions, ready-sorted, ticketed and numbered'.[14] Disraeli snorted at Louis XVIII for thinking that the Westminster model could be simply copied and transported into a foreign country. 'The King of France', he wrote in 1832, 'had no idea that political institutions, to be effective, must be founded on the habits and opinions of the people whom they pretend to govern . . .'[15] It is therefore a poignant irony that while nearly all of this constitutional and political change has been brought about by violence, all France's constitutions except that of the Second Republic, the Second Empire and Vichy, have been inspired by that of Britain.

The Fifth Republic is, surprisingly, only a partial exception to this rule, for General de Gaulle was always an admirer of the British constitution. The bitter defeat of 1940 taught him that national greatness and the strength of institutions went hand in hand. During his state visit to Britain in 1960, he gave a speech to the Lords and Commons assembled in Westminster Hall, which, now that it is has become *de rigueur* to denigrate those same institutions, it is worth recalling. Speaking without notes, his slightly histrionic voice echoing against the ancient stone, the General intoned:

> It is above all your deep national qualities which have permitted you to play an exceptional role in the eye of the storm; but your institutions have counted a very great deal in

your success! Today, allow me, here in Westminster, to give
England her due in this respect as in others.

> Assured of yourselves, almost without appearing to be so,
> you practise liberty in a solid and stable regime. In your
> political system tradition, loyalty, and the rules of the game
> are so strong that your government is naturally cohesive and
> lasting; your parliament has an assured majority for the whole
> length of a legislature; the majority and the government are
> granted permanently; in brief, the legislative and executive
> powers somehow balance each other out and co-operate with
> one another by definition.[16]

Nonetheless, the constitution which the General designed was the
very opposite of the British system, in both theory and practice.
The Fifth Republic was certainly not a simple import of a foreign
model into France, for it was inspired by de Gaulle's belief that
France has an overriding need for a strong monarch. Indeed, one
is tempted to say that Britain and France are both monarchies,
but that in Britain the monarch does not govern. De Gaulle felt
this need especially keenly because of the century-and-a-half of
political turmoil which had preceded the foundation of the Fifth
Republic.

The Third Republic (1875–1940) lasted longer than that of any
other French constitution, yet, uncharacteristically for France, it
was discovered almost by accident. It had been intended to create
an Orléanist constitutional monarchy, but the pretender, the Comte
de Chambord, refused the throne (he would not accept to reign
under the revolutionary tricolour) and so the regime became a
parliamentary republic with a symbolic President. Deputies to the
National Assembly were not directly elected, but nominated from
party lists by proportional representation. By breaking the direct
constituency link on which true parliamentary democracy is based,
this institutionalized the irresponsibility of the political parties, and
the parliament was increasingly felt to be a 'house without win-
dows', cut off from the concerns of ordinary people.

At first, there were usually sufficient parliamentary majorities to
maintain government stability, but from the end of the first decade
of the century onwards, governments seldom lasted for more than a
few months. This instability did not prevent France from negotiat-

ing successful alliances during the First World War, nor from constructing the world's second-largest colonial empire. Initially at least, the constitution enjoyed wide support: as Anatole France quipped, 'I can excuse the Republic for governing badly because it does not govern at all.'[17] In this it resembled post-war Italy. However, from about 1930, things began to change. The regime began to creak considerably, in part because of the huge human losses suffered during the First World War. It became incapable of dealing with the economic crisis, the rise of totalitarianism, and of preparing the country for the next conflict which was looming. Its parliamentary and republican nature was subject to fierce attack by extreme right-wing monarchists in the famous street demonstrations of 6 February 1934, which very nearly pushed the regime over the brink.

As the national consensus began to break down, constitutional reform became a topic of lively political debate. A professor of law at the University of Strasbourg, Carré de Malberg, began to develop a theory which distinguished French from British parliamentarianism, explaining why the former was a disaster and the latter a model to the world. He was to exert a profound influence on the Gaullist constitutionalists, Michel Debré and René Capitant. De Malberg argued that the French parliamentary system had been crucially different from that of Britain ever since 1791. While in both countries, the parliament had wrenched power from the king, in England the process had occurred gradually under a powerful monarchy, and thus parliament had to appeal to popular opinion to augment its own authority. In France, by contrast, the Assembly declared itself sovereign not only with regard to the king but also with regard to the people. De Malberg attributed this to the danger the Revolutionary deputies felt from the sheer power of the people, and to the fact that the weakness of the monarchy made an appeal to popular legitimacy unnecessary. As a result, the Revolutionary assembly often seemed to want to shut out popular sovereignty altogether: Abbé Sieyès had declared on 7 September 1789 that 'The people or the nation can have only one voice, that of the national legislature . . . In a country which is not a democracy, and France cannot be one, the people cannot speak except through its representatives'.[18]

He used the word 'democracy' to refer to Jean-Jacques Rousseau's theories of direct democracy, which was inspired by life in the Swiss cantons. France was too big for this, and so Sieyès perfected the theory of representative government in its place, claiming that the Assembly was always the nation's voice. Grabbing the king's sovereignty – the king having, for at least a century, identified himself with the state – the revolutionaries simply put the 'nation' in the place of the king, thereby falling into the trap, of which Aristotle had warned, of democracy becoming indistinguishable from tyranny if the multitude, and not the law, holds the supreme power.[19] Indeed, inspired by Rousseau's legal positivism, the French Revolution and subsequent practice came to identify 'the law' with 'the general will', a doctrine which subordinates the judiciary to the legislature.

This Revolutionary tradition led de Malberg to draw a distinction between *representative* regimes and *parliamentary* regimes. In the former, the sovereignty of the people, which he believed ought to be inalienable, was completely delegated away to the corrupt and unaccountable Assembly. That this was a profoundly anti-democratic, 'bastard'[20] system, was evident in the Assembly's notorious reluctance to dissolve itself at times of governmental crisis under the Third Republic. Instead of being sovereign, the people were mere onlookers at the political game. Indeed, he thought the system little more than a veil for the domination of the bourgeoisie over the masses. In the British system, by contrast, which he called truly *parliamentary*, democratic elections were capable of producing real governmental change. The aim, therefore, was to restore true popular sovereignty by mixing an accountable parliamentary regime with direct democracy in the form of elections and referenda.

The manner in which the Third Republic came to an end could only confirm de Malberg's view that the essential distinction between constituted power and constitutive power had been abrogated. On 10 July 1940, following the German invasion, the National Assembly, dominated by the left-wing Popular Front, voted plenipotentiary powers to Marshal Pétain, paving the way for the Vichy dictatorship. There could hardly be a starker illustration of the fictitiously democratic nature of the 'representative principle' embodied in France's parliamentary regime, for in voting those powers, the very institution which was supposed to be the depository of national sovereignty had in fact abandoned it.[21] The act was legal in form, yet obviously immoral and unjust in substance, and it epitomized with grotesque clarity the invidious separation of the political class from the people.

The Resistance constitutionalists, especially René Capitant,[22] a professor of constitutional law, and later a Minister of Education, held the national disgrace of Vichy to be the inevitable conclusion of this rupture between the 'legal country' of parliamentary antics, and the 'real country' outside.[23] In contrast to the ephemeral unreality of political life in the Third Republic, those who were active in the Resistance experienced the intense reality of direct political action in their courageous stand against the collaborationist regime.[24] It was to this same quality of unreality that de Gaulle was to refer when attacking Pétain's France in his famous speech at the liberation of Paris. The city, he proclaimed, had been liberated by herself, 'by the *real* France, by eternal France'.[25]

Indeed, de Gaulle's own career can only be grasped as a life-poem on legitimacy and authority, inspired by these experiences. For him, the Pétainist regime, even if 'legal' on paper, was illegitimate because it had ceded inalienable national sovereignty to an occupying power. No French ruler had ever had the right to exercise power if he had alienated the sovereignty from which that power flowed. De Gaulle decided, therefore, that he was nothing less than the personal incarnation of that sovereignty: his appeal to resist, broadcast on the BBC on 18 June 1940, can only be understood as an attempt to keep the tradition of that sovereignty alive.[26] In his estimation of himself as the very incarnation of France, he was to make declarations of which Louis XIV would have been proud. In 1954, he said of his wartime effort, 'I was France, the State, the government. I spoke in the name of France. I was the independence and sovereignty of France.'[27] His colleagues at the time, and in later life, have often testified to de Gaulle's firm belief that, despite being only the leader of a handful of men and a few remote territories, 'he bore a thousand years of history within him'.[28] Because he considered that he embodied national legitimacy, he was able after the war to propagate the myth of its continuity through the Resistance. In the Hôtel de Ville on the day of the liberation of Paris, Georges Bidault, the Chairman of the National Resistance Council, asked him, 'General, would you like to appear on the balcony and proclaim the Republic?' 'No,' replied de Gaulle, 'the Republic has never ceased to exist.'[29]

The need de Gaulle felt for authority to be personified – by himself – was contrary to a central aspect of the French republican tradition. Unlike in the United States, where presidential power was inscribed into the system from the start, French republicanism, once again under Rousseau's influence, came to identify itself with the *impersonal* power of the law.[30] Perhaps it was because of the deep influence exerted on the young de Gaulle by the monarchist-traditionalist philosopher Charles Maurras that he felt very keenly that France herself had been decapitated by the execution of the king in 1792. Indeed, one of his central preoccupations was with the need to restore the authority and political personality of the French state, by giving it a proper head.[31]

The opinion had grown up under the Third Republic that the government should not lead from the front, but be merely an administrative organ under the surveillance of parliament.[32] The British idea that parliament was not a mere assembly of delegates, but an institution capable of leading the nation, by creating and stimulating public opinion, was not current in France.[33] De Gaulle's long-standing belief that the French parliament was incapable of providing such leadership and authority had been vindicated by events, and therefore he considered that the role of the Assembly had to be drastically reduced, and the role of government redefined. As René Capitant wrote, 'It is a strange system, which one might be tempted to call a "limited bureaucracy", where the state is *deprived of a head*, where control is more important than action.'[34]

Anyone who wanted to reinforce the executive was usually suspected of wanting to reinstate royal power. But this was not the only counter-revolutionary element of de Gaulle's republicanism. Far from respecting the secularity which is another traditional corner-stone of French republicanism (also unlike the United States), de Gaulle's language from 1940 onwards was laced with theological and biblical symbolism.[35] The General conceived the national sovereignty of which he was the incarnation as an almost sacred authority. The semi-religious logic of his political action was to be recognized by others. Lady Spears, the wife of the British general Sir Edward Spears, wrote that de Gaulle had 'taken this national shame (of Vichy) upon himself, *assuming it as Christ assumed the sins of the world*'.[36] Later, in 1961, the great liberal political philosopher, Raymond Aron, was able to write in a similar vein that 'This regime, however liberal it may be, is that of a Saviour. It is not democratic in the modern sense of the term'.[37]

But if 1940 and command of the Free French had combined all the essential Gaullist characteristics – authority, dignity, sovereignty, responsibility, personification of power, exceptional circumstances which illuminated eternal truths – the Fourth Republic was spectacularly to ignore all of them. Various attempts were made after the end of the Second World War to make substantial changes to the constitution, but most of these projects were drawn up by party-political politicians with vested interests in preserving the old order, and no serious reforms were adopted. In 1946, when he realized that the Fourth Republic was substantially the same as the Third, de Gaulle resigned from the government, declaring, 'If you do not take account of the absolute necessity of restoring the dignity and authority of the government, you will arrive at a situation where, one day, I predict, you will bitterly regret having taken the path you have taken.'[38]

He was to be proved right. Within twelve years from 1946 to 1958 there were to be twenty-four governments and seventeen Presidents of the Council (Prime Minister). The continuing pressures exerted by the Gaullist movement in the National Assembly were unable to bring about anything but the most minor constitutional changes, and successive fragile government proved incapable of managing the country's finances. After the humiliations of Dien Bien Phu and Algeria, the country found herself on the brink of civil war in 1958. As in 1940, France's weak political institutions were held to blame. The truth which de Gaulle understood had been confirmed: France simply cannot function without strong central authority.

Like many others before him, and like much of the population, de Gaulle was convinced that political parties represented an unacceptable limitation on the power of that central authority. Rather than allowing popular will to be communicated between the people and the government as it should do in a normal democracy, the French 'regime of parties' was only ever an obstacle to the realization of the general interest. Because of the lack of direct responsibility on individual deputies – as a result of proportional representation – political parties in France were mere quarrelsome parliamentary cabals. In a passage which anticipates the behaviour of the Socialist Party under François Mitterrand, de Gaulle wrote,

> Not inspired by general principles, nor even eager to convert people to their cause, they [political parties] will simply lower themselves, shrink, and become the mere representatives of a category of interests ... Their leaders, their delegates and their militants will turn into professional politicians. The conquest of public posts, of positions of influence, and of administrative jobs will absorb political parties, to the point when their principal efforts will be deployed in what they call tactics, but which is in fact nothing but compromise and abandonment of principle.[39]

When de Gaulle insisted in his seminal speech on the constitution at Bayeux in June 1946 that 'the fight between political parties is of such a fundamental character in France that it jeopardizes everything and ignores the superior interest of the country',[40] the audience broke into spontaneous and heartfelt applause.[41] Like Rousseau and the French kings before him, he subscribed to a unitarian view of society, foreign to the 'Anglo-Saxon' tradition, according to which the 'general interest' is something superior to the sum of individual interests which compose it: he did not believe that it could be merely teased out of their mutual conflict.

Although at Bayeux he did not specify that the President be elected by universal suffrage, it was quite clear that he thought that the fundamental legitimacy of the government had to come from the Head of State, and not from parliament as was the British and classic French republican practice, 'because parliament merely unites delegates of particular interests'.[42] By contrast, the President of the Republic, like God, was to be the source of all authority and legitimacy; and, just as the Son proceeds from the Father, so the executive has to 'proceed from the President'.[43] For this reason he held to the rather fictitious view that the Head of State could not come from a political party. He had to be designated by the people.[44]

As a result, in the constitution of the Fifth Republic, the President appoints the government; he presides over the meetings of the Council of Ministers, the equivalent of the Cabinet; he has the right to consult the people either by referendum or by dissolving parliament; and he even has the power to 'take the measures demanded by the circumstances' when 'the institutions of the Republic, the independence of the nation, the integrity of its territory or the execution of its international commitments are threatened' (Article 16).[45] As befits the myth of the President at the head of the nation united, he is himself the guardian of the constitution, in virtue of the catch-all Article 5.[46] Parliament's role was to legislate and to hold the government to account: but it had to cease trying to be the government itself. Thus, parliamentary sessions had to be shortened. There had to be a 'separation of powers' between the executive and the legislature, and ministers had to be debarred from having parliamentary careers, for if the members of the government were members of a parliament with a multiplicity of parties, the government would be divided. In the absence of a solid two-party system like that of Britain or America, and with a very strong extreme Left and extreme Right, France had to achieve stability by other means. One of the constitution's authors, Michel Debré, regretted that the new French constitution could never be built on the same party system as the British, saying that 'Because in France governmental stability cannot come from the electoral law, it must result at least in part from constitutional regulation'.[47]

But for the same reasons, de Gaulle never wanted a fully presidential system. He was not prepared to accept the possibility that the President, as in the US, might be unable to impose his will on the parliament. Fearing interminable blockages if the President's decisions were susceptible to a parliamentary veto, he gave the Prime Minister the role of directing the policy of the government in parliament. Thus the new constitution acquired something which no other constitution in the world has: a bicephalous executive with an irresponsible President and a semi-accountable Prime Minister. The relationship between the President and the Prime Minister was to prove a fatal ambiguity, exploited by François Mitterrand, which perverted the original spirit of the constitution out of all recognition.

On the one hand, the constitution specifies that the Prime Minister is responsible for 'directing government policy' (Article 21). De Gaulle insisted that the President was a mere pole of stability above the political fray, the expression of national unity, not the head of the government. 'When will you understand that

my ambition has never been to be the leader of the majority?'
de Gaulle had asked in 1958. Michel Debré similarly argued that
the President would not actually govern, but intervene in politics only in times of crisis.[48] At a formal hearing into the new
constitution before the consultative committee of the parliament in
1958, de Gaulle was asked whether the Prime Minister, who is
nominated by the President, could also be sacked by him. He
replied,

> No! Because if it were thus, the Prime Minister would not be
> able to govern effectively. The Prime Minister can be dismissed
> by the parliament, but not by the Head of State according to
> the political situation. If it were not thus, the equilibrium
> between the institutions would be compromised. The President
> of the Republic, I must insist, is essentially an umpire (*un
> arbitre*) whose task it is to ensure the proper functioning of the
> institutions of the state, whatever happens.[49]

However, his own practice undermined this claim, as it has that of
all his successors, especially François Mitterrand. It soon became
clear that de Gaulle thought himself responsible for directing the
main orientations of national policy, while the government's executive tasks were subordinate to his commands, and more technical.
How, indeed, could it have been otherwise? After all, the Prime
Minister owed his job to the President, and took orders from him:
his accountability to parliament was minimal by comparison. There
was indeed precious little evidence of de Gaulle ever acting as a
mere umpire, for he increasingly concentrated power in his own
hands. When reproached with violating the constitution, he would
counter with a roguish political incorrectness which showed well
how he viewed the relationship between himself and the constitution
he had designed: 'But can a man be accused of violating his
wife?'[50]

Indeed, despite the explicit assurances he gave to the committee,
de Gaulle himself sacked Michel Debré as Prime Minister, replacing
him with Georges Pompidou in April 1962, because of the former's
disagreement with his Algerian policy. And when in October of
that year, he changed the constitution, introducing the election of
the President by universal suffrage, the National Assembly voted
against the measure by passing a vote of no confidence in the

Pompidou government. It was to be the only vote of no confidence ever to be passed by a National Assembly under the Fifth Republic – to no avail. De Gaulle dissolved the Assembly, called an early legislative election, in which an increased majority of Gaullists was returned, and reappointed Pompidou.[51]

He introduced the election of the presidency by universal suffrage because he felt the constant need for his legitimacy to be confirmed. He also realized that no future President could ever enjoy the same personal authority as he did. Even his own legitimacy, which derived mainly from 1940, would dwindle over time if there were not an election. The presidency, like the Republic of which it was the keystone, could be legitimate only if it positively bathed in popular sovereignty. And yet this device, which was intended to reinforce the Fifth Republic, in fact destroyed two central planks of its philosophy. First, it removed the pretence that the President was above politics, because he would have to contest elections like any other politician. Second, it drastically increased the power of the President against that of the parliament, above and beyond the extraordinary powers of which he already disposed. Indeed, the brazen manner of the reform was itself a conclusive sabotage of parliament's role. The choice of Pompidou as Prime Minister had also already reinforced the constitution's drift towards presidential autocracy, for Pompidou had had no parliamentary experience: he had been the President's *directeur de cabinet*, and under such conditions, it was difficult to pretend that the President was a neutral umpire. Thus, when de Gaulle declared at a press conference in 1966, 'Our constitution is both parliamentary and presidential,' the affirmation was already false.[52] Even by 1964, he had drifted away from the idea that the President was a neutral umpire, such as he had described it in 1958:

> It is the President who appoints the Prime Minister, as well as the other members of the government, who has the ability to change them . . . It is the President who takes the decisions in the Council of Ministers, who promulgates laws, negotiates treaties . . . who is the head of the armed forces, and who makes public appointments . . . The *indivisible* authority of the state is confided entirely in the President by the people who have elected him, and there is no other authority, neither

ministerial, civil, military, *nor judiciary*, which is not conferred and maintained by him.[53]

It seems that de Gaulle did not realize the first consequence of his 1962 reform until François Mitterrand forced him into a second round of elections in 1965 as the leader *of the Left*. The General was shocked. That people should vote against him in the privacy of the voting booth was akin to sacrilege. 'We have built confessionals to try to get rid of the devil. But if the devil is in the confessional himself, that changes everything.'[54] He pretended still to cherish the view that the Head of State was above political parties, but Mitterrand's challenge forced him into a partisan posture he resented. But Faust had concluded a pact with the devil without knowing it: he continued to propagate his unanimist dream for the constitution ('The President is there for the country . . . He responds to something which is common to all the French, their common interest, their national interest')[55] at the very moment when he was perfecting its majoritarian logic: by trying to save the Fifth Republic, he had to give the *coup de grâce* to the *Gaullist* republic.[56] But by doing so, had also planted the seeds of its inevitable downfall, which suggests that it could not have outlasted him under any circumstances.

It is the greatest paradox that the introduction of the election of the President by universal suffrage sealed the anti-democratic fate of the Fifth Republic. The original edifice of the presidency had been built on something magical, de Gaulle's personal historical legitimacy, and his ten-year ability truly to realize it and keep it alive in his political action. His *de facto* accountability was reinforced by the new television age: the Head of State could speak directly to all the French in their own homes, achieving a degree of direct contact with them with no other leader had had in the past. Gaullist supporters still argue that his sweeping powers could be justified because, although there was no mechanism for ensuring the President's political accountability, de Gaulle used referenda and elections very frequently, and when he lost the referendum on decentralization in 1969, he resigned.[57]

But this argument – that the institutions are justified because the General knew the meaning of responsibility, and therefore understood that the contract between the President and the people could and must be broken whenever he ceased to have their trust — assumes that the President is more than a mere umpire. Was there, then, a fatal incoherence in the theory and practice itself? The quasi-sacred unction of universal suffrage was to confer on his successors the indiscrete charm of total irresponsibility, through the institutionalization of practices which made sense only under him. The election of the President only entrenched the subordination to him of the accountable government in parliament, a state of affairs which is intolerable as soon as the President thinks of himself as the leader of a party, as Giscard and Mitterrand clearly did. Inevitably, therefore, they were to lose what elements of legitimacy there existed in the constitution under de Gaulle, and conserve only its dictatorial elements. For this reason, the constitution was to fail to provide for that democratic soundness which de Gaulle himself had given France, at least in the early years of his presidency. By the early 1990s the truth of one of de Gaulle's own remarks about the constitution seemed apparent to all: 'An edifice whose solidity depends upon the presence of one man is necessarily fragile.'[58]

3. The Permanent Coup d'État

François Mitterrand finally destroyed the republican regime by staying in power after the victory of the Right at the legislative elections in 1986. He is incontestably a monarch.

The Count of Paris, pretender to the French throne, 1987

The most vociferous critic of de Gaulle's Fifth Republic, from the moment of its creation, was none other than François Mitterrand. In his most well known, and best-written work, *The Permanent Coup d'État*, published in 1964, he viciously and scathingly attacked the concentration of power in the hands of the President of the Republic. Nonetheless, from the early 1960s onwards, Mitterrand spent his entire political career trying to conquer that same presidency. If he built his political appeal on his tireless opposition to the institutions of the Fifth Republic, once in power, his promises to reform them were abandoned with a sovereign contempt. When reminded of his earlier commitments, he would mutter,

> The political institutions of the country? Oh, I have got used to them . . . There are certain things about them which I have never liked, and which I still do not like. But I do not think that this is the time for reform. It is not a major preoccupation of the French people. It is not one of mine either. I do not want to add another factor of discord to the French who are already divided enough.[1]

His disingenuousness was equalled only by his conceit: 'The institutions? Before me they were dangerous, and after me they shall become so again.'[2]

While in opposition, he had specifically attacked the seven-year presidential term as too long. He also felt that the President should not be eligible for re-election. 'I think that it is an error in our institutions not to have provided for one single non-renewable term of office. Seven years is a long time, but fourteen, that's so

much more . . . All men are fallible, myself included. And I believe
that an excessive power for too long is detrimental to the national
interest.[3] Indeed, his manifesto in 1981, the list of '110 propositions
for France', contained the explicit promise that the presidential
term would be reduced to a five-year term, renewable once, or to
one non-renewable seven-year term.[4] He then proceeded to stand
for re-election in 1988, and stayed in power for a total of fourteen
years himself. Perhaps it was to underline to the French public just
how contemptuously he had led them up the garden path, that he
allowed the republication of *The Permanent Coup d'État* in 1993.
Under his aegis, the very aspect of the constitution which he then
so bitterly attacked, presidential control over policy-making, had
reached its paroxysm, and the quality of French democracy had
declined accordingly. Mitterrand even had the gall to set a pseudo-
process of constitutional reform in motion in 1992, as if it had
taken him eleven years in the Elysée Palace to remember to honour
his most famous commitments.[5] Indeed, if he ever did introduce a
reduction in the powers of the President, it would merely show – as
does his support for the transfer of national policy-making authority
to Europe – that he is determined to be the last man to enjoy those
powers.

The day after Mitterrand came to power, he immediately proceeded to behave in exactly the manner which he had criticised in
his predecessors. On Monday 11 May 1981, he called Pierre Mauroy,
his first Prime Minister, into his office and gave him the names of
the ministers he was to appoint. This was in contempt of the
constitution's requirement that the Prime Minister propose to the
President the names of the ministers he wishes to appoint (Article
8). Mauroy was later to expostulate that he had only nominated one
of his ministers himself, the unknown Jean Le Garrec.[6] Indeed,
Mitterrand hardly even consulted the ministers themselves before
deciding and announcing their appointments. The majority of
them, including such prominent ones as Jack Lang, only heard of
their appointments on the radio.[7] This showed how little importance
Mitterrand attributed to personal capacities for specific portfolios,
no doubt because, in reality, French ministers are used to relying
heavily on their staff, who take most decisions for them. It also was
a means of showing off his own superior power: Mitterrand behaved
in the same way when the government was reshuffled in 1983, and

when he appointed the right-wing cohabitation Prime Minister, Édouard Balladur, in 1993, he did not even ask Balladur to come and see him beforehand. He announced the appointment to the whole country on television instead, before even meeting the new head of government face to face![8]

To be sure, presidential domination of policy dates from de Gaulle, and it has become a well established principle under all Presidents. In 1969, the first year of Pompidou's presidency, the Prime Minister, Jacques Chaban-Delmas was given more or less free rein, and the impression was of a return to parliamentary rule; but by 1972 he was assuring the Assembly that it would be contrary to the spirit of the institutions if a Prime Minister remained in place against the President's wishes. Sacked by Pompidou later that year, he commented, that in 1958, the Prime Minister had escaped from the tutelage of parliament, only to fall under that of the President.[9] Indeed, Pompidou had also said that 'I am sure that future Presidents, whoever they are, will choose Prime Ministers to whom they are closely linked ... I am convinced that they will constantly intervene in the government of the country, and that they will maintain their supremacy in their daily actions.'[10] He was right; and subsequent Presidents have sung the same song. While de Gaulle and Pompidou certainly took charge of the appointment of ministers, Valéry Giscard d'Estaing presented the Chirac government as 'his' government. Having denounced de Gaulle's 'solitary exercise of power',[11] he sent twelve detailed '*lettres directives*' to Chirac during his two years in office, instructing him what to do, and convened fifty-two special councils (like cabinet committees) to direct specific aspects of the government's programme. This was four times more than Pompidou.[12]

But if the decline of the prestige of the Prime Minister has been constant throughout the history of the Fifth Republic, it reached its definitive fall under Mitterrand. The remark by Pompidou, quoted above, assumes that the President will identify himself closely with his Prime Minister, and that therefore he will take some responsibility for the government's policies. Precisely what marks Mitterrand out from the others is that he has changed Prime Ministers as a man might change his shirt. He has had seven Prime Ministers in twelve years – Pierre Mauroy, Laurent Fabius, Jacques Chirac, Michel Rocard, Edith Cresson, Pierre Bérégovoy, and Édouard Balladur.

This is more than the total number of Prime Ministers under de Gaulle, Pompidou and Giscard, put together over twenty-three years, his three predecessors having had only two each.[13] (Indeed, it is a greater turnover even than that of the Queen of the United Kingdom, who has had only ten in forty-one years!) It is significant that Mitterrand should hold the record for the longest-serving President of the Fifth Republic, while his hapless Edith Cresson holds the record for being the shortest-serving Prime Minister.

This game of political musical chairs severely devalues the role of the Prime Minister, but it does not concomitantly increase the President's responsibility for policy, even if it does increase his total domination of it. Rather, it gives the impression that with each new government, a new person is in control. This impression is, of course, false, for it is always he who decides policy. Even though Mitterrand usually refers to his governments as '*mon government*' and '*mes ministres*', it is always they who carry the can if things go wrong, never he, which indeed explains why there have been so many changes. Here again, an increase of presidential power is discernible over time: his first Prime Minister, Pierre Mauroy, was a heavyweight, both politically and physically. Although an old and very loyal ally of Mitterrand's, he was capable of standing his corner in disagreements with him. The most important of these was over the decision on whether the franc should remain in the European Monetary System in 1983, when Mitterrand was initially tempted to leave the system altogether. But Mauroy was in no doubt about who was ultimately in charge. He once asked rhetorically, 'Do you imagine that, in this regime, the President of the Republic is not at the origin of all the great directions, and of all the big decisions? I shall continue to serve in the place where I am for as long as the President of the Republic, *and he alone*, decides.'[14]

With the appointment of Laurent Fabius in 1984, however, decision-making power resided more visibly in the Elysée than ever before. Fabius was essentially a creation of Mitterrand's, without the kind of independent political weight of Mauroy. On the day of Fabius' appointment, *Liberation*'s tart headline was 'Mitterrand is Prime Minister'.[15] Indeed, Mitterrand's attitude to the role of the government and Prime Minister is starkly illustrated by the manner in which he reflected on how to change the guard at Matignon. He asked his personal adviser Jacques Attali to draw up the government's programme beforehand. 'Is your governmental programme ready?' he asked Attali. 'Good. All I need to decide now is which Prime Minister to send it to.'[16] Mitterrand's third Socialist Prime Minister (the fourth in all, including Jacques Chirac), his long-time rival in the Socialist Party, Michel Rocard, who was at Matignon from 1988 to 1991, confirmed that Mitterrand thinks of his Prime Ministers as little more than lackeys. 'At Matignon, you are not the boss. Above you there is someone in charge of planning for the future and setting out the true direction of policy.'[17]

The point is not just that presidential domination over policy is total, for this is inevitable given the constitution. Indeed, it is the *raison d'être* of the constitution. What is objectionable is rather that no responsibility falls on the shoulders of the man who actually takes the decisions, if the President changes the government frequently. Mitterrand has seldom missed an opportunity to emphasize that his Prime Ministers 'must leave the day it is necessary',[18] but at each changing of the guard, the purpose has always been to revive his own flagging political fortunes. This is the opposite of what de Gaulle intended. He appointed Laurent Fabius in 1984 to manage the U-turn on economic policy from statist Socialism to semi-liberalism; he sacked Rocard in 1991 in order to improve his image, and thought that appointing a woman to Matignon would do the trick. Instead, Edith Cresson's unfortunate eleven months in office from May 1991 to April 1992 only marked the nadir of the Prime Ministership. The Prime Minister became little more than the press attachée of the Elysée Palace, and, in Cresson's case, a press attachée with considerable difficulties in communication at that. Finally, the Bérégovoy government, appointed in April 1992 after the Socialists' disastrous showing in the local and regional elections, was composed of eight ministers who had worked at the Elysée since 1981,[19] nine former members of the Convention of Republican Institutions, the party which Mitterrand founded in the 1960s,[20] and two of Mitterrand's closest personal friends.[21] Indeed, one minister even kept an office at the Elysée Palace while continuing to discharge his ministerial functions.[22] Therefore, while real power was concentrated more in the Elysée Palace under Pompidou than de Gaulle, more under Giscard than under Pompidou, it was incomparably more so under Mitterrand than under all his predecessors;[23] and yet Mitterrand, like a snake shedding his skin, was always able to slink away from assuming the consequences.

Not only has Mitterrand set the general direction of policy, as de Gaulle intended, he has entered into the very minutiae of government, and even into its parliamentary activities, all away from the tiresome glare of public transparency. Reporting on the process of ratifying the Maastricht treaty, *Le Monde* wrote in 1992, 'The government, or more precisely the President, *for it is he who in this case decides, down to the very last detail, what will be the parliamentary tactics of ministers,* is giving the impression of not having definitively decided on his strategy.'[24] He also regularly goes through bills crossing bits out which he does not like.[25] Indeed, Mitterrand has often announced specific legislative and political decisions himself without consulting anyone beforehand. In 1984, during a television broadcast, he announced a referendum on private education, which, according to Attali, he had no intention of holding, and which indeed never took place: his closest collaborators and ministers watched the broadcast in the adjoining room, where they heard about the suggestion for the first time.[26] Similarly in 1989, he announced the writing-off of certain African debts, when that decision could only be taken by the National Assembly.[27]

It is revealing that this accretion of presidential domination over policy has occurred because Mitterrand has been able to claim that he is respecting the letter of the constitution. For it is difficult not to conclude that the degradation which has occurred under Mitterrand was programmed into the institutions from the very beginning; or at least that, however well they may have functioned under the General, their steady decline once he left power shows their lack of robustness. Although the Prime Minister and the government merely execute decisions taken by the President, to whom each of its members owes his very job, the pretence is maintained that the Prime Minister is somehow the author of those policies. However, far from being responsible to the parliament or the public, the Prime Minister and his government are responsible only to the President who, in Mitterrand's case, takes no responsibility for himself. Therefore, far from ensuring parliamentary accountability with its hybrid mix of presidential and parliamentary elements, the constitution ensures that there is none. If the Prime Minister were officially recognized as being a mere executor of the President's policies, then that might establish presidential responsibility. But in the present twilight situation, the President gives orders, disguising them as those of his Prime Minister: he can then renounce the paternity of these policies and blame the government if they fail. By respecting the letter of the constitution, Mitterrand has turned its spirit on its head, for de Gaulle understood that spirit to reside in the grand leadership offered by the President, who would leave office if his leadership ever failed. Like one of those tropical blow-fish which are sold puffed-up, dried-out and hollow on the inside, nothing is now left of the constitution but the flimsy and lifeless shell of its former impressive self.

Mitterrand's behaviour has been little more than an up-market version of Clemenceau's colourful remark, referring to his faithful minister, Georges Mandel: 'I'm the one who farts, and he's the one who stinks.'[28] But perhaps the most depressing thing of all is to see this state of affairs actually being justified in political comment. Mitterrand has weakened the role of the Prime Minister so much that many have asked what exactly is the point of even having a Prime Minister at all. In reply, some justify the existence of the Prime Minister by comparing his role to that of a 'fuse' between the President and the people; yet this extraordinary argument seeks to justify precisely the most unacceptable part of the constitution, for it dismissed the whole concept of political responsibility by suggest-ing that if the President's policy breaks down or meets with popular disapproval, the President merely has to appoint another Prime Minister to wriggle out of his political difficulties. The latter thus becomes the sacrificial lamb offered on the altar of public opinion if things get tough for the President. If the doctrine of the 'fuse' is nothing but a justification for shooting the messenger, it received its most gruesome illustration in the suicide of Pierre Bérégovoy in May 1993. He had just led the Socialists to the most crushing electoral defeat in the party's entire history (they obtained 18 per cent of the vote), the most decisive disavowal imaginable of Mitterrand's policies. But by blowing his brains out, Bérégovoy was simply designating himself as scapegoat: within a few weeks, Mitterrand's popularity was above 40 per cent again, as if nothing had happened.

The ambiguous roles of the President and Prime Minister inevita-bly also lead to tensions and distortions in the daily functioning of the government. The Prime Minister spends most of his intellectual energy trying to guess what the President wants, while the President

tends to prefer the Prime Minister least of all his servants, because
he sees him as a rival. He often resents the fact that the latter
believes that he can think for himself. Indeed, the only occasion
when a Prime Minister has resigned of his own accord 'because he
could no longer govern' was when Jacques Chirac fell out with
Valéry Giscard d'Estaing in 1976 – in other words, not because of
disagreement between the Prime Minister and the National Assembly, but between the Prime Minister and the President. Indeed, the
Assembly only heard of Chirac's departure on television.[29] These
tensions in turn sap the Prime Minister's authority within the
government. The other ministers, who know where the real source
of power is, have little respect for their official boss, and so the
make-believe boss is patronized by his make-believe subordinates.
Pierre Joxe, Defence Minister under Michel Rocard, was especially
known for his insolent behaviour towards the Prime Minister in
cabinet meetings.[30]

As a result, the workings of the Council of Ministers can in no
way be compared to that of the British Cabinet. There has been a
good deal of argument among British constitutionalists about
whether the Cabinet still preserves its traditional role of decision-
making body, or whether real decisions are taken in cabinet committees and only brought to Cabinet for ultimate approval. Most of
these charges were exaggerated under Margaret Thatcher's government, because of the obsession of academics and journalists with
her allegedly dictatorial style. However, whatever their partial
truth, they pale into insignificance against Mitterrand's autocratic
treatment of the Council of Ministers. At the very first Council of
Ministers he issued curt instructions to his ministers as to how to
conduct themselves in the meetings. 'Do not read notes, do not
take notes. There is to be no discussion between ministers.'[31] It is
clear that he considered the Council of Ministers to be a rubber
stamp, not a place for discussion. Indeed, he found the meetings a
tedious irrelevance, and rarely listened to what was said.[32]

Instead, he preferred to discuss policy with a small coterie of
friends. Soon after his election to the presidency, he established the
practice of holding a weekly breakfast meeting at the Elysée Palace
on Tuesdays, the day before the Council of Ministers. It was
attended by the Prime Minister, the General Secretary of the
Elysée, the First Secretary of the Socialist Party – all close political

friends – and it became the principal decision-making centre of the state.[33] This way of proceeding is a far cry from the collegiate decision-making process of the British Cabinet, where all opinions of the governing parliamentary party have to be taken into account. Indeed, very often the only reflection on the great public issues of the day took place in Mitterrand's head.[34]

Not only is it unacceptable from a democratic point of view that policy should be made in this way by unelected political favourites – known as the 'elephants' of the Socialist Party – who have no constitutional status, and who correspond to no political constituency; it also shows how the constitution was unable to resist the abusive pressures which Mitterrand exerted on it. Under his reign, the original anti-partisan logic of the presidency has been perverted out of all recognition. While it would have been inconceivable for de Gaulle or Pompidou to meet every week with representatives of the Gaullist parties, the UNR and later the UDR – it would have been incompatible with their unanimist concept of the presidency – one is forced to admit that, despite de Gaulle's famous dislike of political parties, the constitution gives them about as much power as one can imagine.[35] One especially vicious commentator savages this aspect of the constitution:

> De Gaulle was convinced that the powerful office he was creating, which would be one of arbitrage and legitimacy, was the only way to overcome the 'scheming of political parties'. This has proved to be a tragic error, which thirty years on has delivered us the sinister totalitarianism of Giscard and Mitterrand, with the absolute power of an old despot reigning over an explosion of clans and of rival bands.[36]

But perhaps the clearest illustration of Mitterrand's abuse of the spirit of the constitution is the practice of 'cohabitation' with a right-wing government, introduced for the first time in the history of the Fifth Republic in 1986–8 under Jacques Chirac and repeated in 1993 under Édouard Balladur. It is perhaps significant that the metaphor of cohabitation is a bad one: in the modern world, vacuous figures of speech often stick in common usage, underlying the degree to which language is abused, and such abuses often betray an unclarity of understanding, or an attempt to obscure contradictions. When two people cohabit, they do so because they love each other, and because they do not care much for the institution of marriage. By contrast, the political 'cohabitation' between a President of one political persuasion and government of another demonstrates the primacy of institutions over affections.

The reason why 'cohabitation' is the ultimate perversion of the constitution is that it allows the President to remain in power, albeit slightly enfeebled, even after clear disavowal of him by the electorate. This is clearly incompatible with the logic of a centralist constitution, whose whole legitimacy reposes on that of the President, and on regular plebiscitary consultation. Indeed, de Gaulle had explicitly ruled out the legitimacy of 'cohabitation'.[37] René Capitant made it clear that

> To admit that the Head of State could remain in power against the will of the people would be to commit an attack against the regime. The French people has the right to overthrow the President of the Republic during the course of his seven-year term of office. It has the right to do this by sending to the Assembly a majority hostile to the policies of the President.[38]

In a sort of half-way house between this clear statement of the Gaullist position and Mitterrand's practice, Valéry Giscard d'Estaing, contemplating the possibility that a left-wing parliament might be elected in 1978, had said that he would transform himself into a neutral chairman of the Council of Ministers. He even said that he would have left the Elysée except for formal purposes, to underline his purely symbolic role, and that only the Prime Minister would attend European summits, while as President, he would attend international summits only when no negotiation was necessary. In his view, the President's signature on bills was the equivalent of royal assent in Britain, not an act of political approval.[39]

Mitterrand had no such scruples. When the Right seemed likely to win the elections in 1986, he expressed his determination to stay in power. Indeed, before the elections were held, he altered the voting system by introducing proportional representation, even though he had expressed his hostility to PR in 1948, 1950, 1951, 1953 and 1958.[40] This was in order to minimize the scale of the Socialist defeat, and to disorientate the Right by allowing the National Front to win parliamentary representation. (In the event, the Front won thirty-five seats.) Mitterrand knew well that a strong

National Front presence would put the centre-right parties under pressure to come to a pact with the extreme right, which he hoped would be politically suicidal. Once the Right was in power, Mitterrand did everything to wreck the activities of the Chirac government and to maintain his own grip on power, justifying his actions in the name of respect for the constitution. Chirac, of course, defended and demanded the right to govern, which gave rise to the paradoxical situation of Mitterrand, the Socialist and veteran opponent of de Gaulle's presidential constitution, defending the rights and powers of the presidency, while Chirac, the Gaullist, insisted on those of the parliament and government.

Mitterrand thus remained in office throughout, and played the role of being in power and opposition at the same time, refusing to consider the Socialists' electoral defeats of 1986 and 1993 as his own. He repeatedly wrong-footed Chirac by publicly undermining the government's activities and stuffing public posts with his own appointees. In 1986, when Chirac was Prime Minister, he publicly supported student leaders in their protests against the right-wing government. He also made use of the power of veto which the constitution gives him on certain decrees and ordonnances,[41] refusing to enact certain aspects of government legislation, saying that he would act as a brake on the government's supposed 'excesses', and that he would protect what he misleadingly called France's 'social achievements'. He co-ordinated his obstructive tactics with Socialist deputies.

Some admired Mitterrand's brazen political skill during 1986–8, and the strategy resulted in his re-election as President after two years. But it is worth pondering the fact that this strategy was to undermine the government of the republic of which he was the President. This is clearly incompatible with the primary role of the presidency, which is to assure the smooth functioning of the institutions. That he should disguise his wrecking operation against Chirac as respect for the letter of the constitution only adds insult to injury, for his 'interpretation' of his role betrays precisely the 'representative' understanding of political institutions which the authors of the Fifth Republic had wanted to destroy. Without considering the specific French background, there can surely be no justification for the existence side-by-side of two mutually antagonistic politicians fighting over ill-defined areas of responsibility at the head of a country's executive.

It is significant that the first person publicly to theorize the possibility of 'cohabitation' was Édouard Balladur in 1983. His introduction of the idea into the political arena showed that he shared the same un-Gaullist conception of the constitution as François Mitterrand. It was no surprise, therefore, that Balladur should have accepted so many constraints on his own premiership in 1993. Before nominating him, Mitterrand insisted on continuity in the most important domain of all, European policy. This constraint, which Balladur had already decided to accept, meant that he was unable to change either France's foreign or economic policy, and that he therefore had to preside both over the economic collapse caused by the pursuit of the policy of the *franc fort*, and over an increasingly meaningless foreign-policy attachment to the Maastricht process. By March 1994, the perverse effects of this were becoming clear: the education issue blew up again, and student demonstrations were organized by the leaders of SOS-Racisme (a left-wing front organization set up by the Elysée) in order to protest against the reduction of the minimum wage for students entering employment. As on a number of other issues, Balladur was forced to climb down; but what was also striking was that 3,000 police officers failed to prevent widespread looting and rioting. This was doubtless because the government was terrified of a repeat performance of 1986, when during student demonstrations a young Arab had died after being arrested by the police. (The incident was one of the major causes of the Right's subsequent defeat in 1988.) The impression grew current of a powerless government presiding over the rising fortunes of the Left.

In no other country is the elected government prevented from taking the measures for which it has been elected. A cohabitation Prime Minister is just as absurd a concept as one who is nothing but the President's poodle. Indeed, it is a mistake to think that the 'cohabitation' radically changed the interaction between the Prime Minister and the President. Mitterrand's relationships with his Prime Ministers have seldom been tranquil, even when they have been Socialists. In 1988, he appointed his old rival in the Socialist Party, Michel Rocard, to the post of Prime Minister. His treatment of Rocard was very similar to that of Jacques Chirac, his main rival on the Right, and then subsequently to that of Édouard Balladur. In 1990, Mitterrand exploited an education crisis in similar ways to his own advantage, his impervious presidential perch allowing him to intervene from on high: he humiliated the Rocard government by receiving student protesters at the Elysée Palace, and then sending them to the Minister of Education with instructions from himself.[42]

However, the Balladuro-Mitterrandian understanding of the constitution did not cease to gain ground. This was demonstrated by the futile debate about whether the presidential term should be five years or seven, which Mitterrand caused to be re-launched in 1992. The debate is futile because the Gaullist understanding is that the fundamental contract between the President and the people can and must be broken the instant the President no longer enjoys popular legitimacy. Fixing terms is therefore contrary to its spirit, whatever those terms are. René Capitant had also made this quite clear:

> It has often been said that seven years is a long time for a presidential term of office. It is true, but it would be better to speak in the conditional. It would indeed be a long time if during those seven years the President was not responsible before the people, and if the people did not have the possibility to break off the seven-year term, as they did in 1969.[43]

Capitant's interpretation has the double advantage of corresponding both to de Gaulle's own practice, as well as to an effective and democratic conception of the institutions. However, his theory also reinforces the view that the constitution was bound to self-destruct anyway, for even de Gaulle's laudable decision to quit after losing the referendum in 1969 shows that it is the President himself who decides whether or not he still has legitimacy. Normally, such a decision should not be in his hands. At the same time, de Gaulle had himself planted the seeds of the constitution's own destruction because Mitterrand would not have been able to stay in power through the cohabitation if the General had not invented the myth of the 'President of all the French'. After the 1967 legislative elections, the Gaullist UNR party found itself returned with a reduced majority. The General had refused beforehand to accept that this would represent a setback for himself, because, in conformity with his conviction that a parliamentary election was not a truly national one, he declared, 'I will not put my mandate into question. There are to be 487 local elections. They cannot prevail over the national election.'[44]

The idea has persisted that the President, when so elected, has a superior and all-embracing legitimacy to that of any other elected body, and Mitterrand himself has certainly used the label 'President of all the French' quite often, especially when confronted in a contest with a difficult opponent.[45] In other words, the ultimate contradiction of the original logic of the constitution was made possible only because one of its founding myths was alive and well. Having conquered power on a partisan basis, Mitterrand remained in power in 1986 after his party's electoral defeat only because he could pretend that the myth applied to himself too, and that the Socialists' defeat was not his business. Indeed, his defeat paradoxically reinforced him in his new role: having for five years been steeped in ideological confrontation with French society – in virtue of his nationalizations, his pursuit of statist Socialism from 1981–3, his attempt to integrate private education within the state – he started to adopt a totally new presidential practice. Having claimed to have been elected by the '*people* of the Left' ('*le peuple de gauche*'), he started to play the role of the President of all the French, and every day, the cohabitation reinforced the President who had been disavowed in the election of 1986. In 1984 he declared, 'I was elected by people on the Left, but I shall be the President of all the French. By changing my office, my obligations change.'[46] As one critic remarks, 'The authors of the constitution in 1958 had chosen political effectiveness. The general interpretation of the constitution in 1986 was one of political surrealism.'[47] Cohabitation did not merely allow irresponsibility: it encouraged it, and imparted new strength to the President. Mitterrand went on to campaign successfully for re-election in 1988 with the slogan '*La France unie*'.

The myth was the main, perhaps the only, justification for the extraordinary powers the President enjoys. However, those powers can be legitimate only if he resembles a monarch and not an ordinary politician – an evident absurdity when one reflects on what happens in a presidential election. De Gaulle's 1962 reform introduced a two-round election, for fear that the Left might unite under one candidate, and a Communist thereby be elected, if there were only one round. In all five presidential elections (1965, 1969, 1974, 1981 and 1988), no President has been elected outright in the first round. The successful candidates have won only in the second round, with the help of votes from people who did not want him as their first choice. Moreover, the margin by which the candidates have beaten their opponents has often been very small. In 1974, Giscard received 50.81 per cent of the vote in the second round, less than 1 per cent more than François Mitterrand. In 1981, Mitterrand himself only beat Giscard by 3.5 per cent, and that was with the help of some Gaullists who were determined to vote tactically against Giscard. This is hardly grounds for political omnipotence.

Part of Mitterrand's operation against Chirac's government during 1986–8 centred on another mysterious doctrine, that of the so-called 'reserved domain'. The doctrine is as widely recognized in practice as it is denied in public: it is that there are certain areas of policy which are officially the President's personal and exclusive preserve, notably foreign affairs and defence. All Presidents have seemed to assume that they have a special or exclusive role in these areas, even if their declarations on the issue have been contradictory. (De Gaulle both affirmed and denied at different times that there was a reserved domain.)[48] But Mitterrand built a good part of his political career in opposition by attacking the doctrine. In 1965, he declared, 'Despite what I read every day, I reject . . . the very idea of a "reserved domain". There is no "reserved domain". There is the constitution and the national interest.'[49]

It is odd that there should even be any debate on the matter, for the constitution makes no mention whatever of a special role for the President in foreign affairs, except inasmuch as he signs treaties as Head of State. Indeed, it even states explicitly that the Prime Minister is responsible for National Defence (Article 21), an indication, perhaps, of the way in which the French fascination for written constitutions is equalled only by a considerable degree of contempt for their content. However, once Mitterrand got into power, his attitude on this, as on other constitutional matters, underwent a total change. Although he occasionally still claims that he is opposed to the doctrine,[50] his behaviour has suggested otherwise. On a trip to Pakistan in February 1990, when he decided to sell a nuclear centre to the country, doubts were expressed at the press conference as to whether this was wise. Mitterrand just snapped, 'If these people have doubts, why are they here? I'm the expert.'[51] Indeed, just before the expected election of a Gaullist-Liberal government in 1986, he declared bluntly, 'If there were any

confiscation of foreign policy by anybody following a change of
majority in parliament, that would be a *coup d'état*.'[52]

Whether this was an inadvertent or contemptuously deliberate
reference to his book, *The Permanent Coup d'État*, in which he
expressed the opposite view, is difficult to tell. At any rate, he
vetoed Chirac's ministerial appointments for Defence and Foreign
Affairs, no doubt to underline his determination to preserve the
'reserved domain' in those areas. As a result, Prime Minister Chirac
found that he was able to influence foreign and EEC policy only
marginally, despite having created a seven-person-strong diplomatic
unit at Matignon.[53] And after the first Council of Ministers with the
Balladur government in 1993, Mitterrand tarried publicly with the
two new ministers of Defence and Foreign Affairs, presumably for
the same reason, having announced prior to the elections that he
would only ever appoint a Prime Minister who was in absolute
agreement with his European policy.

Indeed, Mitterrand has not only preserved the doctrine of the
presidential domain, he has actually enlarged it beyond defence and
foreign affairs. At the beginning of the presidency, his adviser,
Jacques Attali, noted in his diary, without comment, that 'The
reserved domain was well defined: foreign policy, defence policy,
the international economy, Europe, and the principal public appointments.'[54] He should have added 'culture', for the President was to
devote himself to a number of prestige quasi-cultural building
projects,[55] on a scale unparalleled by any previous President, even
though he had attacked the omnipotence of the President while in
opposition, saying that he 'busies himself with everything, even
with the gardens along the banks of the Seine'.[56]

Even de Gaulle himself realized the truth of which the
seventeenth-century Dutch philosopher Spinoza had been per-
suaded: 'A dominion whose well-being depends on any man's good
faith, and whose affairs cannot be properly administered unless
those who are engaged in them will act honestly, will be very
unstable.[57] Either the degradation was inevitable, or de Gaulle's
legacy was insufficiently strong to withstand increasing abuse: but
both judgements are an unfavourable assessment of the constitution
itself. Perhaps one should forget the mitigating historical circumstances of the constitution's creation, and concentrate on the essential point: whoever assumes the office, the power of the French

President is incompatible with the basic democratic principle that power should not be exercised without responsibility. This is certainly the view of one commentator:

> I intend here to defend François Mitterrand against his detractors. I certainly recognize that, in the exercise of his presidential functions, he has joined in a disastrous marriage the abuse of power with the powerlessness to govern; arbitrariness with indecision; omnipotence with impotence; democratic legitimacy with the violation of laws; the republican state with monarchical favouritism; length of stay in office with inefficiency, failure and arrogance, unpopularity and self-satisfaction. I recognize all this, *but . . . the guilty partner is not the man but the institution.* It is the role of the President, as it is defined in the constitution.[58]

Mitterrand built his whole career on his opposition to de Gaulle, and he seems obsessed with outdoing his memory. But it is clear at the end of his reign that within the veteran challenger to the omnipotent General, and to the autocratic constitution he designed, there slept a disciple who surpassed even the master himself.

4. The House of Mitterrand

Administrative officials form a class apart, with their own feelings, traditions, virtues, and notions of honour and pride. They constitute the aristocracy of the new society. A marked characteristic of the French administration is the violent hatred it bears towards everyone who presumes to meddle in public affairs without its knowledge . . . It objects to people looking after their own concerns; it prefers sterility to competition.

Alexis de Tocqueville, *L'Ancien Régime et la révolution*[1]

If Mitterrand's behaviour in power has betrayed and magnified many of the constitutional abuses which he used to criticize under de Gaulle, this is only one instance of a general trend. His political rhetoric is in general laden with Manichaean metaphors of Right and Wrong. Like a classical gnostic, he divides the political universe into Good and Evil principles, with himself, the Left and the People in the former category, and the Right, Money and his political enemies in the latter. In fact, however, this habit often leads him to denounce in others, sometimes in the most violent terms, precisely those faults which he himself epitomizes.

His curious propensity to attack his enemies as 'clans' is an example of this. He has gained considerable electoral advantage by evoking the image of his opponents as 'factions', 'bands', 'groups' and so on, and to imply that he represents a more unitary force himself. In *Le Coup d'état permanent*, he wrote, 'Before de Gaulle, they say that France was governed by committees. Now, because of him, she is governed by commandos – at least until the moment when the people takes back its rights.'[2] Twenty-four years later, during the 1988 presidential election campaign, he was still attacking Jacques Chirac, and his party, the RPR, with the same old song: 'I want France to be united; and she will not be united if she is taken over by intolerant people, by parties who want everything, by clans or gangs.'[3] He was even able, at one point, to describe Chirac as 'the man who wants everything'. Then Prime Minister and Mayor of Paris, Chirac was perhaps vulnerable to such a charge; but it was ironic that the man who really did have everything should have been able to make such an attack with impunity. In a similar vein, Mitterrand's success in keeping alive the fear of the 'Gaullist state', in which the government supposedly achieved control over all the levers of state and civil society, is astonishing in view of the way that the Socialist Party devoted itself, largely successfully, to doing the same thing itself. Indeed, many would say that Mitterrand surpassed even the General.

In order to understand how a political party can attain near-total control over the levers of state power, it is necessary to grasp the exceptional power of the administration in France. The administration has enjoyed inordinate strength in France since the *Ancien Régime*.[4] Indeed, it is a charming irony that, despite the rural image of their country which the French like to project abroad, and in which they still believe themselves, France now has more civil servants than peasants. The administration's domination extends well into areas beyond its immediate ambit, like the media, with which it shares structural and personal affinity. It is exacerbated by a striking permeability between the administration, politics and industry, which leads both to the politicization of the bureaucracy and to the bureaucratization of politics.

The politicization of the administration is totally contrary to British practice, where the neutrality of the civil service is an essential constitutional principle. Indeed, to someone steeped in the ways of French politics it is almost incomprehensible that the most senior official in the British civil service, the Cabinet Secretary, as well as the overwhelming majority of all other civil servants, should stay at their posts when the government changes.[5] The tradition in France is for incoming French governments to clear out whole swathes of the civil service, the media, press, the nationalized industries and banks.

An appointment in France is used simply as a means of increasing the power of the appointer. Mitterrand's acolyte Jacques Attali positively drools over 'the drunkenness of the only true power: appointing people',[6] by which he presumably means that a network of the right friends in the right places is the most effective means of ensuring control over government and society. Indeed, if commenta-

tors are agreed on one thing about Mitterrand's character, it is that
he is exceptionally attached to his personal friends. Once, during
the Fourth Republic, Mitterrand had declared that he just needed
'fifty well-placed friends in order to run the country',[7] and he has
not varied much from this since. Indeed, he is well known for
maintaining complex intersecting circles of friends of greater and
lesser intimacy: there is the circle which is invited on Sundays,
there is the private circle in Paris, there is the circle which is asked
to stay at his country house at Latché.[8]

Most Presidents of the Fifth Republic, starting with de Gaulle,
have been the victim of press derision about their monarchical
behaviour, and their tendency to construct a 'court' around themselves. Here, too, Mitterrand has outdone his predecessors, especially where the rewarding of flattery is concerned. No hyperbole is
enough for those who wish to make their way to the top under
Mitterrand. Harzoun Tazieff was made a Secretary of State after
declaring, 'I have lived through some great moments in my lifetime
– the Popular Front, the Allied Landings in 1944, the Liberation
. . . But what I have just experienced today [10 May 1981] is greater
than all those things, for today France has regained democracy and
liberty.'[9] On the same day, Pierre Mauroy declared that 'A new
dawn has broken. With us, the truth has risen':[10] he was appointed
Prime Minister. Jacques Fauvet, the Director of *Le Monde* proclaimed that the Socialist victory was 'the victory of morality':[11] he
was awarded the Légion d'honneur and made the President of the
Commission on Information and Liberties. Given such apparently
successful flattery, it is hardly surprising that in 1986 Mitterrand
was to half-admit, 'I have courtesans, but no court.'[12] To deny it
would have been impossible!

That he should have behaved in this princely way has been a
source of great disappointment to some on the Left who were
enthusiastic at his election in 1981, especially because they had
pretended that favouritism was the preserve of the Right. One of
the first to experience such disappointment was Serge July, the
editor of the left-wing daily, *Libération*. It is he who first identified
that Mitterrand 'feels greater solidarity to men than to ideas'.[13]
Surveying the gathering of the Mitterrand faithful at his first
presidential garden party at the Elysée Palace in 1982, July wrote
(in an article entitled 'The Converted Godfather'), 'Mitterrand does

not have confidence in ideas in order to govern the world. It is not the Socialist Party which is directing the affairs of France, it is François Mitterrand alone with his 'family' of faithful friends, who have been sifted out with his instinctive mistrust.'[14]

Like his other powers, the President's power of appointment is vast. Those who complain of the power of patronage of the British Prime Minister, referring usually to his ability to give out knighthoods, peerages and other baubles, should compare this with the power of the French President to appoint people to positions of real power throughout the whole apparatus of the French politico-industrial complex. Moreover, whereas executive appointments by the American President are subject to the approval of Congress, in France, none of these appointments is subject to the approval of anyone. Above all, the overwhelming bulk of these appointments are the *personal* responsibility of the President, not even of the government. Inevitably, therefore, it is easy for the solemn task of attributing public appointments to degenerate into a mere abuse of the state as an immense machine for distributing situations, incomes, material advantages, costly favours and so on.[15] A former adviser to Pierre Mauroy has testified that

> During the three years I spent at Matignon, not one single significant public appointment was announced by the Prime Minister. The lucky person chosen always received a phone call from Mitterrand. The President of the Republic has taken great care in distributing his favours and he always lets people know to whom they owe their job. The nepotism which he has practised is worse than under Giscard.[16]

On coming to power, Mitterrand had claimed that he would not purge people in the administration for political reasons, and that he would manifest tolerance towards 'those who have chosen to serve the state'. But like most of Mitterrand's promises, it was an empty one.

It is not difficult to guess at the effect of this practice. Anyone in the system who finds himself rewarded with a post in the government, the upper echelons of the national administration, or in industry, is not someone to whom a task is being given in order that it be executed, and who will be judged on the integrity and efficiency with which he fulfils it. On the contrary, it simply means he is a friend who is being recompensed for his loyalty to the President. If one looks at the curricula vitae of the directors of nationalized companies and of the senior officials in the administration, the especially young or successful ones have very often worked either in the private office of the President of the Republic or of the Prime Minister. In other words, those who execute the policy of the nation from the highest positions of power are more widely recruited from among the President's personal friends and favourites than from true political figures who possess a genuine base in the electorate and who are motivated by the convictions which come from there. In the words of one harsh critic, 'Presidential favouritism has replaced universal suffrage as our basic constitutional principle.'[17]

The list of major appointments over which the President has direct control runs to several pages. He is responsible for over 500 jobs in the upper echelons of the civil service.[18] The posts include officials at the Council of State, prefects, directors of the central administration, generals, university rectors, ambassadors. He picks the heads of banks, insurance companies, transport agencies, nationalized industries, universities, museums, the *Grandes Écoles*, libraries, operas, theatres, music companies, and of the media and press agencies. Then there is a host of rather ridiculous auxiliary posts, including the director of the port of Dunkirk; the National Hunting Office; the National Office for Fruit, Vegetables and Horticulture; the Director-General of Submarine Cables; and the National Interprofessional Office for Aromatic and Medicinal Plants. No other head of state or government in the world has as much power as the French President to award patronage to his clients and flatterers. According to the Academician and parliamentarian, Jean-François Deniau, it surpasses even that of a South American dictatorship.[19] The result, in the words of one critic, 'is that the system combines the worst aspects of old Italian-style *partitocrazia* and the French-style presidential system, for there is a conjunction of two mafias: the swarm of the prince's favourites, somewhat in the manner of the degenerate *Ancien Régime*, and the fratricide clan of the feudal barons of the political parties'.[20]

However, the power of appointment is not just a means of ensuring the servility of individuals. It can also be used to attenuate the results of electoral misfortune. In 1985, anticipating the defeat of the Socialists, he made sure that as many friends as possible were nominated in jobs over which he had exclusive power.[21] In the same way, just before the Socialists' defeat at the legislative elections in 1993, he stuffed public posts with new appointees in order to soften the anticipated blow, sure in the knowledge that the incoming emollient Balladur government would not dare purging the administration while he was still in power. The most prominent of these appointees was Pierre Joxe, the former Defence Minister, who was made President of the Court of Accounts, the highest financial body in the land. But there were hundreds of lower-scale appointments as well. Indeed, on the last day of the Socialist government, the government published thirteen pages of such appointments to a whole range of posts in the *Journal Officiel*.[22]

Mitterrand has also been very adept at applying the same principle to institutions over which France has no legal control whatever. The most obvious examples of this are the European Commission in Brussels and the European Bank for Reconstruction and Development in London. As the British suspect, Jacques Delors, who owes his job to François Mitterrand, seems to act largely as if he were working for France rather than in the general interest. That this is so is clear from the way Mitterrand discussed the appointment of new European Commissioners in 1984. He and his advisers reflected on what areas of European policy France wanted to continue to control directly, and which areas would have to be sacrificed.[23] This approach is incompatible with the oath of independence which European Commissioners must swear on taking office.

Jacques Attali's own ill-fated stint at the EBRD, and the subsequent appointment there of the former Governor of the Bank of France, Jacques de Larosière, demonstrate how determined France is to have a political counterweight to the feared economic and political domination of Eastern Europe by Germany. The plan to put Attali there (conceived in part by Attali himself) must count as one of Mitterrand's most spectacular failures: the former's fate at the hands of a press and public opinion unused and hostile to the megalomania and authoritarianism of French politicians was a delightful come-uppance to observe. But it was also amusing to observe Attali trying and failing in a French radio broadcast[24] to convince his interviewer that he was the head of an international organization, and not the placeman for Mitterrand or even for

France. One was simply tempted to murmur, 'He doth protest too much, methinks.'

Mitterrand's favouritism has even extended to members of the Mitterrand family, and to that of his wife. In 1981, the newly elected President Mitterrand sent his brother, General Robert Mitterrand, as a special envoy to see the King of Saudi Arabia. He also followed this brother's advice for the appointment of the head of the army.[25] The same brother had been François Mitterrand's *directeur de cabinet* from 1947 to 1949, when Mitterrand was already a minister in the Fourth Republic. Mitterrand's son, Gilbert, was elected a deputy in 1981. His great-nephew, Jérôme Lambert has been a deputy for the Charente since 1986. Most striking of all is the appointment of his son, Jean-Christophe Mitterrand, as his personal adviser at the Elysée Palace on African Affairs. The son's frequent trips to the black continent earned him the nickname 'Papamadi', which roughly translates as 'Daddy said'. Mitterrand himself has reacted with irritation when people have reproached him with this nepotism, saying that his son had spent much time in Africa while working as a journalist, and that he was therefore perfectly qualified for the job. As *Le Canard Enchaîné* remarked, it is a good thing he did not work on the economics desk of Agence France Presse, or else Mitterrand might have appointed him Minister of Finance.[26]

Another of his favourite tricks is to appoint people who have lost elections, or who have otherwise been ejected from power, as if the new nomination were consolation for the unfairness of being thrown out.[27] Conversely, ministers can be dropped for the most personal reasons: Lionel Jospin was sacked not for being a bad minister, nor even for being defeated in an election, but simply for having contradicted the President in private.

It is inevitable that the same way of behaving filters down through the whole political apparatus. Within individual ministries, the power and practice of patronage is huge. When they came to power, it soon became obvious that the Socialists, with the support of the government and the President, intended to place their friends in a whole range of essential posts, to a degree which had never been seen before. In the Foreign Ministry this desire for control seemed to concern not only important posts, but also others of lesser and even very little importance, both in the main embassies and also in the central administration. In other words, it was not a matter of controlling merely the essential cogs of the administration, but of placing one's friends in power at all levels.[28] The turnover of officials shot up, creating confusion and disorientation in French diplomacy, an area where Mitterrand had claimed to want to put a premium on stability and continuity. Moreover, the speed at which the posts were attributed meant that their occupants were often chosen with very little attention, and certainly not according to merit. This atmosphere of upheaval did not let up, even with the passage of time and the change of minister. In the nine years of Mitterrand's reign, out of more than 500 changes in diplomatic postings which were announced during this period, nearly half (47 per cent) occurred within two years of the person's appointment to the post; in almost one case out of five (18.7 per cent), between six months and two years. This is a figure far greater than that which can be explained by illness, death, accidents or diplomatic incidents. The abuses included removing one ambassador who had been in place for a mere six months, even though the unfortunate man removed had been a non-political appointment of Michel Rocard's. Another ambassador who was recalled suddenly assumed that he was being punished. When he asked for an explanation, he was abruptly told, 'There are certain questions that one does not ask!'[29] Thus even new arrivals in their posts felt unstable because they could not be sure of serving their normal term. The fact that these practices occurred under more than one Foreign Minister shows that it was a management style which suited Mitterrand himself.[30]

In order to understand how this sort of control can be achieved, it is necessary to grasp that France has a strong administration which is fed by a very hierarchical and closed élite, from which such favourites could be drawn and put into positions of power. Indeed, it is widely recognized that France suffers from an excessively élitist concentration of decisions, responsibilities and privileges.[31] The most striking aspect of French élitism is in the tertiary education system, which is divided between ordinary universities, where admission is universally open to all, and the prestigious *Grandes Écoles*. It is often a surprise to learn that such a self-professedly egalitarian country should maintain such a system of state-sponsored élitism.

The oldest and one of the most prestigious *Grandes Écoles* is the

École Polytechnique, originally an engineering academy for army officers, founded by Napoleon. Equally prestigious is the École Nationale d'Administration, set up by General de Gaulle in 1945 in order to give France a civil service comparable in quality to that of Britain, which de Gaulle had so admired while in London during the war. He had also wanted ENA to widen the social base of the French administrative élite. Then there is the Institut d'Études Politiques de Paris (known as 'Sciences-Po'), set up in 1872 to strengthen the quality of France's political élite after the humiliation of the defeat at the hands of Prussia in 1871, and which now has a near monopoly on preparing students for ENA. In addition, there are various technical, scientific and humanities schools such as the École Normale Supérieue for teachers and the École des Langues Orientales for linguists and Orientalists.

The first three had as the prime motive behind their foundation the desire to inject a strong dose of intelligence and professionalism into France's political bloodstream. But Polytechnique, as its name implies, is a technical college, where students study natural sciences like chemistry and physics. ENA, as it name also suggests, teaches people to become administrators, while at 'Sciences-Po', the term 'political science' indicates not so much the study of politics as a phenomenon but more the study of the *science of how to do politics*. In other words, these schools are based on the assumption that politics and administration are fundamentally the same, and that they are both comparable to natural science. This is what gives the French political and administrative class its overwhelmingly technocratic bent: if politics for Bismarck was the art of the possible, then for the French élite educational system, it is the science of the necessary. This is in striking contrast to the British assumption that a knowledge of history, the law and the classics are a better preparation for government than science or engineering.[32]

These schools dovetail with France's strongly corporatist and hierarchical structures. As in Britain, birth and inherited money are still important for the attainment of social status and power. Seniority in certain sectors of big business, or association with a powerful politician, can have the same effect. But the biggest and surest way to the top is to become one of the great mandarins of the French state. The *Grandes Écoles* are the way to get to the top by this last means. Moreover, while several decades of effort have been devoted to enlarging the ambit of the system of national education, during which time the number of students in the universities has certainly increased, the social composition and prestige of the *Grandes Écoles*, and their concomitant sense of superiority over the universities, has only continued to rise. Moreover, the relationships between *énarques* when they encounter each other is governed by elaborate and clubby codes of conduct whose purpose and effect is to exclude non-*énarques* in later life. Ties with the old school are strong: few *énarque* ministers ever miss the school's annual old-boys' dinner, nor the opportunity to address the appropriate Sub-Prefect as 'tu', a practice allowed among students of the same graduation year, which is avidly guarded even when the formality of the occasion would demand otherwise.[33] It is difficult to exaggerate how great and insurmountable is the handicap of not being an *énarque* to those who wish to rise within political circles.

The supposedly meritocratic ENA has not opened the upper echelons of the administration to a wider social base of the population, even though this was one of its original aims. Today, 80 per cent of *Inspecteurs des Finances* and members of Conseil d'État (the most prestigious posts) are from upper-middle-class backgrounds, with 40 per cent of them from Paris. Women were not admitted as Inspectors of Finances until 1975. This rise in the social level of senior officials is a long-term trend: already in the 1970s, one commentator had concluded that ENA had become 'more bourgeois, more Parisian, and more Sciences-Po'.[34] Sciences-Po itself, where nearly all future *énarques* study before sitting the entrance examination, is overwhelmingly and increasingly bourgeois: it has fewer students from modest backgrounds than it did in the 1950s.

This has occurred for a surprising reason: family background becomes more important as soon as the public-education system enters a state of crisis, as it has done increasingly during recent decades. In this as in so many other domains, there is a mistaken tendency in Britain to assume that things in France work better; yet many parents regard the current state of the national education system as disastrous.[35] The Ministry of National Education is widely regarded as a bureaucratic Moloch which is as easy to reform as the Red Army. It swallows money without any effective control or even knowledge of curricula and teaching. During the demonstrations against the Balladur government's proposal that local authorities should be allowed partially to finance private schools (the proposed revision of the famous *Loi Falloux* which sets a low upper limit of 10 per cent to such financing), it became clear that state schools, with their leaking roofs and poor resources, were heavily in need of resources themselves. The problem of drugs in suburban schools is also especially grave. The result of the degradation of the state sector is a cruel paradox: the quality of a child's education depends increasingly on where the family lives, on their catchment area, and thus *de facto* increasingly on their income. Social selection therefore occurs at a very early age. Because the average school no longer provides a sufficient level of education, many young people of modest backgrounds can no longer envisage making the grades for the main administrative examinations.[36]

Élitism (not meritocracy) thus begins at an early age, for the *Grandes Écoles* provide recruits for the whole administration. It is positively institutionalized within the administration itself, however, within which there are clearly defined hierarchies. Certain ministries and departments of state are more prestigious than others. At the summit of this hierarchy there are the Council of State, the Court of Accounts and the Inspection of Finances, as well as the great ministries, especially the Quai d'Orsay and the hugely powerful Ministry of Finance, which has been called 'a state within the state'.[37] Slightly lower down come the other *corps*, the *Corps* of Prefects, the magistrature, and the engineering *corps*. The lowly ministries include those of the Interior and Justice, even if for politicians these count as among the most important.

The non-governmental *corps d'état* dominate the administration of France, and, with the exception of the Inspection of Finances, they are all directly descended from the days of the French monarchy. Perhaps this is why they have been described as 'aristocratic and corporatist'.[38] The Prefects, for instance – officials of the Ministry of the Interior who enforce central-government control over each *département* – are merely the revolutionary replacement for the royal *Intendants*. It is precisely because of the traditional centralism of the French state that it is easy for one homogenous group of people to gain control of the main levers of power over it. Previous French republics have been identified with certain dominant classes, as their power rose against that of the traditional hegemony in the provinces of the local worthies (*les notables*). Labels such as the 'republic of dukes', the 'republic of comrades', the 'republic of schoolteachers' and the 'republic of lawyers' were applied successively to the Third and Fourth republics.[39] But whereas in those republics, the administration was strong because parliament and politicians were weak, the Fifth Republic has seen a continuing blurring of the distinction between the political and administrative worlds. Indeed, there can be little doubt that the Fifth Republic has proved, more than any other, to be the 'republic of officials'. It is perhaps the central paradox of the evolution of the Gaullist constitution that despite the apparent premium which it set on political action and political responsibility, it has in fact seen the increasing encroachment of the power of the bureaucrat (or the bureaucratically minded politician) over the essential levers of governmental power. In the thirty years since 1958, the sphere of intervention of the class of senior officials has been ceaselessly enlarged, with senior politicians being drawn increasingly from its ranks. As a result, in the words of one expert, 'Always having been plutocratic, France has now become technocratic.'[40]

The domination of the administrative élite throughout the political class is now breathtaking. *Énarques* very often undertake political careers rather than just administrative ones, and sometimes they flit between the two. In the parliament elected in 1986, 47 per cent of deputies were civil servants. This percentage is 600 times higher than that for the population as a whole. But the domination of ENA is clearest right at the top of the pyramid, where political life is dominated by a very small number of potential presidential candidates ('*les présidentiables*'). Once a politician has credible pretensions to the highest office in the land, he devotes his entire life to the pursuit of the ultimate prize. These people are constantly given massive time and space on the media and in the press. Both on the Left and on the Right, these people are nearly all *énarques*. Lionel Jospin (Socialist Minister of Education), Pierre Joxe (Socialist Minister of Defence, Minister of Interior), Michel Rocard (Socialist Prime Minister), Laurent Fabius (Prime Minister, General Secretary of Socialist Party), Jean-Pierre Chevènement (Socialist Minister of Defence), Jacques Chirac (twice Prime Minister, President of Gaullist RPR, Mayor of Paris), Alain Juppé (RPR Foreign Minister, Secretary General of RPR), François Léotard (Minister of

Defence, President of Republican Party), Philippe Séguin (RPR
President of the National Assembly), Édouard Balladur (RPR
Finance Minister, Prime Minister), and Valéry Giscard d'Estaing
(former President and Finance Minister, President of the UDF
party) are all *énarques*, to name only the most prominent under
Mitterrand (who is not one himself!). This is in spite of the fact that
ENA is tiny: it has a mere 80 graduates a year, compared to about
8,000 a year from Oxford and Cambridge. Under such circumstances, it is rather charming to hear people reproaching Britain for
being an excessively élitist society.

Under such circumstances, it is hardly surprising that the political
life of Mitterrand's France should be notable for its overwhelmingly
bureaucratic flavour. When in opposition, the future President
harped on the overall need to overcome the dominance of the civil-
service élite, but once in power he made no real effort to change
the system. Indeed, the percentage of *énarques* in the top three *corps
d'état* has increased greatly in recent decades. Whereas they ac-
counted for about 40 per cent of the officials in the 1950s (ENA
had only just been founded), this figure had risen to between 75
per cent and 90 per cent by the 1980s.[41] Having spent twenty
years promising that he would abolish the institution of the Prefect,
claiming that the level of control which the government exercised
over the country through Prefects was excessively centralist and
authoritarian, Mitterrand was to be seen within days of his election
being conducted on his visits around the country by the local
Prefect resplendent in his uniform, just like any other President
before him. Moreover, the presence of senior officials-turned-politi-
cians in Mitterrand's governments has remained high. Their increasing power is a long-term trend: in 1958, about a third of all
ministers came from the civil service; during the 1970s, it rose to
above a half. Valéry Giscard d'Estaing and Raymond Barre, his
Prime Minister, earned themselves reputations for being technocratic and for instituting government by experts: in 1978, fifteen
out of the twenty government ministers (75 per cent) were senior
civil servants. Barre himself was a professor of economics at
Sciences-Po. But even under Pierre Mauroy, the first Socialist
Prime Minister, the figure was still 60 per cent. This was because
many leading Socialists were from the *énarque* élite anyway, and in
some cases from privileged family backgrounds themselves. For

instance, the Attali brothers, Jacques and Bernard (the former was personal adviser to Mitterrand, the latter Chairman of Air France) went to the same exclusive upper-middle-class school in the bourgeois 16th arrondissement of Paris as Jean-Louis Bianco, another Mitterrand favourite who was nominated Secretary General of the Elysée Palace and later Minister of Transport. Laurent Fabius, Mitterrand's second Prime Minister, also attended the same school. Alain Boublil, a Mitterrand crony who was *directeur de cabinet* to Pierre Beregovoy, was also an old friend of Jacques Attali's.[42] Thus, far from being the enemies of the administrative class, the Socialists, with their ideological bent towards the ever greater technocratic administration of the whole of society, soon turned out to be their natural allies. After all, there is an ideological affinity between Socialists and administrators anyway. Following in the tradition of the French positivist, Saint-Simon, Friedrich Engels hoped that Socialism would substitute 'the government of persons with the administration of things'.[43]

The presence of *énarques* in the private offices ('cabinets') of ministers is also immense. Ministers seem to like to surround themselves with ambitious young technocrats doing time in politics before being 'parachuted' from there – as they often are – into some high-flying job in industry or elsewhere in public administration. Often recent graduates from ENA enter the service of ministerial cabinets before they are allowed to do so: the law requires that they remain for four years after graduation in the ministry to which they are allocated. The power of the members of these *cabinets* is in proportion to the power of the minister and his ministry: it reaches its paroxysm with the President of the Republic. During General de Gaulle's first term of office, a quarter of the Elysée staff were from ENA; a third in his second term; half under Georges Pompidou; two-thirds under Valéry Giscard d'Estaing; only to fall back slightly to a third under Mitterrand. During the Chirac government of 1986–8, there were no fewer than 115 *énarques* in ministerial *cabinets*: under the previous Socialist government of Laurent Fabius, there had already been 94. Chirac's *Cabinet* itself was composed of 35 officials, of which 23 were senior officials, more than half of them *énarques*. In Edouard Balladur's *cabinet* (he was then Finance Minister), there were 16 members, of which 12 were senior civil servants, most of them *énarques* too.[44]

But the point is not simply to describe French élitism. It is important to understand that the effect of this hegemony of one politico-administrative class, especially when it exercises its power behind the scenes, is to blur the lines of responsibility within the political system. In other words, the failure to accept personal responsibility for decisions, which has characterized Mitterrand's own behaviour, is institutionalized in the system of politico-administrative hegemony over which he presides. Jobs in ministerial *cabinets*, for instance, are very powerful indeed. Because of the practice known as '*le cumul des mandats*', whereby senior politicians accumulate a series of different political jobs, ministers tend to delegate large areas of power to their officials. Often, they have so many jobs that they cannot realistically do any of them properly. The entrenchment of this practice means that the politician who is supposedly responsible can in fact no longer answer for anything. Each mandate which he receives from the people simply leads him to feign competence, and to read what others have read. As one polemicist puts it, 'Such is the lie of power which pretends to be able to do what it cannot, and which pretends to represent citizens with whom it cannot concern itself, and to manage an administration which it cannot understand . . . The whole system of *cabinets* leads to ignorance and blindness.'[45]

It can also lead to outright anti-democratic behaviour. One clear illustration of this came in December 1989, in one of those grotesque affairs which constantly bedevils French politics: a group of demonstrators, including several deputies of the National Assembly and Senators, were demonstrating outside the National Assembly in favour of General Aoun of Lebanon. The CRS riot troops had been given the order to disperse the demonstration, and they moved in with their truncheons. Several deputies were hit – but the Minister of the Interior had been abroad and had taken no decision himself. In other words, the order to use force against the democratically elected representatives of the French nation was given by an anonymous and unaccountable technocratic adviser sitting in the private office of the Minister of the Interior.[46] No doubt it was because he understood the power of such anonymous officials that Charles Hernu, the former Defence Minister, once said, 'I do not ring Mauroy [the Prime Minister] any more. I have not rung him for ages. I prefer to ring his *directeur de cabinet*, Michel Delebarre. He's the real Prime Minister.'[47]

But the hegemony of the politico-administrative class does not stop at the political organs of the state: it extends well into industry as well, both public and private, as well as into banking and the media. For there is a well established system, known in the slang of the École Polytechnique as *'pantouflage'* ('slipper-money'), according to which a graduate from one of the *Grandes Écoles* may perfectly legitimately buy his way out of his contract to work for the state for ten years, and enter the private sector. The scale of this practice is staggering. The managing directors of 27 of the top 50 (and 42 of the top 140) industrial groups and companies in France are senior civil servants.[48] Directors and managing directors of the following groups are former civil servants, either from ENA or from Polytechnique, who have all spent time working in the *cabinets* of ministers: Gaz de France, Chargeurs réunis, Peugeot-Citroën, Thomson, Lazard, Crédit du Nord, Renault, SNCF, Paribas, GAN, EXOR, UTA Airlines, Air France, Banque Nationale de Paris, Credit Lyonnais, Société Lyonnaise des Eaux, Péchiney, Charbonnages de France, Hydroénergie, France-Manche, Ambroise-Roux, Stern, UAP, Credit National, Pennaroya, Société Générale, COGEMA. This represents practically the entirety of French banking and industry.[49]

One of the greatest practitioners of this is Édouard Balladur, François Mitterrand's last Prime Minister. Although his achievements are exceptional, the basic pattern of moving between ministerial *cabinets*, private enterprise, the public sector, the administration, and government itself, is typical. A graduate of ENA, he spent four years in the *cabinet* of the then Prime Minister, Georges Pompidou. From there he became chairman of the construction company building the tunnel under Mont Blanc. After five years back in politics as General Secretary of the Elysée Palace under President Pompidou, he joined the nationalized Compagnie Générale d'Électricité in 1982, where he became Chairman of two of its branches. As Finance Minister from 1986–8, he was responsible for privatizing the CGE; he spent a few years preparing his return to power between 1988 and 1993, and duly became Prime Minister in March 1993.[50]

Another classic example of *pantouflage* was manifest during the Air France crisis at the end of 1993, when a strike paralysed the two main international airports in Paris, and added to Air France's chronic debt. Indeed, it very nearly finished off the airline, which had been on its knees for several years. All the main actors in the drama, which resulted in an immediate government climb-down, were typical representatives of the politico-industrial class, starting with the Prime Minister, Édouard Balladur himself. The negotiations were not conducted by the Minister of Transport, but by his *chef de cabinet*, Jean-Pierre Beysson. Beysson had previously been the head of *Aéroports de Paris*. Bernard Attali, the incumbent President of Air France, sacrificed by the government at the high point of the crisis, had himself worked in the airline industry, in insurance, at the Court of Accounts (civil service), as *directeur de cabinet* of the Commissioner General of Equipment and Productivity, and at the Ministry of National and Regional Development. His replacement, Christian Blanc, was appointed as the new President of Air France because of his clearly defined political orientation: he was known to be a Rocardien Socialist, and had earned a reputation as a 'man of dialogue', having been responsible for negotiating an end to the colonial uprising in New Caledonia in 1988 while working for Michel Rocard at Matignon.

Some commentators, especially British admirers of the power of the French administration, have praised the ease with which civil servants move between the industrial sector and the civil service, holding it to be one of the strengths of the French system that civil servants thereby come into contact with the outside world.[51] They also argue that this enables government and industry better to know what the other is doing. Such a view commits a number of errors, the greatest (a very common one) being to assume that government and the management of industry are similar tasks. Indeed, it assumes that government should or can run industry, a mercantile illusion which led Britain into the economic morass of the 1970s. As the Air France crisis shows, France will not be spared the same fate, for far from making French industry more efficient, these assumptions merely entrench the deeply corporatist instincts of the French government and industry. If France seems to have survived well with such a model in the past (and the extent of the planning of the French economy in the post-war period is truly stunning: Jean Monnet even set up a Planning Commission, the Commissariat Général du Plan, which was only demoted to an advisory role in the late 1950s), then it is mainly due to the high growth rate generated over thirty years until the 1970s by the post-war reconstruction of the country. As the country prepares to face increased international competition within Europe and in the wider world, however, France will have to learn the same lesson that Britain learned under Thatcher, that government and industry have fundamentally different roles in society. It is the task of the former to create the conditions which permit the free development of the economy by upholding the law, not to act as an economic agent itself.

However, the practice of *pantouflage* produces another, more surprising defect. These technocrats often lack the *political* skills which are needed in industry as much as in government. Once again, the comparison between British Airways and Air France is illuminating. When Sir John (now Lord) King was appointed in 1980 to lead British Airways out of crisis, he did it by revamping the whole company's work ethic, as well as by taking the tough economic decisions necessary, such as reducing personnel. Such stimulating and energetic leadership galvanized the staff into action, and re-implanted basic notions like customer service, which were absent from British industry at the time as they are from Air France to this day. Bernard Attali, by contrast, did nothing of the kind. Such leadership qualities are hardly fostered by a system which places a premium on the science of administration. He simply introduced an austerity plan to sack 4,000 low-paid employees, which produced a predictable result: staff were outraged at what they saw as the brutality of the plan, and, in the absence of any sense of direction from the management, their strike was widely supported within the airline. Instead of inspiration from the top, there was merely the dull thud of the technocrat's rubber stamp.

The ultimate irony is that *pantouflage* undermines the whole logic of having an élitist and talented civil service in the first place. First, it means that the talents of young *énarques* are often lost by the public sector, for which they were trained. Second, the very reason why they are recruited into the private sector is less for their abilities (though these are doubtless considerable) but more for their contacts within the administration and in government. Any self-respecting enterprise needs to have a few *énarques* and *polytechniciens* on its pay-roll in order to be able to profit from their address-book and their network of contacts in government. Indeed, it is often quicker for an ambitious *énarque* to get to the top by working in politics first, and then being poached by industry, than to start at the bottom of the industry in question. It is difficult to see how this is compatible with the notion of the selfless and neutral senior civil servant if he increasingly resembles a highly paid trafficker of influence.

Faced with a general degradation in the political life of a country, people may place their faith in something supposedly superior, but this belief in the supposed wisdom of an unaccountable administration[52] – the contemporary equivalent of the support given to enlightened despotism in the eighteenth century – makes the false assumption that the administration is free from the vices of short-termism and corruption with which politicians, in France as in many other countries, are often reproached. When the administration is as closely integrated within the political world as it is in France, it cannot pretend to be free from its vices, and thus there should be no premium on unaccountability. However much *fonctionnaires* may think of themselves as representing some neutral, rationalistic body of experts running the country for its own good, it is clear that the attribution of posts, and the promotion of senior officials, depends on the backscratching and internal politicking which is inevitable in any opaque bureaucratic system.

Illicit practices creep in whenever accountability is not ensured, and these can provide the vectors for straightforward corruption. *Pantouflage* between the private and public sectors, for instance, creates conflicts of interest which are both morally dubious and often break the rules. It is, for instance, illegal for a civil servant to work in a part of the private sector which is connected with the work he did in the public sector, but this provision is often simply ignored. Cases which a few decades ago would have brought about prosecutions and convictions are now to be found throughout the pages of *Who's Who* and in professional directories. A senior civil servant in the Ministry of Health finds himself a job in the pharmaceutical branch of a leading multinational; two senior figures in the Ministry of Post and Telecommunications move to electricity and telecommunications companies; a former senior official in the Ministry of Defence goes to work with an aeronautical company; former officials at the Ministry of Finance go into banking.[53]

Above all, perhaps, the system's hierarchical values also undermine its own *raison d'être*. A young ambitious *énarque* will choose to go to the Council of State not because he is a lawyer, nor even because he wishes to specialize in constitutional and administrative law, but more because he knows that it is the best strategic career move that he can make.[54] This means that the talents most highly valued by the system are indeed general *administrative* ones, rather than ones adapted to the task in hand, such as legal ones for the Council of State. The more senior the official, the more he is a generalist: but this makes a mockery of the whole purpose of the *Grandes Écoles*, which is to create a highly trained élite for specific purposes.[55] Moreover, because the main expertise of the most brilliant *énarques* is their general knowledge of the complex machinery of the state, they have a professional interest in running and perpetuating their own system.[56] The more the upper echelons of the public administration, industry and politics is a closed world, ruled by a small élite, not open to public scrutiny, and the more complicated and technocratic the business of government becomes, then the only way to make the system work is to have *cognoscenti* in the know running it, and so the spiral continues. At that point, only acquaintances, complicity and the old-boy network can oil the wheels.

Members of the establishment often argue in favour of maintaining the unity and power of the élite. On the occasion of the school's fortieth anniversary, the director of ENA justified its activity by saying that 'The great problems of a nation go beyond even the longest electoral timetables. The senior civil service, thanks to its cumulative memory, its far-sighted perspective, its competence in the preparation and execution of decisions, is the legitimate manager of the "long term" of the Nation.'[57] A noble sentiment, perhaps, were it not that it is but a short step from this to a contempt for the democratic political process itself. No one would doubt the admirable public ethic in the French administration – perhaps lacking in that of other countries – but there need to be checks and balances even on this. It betrays a less than wholehearted attachment to democracy to want to place the control of society in the hands of a homogenous group of people not subject to control. Throughout history, unaccountable institutions, like the Prussian army or the European Commission, have displayed a tendency to think of themselves as the ultimate depository of the nation's or the community's values.[58] Indeed, Christian Pierret, another *énarque*, comes to just such a conclusion:

> The permanence and the ethics of the senior civil service contributes to a smoothing-over of political problems. *Énarques* are men of quality who have been brought up for the service of the state. When one looks at France since the war, who has remained solid, who has decided without political pressure, who has kept to the straight and narrow in comparison with the vacuity of politicians? The administration![59]

Here, in all its splendour, is the explicit self-justification of the bureaucrat. It is a sad comment on France that the traditions and collective political memory of the nation are contained in the administration, where lines of responsibility are the least clear. In Britain, it is in parliament – i.e. in the public and democratic domain – that these permanent values are supposed to reside. It is even sadder to see such men clearly making the claim that *true national legitimacy* resides not with the democratically elected leaders of the government but with the unelected and unaccountable bureaucracy.

These trends have all been aggravated under Mitterrand, and the resulting politico-administrative mafia represents an increasing drag on real political change. This is why the Mitterrand years have been notable for their reactionary lethargy. The natural strength of the French administrative apparatus has been compounded by the bureaucratization of political mentalities, and by the basic vacuum at the heart of the Mitterrandist 'project'. It is possible that the administration might one day be galvanized into action by a strong and visionary Head of State, but in the absence of such leadership, the power-structure becomes only self-serving: 'The political class, instead of basing the administration of the state on merit, thinks of nothing than how fruitfully to organize itself into mafioso and clientilist networks.'[60] And when the habits of bureaucracies colonize the political world, as they have done in France, then the electorate's control over those in power suffers accordingly. The Fifth Republic began with the collapse of the Fourth, which occurred when the attempt to substitute weak political leadership by strong administration led eventually to directionlessness and national collapse. De Gaulle's republic is likely to end for the same reasons it began, for far from giving back to France that political *élan* and leadership which he himself embodied, ENA has reinforced the bureaucratic nature of the French state. One historian described the Fourth Republic thus:

> The change of Cabinet in France, as compared with Britain, resembles the change of scene in a French play as compared with an English one. In the latter, a change of scene means just what it says: the *venue* has altered. In a French play, every time a new character comes on, or goes off, this is labelled as a change of scene, though the place may be exactly the same.[61]

An observer of the contemporary scene remarks, 'The administrative élite is so powerful that it no longer consents to being the expiatory victim of political change . . . In France the changing of the political guard takes place within one same world, exclusively the senior civil service. That which politics destroys, corporatism and the old-boy network reconstructs.'[62] *Plus ça change, plus c'est la même chose.*

5. The Death of Politics

This ancient French propensity of dissipating one's efforts in
verbiage, playing political games as if in a circus, and trying
to climb the greasy pole . . .

Charles de Gaulle[1]

It has been said that France is a tranquil country agitated by
legislators. It was to restore that tranquillity, and to overcome the
'dictatorship of the National Assembly' that the Gaullist constitution reduced the powers of the parliament, while leaving the role of
governing to the government, and especially to the President. Over
time, however, the increasing domination of the presidency has
sapped what little role the parliament retained, so much so that
France's leading constitutionalist (a long-standing critic of the Fifth
Republic) writes bluntly, 'The parliament has almost no role in
politics any more.'[2] Thus it now seems that the constitution may
have overcome the Assembly, but not the dictatorship. Therefore,
some have not hesitated to call the Mitterrand state 'totalitarian'.[3]
While there may be a long tradition of anti-parliamentarianism in
France – one historian remarks that 'the French are democrats, they
are not parliamentarians'[4] – it is doubtful whether one can continue
being the former without being the latter for long.

Twenty-nine of the eighty-nine articles in the constitution limit
the parliament's power. The most notorious and controversial is
Article 49.3, which enables the government to declare a bill a
matter of confidence. In this case, the bill is automatically accepted
as law, without even a debate or a vote, unless the government is
overthrown by a vote of no confidence within twenty-four hours.
The motion must be signed by one tenth of the Assembly, and
passed by an absolute majority of votes (i.e. abstentions count as
votes of confidence). The signatories of such a motion are subsequently forbidden from putting down another one in the same
session.

In December 1979, Mitterrand pointed out that the article undermines the very function of the parliament which the constitution was supposed to reinstate, that of voting laws. 'What kind of a democracy functions without a parliament, and without law as the parliamentary system understands it?' he complained. 'Are we going to admit . . . that it is the government which makes the law?'[5] Here as elsewhere, the sharpness with which he attacked such procedures in opposition has been exceeded only by the enthusiasm with which he embraced them in power. During 1988–93, the use of this brutal measure, which previously had been used only in exceptional cases, became completely banal: in 1991 it was used nine times for four bills, and only two censure motions were put down in response.[6] The Communist Party consistently refused to endorse these no-confidence motions, despite its numerous disagreements with the government, and was thus responsible for keeping the minority Socialist government in power, and for entrenching the desuetude of the Assembly's power to censure the government.

The article contains at least two objectionable elements. The first is that a single piece of legislation should not be declared a matter of confidence, for this fatally reduces parliament's power to deal with legislation as it wishes.[7] The second is the fact that the Assembly's ultimate confidence in the government is invoked to pass a law only reinforces the illusion that government is ultimately subject to the approval of parliament. It is an illusion precisely because the real head of the executive, the President, is in fact not responsible to parliament at all: were a government to be overturned by a vote of no confidence, then the President could appoint another Prime Minister or dissolve the Assembly and keep the same Prime Minister, subject to new elections. This is what de Gaulle did in 1962.

Moreover, having the theoretical power to dismiss the government is not enough. That the French National Assembly has this power distracts attention from its weakness in other areas, most notably from its ineffectiveness in ensuring the kind of daily accountability in the normal course of government for which the British parliament is rightly noted, or even in debating policy. It is perhaps significant that in his attacks Mitterrand omitted to mention that the article prevents even *debate* from taking place on the bill under consideration.

But there is an array of other articles which reinforce the government's domination over the Assembly. Article 44 allows the government to require the parliament to vote on the whole or part of a text in its entirety, disallowing all amendments except its own. This has the effect of bypassing all scrutiny or amendment proposals in committees. In any case, Article 43 limits the number of permanent legislative committees to six in each chamber. This has had a disastrous effect on parliamentary accountability, partly because the committees are simply too big to be effective, (each committee has about 100 members), but also because nobody goes to the meetings anyway.[8] There is thus practically no parliamentary influence on the elaboration of law or policy, and no collective control of ministerial or governmental action.[9] There is certainly no room for legislative initiative on the part of individual deputies; but even to get an amendment to a bill adopted, it is more effective for a deputy to negotiate directly with a technical adviser in the Elysée Palace or at the Hôtel Matignon than to table an amendment on the parliamentary timetable. This means that debate vanishes from the open, parliamentary domain into the obscurity of the corridors of power.

Another critic has written acidly of how, 'Everyone is struck by the caricature of transparency which the parliament represents: it watches measures passing like trains without voting on them, and thus it becomes a humiliating fiction of democracy.'[10] Where the scrutiny of European legislation is concerned, for instance, its record is lamentable: despite France's thirty years of membership of the EEC, 90 per cent of European legislation is still passed without any involvement of the National Assembly whatsoever, via the government's 'power of regulation'.

This is because of another general limitation on parliament's power: its areas of competence, defined as 'the law', are laid down in Article 34. The ostensible aim of this article was to restore a degree of dignity to 'the law' by leaving technical and administrative regulation to the government, and concentrating the activity of parliament exclusively on legislation. But in reality, it has successfully reduced the number of areas in which the government had to seek the approval of parliament for difficult and unpopular measures. In national legislation, this removes from the parliament a large area of competence in fixing, or even in discussing, the technical and regulatory aspects of the application of legislation, leaving an unhealthy margin of manoeuvre to those executive officials – bureaucrats or ministers – whose job it is to apply the law.

This has led some people to comment sarcastically that what matters in France is not to know the law, but to know the person responsible for applying it. While it may be good practice and common sense to leave to the regulatory authorities the task of entering into details which are often technical, it is obvious that the legislator should reserve the discretionary right to be more precise when he decides, rightly or wrongly, that an explanation is necessary to clarify a text or to dissipate its ambiguity.[11] The explosion of regulation is a very widespread problem in modern democracies, and Britain suffers from it as much as most countries.[12] In France, the government's pre-eminence is further enhanced by its wide powers to pass executive acts by decree, and it can also pass legislation itself (by *ordonnances*), under formal delegation from the parliament, even in those areas which are the parliament's normal exclusive competence.[13] Article 41 permits the government to declare a bill or an amendment outside the competence of the parliament, and thus to override any parliamentary objections; while Article 45 permits the government to interfere with the discussions between the National Assembly and the Senate if there is a disagreement between them. One is reminded of the words of the Lord Chancellor in *Iolanthe*:

> The Law is the true embodiment
> Of everything that's excellent.
> It has no kind of fault or flaw,
> And I, my Lords, embody the Law.[14]

Article 48 gives the government a complete monopoly in deciding the parliament's agenda: there is no 'opposition time' at all. This was no doubt introduced because under the fractious Third and Fourth Republics, each chamber had complete control of its timetable, but it is typical of France's political development that it should have swung from one extreme to the other.[15] The clear result of these constitutional provisions is that the representatives of the nation hardly have any power to discuss – and even less to adopt – bills which do not have the support of the government.[16]

Because the government can always impose its will on parliament, most governments treat the parliament with considerable contempt. The Socialist governments of the 1980s have been especially bad in this regard. In December 1990, for instance, the Minister for Relations with the Parliament reported that over 2,000 parliamentary questions which had been put to the government over the previous six months had been simply left unanswered. Over 800 questions remained unanswered for up to a year, 500 for eighteen months, and nearly 400 questions had been waiting two years for a reply.[17] No doubt this was why the Council of State, the organ responsible for surveying the way the administration functions, severely reproached the Socialists with 'Exclusive responsibility for having usurped the legislative power of the state, especially where the brevity of consultation and the insufficient preparation of texts is concerned'.[18]

A classic case of the contempt with which parliament is treated was the fiasco over the Schengen agreement. The accords, signed between France, Germany, Italy and the Benelux countries (and later by Greece and Spain) was supposed to abolish customs and immigration controls at the borders between those countries, and to replace them with an Orwellian system of internal surveillance by computer and police registration. (Tourists from non-Schengen countries, such as Britain, would have had to register with the police within three days of their arrival, and would have had to carry papers proving registration on them for presentation to the police on demand.)[19]

The Socialist government used Article 41 to overrule the Senate's objections to the agreement on 27 June 1991, and thereby to force its ratification through. There were then to be no fewer than six acts of parliament ratifying the accords, plus a formal amendment to the constitution, voted by the deputies of the National Assembly and the Senators meeting in formal congress at Versailles. (The Constitutional Court had ruled that the agreement was contrary to the constitution's provisions on asylum policy, so the constitution had to be changed.) And yet, despite having engaged the legislative and even constitutional powers of the state for two years on the matter, the new right-wing government announced in early 1994, without prior parliamentary consultation, that the accords would not be 'applied' for technical reasons, even though all the appropriate laws had been passed. Apparently the computer which was to have monitored the movements throughout the whole Schengen area did not work.[20] Other countries suspected that France had pulled the plug on the computer because the new government was thought to be hostile to it. Whatever the truth, there can be few clearer illustrations that executive and legislative power resides exclusively with the government, because it has a life-or-death say over the application of laws.

Small wonder, then, that the National Assembly is one of the few places in the country where the great political issues of the day are never discussed.[21] As the President of the National Assembly, Philippe Séguin, wrote (while in opposition),

> Everything takes place in the obscurity of ministerial private offices, in the corridor, in secret. Public debate is eluded, confiscated, dodged. Decisions are announced as being only of limited importance, but it is only after they have been taken that they explain to us that the consequences are, in fact, incalculable. A truly infernal machine has been set in motion, over which we no longer have any control.[22]

Indeed, it is this lack of public debate which is the most striking difference between the British and the French parliaments. Debates are held, without a vote, only after government statements. These are very rare: there are maybe two or three a year, while Michel Rocard's government made only one during the whole of 1988. There is a weekly session of 'questions to the government' which is meagre by comparison with the daily questioning of ministers, and the twice-weekly questioning of the Prime Minister, at Westminster. Until a recent reform, introduced in 1993, which has tried to reinvigorate parliamentary life by restricting the length of time for each question to the government, this session, which lasts for about two hours on Wednesday afternoons, was more of a set piece than a real parliamentary occasion. In the Assembly elected in 1993, how-ever, the Socialist opposition was so tiny (about eighty members) that the reformed session became more of an occasion for self-congratulation than the ministerial gruelling it should be.

The French parliament is therefore in a state of living death. This is in turn both cause and effect of the endemic problem of absentee-ism, which is tolerated and encouraged by the iniquitous practice of voting by massive proxy. One or two deputies from each party used to be delegated to vote on behalf of the whole parliamentary group by turning the keys in the voting machines at their seats. This practice was also abolished by the incoming President of the National Assembly, Philippe Séguin, but not before it had gone on for thirty years, in flagrant contravention of Article 27 of the constitution. In other words, for the last three decades, France has been governed *without a parliament whose members actually voted for its own laws.* In Westminster, MPs must be present for their vote to count. It is hardly surprising, given the inability of deputies to intervene or to vote individually according to their convictions, that one commentator has called the French parliament 'The place of great disillusionment . . . The most disappointed people are the deputies themselves, who are the playthings of a system which makes them collectively indispensable but individually useless'.[23]

As a consequence, the overwhelming majority of them take on other political jobs at regional or local level. This practice, called '*le cumul des mandats*', has two main motives: money and power. A deputy receives nearly 40,000 francs a month, most of it untaxed (about £55,000 a year). He may also take a local post, usually a mayorship or a seat on the Regional Council (90 per cent of deputies have a local post as well), and these are also handsomely remunerated. If he is lucky enough also to have a seat in the European parliament, he can add on another fat tax-free salary. Presidencies of Regional Councils, mayorships, and other senior local posts, also carry official cars with them, and a successful politician – a minister, say – may travel to his constituency in his ministerial car only to disembark and get into his mayoral car instead. An indication of the gilded life style which French ministers enjoy came from Edith Cresson, who, when the Socialists were ejected from power in 1986, declared with her habitual frankness, 'I did not even know how to take a taxi any more.'[24]

It is important for a deputy to have a local power-base upon which to build his national political career. This anchors him to a particular part of the country in a more solid way than merely representing a constituency does. Despite a strong centralist republican tradition according to which deputies represent the entire nation, and not merely their constituency, there are some notable examples of local barons, whose national profile is strongly underpinned by a powerful regional fiefdom. The most striking examples of this are Jacques Chirac, the Mayor of Paris; Jacques Chaban-Delmas, who has been Mayor of Bordeaux for about forty years; and Pierre Mauroy, the Mayor of Lille, whose own large physical circumference is the bulky embodiment of his political weight, which sits firmly on the northern industrial region of the Nord-Pas-de-Calais. The accumulation of posts, which has excited considerable criticism, has recently been legitimized by a law limiting the number of such jobs any one person may hold to three. Before that law Jean Lecanuet, an RPR politician, held the record for being simultaneously Mayor, Senator, member of the European parliament, President of a General Council, and a regional councillor, having also served as a minister. At the time, he earned upwards of 60,000 francs a month as a result, in other words about 30 per cent more than the President of the Republic or the Prime Minister.[25]

The accumulation of posts allows most politicians to put themselves into the top 5 per cent of earners. Parliamentary salaries are extremely comfortable, especially considering their tax exemptions.[26] As a result, taxes are voted, applied and modified by parliamentarians, managed by local politicians, and applied and collected by senior officials, who have all in part or totally ceased to pay tax. This breaks all democratic attachment to the raising of tax and all psychological understanding of tax as it is experienced by ordinary people.[27]

The practice also means that deputies cannot do any one of their several jobs properly. They certainly cannot be good deputies, and therefore their absenteeism from the National Assembly in turn encourages voters to desert the ballot box.[28] Indeed, while President of the National Assembly, Laurent Fabius bemoaned the low esteem in which his own country's parliament is held. Speaking in Lithuania in September 1991 he said, 'I observe with great enthusiasm that in many countries citizens are making human chains to protect their parliament, while at the same time, in my own country, as in many neighbouring countries, the parliament is a neglected and even despised charade.'[29]

Perhaps the most striking effect of what one Socialist deputy has called 'the near-total functional paralysis of the Assembly'[30] is the deleterious effect it has on the quality of the debate in the media. Within the parliament there is little but a sort of caricature of a contest between the Right and the Left. The impression is given that this is a mere fig-leaf for a profound lack of ideas, a general failure of political imagination, and, once the anxiety and the challenge of elections has passed, a complicity between parliamentarians of different political persuasions.[31] As a result of this – and this is perhaps the key to the death of politics under Mitterrand – the quality of political debate in French politics is strikingly low. This in turn has a fatal impact on political accountability: the right questions are not being asked because they are not being aired. Lacking a parliamentary stimulus or crucible, the French media under Mitterrand have sunk slowly and ungracefully into irrelevance. They thus fail to fill the gap in political accountability which the parliament's inactivity leaves so spectacularly open.

The first reason why this is so is structural. Whole swathes of the media, the press and publishing, are in the hands of the politico-administrative class, and there is therefore a natural affinity between the media and politicians. The largest French publishing-house, Hachette, is directed by an *Inspecteur des Finances*, Yves Sabouret, who worked for seven years in various ministerial *cabinets*, including that of the Prime Minister, Pierre Messmer. It is rather as if Penguin were directed by a former Head of the Policy Unit at 10, Downing Street. His predecessor at Hachette, Simon Nora, now the head of the École Nationale d'Administration itself, is an *Inspecteur des Mines* and a former member of the *cabinet* of the former Prime Minister Jacques Chaban-Delmas. Other members of the Hachette board are in the same category, while the directors of Editions Mondiales as of Editions du Cerf are also graduates of ENA who have worked in other *cabinets*. The important French radio station, RTL, is directed by Jacques Rigaud, an *énarque* who worked at the Council of State, then for six years in a ministerial *cabinet*. Jean Drucker, another *énarque* also presides over the television channel associated with RTL, M6. The same applies to Radio Monte-Carlo and to Antenne 2, the television channel. Even the press does not escape their influence. The senior directors on the editorial boards of the leading newspapers, *Le Figaro*, *Le Monde*, *L'Express* and *Le Point* are also often *énarques*, Inspectors of Finances, and so on.

Apart from a strong natural complicity between the political and media classes, there is also a large measure of direct government control over the media. The laws on press freedom are notoriously draconian, for they not only prohibit coverage of the private lives of politicians, but also contain such extraordinary crimes as 'defamation of a minister' for which even cartoonists can be prosecuted.[32] Direct political control takes several forms, mainly the political nomination of the heads of radio and television channels. Upon his election, Mitterrand himself was determined to remove his enemies in radio and television, and Jacques Attali testifies to his 'literal obsession' with placing the entire TV and media network in the hands of his supporters. Maurice Ulrich was replaced at Antenne 2 by Pierre Desgraupes; Jacques Boutet replaced Jean-Louis Guillaud at TF 1; and the President of FR 3, Claude Contamine, and the director of information at Radio France, Roland Faure, were also sacked and replaced by his nominees. To add insult to injury, Attali compares the Socialists' record to that of the Right in 1974, saying that the former's changes at the top of the TV world were modest by comparison.[33] In a similar vein, within a year of his appointment as Prime Minister, Édouard Balladur was facing attacks from the Left, denouncing the way the government had 'stitched up' the media, appointing his personal or political friends to the heads of the important TV stations.[34] Balladur's approach may have been more piecemeal – he generally appointed one or two friends to important posts each month – but the principle is the same.

The effects of this are not hard to predict. During his extraordinary adventures in uncovering the Urba corruption scandal, [35] the police inspector Antoine Gaudino realized that the information policy of the state-controlled Agence France Presse was under political supervision. The Director of General Information, Pierre Feuilly, was a well-known Socialist militant, close to Jean Poperen, a former minister who heads a minor 'current' in the Socialist Party. Gaudino recounts how he spent three hours on the telephone persuading Feuilly to give an accurate account of his own declaration on an important issue during the development of the affair. After a long argument in the early hours of the morning, Feuilly finally capitulated; but Gaudino believed Agence France Presse was waiting for government approval first.[36]

There is also significant government influence over the private press as well. Recent decades have seen a collapse in the quality and circulation of the press. France probably now has the worst national dailies of any major Western European country. Her inferiority to Britain in this respect is widely acknowledged. One of the main reasons for this is that the government subsidizes the press to the staggering total of 5 billion francs a year (£600 million). It mainly takes the form of direct payments, and preferential rates for the post and telephone, but there are also direct subsidies. In 1993, when the right-wing *Le Quotidien de Paris* seemed in danger of going bankrupt, the Minister for Communications, Alain Carignon, suddenly and opportunely announced the creation of a 20-million-franc fund to support the paper. When such subsidies represent a greater income than that from copy sales, it is hardly surprising that journalists admit that they care more about the subsidies than about the interest value of their papers, nor that they are loath to bite the hand that feeds them.

In this context, it is amusing to observe the impotence of the various commissions which have been set up to run the media and to 'monitor' press freedom. (One would have thought that the absence of such commissions would be the best way to achieve this.) When the High Authority for Audiovisual expressed its opposition to the appointment by President Mitterrand of Jean-Claude Héberlé as head of Antenne 2 in 1984, Mitterrand went ahead and appointed him anyway.[37] Such institutions are often populated by members of the political establishment anyway. The Commission Nationale de la Communication et des Libertés set up by the Chirac government of 1986–8 was dominated by *énarques*. There was ex-officio representation from the Council of State, the Court of Accounts and the Court of Cassation (Supreme Court of Appeal). Its chairman, Prince Gabriel de Broglie, a cousin of General de Gaulle, was an *énarque* who had worked at the Council of State, and then in a ministerial *cabinet* for four years, before becoming Director-General of Radio France. The nine members of the commission included an *Inspecteur General des Finances*, a Master Councillor at the Court of Accounts, and a Civil Administrator, the last two having been nominated by François Mitterrand. The small minority who were not civil servants included one *polytechnicien* and former Chairman and managing director of Thomson, and another who spent nearly the whole of the Fourth Republic in the *cabinets* of ministers before becoming an official in the company directors' union, and who was briefly the Chairman and managing director of

Agence France Presse.[38] When in 1988, the CNCL was replaced by the Conseil Supérieur de l'Audiovisuel, the new body immediately joined the Conseil d'État, the Conseil Constitutionnel and the Cour de Cassation as one of the most august and powerful bodies of the state: populated entirely by the élite, of course.

The weakness of the mass media has very deleterious effects on political accountability. In a television age, they have a very important role to play in ensuring the quality of the political debate. France under Mitterrand comes out just as unfavourably here as she does in other areas. Mitterrand is not only more powerful than de Gaulle, but is also even less accountable and accessible. Presidential press conferences are the only time the President is ever questioned on his policies by anyone: they occur at his initiative, and on his agenda. He has held far fewer than the General. When in September 1991, he held a press conference in one of his many attempts to relaunch his own failing fortunes, commentators pointed out that this was only the sixth such conference he had ever held. De Gaulle, during the same period, had held seventeen; Pompidou and Giscard had held eighteen in twelve years between them.[39]

Political habits at national level are reflected, indeed copied, by the media. In Britain, where parliament is based on the institutionalization of the two-party system, and where the dualist model of government and opposition provokes lively debate and opposition, television and radio interviews always contain substantial questions, and always allow at least two points of view to be expressed. Often two politicians of opposing tendencies are invited to debate at the same time. It is, indeed, the secret of the success of the two-party system, to which all mature democracies in time evolve, that the political system *assumes* that there is always a 'yes' and a 'no'. This is in contrast to the more unitarian model encouraged by 'proportional representation', which is predicated on the illusion of a single response and a single purpose for the whole of society. Although there is no PR at national level in France, there are hardly ever interesting debates between politicians of different viewpoints: usually only one politician ever speaks at a time, and then often for far too long. Partly suppressed from on high, partly because politicians themselves refuse to appear on them, those programmes where there was real debate have disappeared one by one, and there are now none left.

Oddly enough, Mitterrand is thought to have welcomed the disappearance of a lively radio debate between political commentators on Friday evenings. This recalls his decision in 1948, when Secretary of State to the President of the Council (the Prime Minister) and thus *de facto* Minister of Information, to close down radio programmes, especially the ones with most lively discussions between parliamentary correspondents, because he thought that the journalists merely insulted each other. He was not averse to censuring programmes and sacking troublesome journalists either. He justified these actions by saying that they were necessary to respond to the threat of Communist domination within the radio. For, as he made clear in a debate in the National Assembly on 19 July 1949, he considered the radio to be a form of government.[40]

The result today is media practices which seem to owe their form to the declamatory tradition in French politics: when someone speaks in the National Assembly, he mounts a podium, whereas in Britain he remains in his place, and has to compete with the general hubbub from his usual seat. As one Socialist deputy has argued, 'Ministerial press conferences, grand juries and other televized festivities, all manifest the same terrifying characteristic of being occasions where only one person speaks, or where caricatures of fixed opposing positions are expressed . . . It is sometimes difficult to admit to ourselves the extent of our own decadence in this regard.'[41] Indeed, individual politicians sometimes even have their own programmes or other media outlets: the local radio station in the constituency of the Minister of the Interior, Charles Pasqua, is practically Radio Pasqua; and the former Prime Minister, Laurent Fabius, organized his own chat-show, 'Parlons France' in which he replied to planted questions.[42]

Almost all commentators make reference to the 'oligarchical drift away from democracy'[43] or to the fact that 'the immense majority of the population does not feel itself involved in politics and regards the combat as a mere spectator'.[44] This is largely due to the extreme homogeneity of the politico-mediatic class, which discusses political issues in such a way to be unintelligible to the man in the street. One of the clearest demonstrations of this alienation came during the Maastricht campaign, when President Mitterrand took part in a $2\frac{1}{2}$ hour broadcast from the Sorbonne. Brought into the studio by the compère with the ineffable phrase 'And now, Mr

President, you will meet the French people', Mitterrand was indeed subjected to some fairly lively questioning by ordinary folk. However, when three professional journalists took the floor and began to discuss politics with the President in their opaque language, the interest value of the broadcast plummeted, for there can have been few more grotesque spectacles of the mediatico-political class gazing at its own navel.

On another particularly memorable occasion, on 12 April 1992, President Mitterrand decided to give a television interview. Here was the politics of vapid spectacle at its most disgusting. It was shortly before the debate over Maastricht began, and his only desire was to divide the opposition and dazzle the French with his omniscience about Europe. But even that long-suffering people, used to the clubby world of politicians and journalists treating them with contempt, were taken aback to see their President being questioned in tones of wonder by three of France's most prominent journalists, Anne Sinclair, Christine Ockrent and Ivan Levai. The reason for their shock? Anne Sinclair is the wife of Dominique Strauss-Kahn, then Mitterrand's Minister of Industry; Christine Ockrent is the wife of Bernard Kouchner, then Mitterrand's Minister of Health and Humanitarian Aid; while Ivan Levai, a well-known and active supporter of the Socialist Party, had been previously married to Anne Sinclair. His questioners omitted any untoward mention of the kickback scandals which were then rocking the Socialist Party, or of the amnesty law which the government had voted itself in order to wriggle out of them.[45]

Rather than offering any serious counterweight or challenge to political power, French journalists are too often so fascinated by its power that they only magnify its irresponsibility. Instead of interrogating politicians on matters of policy, they often seem more interested in petty political intrigue. It is a common symptom of this fascination with the corridors of power for journalists to dwell at great length asking politicians, or sometimes even other journalists, meticulous questions about their relations with or opinions about other politicians. This obsession can reach pornographic proportions. When interviewing Jacques Attali while he was still President of the European Bank for Reconstruction and Development, Ivan Levai insisted on asking him about his relations with Delors, Balladur, Chirac and so on, even though Attali made it clear that he did not want to enter into the internal French electoral debate.[46] A prominent TV journalist, Patrick Poivre d'Arvor, devoted an entire fifteen-minute interview with Margaret Thatcher to questions about her opinion of French politicians, religiously and obsessively going through the whole list, asking 'What did you think of Giscard, Mitterrand, Barre, Chirac, Delors . . .' and so on. Or again, reporting on a long television interview with Mitterrand in late 1993, the news bulletin on France 3 selected *only* the bits where Mitterrand spoke of his relationship with Jacques Chirac and Michel Rocard.[47] Whole boxes of pages in the press the next day were devoted to the same thing.

The media's concentration on personal intrigue entrenches one of the strangest characteristics of French politics: its sheer unreality. One manifestation of this is the prepared interview. When the prolific journalist Franz-Olivier Giesbert was being interviewed on television about his book in October 1993 (it is extraordinary how much free airtime the most famous journalists get to publicize their works), he and the interviewer went through the same inevitable list of prominent politicians, Giesbert obligingly providing his prepared one-liners off pat. Similarly, on the main evening news programmes at 8 p.m., there are occasionally 'interviews' with other journalists, but it is always clear from the open-ended nature of the 'question', and from the tone and length of the 'answer', that the second journalist is reading a prepared text from an autocue. In this unreal, trivial world, there is, in fact, no debate or interview whatever.

Indeed, belonging to the élite themselves, journalists – especially the prominent ones – are often insufferably smug. On a well-known radio phone-in programme, 'Le Téléphone Sonne', a group of journalists tried to defend their profession's reputation against persistent evidence that the French hold them in low esteem, believing them to be arrogant and untrustworthy political lackeys.[48] The defence on this occasion was better than any prosecution: during the 45-minute programme, they only took three calls! Accused of having been biased over Maastricht, they defended themselves by saying that all they had been trying to do was to explain objectively why people should vote 'yes'.[49]

An important consequence of the structural defects of French political institutions and the weakness of the media is the obsessive attention devoted to opinion polls. All countries have opinion polls, but in France they are published at very regular intervals, frequently making the front pages of magazine articles which claim to show that 'the French' think this or that. The subjects under discussion are often very ephemeral, but it is curious to devote so much analysis to what people supposedly *think* about certain facts, rather than on what the facts actually are. One prominent radio journalist once announced that the weekly magazine *L'Express* had produced 100 suggestions for reducing unemployment. Then he said, 'But it's not very interesting. What is far more interesting, however, is an opinion poll published at the same time on the attitudes of the French to the question of how to reduce unemployment.'[50]

Opinion polls dictate the rhythm of political life to such an extent that the country lives in a permanent short-circuit between public opinion, which is constantly solicited, measured, and polled, and the government. This system gives a very exact indication of the institutional weakness of France: because social dialogue is insufficient, because there are no respected and influential intermediary bodies, and because there is no separation or even balance of powers, political life is dictated by an irrational, passionate and sterile confrontation between the government and public opinion.[51] Even the word in French for opinion poll, '*sondage*', is illustrative of the problem. It comes from 'to sound out', as in a nautical sounding, just as if the French political class, rather like a boat containing a small band of trepid adventurers, bobbing about on the seething, unconstituted mass of public opinion, were occasionally to let down fathom-lines into it, bringing back bitty scraps of information. But such data can never predict the coming of the storm by which they are liable at any moment to be engulfed.

The most charitable thing one can say of the journalists is that their concentration on personalities and on the pseudo-science of opinion polls reflects the way in which politicians themselves think. Because of the monarchical constitution, all political debate is dictated – almost to the exclusion of all other considerations – by the race for the presidency. Indeed, French politicians rather resemble the nobility under the *Ancien Régime*: because the monarch is absolute, everybody else remains in a state of exquisite powerlessness, and their only roles are to watch the royal spectacle, or to engage in intrigue. Versailles was constructed by Louis XIV as a means of neutering the nobility by forcing them to play the elaborate rituals of the court and drawing them into webs of ultimately futile scheming: the French political system has much the same effect on presidential hopefuls because, as at Versailles, advancement depends on the favours of the king.

Indeed, it is one of the most perverse effects of the presidential system that any politician with an ounce of talent immediately gets put into the category of *'présidentiable'* – a possible candidate for the highest office. From that point onwards, for twenty or thirty years, the man will not apply his talent to anything else other than to his attempt to put himself in a position to conquer the presidency. He will not, in other words, do what a British politician does: use his talents to the best of his ability in his ministry, trying to do a good job there before, as he hopes, moving upwards. To this end, the French politician will hold several ministerial portfolios, and a clutch of other jobs at local and regional level for these twenty or thirty years, but he will exercise them only with respect to his principal objective, not for their own sake. What matters to him is their utility in helping him to prepare his candidature, and above all to avoid compromising it by forcing him to take risks. His political style will therefore be wily and biased, dictated by the single desire not to alienate any future electoral clientele and in order to embellish his 'image'. *'Présidentiables'* lose the habit of speaking as a function of the portfolios they hold. Indeed, they lose the habit of even thinking about them, in order to consider only the effect which the positions they take might have on their chances of getting elected. The perspective of attaining near-absolute power for fourteen years destroys the normal democratic competition of powers, which ought to be more frequent, fairer and more diverse than it can ever be in France.[52] In other words, France has given herself a granite constitution with huge powers vested in the hands of one man, with a view to making great projects realizable, and yet in practical terms her political life is dictated by the ephemeral and provisional calculations of the present, based on a very long-term and perhaps unrealizable personal future.

Journalists, for their part, devote more attention and discussion to a politician's supposed ulterior motives in making a declaration – as a result of the way he might be positioning himself against his rivals, for instance – than to the substance of the declaration itself. And this, in turn, reinforces the sense of weightless trivia which afflicts French politics. The author of a book entitled *La Démocratie Malade du Mensonge* (*Democracy Sick from Lies*), writes,

> In France, the political world is a little world which evaluates signals according to the games played within itself. In the daily life of ministerial *cabinets*, priorities are all determined in accordance with the exercise of power. If one section of the Socialist Party seems to be overtaking the Jospinistes, the Rocardiens will stick their oar in to prevent it. Their urgencies are not democratic, they are microcosmic. And they spend all their time thinking about such things rather than governing. The same is true of the opposition. In this democracy, politicians' lives are composed of a thousand concerns which distance them more and more from citizens' daily concerns.[53]

To be sure, all countries' political systems have an element of this: speculation about the future of John Major in Britain was feverish for several years. But it must be remembered that, unlike the British case, such speculation in France truly is futile, because nothing can change for seven years. At least there was a chance that the Conservative Party might ditch its leader.

These distortions also give French politics an in-built stagnancy, which a glance at the physical and political longevity of French politicians will confirm. The same small clutch of politicians has monopolized the political world for the last twenty years or so: Mitterrand, Giscard, Chirac, Barre, Balladur, Delors, Fabius and Rocard. Their presidential ambitions paralyse the whole political system, as Jacques Delors inadvertently made clear in an interview in 1992. Looking back, he said, 'When the possibility was raised that I might be Prime Minister last year, some of the political friends to whom I feel close enough to make a plan for the next five years, said, "We should not move until the next presidential election."'[54] In other words, the presidency, and the political system generally, operates in such a way as to dissuade those who aspire to government from 'moving' three years before the next election date! Three years is the greater part of the term of a British parliament, and three-quarters of the term of an American President. The problem is endemic: in 1985 the centrist Edmond Alphandéry

(who subsequently became Minister for the Economy in the Balladur government in 1993) appealed to people to vote for the Right
in the 1986 legislative elections as a sign that Mitterrand should go.
But other right-wing potential presidential candidates thought that,
if Mitterrand went, then Raymond Barre would win, and so they
decided to hold their fire until the presidential election itself, and
not campaign enthusiastically for the Right. This weakened right-
wing support in the 1986 elections, enfeebled the Chirac government, and paved the way for his humiliation and Mitterrand's re-
election in 1988.

The system, then, is the victim of a cruel double paradox: the
omnipotent presidency in fact makes effective decision-taking very
difficult. Potential challengers for the presidency think so far into
the long term that all their short-and medium-term activities are
neutered. Mitterrand, for his part, excels in this world because,
having grown up in the atmosphere of intrigue and compromise
for which the Fourth Republic is notorious, and having spent a
total of fifty years in politics, he knows the rules better than anyone
else. And so, his long period in office has been marked by an
obsession with destroying his enemies, at France's expense. In
the second presidential term, as we have seen, he appointed Michel
Rocard as his Prime Minister with much the same intention as that
with which he brought the Communists into the first Mauroy
government in 1981: to destroy him. He dedicated himself to this
task with address for two years, much as he had spent the cohabitation period successfully undermining Jacques Chirac and the right-
wing government which the people had elected. He finally sacked
Rocard in 1990, to replace him with Edith Cresson. This dismissal
of a capable politician who had been Mitterrand's rival in the
Socialist Party for thirty years led one critic to write, 'Mitterrand
has a sense of sacrifice. In order to preserve his power, he has
sacrificed everything: his party, his country, and even his own image
in the eyes of history.'[55] In other words, the presidency of the
republic prevents France from being governed. It does not function
properly itself, and it prevents the rest of France from functioning
too. In a world where the vapidity of 'communication' reigns
supreme, the illusion dominates that words alone or tinny symbols
are sufficient in politics. Nothing is valued for what it is, only for
what it seems. The appointments of Edith Cresson and the

businessman-politician-football manager, Bernard Tapie, as ministers, seemed to be little more than public-relations exercises, or kitschy 'symbols' of 'progress', 'youth', or 'a simple man who has succeeded'. Mitterrand is even thought to have flirted with the idea of making Jack Lang Prime Minister.[56] In such a world, where the illusion of 'communication' replaces true political action, stagnation, nepotism, and sheer wastage of resources are the result.[57]

Mitterrand lives and breathes the medium of the spoken word, for it is ideal for him: it is transitory and quickly forgotten. His speech is used to create a 'sensation', rather than specific proposals, and he does not consider that the utterance commits him to anything. What counts as action in his political world does not count as action in the real world: after the Socialist Party's severe defeat in regional elections in March 1992, for instance, Mitterrand said he would 'go on the offensive'. This involved simply speaking on the radio and television. He used the occasion to emphasize that he would continue until the end of his term of office, merely underlining his political irresponsibility. Here, too, then, de Gaulle's republic has been undermined from within by his oldest rival. De Gaulle, the man of action, has found his antithesis in Mitterrand, the man of mere talk. De Gaulle was a great orator, but he spoke in such a way that changed things. All that Mitterrand's speeches do is to enable him to wriggle out of a tight spot, reinforce his own power, or destroy an opponent. Under him, the politics of spectacle has triumphed.

Within such a framework, sensible government is impossible: 'In the Mitterrand-state, as in the now defunct regimes of Eastern Europe, a law's value depends less on its provisions than on the simple proclamation of its existence: in each case, it is a matter of satisfying a clientele or satisfying people's ideological prejudices.[58] The same activities percolate down throughout the whole mechanism of government: ministers imitate the President. They invent laws or pseudo-laws which are not applied, cannot be applied, or are incomprehensible, in order to make people talk about them, and hopefully to ask them on television to 'explain' their new bill. Unsurprisingly, this produces legislative inflation, and the French parliament passes more than a 1,000 laws a year; all of them are initiated by the government. This is about as many as Rome had during the whole of two millennia. In such circumstances, it is hardly surprising that the respect for parliament has declined.[59]

Just as the Fifth Republic has collapsed institutionally from the Utopian vision which Charles de Gaulle had of it – submerged by grubby politicking, the regime of parties, and the soporific under-pull of technocracy – so the old French habits which he wanted to overcome have overwhelmed the republic he created. In particular, the old and invidious gap between the real country and legal country persists, between ordinary people and the political class. Commentators are nearly unanimous on the perverse effects of this. One critic is particularly lucid:

> French citizens no longer have any choice between policies, between different social projects, or between different perspectives on the future. They watch the daily management of the state, passively and sceptically. As far as political debate is concerned, it is at best a confused mixture of statistics, the perception of which becomes more and more abstract as they continue to be manipulated, at worst a puzzle of sound bites, artificially fabricated by a media system which is submerged by the influence of television, sinking into mere spectacle . . . The political debate closes in on itself because whole swathes of society no longer feel themselves represented and not even cared for.[60]

6. *An Inspector Calls*

Listening to these so-called republicans talk of liberty and
virtue is like watching some faded courtesan affecting the rosy
blushes of virginity.

Joseph de Maistre, *Considérations sur la France*, 1797[1]

The curious sense of unreality which Mitterrand has imparted to
French politics began at the beginning. On 10 May 1981, the day of
his election to the presidency, there was a demonstration on Place
de la Bastille. The Right had been in power since 1958, and the Left
lost no opportunity to emphasize that a new age had dawned.
Mitterrand had been elected in part simply because of the Right's
long tenure, but also because Valéry Giscard d'Estaing's scandal-
ridden reign and authoritarian behaviour had given the Right a
shabby and autocratic image. The incoming Socialist promised a
moral renewal of French politics,[2] and one of the '110 propositions
for France' on which Mitterrand campaigned was an undertaking
to pursue judicial inquiries into politicians suspected of corruption.[3]
Assorted lefties carried banners saying, 'Mitterrand, give us sunshine.'[4] Jack Lang, who was to prove a constant source of grovel-
ling hyperbole, declared, 'This day, France has crossed the frontier
which separates night from day.'[5] Shakespeare's *Richard III*, which
describes the ruthless ascent to power of a schemer, also begins
with references to sunshine, day and light ('Now is the winter
of our discontent made glorious summer by this sun of York'),[6] and
those who think that the dwarfish Mitterrand was to prove at least
as villainous as his predecessor might do well to recall the event.
For, although the Place de la Bastille was chosen as being symbolic
of the people-power which Socialism is supposed to represent, the
'spontaneous' demonstration, had, in fact, been organized and pre-
planned three weeks in advance.[7] It was to be only the first example
while he was in power of one of Mitterrand's most notorious hall
marks: make-believe.

His promise to clean up French political life was to prove just as ineffective, as was his pretence that corruption is endemic to the Right. For far from creating a moral renewal in French politics, the Socialists' conviction that morality is on the Left seems only to have legitimized an orgy of clientilism and other abuses of power. There has been a huge literature on the subject,[8] and the title of one major book on corruption under Mitterrand, André Routier's *La République des loups* (*The Republic of Wolves*),[9] deliberately evokes the titles of a series of books attacking the Third Republic, written during the 1920s and 1930s.[10] Indeed, many of the criticisms levelled at the political system during that scandal-ridden period in French history have reappeared under Mitterrand, and some have drawn direct parallels between then and now, one commentator writing that 'This *fin de siècle* in France seems once again to be bathed in a sweet air of moral decadence'.[11] Some even believe that Mitterrand's France is more corrupt than any previous regime, others even that France is now among the most corrupt countries in the world, just after Africa and more corrupt than Italy.[12] Two out of three French people now believe that their political leaders, across the political spectrum, are dishonest.[13]

That this is so is addedly ironic considering that throughout Mitterrand's life, one theme has recurred in his speeches: a constant and obsessive denunciation of the role of money in society. His declarations on this are of an astonishing virulence. In his autobiography, for instance, he claims that his family thought that hierarchy based on the privilege of money was the worst of all disorders. 'It was unacceptable and revolting that money should be able to outdo other values which ought to have been its natural points of reference: *la patrie*, religion, liberty, dignity. Money was the enemy, the corrupting force with which one ought to have nothing to do.'[14] On many subsequent occasions, he would rail against 'the money-king' or 'international money', whose 'net is closing, the net of gold, the net of blood', insisting that France would not be free until liberated from this 'enemy'.[15] In keynote speeches he would thunder against 'The money which corrupts, money which buys, money which crushes, money which kills, money which ruins, money which rots right through to the conscience of men'[16]; or evoke 'The money which flows on all sides ... Money, money, money, everywhere'.[17] As late as 1981, the 110 propositions made the same incantatory reference to how *le grand capital* enslaved man and devoured his essence, and throughout the following decade he was still given to strongly worded expostulations on the matter, such as when people reproached him for having pursued 'monetarist' policies.[18] He even on one occasion claimed that money played such a little role in his own life that he lived only off his presidential salary, and did not have any savings or investments, an unlikely assertion.[19]

It is worth dwelling on the peculiar Frenchness of this obsession, for it is one which unites both Right and Left. In particular, it has a distinguished pedigree in the provincial, Catholic tradition which characterized Mitterrand's own background, and of which the extreme Right is an excrescence. Both traditions were influenced by the papal encyclical *Quadragesimo Anno*. Published in 1931, only two years after the Lateran accords signed between the Vatican and Mussolini, and no doubt inspired by the warm relationship between the Church and the fascist state, that encyclical contains a vigorous denunciation of political liberalism.[20] Similarly, the essence of the political doctrine of the Vichy government was its rejection of the liberal capitalist order as if it, and not Communism, were the main enemy. Vichy rightly identified liberal individualism with democracy, which it hated.[21] The hatred of money was indeed one of Marshal Pétain's favourite themes, and, like Mitterrand, he painted his own '*combat*' in the colours of national emancipation, declaring, 'I intend our country to be liberated from that most miserable tutelage, that of money'.[22] Charles Maurras, the leader of the extreme right-wing traditionalist-monarchist party, Action Française, also blamed the all-pervasive power of money for the democratic order which he so detested.[23] Indeed, even de Gaulle declared to André Malraux after his defeat in the referendum in 1969, that 'I was faced with the real enemy which I have had all my life, and that is Money'.[24]

Perhaps the persistence of this obsession can be explained because, throughout history, French politics have, indeed, often been financially corrupt.[25] Traditionally, French *affaires* are affairs of state or business, rather than affairs of the heart, although there have been some famous scandals in the last category: in the Third

Republic, President Félix Faure collapsed and died while entertaining his mistress at the Elysée Palace; the second Madame Caillaux shot dead the editor of the *Figaro* for publishing love letters written to her by President Caillaux during his first marriage.[26] People were understandably preoccupied to learn that Valéry Giscard d'Estaing had accepted gifts of diamonds from the cannibalistic Emperor Bokassa, but in general the sexual peccadilloes of politicians are not considered scandal-worthy. On the contrary, many members of the public seem to consider it appropriate for a political leader to demonstrate his virility by having many lovers. When confronted with the extra-marital dalliance of one of his ministers, de Gaulle once dismissed the rumour, saying, 'Well, he's only doing a man's job.'[27] The fact that François Mitterrand lodges a female friend in a grace-and-favour apartment provided for by the state (a presidential favour) has passed almost without comment.[28] In any case, any journalist who decides to pry has the shackles of France's strict privacy law to contend with, for the private lives of politicians are a secret of state.

But Mitterrand's ritualistic denunciations of the role of money in society are even odder when one realizes that corruption in France is as widespread as it is structurally inherent to the system. It flows mainly from a failure to distinguish between the public and the private domains, i.e. between powers and privileges which accrue to a man in virtue of his office on the one hand, and to him as a private person on the other. This leads to the abuse of public money for private or party-political purposes, a practice which has become so widespread that it seems as if the distinction between the legitimate and illegitimate use of such money has become completely blurred in politicians' minds. This in turn eats away like a cancer at public respect for the political institutions and processes of the state. As one expert on the matter has concluded, 'Corruption is by no means novel in French politics. What is different today is that corrupting practices are seeping through the public arena, are gaining an unhealthy degree of public acceptance, are unsanctioned by the high officials of the parties and the state, and, finally, are uncontrolled by political institutions.'[29]

Consider the official sanction of the practice of providing ministers with so-called 'secret funds'. These are sums of money which are legally put at the disposal of the government, although their actual spending is not monitored by anybody. The sums involved are staggering: they amount to 400 million francs per year (£45 million). Of this, 100 million goes to the Elysée, 200 million to Matignon and the rest to other ministries. Each ministry receives between 50,000 and 300,000 francs each month, with a good 25,000 francs (£30,000 a year) for the minister's personal use. The money is usually delivered in cash, in brown envelopes, so that its exact use is never traced.[30] In addition to private consumption, much of the Matignon money has been used to pay for the functioning of the party in power. One of the founders of Giscard's party, the Union for French Democracy, has admitted that 'When the UDF was founded, it was financed entirely by the secret funds from Matignon: about 200,000 francs per month (£240,000 per year) to pay for offices in the Boulevard Saint-Germain, the staff, and so on'.[31]

These and other practices have continued under the Socialists. For instance, the National Assembly also has huge funds, which are used to help deputies with their private finances. Sometimes the use of this money has no hint of legitimacy about it. [32] Indeed, it was rather amusing to observe that, at the time when unseemly public pressure was being mounted in Britain for the Queen to pay taxes, the inhabitants of the two royal palaces in Paris, the Bourbon Palace (National Assembly) and the Luxembourg Palace (Senate), graciously agreed that, like her, they too ought to pay taxes on their fortune – of whose very existence the man in the street had probably been hitherto unaware. The most obviously corrupt use of such payments, however, is to ensure political compliance. One official at the Ministry of Finance makes the astonishing admission that

> Each year when the budget is being voted on, we put a little envelope aside for the deputies' good works . . . In order to encourage the deputies not to put down any amendments which might be irritating to the government, we use the money to distribute little presents to them for their constituencies or for their political friends during the course of the debate in the parliament.[33]

These practices explain why anyone who visits the office of a leading French politician will be struck by their palatial premises.

Money, indeed, seems to cushion the successful French politician at every moment: when the President travels abroad, his train comprises two or three Boeing 747s, or perhaps the presidential Concorde – far more than that of the Queen of the United Kingdom or the King of Spain.[34]

However, the biggest factor in undermining public confidence in the political class under Mitterrand was the so-called 'Urba affair'. Urba is the shorthand name for three companies, Urba-Conseil, Urba-Technic and Urba-Gracco, which belonged to a holding company with the otiose name of Management of the Companies in the Group (Gestion des Sociétés Regroupées). It was set up in 1972 by François Mitterrand, one year after he had founded the Socialist Party at the Epinay Congress, when he realized that the money for his own self-promotion would have to come from somewhere. Urba was ostensibly a consulting company belonging to the Socialist Party. In fact it was a phantom organization which acted as instrument of the party's traffic in influence. The method of operation was simple. A Socialist local authority which desired to award a contract would invite companies to submit proposals for the work. The chances of success of these proposals would be increased if they paid for the services of the 'consultancy group'. These companies took their commission – anything between 3 per cent and 15 per cent of the cost of the contract[35] – and passed the money on to the Socialist Party. The local authority, subverting the law and public procedure, would then award the contract to the company which paid the biggest bribe.[36] One of the main actors in the affair, who was later imprisoned, has confirmed that these illicit practices brought between 38 and 58 million francs a year to the party.[37]

The decentralization of some powers to local and regional authorities, which occurred under the Socialists in 1983, oiled the wheels by which this corrupt behaviour could occur. One practitioner of pay-offs has explained that 'Bribery has obviously increased with the decentralization laws [passed in 1983], which have increased the competencies of the mayors in questions of town planning . . . Back-handers have become the rule. And local politicians now need more money for their electoral campaigns'.[38] Ten years ago, for instance, the back-handers required for building a supermarket represented 1 per cent of its total cost. Now the average is 10 per cent, or about 1,000 francs per square metre of shop premises.[39]

Urba's name first began to appear in the French press in 1982, when a property developer wanted to undertake a development in Spain. He applied to the Finance Ministry for the necessary authorization, and was turned down. A friend encouraged him to turn to Urba for help. The developer paid Urba 510,000 francs, and the application was re-examined, but the Minister of Finance, Jacques Delors, refused a second time. Urba returned the money in embarrassment at its failure.[40] The name appeared again in 1983, when a police inspector, Antoine Gaudino, discovered that a company had obtained public contracts after paying 6 million francs in false invoices to various consultancy groups in the Hérault region, including Urba.

Six years later, the same Inspector Gaudino was to discover the iceberg of which his previous discoveries turned out to be the mere tip. On 17 April 1989, he came across the so-called Delcroix papers, in the course of his investigations into a scandal concerning false invoices in Marseille (the so-called SORMAE affair). Joseph Delcroix had kept minutes of all the meetings of the steering committee of the various branches of Urba, the Group of Economic Interest (GIE). The content of his notes was explosive, for they proved what Gaudino had always suspected: 'Purpose of Urba: to provide money for the Socialist Party, the subscriptions being insufficient, and there being no aid expected from business.'[41] It is no coincidence, therefore, that the expenditure of the Socialist Party rose from 90 million francs in 1987 to between 173 and 250 million francs in 1991, excluding the cost of electoral expenses. These figures were part of a general increase in expenditure by French political parties: perhaps it is unsurprising that, during this period, the numbers of members of political parties fell and the general gap between people and politicians widened.[42]

However, the really explosive finding was this: the Delcroix papers also showed that François Mitterrand's presidential campaign in May 1988 had been financed by Urba to the tune of 24 million francs (nearly £3 million). (The campaign had cost a total of 100 million francs.) Indeed, the contact man at the Elysée Palace for Urba was none other than Jean-Claude Colliard, the President's *directeur de cabinet*.[43] The papers also showed that an official at the

Court of Accounts, David Azoulay, had transferred the money to a front company, Multiservices. The company had been dissolved within a few hours of its creation, in order not to leave any documentary trace of its existence,[44] and Azoulay had subsequently deposited falsified official accounts of the election campaign with the Constitutional Court.[45]

'*Le pouvoir*', as the French charmingly call the government, was not slow to react. Antoine Gaudino and his fellow policeman Alain Mayot were immediately taken off the case, and the inquiry was canned. A month later, the government introduced an amnesty law, which was passed on 15 January 1990. It complemented a previous amnesty law, passed in July 1988, which retrospectively exculpated all politicians from corruption charges, except in the case of personal enrichment, trading favours or interference in the course of justice.[46]

Inspector Gaudino published a book on 10 October 1990, *L'Enquête impossible*, in which he explained Urba's methods. As the law requires in France, a copy of the book was deposited with the local prefecture, the antenna of the Ministry of the Interior, two weeks before publication. Within days, police were sent round to the printers to rummage through the premises. A week before publication, on 3 October 1991, a new Minister of Justice was appointed. As Gaudino himself remarks, 'Political cynicism can lead to mistakes which surpass all understanding':[47] the new minister was none other than Henri Nallet, the former treasurer of Mitterrand's presidential campaign, the very campaign which Urba had financed!

Two days after the book was published, Gaudino was suspended from the police force by the Minister of the Interior, Pierre Joxe, himself also a former Treasurer of the Socialist Party. He was finally sacked on 18 March 1991, after a hearing at a police tribunal, where the president of the tribunal had to use his 'golden' vote to obtain the sacking, there not having been a majority on the committee. Later that evening, the Director-General of the police, François Roussely, declared on television that the decision had been taken by simple majority. Roussely had previously been the *directeur de cabinet* of Pierre Joxe, the Interior Minister.[48]

From then on, Gaudino's life took on a Keystone Cops aura, which would have been funny had it not been all too real. He had contacted the investigative journalist, Jean Montaldo, and the dynamic politician, Philippe de Villiers, in order to bring the case to the public's attention. They would speak in code language on the telephone, suspecting that they were being listened to. They never used fax machines for the same reason. They were followed by policeman in raincoats and sunglasses whenever they met in cafés. After one such meeting, in an attempt to see how many people were following him, Gaudino turned into a deserted street: twelve men were on his tail. Recalling the existence of the notorious 'anti-terrorist cell' at the Elysée Palace,[49] Gaudino thought with a sinister flash, 'I suddenly remembered the disappearance of the Pastor Doucé,' a reference to a priest who, it is suspected, was murdered by the French secret services, the Renseignements Généraux in 1990.[50]

Indeed, Gaudino was witness to the following exchange between Philippe de Villiers and one of his friends in the UDF, Pascal Clément. Clément asked Villiers, 'How far are you prepared to go in this business?' Villiers replied that corruption was an evil which threatened the very core of democracy, and that he was prepared to go as far as necessary. Clément then gave the following friendly caution, 'Don't forget, Philippe, that there was the Fontanet affair, and the Boulin affair. With the way you're carrying on, there might be a Villiers affair as well.'[51] Fontanet and Boulin were both politicians who were found dead under suspicious circumstances. Robert Boulin, the Employment Minister under Prime Minister Raymond Barre and President Valéry Giscard d'Estaing, had been found drowned in a lake in the forest of Rambouillet, the same forest, which belongs ex officio to the President, where Pastor Doucé was found murdered. It seems that Boulin was about to accuse a government minister and a magistrate of leaking secret details gleaned from a judicial investigation which incriminated other members of the governement. While the coroner returned a verdict of suicide on Boulin a week after his death, his family contested this. They evidently believed that he had been murdered by someone interested in shutting him up. Even given the suspicion that political murders have taken place in recent French history, Gaudino was understandably astonished to hear Pascal Clément warning Philippe de Villiers that he was seriously concerned about the danger to his life.

But Villiers and Gaudino also received threats. Six months later, a former Minister of the Interior explained how he would have dealt with Gaudino: 'Twelve bullets in the head.'[52] A serving minister said to Villiers, 'If you carry on, we will smash you.'[53] Finally an old friend of Villiers came to see him, and said to him, in secret,

> My dear friend, you know how much I admire your fight. I share all your motivations. For the honour of our country, it is essential that the trading of favours which you denounce should cease. At the same time, I must say to you that this is having a bad effect. This scandal will involve everybody. I appeal to your reason to stop, knowing that you understand politics too well not to know what is at stake. I appeal to your reason because you are well aware how big this thing is. In addition, for some people, human life is cheap.[54]

Despite these threats and warnings, the Urba farce continued. On 13 April 1991, Mitterrand's friend, the businessman-politician, Bernard Tapie, who was later to enjoy a fifty-day spell as Minister for Towns in the Bérégovoy government in 1992 before resigning pending investigations into his financial affairs, asked to meet Gaudino in secret. Led to a hotel room in Marseille by Tapie's personal bodyguard, who, in true mafioso style, had a gun visibly bulging under his jacket, Gaudino taped the conversation as a precaution, fearing that he might be framed by Tapie. Tapie freely admitted the corrupt activities in which the Socialists were involved – he was himself already under suspicion for numerous shady deals – and recounted a story told him by Jean-Paul Huchon, the *directeur de cabinet* of Michel Rocard, the Prime Minister. Huchon had said,

> I swear on the life of my children that four months ago, at Matignon, Rocard said to me, 'We must absolutely allow the inquiry to continue. That will allow us to demonstrate our honesty, and those who cannot, worse luck for them.' Mauroy agreed. But the next day, Mauroy and Jospin came back, having been to see Bianco. They said, 'It is absolutely out of the question.'[55]

'Bianco' is Jean-Louis Bianco, the Secretary-General of the President of the Republic. He was transmitting to Rocard his boss's decision to forbid the inquiry to continue. In other words, the decision had come from Mitterrand, whose role as President and

First Magistrate of France makes him the guarantor of the independence of the judiciary.[56]

The case may have run into the sands of political obstruction had not a young magistrate, Thierry Jean-Pierre, been working on a case involving the accidental death of two workers on a building site in Le Mans. An anonymous telephone caller informed him that the building company involved had been paying bribes to politicians. Over the coming years, this young judge was to make a name for himself in the tenacious pursuit of this and other cases of corruption. His investigations confirmed that Urba received commissions for the successful planning applications with which it dealt, 40 per cent of which it kept, 30 per cent of which went to the central organization of the Socialist Party, and 30 per cent to the local Socialist deputy. Indeed, in time, even the head of Urba, Gerard Monate, was to explain, 'The link [between the PS and Urba] is simple. I was designated by the party. The party is informed, the Treasurer knows what I do, the control commission comes to examine the accounts but it is I who distributes the money in all clarity.'[57] Later, he added, 'Monsieur Nallet, treasurer of Monsieur Mitterrand's campaign, asked me to call on my regional delegates [i.e. of Urba] to collect funds.'[58]

On 7 April 1992, Thierry Jean-Pierre decided to arrest Monate. In anticipation of the magistrate's arrival at his house, Monate was placed under police guard. But while Jean-Pierre was on the way to the man's home, the Minister of Justice – who is responsible for ordering public prosecutions and investigations – telephoned the public prosecutor at Le Mans and ordered Jean-Pierre to be taken off the case. The latter learned of this when he got to Monate's home. He thus went instead to the head office of Urba in the 9th arrondissement of Paris, entered the building, had the locks changed, and three hours later he left with five boxes of documents. For this, the Minister of Justice, Henri Nallet, accused him of 'judicial burglary'.[59] He was also implicitly censured by the Foreign Minister, Roland Dumas, who doubtless had him in mind when he hysterically attacked what he called the climate of 'pre-fascism' in France in February 1993.

Having taken Jean-Pierre off the case, Nallet tried his luck again, by trying to close the case altogether. But the Chamber of Accusation of the Court of Appeal at Angers refused, although it confirmed the removal of Jean-Pierre. Thus, a different judge was put on the case. It might have died down had not a lawyer friend of Gaudino's realized that parliamentarians could take a municipality to court for abuse of funds. (It is nearly impossible for private citizens to bring cases to court against the wishes of the Ministry of Justice.)[60] A Green Party MEP in Marseille agreed to take the city council to court, using Gaudino's book as evidence for his charge that the company Borie SAE had paid a 5,700,000-franc commission to Urba, of which 80 per cent had gone to three Marseille deputies.

But the case still met with further political obstruction. Deputies enjoy immunity from prosecution during the parliamentary session, unless the case has been opened before that session. A trial was thus opened in haste by the Court of Appeal in Lyon on 27 September 1991, a few days before the session began. In the meantime, one of the deputies, Michel Pezet had appealed to the Council of State, asking them to reject the original case brought by the MEP: the Council of State is advised in such cases by the Ministry of the Interior. It stopped the case by decree on 15 November 1991, the decree being signed by the Prime Minister and the Minister of the Interior.[61] In other words, an administrative measure had been used to obstruct a criminal measure. This unprecedented abuse of this organ of state was made even more flagrant by the fact that the Councillors were reported to have said in their communiqué that there were no grounds for pursuing the inquiry, an opinion which it lay quite outside their remit to give. It was not until 12 May 1992 that the Supreme Court reopened the case, overturning the decision of the Council of State. Throughout 1993, senior Socialists were called in for questioning, including the former President of the National Assembly, Henri Emmanuelli (who had been under investigation while President of the National Assembly). The case continues.

Perhaps a country should be judged not by the number of scandals which it has, but by the way the country reacts to their discovery. In this respect, Mitterrand's France comes out with very low marks. When faced with conclusive evidence that the Socialist Party had a Mafia-style organization attached to it, upon which it depended for a large part of its revenue, many commentators and politicians tried to whitewash the matter by claiming that the problem of political corruption was part of a general decline in social values. This extraordinary defence – which met with the rude rebuff of judges in the similar 'clean hands' revolution going on in Italy at the time – suggests that the whole of society, itself a victim of the systematic extortion practised upon it by the governing party, is in some way culpable for the illegal activities of identifiable individuals and organizations.[62]

Indeed, perhaps the most astonishing thing about the affair is the complicity of influential parts of the press. Not only did many newspapers and other media fail to register the appropriate degree of protest, but many of them, especially left-wing ones, preferred to cover up the criminal activities of their Socialist friends with semantic fog, by talking about 'illicit practices', 'parallel financing' and so on. Another line of defence has been to say that all French political parties are corrupt. This argument is rather like the one blaming what happened on a general decline in social values, inasmuch as both arguments seems to ignore the most basic notions of individual responsibility for specific criminal acts. Indeed, both arguments are rather like a murderer defending himself by saying that all men are sinners.

It is not a large step from this kind of thinking to a contempt for the very institutions of justice themselves, a contempt which is unfortunately all too much in evidence. In January 1992, the headquarters of the Socialist Party itself were raided by investigative magistrates – as if Conservative Central Office in Smith Square were to be visited by the fraud squad. The normal reaction to this would be simple outrage that those in power should abuse their position. Instead, Jean-Marie Colombani, one of France's most prominent political commentators, wrote,

> It would obviously be abusive to claim that behaviour of the political 'class' is governed only by amorality [sic]. It would similarly be dangerous to search with all one's strength for a purity which is itself foreign to democracy, which is made up of a process of pacifying the conflicts of interest created by a society. From this point of view, the 'crusade' of certain judges, and now being led by politicians such as Philippe de Villiers, taken to its logical conclusion, is an abusive enterprise. Justice is itself a power, and an imbalance can manifest itself exaggeratedly to the detriment of the executive.[63]

This kind of apparatchik comment would not have been out of place in the pages of *Pravda*, which in some respects *Le Monde* resembles. But Colombani's contempt for judicial institutions and practices is equalled only by his contempt for notions of natural justice: 'One forgets that before the new [amnesty] law, illegality was obligatory.'[64]

It is, of course, rubbish that there were no laws against corruption within the ordinary legal framework of France,[65] but the widely believed pretence that this is not so provides a convenient escape clause for guilty politicians. Above all, however, the notion that legality or illegality can be conjured up by government *fiat* is compelling evidence of moral leprosy. Indeed, a hysterical fear of rocking the boat seems to pervert so much journalistic comment and political comment, as if journalists were not supposed to do just that in the name of truth and justice. The centre-right commentator, Alain Duhamel, has written, 'The systematic, extreme and psychodramatic exploitation of the "affairs" by a handful of cursing politicians does not only constitute a permanent demonstration of intellectual dishonesty, a nauseous river of mud and of scum, a pathological cry of hatred, *but also an incomparable machine for collective self-destabilization*.'[66] Indeed, at one stage in the Urba affair, Philippe de Villiers explained to Antoine Gaudino that the French attitude to justice has remained basically unchanged since the Dreyfus affair: 'Better an injustice than disorder.'[67]

However, there are very good reasons why politicians might fear such disorder: corruption being widespread, they have indeed got much to lose if ever justice were to be done. Indeed, it is precisely because it is widespread that the Socialist Party was able to get away with its illicit practices. Opposition politicians have usually preferred not to stir things up too much. Instead, political parties operate on the principle of mutual deterrence. Each party accumulates information relating to a potential scandal. The revelation of any '*affaire*' by one side immediately leads to reprisals, that is, to the unleashing of other '*affaires*'. Mutual blackmail keeps the system going. When the Minister of Co-operation in 1986, Michael Aurillac, revealed the scandal of Carrefour du Développement (another slush fund used by the Socialist Party),[68] his own colleagues advised him against making a fuss about the misuse of funds by the Socialists (by then in opposition). They considered several million dollars a minor infraction; but more importantly, they feared retaliation. Similarly when the Péchiney scandal broke in 1989 (involving insider trading by some of Mitterrand's closest associates),[69] the (right-wing) opposition remained almost silent. A major potential financial scandal that apparently implicated the Left was unexploited by the Right because it feared that the information that the Left had gathered on the conduct of the privatization programme in 1986–8 would be the retaliation, and this would implicate the RPR, as well as many of its friends who had ostensibly benefited from the programme.[70]

Another tactic is to seek refuge in frankness, as if admission of the crime expiated it. Speaking of his own prosecution, Henri Emmanuelli, the former President of the National Assembly said,

> If I have understood correctly, it is a matter of showing that there were links between Urba and the Socialist Party. It is a curious anxiety, a strange demand, a bizarre preoccupation, to want to demonstrate well known facts, which we have never contested. Yes, Urba existed, like many other consulting groups linked to political parties. And I maintain, at the risk of shocking people, that among all the methods of parallel financing which existed at the time, this was the least bad, the most transparent, and the best one capable of preventing corruption.[71]

Indeed the former head of Urba, Gerard Monate even suggested that Urba's practices should be legalized outright, and merely subjected to a tighter control.[72]

Henri Nallet made the following remarks about the affair: 'I have never had recourse myself to Urba, nor to the Société Multiservices whose name has been occasionally mentioned. Urba participated in the financing of the campaign of the Socialist Party in favour of François Mitterrand.'[73] By this, he means that he has never used the money personally. Such a defence has been encouraged by the two amnesty laws which the government passed in 1988 and 1990. They were objectionable not only because they legally exculpate what are deplorable activities, but also because they established a spurious distinction between organized Mafia-style corruption by a governing party, which they excuse, while only declaring personal enrichment to be criminal. François Mitterrand has had frequent recourse to this line of argument: 'Out of the 58 deputies ... who are now involved in judicial investigations, only 4 or 5 are being investigated for personal enrichment. The others are being investigated for having obtained money for their political party, which is completely different.'[74] But the pretence that only personal enrichment is culpable is moral and legal nonsense, because what is shocking about the affair is precisely that the Socialists' method was systematic. The mechanisms of Urba were not original, because other parties had used similar ones. What was special was the centralization of the operations of the Socialist Party, using consultancy groups which everybody in the political world knew to be front organizations for the PS. The novelty was therefore that corruption ceased to be an individual, marginal or deviant phenomenon, and became instead a normal, systematic and collective practice.[75]

Another tactic of Mitterrand's has been to claim that there are as many or more right-wing politicians under suspicion than left-wing ones. Interviewed on television about the corruption scandals, he said,

> I have checked – because I was obviously expecting a question on this – there are 58 parliamentary deputies involved (I do not say guilty) in judicial inquiries. Out of those there are 30 who belong to the [right-wing] opposition and 28 who are in the presidential majority [the Socialists]. I must say that one hears far more about the latter than the former.[76]

Once again, the suggestion that all politicians are corrupt is only partly true. Although the right-wing politician, Alain Madelin, once declared with insolent frankness, 'The false invoice is to the political world what air is to a normal human being'[77] (during 1994, his party was under investigation for having used illicit money to purchase the property it used for its headquarters),[78] this cannot hide the fact that the Socialist Party was the only one to have an organization *structurally* integrated within it, and which traded in favours, perverting the course of justice which it, as the party of government, was supposed to uphold.

Mitterrand has systematically treated with contempt the succession of question-marks which have been raised over the morality of his party. In January 1992, he 'did not hide his exasperation with the polemic over the political scandals,'[79] as if such a reaction were appropriate given their basis in fact, and as if the public's feelings counted nothing. Often, he would just refuse to answer questions. When faced with allegations of corrupt activity against Bernard Tapie, Mitterrand would just stonewall, 'He was a good minister and a good football manager. I know nothing about the judicial investigations.'[80] Indeed, more than any politician, Mitterrand seemed to want to dismiss the very concept of right and wrong: 'Is there a greater proportion of dishonest people under the Fifth Republic than under the Fourth? Who knows? I cannot say, it is unlikely, it must be about the same . . . You know that immorality was not born yesterday.'[81] One might as well say that there has always been murder, and that in the past it may have gone unpunished more frequently than today. Mitterrand's whole political personality depends on the blurring of distinctions, political as much as moral, and on the refusal ever to be pinned down to any single position on anything. Few phrases, indeed, epitomize his moral cynicism better than when he refused to accept that there was anything wrong with his continuing to frequent his old friend, René Bousquet, the former Chief of Police under Vichy: 'You think that life is black and white? No, it is light grey and dark grey.'[82]

It was against this background of moral chaos that François Mitterrand reluctantly appointed Pierre Bérégovoy Prime Minister in April 1992. Bérégovoy had been the only senior Socialist untainted by the revelations. His supposed integrity made him seem ideally suited to disperse the rank stench of corruption in which French political life was suffocating, and one of his first actions on assuming office was to announce that he would lance the boil of systemic illegality in French politics. Like the Lord High Executioner in *The Mikado*,[83] he mounted the tribune of the National Assembly waving a list of names – which he did not reveal – of politicians who were likely to be prosecuted. He hoped thereby to begin to turn around the flagging political fortunes of the Socialist Party in time for the general election in April 1993.

Twelve months later, Mitterrand's last Socialist Prime Minister was to take a gun out of the glove compartment of his ministerial car, walk along the banks of a canal with it, and blow his brains out. Far from saving the party by causing heads to roll, Bérégovoy chose to execute himself. The Socialist Party had itself been massacred at the hands of the electorate, winning scarcely 18 per cent of the vote. The election has reduced them to a rump of some 80 deputies in a National Assembly of nearly 600, giving the right-wing parties the biggest majority of any party in parliament since the early nineteenth century. It seemed that, as Mitterrand contemplated his own departure from power, he was prepared to leave the Socialist Party in the same state in which he had found it in 1971 – total disarray.

Both the date and place of Bérégovoy's suicide were highly symbolic. He killed himself on 1 May, no doubt in reference to his Socialist convictions. It was an open secret that he resented the patronizing attitude adopted towards him by the snobbish over-educated élite of the Socialist Party. Many of them seemed themselves overtly hostile to him, a man who had got to the top from genuinely working-class beginnings. He had worked as a welder before going into politics, and often felt like the gasman who had ended up in the jet set.[84] They nicknamed him 'the little man', '*la petite chose*'.[85] Indeed, similar attitudes had been detectable when Bernard Tapie resigned from Beregovoy's government in June 1992, for many seemed to gloat over his downfall. As with Bérégovoy, Tapie's lowly origins excited almost obsessive comment, an indication of how difficult it is, even in the Socialist Party, for ordinary people to succeed.

Nor had Bérégovoy ever belonged to Mitterrand's closest entourage, the presidential court being divided into circles of greater and lesser intimacy. The President had passed him over as Prime Minister, choosing him only when there was no one else left after the disastrous failure of Edith Cresson. Indeed, Mitterrand had also passed him over in 1983, when Bérégovoy entertained ambitions of replacing Pierre Mauroy in March of that year.[86] In 1981, Mitterrand had also deprived Bérégovoy of the grace-and-favour appartment on the Quai Branly in the expensive 7th arrondissement of Paris, which was his due as Secretary-General of the Elysée Palace, a post he occupied at the beginning of Mitterrand's reign. The President decided instead to give it to his close friend and adviser, François de Grossouvre. After the crushing electoral defeat in April 1993, Mitterrand had further exacerbated Bérégovoy's sense of exclusion from presidential favour by refusing to see him or even to talk to him on the telephone.[87]

The place, the bank of a canal in his constituency in the Nièvre, was also symbolic. He had had himself photographed there by *Paris-Match* in June 1992 as part of his personal campaign to improve his image and that of his party. When he died, the photographs of him there were reprinted everywhere. But there was also a deeper resonance: he was the son of a Ukrainian immigrant, and the surname 'Bérégovoy' means 'on the bank' in Russian.

In fact, Bérégovoy was found still alive. For some reason, it was decided to transport him to the Val-de-Grâce hospital in Paris by helicopter instead of conducting him to the local hospital. (The Nièvre is about two hours from Paris by car.) The decision is addedly strange because the weather was so appalling that the helicopter very nearly lost its way in the cloud on the approach to Paris. According to the later official account – the exact events were very unclear at the time, for the initial reports were that he had been killed outright – Bérégovoy finally passed away in the helicopter itself.

However, the reasons for his death were not simple humiliation at the Socialists' defeat, nor even despair at France's chronic and rising unemployment. No doubt it was unbearable for Bérégovoy to watch his life's vocation as a Socialist – the defence of the interests of the working man – crumble before his eyes. It must have been especially galling that he had personally identified himself with the policy of the *franc fort* which was directly responsible for the lengthening dole queues. He felt addedly resentful that he had been forced to play along with what he called 'that huge con-trick, the Maastricht treaty'.[88] There was in addition a deeper personal reason for his despair: his own increasing personal implication in another financial corruption scandal, the Péchiney affair. His former *directeur de cabinet*, Alain Boublil, was one of the three main defendants accused of insider dealing.[89] Had Bérégovoy not killed himself, it is likely that he would himself have been called to testify at the trial, for he had been linked to the main criminal at the centre of that, and other, financial scandals, Roger-Patrice Pelat.

On 3 February 1993, shortly after Bérégovoy had been put in charge of the Socialist Party's doomed election campaign, *Le Canard*

Enchaîné revealed that in 1986 he had accepted an interest-free loan
of 1 million francs from Roger-Patrice Pelat. The loan had been
registered with a lawyer and was to be repaid before 1995. Bérégovoy had needed the money to buy a large apartment in the
expensive 16th arrondissement of Paris: after having been refused
the grace-and-favour apartment by Mitterrand in 1981, he had lived
in modest circumstances, unbecoming of the Finance Minister
of France.

Pelat had been a close friend of François Mitterrand. He had died
in 1989, while facing criminal charges for insider trading in the
Péchiney affair. The friendship between Mitterrand and Pelat had
been sealed in youth, sadness and adventure. They had been prisoners of war together in Germany in 1940, and had even escaped from
the prison camp together. After the war, they remained friends, and
were linked in other ways. Pelat had introduced Mitterrand to
Danièle Gouze, who was to become his wife; and he was one of the
very few people whom Mitterrand ever addressed as '*tu*'.

Because of Pelat's presumed guilt in the Péchiney scandal, the
mere association between Bérégovoy and Pelat was a thunderbolt
to the reputation of the man who had taken it upon himself to clean
up the image of the Socialist Party. But worse was to come. On 2
February 1993, in evidence given to the investigating magistrate,
Thierry Jean-Pierre, Pelat's son, Olivier, claimed that Bérégovoy
had repaid half of the loan between 1986 and 1988 in the form of
'books, antique furniture and *objets d'art*.' The remaining 500,000
francs had been settled by a personal cheque at the end of 1992, by
which time investigations into Pelat's finances were well under
way.[90] But the judge had been unable to find any record of this
supposed repayment, nor any list of the objects of value in
question.[91]

Olivier Pelat's declaration, which took Pierre Bérégovoy totally
by surprise, was never substantiated by any list of the *objets d'art*.[92]
Bérégovoy confided to friends in private that the suggestion that he
had repaid the loan with bric-à-brac was '*imbécile*'.[93] Olivier Pelat
must therefore have thought that they would help Bérégovoy
out of a tight spot. Perhaps he recalled the explanation that had
been given for a cheque for 150,000 francs, which Roger-Patrice
Pelat had been discovered to have made out to François Mitterrand
in 1989, which, it had been claimed, was for 'books bought by the

President for his friend, while on a foreign trip'. That cheque had been discovered by police investigating Pelat's affairs in connection with the Péchiney scandal.[94] Indeed, if the then judge, Elizabeth Boizette, had pursued her investigations into that cheque further, she might have discovered the Bérégovoy loan even earlier. Similarly, the judge, Thierry Jean-Pierre, who did discover the Béré-govoy cheque, had found it during the course of his investigations into the false-invoices scandal. Bérégovoy was thus directly linked by association with the very corruption scandal of which he was supposed to be the antithesis.

The noose was tightening around Bérégovoy for other reasons. By the time he became Prime Minister, two of his closest colleagues, Jean-Charles Naouri and Alain Boublil, both former *directeurs de cabinet* of his at the Ministry of Finance, had each been charged for involvement in an insider trading scandal, Société Générale and Péchiney respectively. Pelat was directly implicated in the latter. In many other Western European countries, and certainly in Britain, such a close professional association with suspected criminals would have destroyed any politician immediately, and certainly made him unsuitable for high office. This is not so in France.

Indeed, with a contempt for such niceties which bordered on the insolent, Bérégovoy also had in his government a man, Bernard Tapie, as Minister for Towns, who was himself facing serious allegations at the time of his appointment in connection with his football club, Olympic Marseille. Judging from President Mitterrand's well honed practice of dictating to the Prime Minister the content of his *cabinets*, and knowing that it was Jacques Attali, the president's personal adviser, who had originally brought Tapie into the orbit of the Elysée, it is likely that it was Mitterrand himself who secured his post in the government. That Tapie resigned within fifty days of his appointment suggests that Mitterrand cared little for the fact that judicial investigations were pending.

Another scandal concerned Vibrachoc, a small industrial company which had been founded in 1953 by Roger-Patrice Pelat and Robert Mitterrand, the future President's brother.[95] Within a year of François Mitterrand's election, in July 1982, the company was bought by Alsthom, a subsidiary of the recently nationalized Compagnie Générale d'Électricité (CGE), on the suggestions of officials at the Elysée Palace. CGE had recently been nationalized by the government.[96] An initial offer for the company prepared by Mitterrand's officials was rejected by Pelat; it was subsequently improved. Some senior executives at Alsthom thought that the price was excessive, and they alerted the Prime Minister's office, thinking that the idea was an eccentricity from the President's personal adviser on industrial matters, Alain Boublil. Pierre Mauroy therefore decided to ask Mitterrand directly for instructions.

At a subsequent meeting on the matter, Mauroy dealt with the issue very rapidly, slipping it into the agenda between two other issues. He said that it was not just Boublil's idea. (Indeed, Boublil subsequently denied that he had been responsible for having instigated the takeover.)[97] On the contrary, said Mauroy, the Vibrachoc sale had to go ahead, because the President wanted it. 'He has old debts to settle,' he explained.[98] It was subsequently revealed that Mitterrand himself had been paid tens of thousands of francs by Vibrachoc in his capacity as a 'legal adviser' before his election in May 1981, and that Pelat had also met some of Mitterrand's secretarial and transport costs.[99]

Vibrachoc was finally bought for 110 million francs in July 1982, the funds having been raised by two nationalized banks, the Banque Nationale de Paris and the Credit Lyonnais. And yet, six months after being sold, Vibrachoc had to make a 60-million-franc provision for its losses, and its assets were valued at less than 2 million francs.[100] In 1988 it was making a loss of 14 million francs a year.[101] It is estimated that the company had been overvalued by about 20 million francs.[102] The strategic takeover department at the Compagnie Générale d'Electricité had never been consulted. Instead, the takeover was arranged by two officials at the Elysée – a curious use of presidential staff, considering that the company was so small, comprising only some 450 employees.[103]

When Mitterrand was later confronted about his friendship with the man whose company the government had bought for 20 million francs more than it was worth, he would emphasize Pelat's poor background.[104] The implication was that he had worked hard since the war and made a fortune. However, it was only *after* the sale of Vibrachoc that Pelat, 'like an excited boy', took people around his newly acquired château in Sologne with 850 acres of land, kitted out with a helicopter pad which Mitterrand himself was to use for his frequent visits there.[105] From then on he was to become very closely involved with the President's daily work, and was nicknamed 'the Vice-President' by the staff at the Elysée.

But the general public did not know his name until a second scandal, Péchiney, broke. At the end of December 1988, the New York Securities Exchange Commission was investigating the sudden purchase of shares in an American packaging company, Triangle, only days before the director of the nationalized group, Péchiney, announced its takeover of Triangle on Monday 21 November 1988. Péchiney bought the shares for $56 each; considering that before the weekend the shares had been quoted on the New York Stock Exchange at $10.375, one did not have to be Sherlock Holmes to realize that something was up. The SEC estimated the total gains of the operation at 47 million francs.[106]

This was a massive takeover, representing an acquisition of more than 6 billion francs. Michel Rocard had described it as 'very good news for France'. Clearly such a takeover demands considerable preparation, and all the main protagonists were closely connected. Alain Boublil, who by this time had been sent from the Elysée to be Pierre Bérégovoy's *directeur de cabinet*, was intimately involved. Indeed, it was he who suggested the purchase to Péchiney in the first place,[107] and who conducted the negotiations between Péchiney and Triangle in July 1988 on board a yacht belonging to a Lebanese businessman living in France, Samir Traboulsi. Traboulsi was decorated with the Légion d'honneur on 3 October 1988 by Bérégovoy 'in the name of the President of the Republic' for his role in the liberation of French hostages in Lebanon, and he had acted as the intermediary for the Americans who were selling Triangle.[108] Robert Mitterrand gave the speech in Traboulsi's honour. Moreover, on Sunday 13 November 1988, two days after the deal had been secretly concluded in New York, and a week before the official announcement of the deal, Pierre Bérégovoy and his wife held a party for about sixty friends to celebrate their fortieth wedding anniversary: Pelat, Traboulsi and Boublil were all present.[109] At that party the Lebanese businessman Charbel Ghanem was also present. He owned a Swiss company, Socofinance, through which 91,000 Péchiney shares were bought, on the account of an unknown buyer domiciled in the Caribbean tax haven of Anguilla, a purchase which made a profit of 21 million francs. This unknown buyer had even better information than the others, for his shares were bought throughout the summer of 1988.[110]

Another old associate of Mitterrand's, Max Théret, who during his long life had been a bodyguard of Leon Trotsky, a founder member of the Socialist Party, an owner of the Socialist paper, *Le Matin de Paris*, and the owner of the FNAC record store, also bought Péchiney shares, and made 8.8 million francs out of the affair.[111] Théret always claimed that the *coup de Bourse* had been just his good luck: the investigating magistrates found this unconvincing, and in the initial trial he was eventually convicted for insider dealing.

On 31 January 1989, the Committee for Bourse Operations (Commission des Opérations de Bourse), the French Stock Exchange watch-dog, revealed that among those who had bought shares at the last minute was none other than Roger-Patrice Pelat, who had bought 10,000 of them on 16 and 17 November 1988, i.e. in the intervening days between the secret conclusion of the deal and its official announcement.[112]

The decision to go ahead with the takeover was made only at the last minute. Mitterrand, who in this as in all matters, took the final decision, had – typically – had difficulty making up his mind. Bérégovoy and Rocard were in favour, but Mitterrand hesitated until the morning of Friday 18 November before finally giving the green light, by which time Pelat had bought his shares.[113] There are few prizes for guessing who might have influenced him to make the final choice.

A persistent rumour also maintained that Pelat had bought a further 20,000 shares in the company via a company of his based in Switzerland, even though he swore in public, and to his friend François Mitterrand, that this latter rumour was untrue. On 20 February 1989, he was charged with insider trading, but died on 7 March.[114] Two and a half years later, in September 1991, it became clear that Pelat had been lying. The investigating judge, Elizabeth Boizette, received documentary evidence from the Swiss authorities that 20,000 shares in Triangle had been bought by a company, Experta Treuhand, which was owned by Pelat.[115]

In other words, Bérégovoy was connected with Pelat, a criminal. The revelation of the loan from Pelat only added to his difficulties. However, he did not deny Olivier Pelat's story in public. Perhaps he calculated that if he had done so, it would have made the whole loan – and his failure to repay it – look even more suspicious. Indeed, it is likely that he repaid the first half only because he realized that the investigations into Pelat's affairs would discover the loan sooner or later. He merely protested again and again in public that everything had been registered legally: so much so, indeed, that one felt he was protesting too much. In private, he was said to be in agony over the matter.[116]

The way in which a scandal is dealt with is often as revealing as the content of the accusation itself. At the time of the revelation of the Pelat loan, commentators rushed to argue that Bérégovoy was an innocent man in a den of vipers. Some said that it proved that he cannot have been personally corrupt if he needed to borrow such a 'small' sum of money as 1 million francs to buy a flat costing 'only' 2.4 million francs, a defence which only serves as an indication of the riches associated with French politicians. Bérégovoy's own denials of culpability were also inadequate. They betrayed the same basic lack of understanding of the notion of political responsibility which had been in evidence in politicians' reactions to the Urba affair. First, his insistence that the loan was all above board and that he was entitled to borrow money from whomsoever he liked without being beholden to him distracts attention from the fact that an interest-free loan of 1 million francs over a period of nine years represents a *gift* of over 1 million francs, when compound interest is calculated.

Second, and above all, the loan was a supreme political hypocrisy, for Bérégovoy had made his very name synonymous with the policy of the *'franc fort'*, a policy whose main effect was to maintain interest rates artificially high within the European Exchange Rate Mechanism for foreign-policy purposes. While ordinary home buyers and industry had to bear the burden, the man actually responsible for the policy borrowed money for free from the rich friends he made in the gilded circles of power, rather than meeting the true costs out of his own pocket.

Bérégovoy thus refused to provide a list of the *objets d'art* in question, for the very good reason that they cannot have existed. Instead, he tried to prove that he was not in hock to Pelat by publishing in *Paris-Match* a letter from himself, dated 6 September

1984, to the then Prime Minister, Laurent Fabius. In it, he expressed his hostility to the provision to North Korea of a loan by the Compagnie Française d'Assurance du Commerce Extérieur (COFACE), the French public organism which finances exports, in exchange for a contract with Campenon Bernard, a public-works company. Bérégovoy was trying thereby to disentangle himself from a web of connections between himself and Pelat.

In 1985, the investigating magistrate, Thierry Jean-Pierre, had discovered the existence of 20 million francs' worth of work that had been done for free on Roger-Patrice Pelat's private château at Sologne, at which President Mitterrand was a frequent guest,[117] by Campenon Bernard, as a 'commission' in exchange for a contract in North Korea, which Pelat had obtained for the company. Jean-Pierre was concerned to ascertain whether any improper role had been played in the affair by COFACE, which is controlled by the Ministry of Finance, Pierre Beregovoy having been the Minister of Finance at the time.

Instead, Jean-Pierre's investigations were later to reveal that François Mitterrand had been directly involved. Before his election to the presidency in 1981, Mitterrand had visited North Korea, and the question of diplomatic recognition by France was raised. Once elected, the new President received an enormous bouquet of flowers from the North Korean delegation in Paris. Mitterrand's close friend and adviser, François de Grossouvre, received the flowers and the delegation, and became the interlocutor between the North Koreans and the President. In 1982, Grossouvre himself visited North Korea on Mitterrand's behalf, bringing, among other things, the personal birthday good wishes from the French President to the last and most vicious Communist dictator in the world, the Great Leader, Kim Il-Sung. When a return visit was paid by the North Korean delegation in Paris, the idea was conceived of building a large tourist/cultural centre in Pyongyang. North Korea was desirous of obtaining diplomatic recognition, although Paris could not risk the degradation of her relations with South Korea unless there was some economic reason for the step. (Indeed Mitterrand even confided to the Secretary-General of the Chinese Communist Party in 1983 that he wished France to be the first country to recognize North Korea.)[118] At this point, Roger-Patrice Pelat intervened to suggest the construction of a luxury hotel, which eventually satisfied all parties.[119]

Thierry Jean-Pierre was of course the same man who had been conducting the investigation into the corrupt financing of the Socialist Party. He was also investigating suspicions that the Socialist Party had been involved in illegal arms deals, part of a European network selling weapons into Africa.[120] The Minister of Justice, Michel Vauzelle, tried to close the investigations into the COFACE issue, just as his predecessor had taken him off the Urba affair.[121] He pursued his investigations, finally revealing that Pelat had made regular payments to François Mitterrand from 1972–81, and then to Mitterrand's son, Gilbert Mitterrand, the President's personal adviser on African affairs at the Elysée Palace, from 1981–9. Pelat had also made regular payments to the daughter of Pierre Beregovoy in 1984 and 1985 and one substantial payment to a woman named only as Madame P., to whom the French press demurely refer as 'a close friend of the President'.[122]

In other words, the publication of the letter to Fabius in *Paris-Match* seemed to contradict the suspicion that Beregovoy might have accepted the famous loan from Pelat in payment for his efforts in securing the contract. Instead, the magazine reported that three months later, Laurent Fabius announced that the loan would go ahead: it claimed that Beregovoy's advice had been overruled by the Elysée. In his report, the magistrate Jean-Pierre asked the following leading questions: 'It remains to be determined by what route the very probable persuasion by Roger-Patrice Pelat of the Prime Minister, Laurent Fabius, occurred: Did he speak to him directly? Was the persuasion passed on by a third party? Was this third party the Elysée Palace?'[123]

Following the publication of that report in the press, Philippe de Villiers, the deputy who had made a name for himself as a dynamic anti-corruption campaigner, made a formal request that the National Assembly instigate a parliamentary inquiry into the consequences for the institutions of the republic of the financial relationship between Roger-Patrice Pelat and François Mitterrand. The request was turned down by the President of the National Assembly, Philippe Séguin, who replied to Villiers that 'Republican tradition ... forbids that the Head of State be put into question by the parliament'.[124]

François Mitterrand's own reactions to the mounting evidence against himself has hardly been edifying. His increasingly testy

reactions to questions about Pelat and Péchiney seem to indicate an
uneasy conscience, and Freudian slips are never usually reassuring
signs of someone's innocence. On 12 February 1989, he appeared
on '7 sur 7', a well known interview programme with Anne
Sinclair. Being of great topicality, the Péchiney affair was raised.
Mitterrand spent a long time describing the dramatic conditions
in which he had met and befriended Pelat in Germany in 1940.
Then this,

Anne Sinclair:	If there are question-marks over Patrice Pelat, it is not because he played the Stock Market, not because he owned shares, not because he increased his own capital, but because he was close to those in power, and had . . .
Mitterrand:	No, no . . .
Anne Sinclair:	Well, close to you . . .
Mitterrand:	No . . .
Anne Sinclair:	Otherwise, his name would not have been mentioned . . .
Mitterrand:	What do you mean? That I informed him?
Anne Sinclair:	No! Goodness! Nobody said that . . . !
Mitterrand:	Why are you suggesting it now, then?
Anne Sinclair:	I am not suggesting . . .
Mitterrand:	I could not have done it, because I did not even know about it myself. But in any case, it is a private matter which we cannot discuss this evening.
Anne Sinclair:	The question is whether he benefited from information . . .
Mitterrand:	It is possible. I know nothing about it.[125]

Mitterrand's claim that he knew nothing about a 6-billion-franc
takeover is extraordinary. One harsh critic of Mitterrand has even
said of him: 'He has a natural penchant for lying: even better, a
taste for inventing, a facility for accumulating fabrications rather in
the way that one tells stories to a child who is falling asleep.'[126]
Indeed, this might recall what an Italian journalist wrote about
Giulio Andreotti: 'For as long as the liar has power, the lie will win

out over all suspicions, because it is not the truth which is at stake, but power.'[127]

On 7 April 1994, at around 8.00 p.m. in the evening, François de Grossouvre went to his office in the Elysée Palace. A shot was heard, and moments later, Grossouvre was found dead in his office with a gun in his hand.

Like Bérégovoy, Grossouvre had been frozen out of the favours of President Mitterrand. For several years he had been speaking openly about the vicissitudes of his relationship with François Mitterrand. They had been friends for many decades, having originally met in Vichy in 1942. Like Mitterrand, Grossouvre initially collaborated with the Pétainist regime before entering the Resistance in 1943. During the years of Mitterrand's presidency, he had been the arch-*éminence grise*. He had acted as his special envoy to North Korea and in other sensitive areas. He was especially interested in the secret services, and in information on individuals. Although apparently demoted to looking after the 'Presidential Hunts' in July 1985, he continued his close collaboration with Mitterrand. In particular, Grossouvre was intimately involved with the financing of Mitterrand's four presidential election campaigns (1965, 1974, 1981 and 1988).[128]

But increasingly the long friendship between the two men turned sour. Grossouvre had even said of Mitterrand, 'The only things which he is interested in these days is money and death.'[129] He had been writing his memoirs at the time of his death, and Mitterrand had asked him to place a copy with one of his advisers. Grossouvre refused. He must have known every single secret detail about life in the Elysée Palace from 1981 onwards. He was convinced that he was about to be framed. 'I am going to be attacked,' he would say.[130] He had even said to two journalists on repeated occasions, 'If anything happens to me, it is because I have been killed.'[131]

Mitterrand had taken great exception to Grossouvre's attacks against Roger-Patrice Pelat and against his eldest son, Jean-Christophe Mitterrand. The President was especially outraged when Grossouvre agreed to see the magistrate Thierry Jean-Pierre in his apartment at 11, Quai Branly (where Grossouvre had a grace-and-favour apartment in the same building in which Mitterrand lodges his mistress). The link with Jean-Pierre is essential, because the magistrate's report had explained how Grossouvre has arranged the building contract in North Korea for Pelat – the deal to which Beregovoy had expressed his opposition. In other words, by April 1994, the three main actors in the Pelat affair, Grossouvre, Bérégovoy, and Pelat himself, were all dead.

7. Cry 'Havoc' and Leash the Dogs

France is like Italy – only without Italian judges.

Philippe de Villiers[1]

Mitterrand's oration at Bérégovoy's funeral was highly political and extraordinarily vicious. He had come not to praise Beregovoy, but to try to bury the journalists and judges upon whom he tried to place the blame for his death. At first, he dwelt at length on the so-called economic success of France under successive Socialist governments, and read out a series of quotations from foreign newspapers praising France's economy to prove his point. There can seldom have been a clearer illustration of that peculiar loathing and fascination with which foreigners' opinions about France are treated, than to hear editorials from the *New York Times*, the *Frankfurter Allgemeine Zeitung* and the *Wall Street Journal* being read out at the state funeral for a Prime Minister.

But his true aim soon became clear. Turning to the treatment Bérégovoy had received at the hands of the French press and magistrature, he tried to present Bérégovoy as an honourable man.

> His record authorizes me to restate the capacity of this statesman, the honesty of a citizen who preferred to die rather than to suffer the effrontery of doubt. All the explanations of the world cannot justify *throwing to the dogs* the honour, and finally the life, of a man, at the price of a double infraction by his accusers of the fundamental laws of the republic, those which protect the life and liberty of each and every one of us.[2]

The 'dogs' in question were the French judiciary and the media. Few speeches could have better illustrated Mitterrand's hatred for both institutions. He clearly thought that the slightest investigation into the systematic extortion of the French population practiced by

the party of which he was the leader, or into the criminal activities
of one of his closest friends, was quite unacceptable. As *Le Canard
Enchaîné* put it, 'The political class dresses in black in order to
whitewash itself.'

Mitterrand's reaction was all the more grotesque when one
considers that precisely what the Urba affair showed was that the
judicial process can still be the object of political interference in
France, and that elected politicians, magistrates and policemen
involved in investigations could be subject to death threats. Indeed,
there is a long tradition of political interference in the judicial
process. Despite all his simpering protestations of innocence,
Bérégovoy had himself been implicated in one such case, although
it does not seem to have aroused much comment. In 1992, the
Nouvel Observateur published a story recounting a telephone conversation between Bernard Tapie and Pierre Bérégovoy. The author
of the tale had been in the room with Tapie when Bérégovoy
telephoned, and the phone's loudspeaker was left on. He was thus
able to hear the then Finance Minister and future Prime Minister
apologizing to Tapie for not having acted to prevent his prosecution and conviction for breaking France's exchange-control laws. If
the Finance Minister can interfere in the judicial process, then
presumably they all can. But the press's role is, once again, curious:
the event had occurred in 1985, but the magazine did not report
it until seven years later.[3] In any case, when it does occur, publication by the press of such incriminating behaviour usually just
slips off French politicians like water off a duck's back. When
Edith Cresson was Minister of Agriculture, she was well known to
have written to Robert Badinter, then Minister of Justice, on official
ministry writing paper, and in her ministerial capacity, to ask him
to take an investigating magistrate off a case. This was because the
person under investigation was a 'friend of the Socialist Party, who
has done a lot for us'. The letter was published in the press twice,
on 27 April 1988 and on 18 January 1989,[4] and yet this did not
prevent or even mildly hinder her appointment as Prime Minister
in 1991.

Mitterrand's harsh language encouraged other politicians on
both Left and Right to join in the hysterical tirade against the
judiciary and the press. The dead man's brother, a Socialist deputy,
claimed that the judges and journalists had 'killed him'.[5] Michel

Charasse, a former minister under Bérégovoy, and a close adviser of Mitterrand, said, 'If I were a judge or a journalist, I would not sleep well tonight.'[6] The former Justice Minister, Michel Vauzelle attacked 'the media system, of which we are all the slaves and the victims', and asked heavily, 'Do we have the right to allow such a system [i.e. the media] to continue when it can break the best of us, and possibly break democracy itself?'[7] Laurent Fabius, who was still awaiting investigation into his role in the contaminated-blood scandal, sung the same macabre song:

> There are words, caricatures and images which have the same force as bullets ... I sense the injustice all the more ... because the same people who have dragged his name through the mud, are today making benign declarations, filling the airwaves with their sorrows, usually talking more eagerly of themselves than of Pierre, thus robbing him of his death in the same way as *they destroyed his life*.[8]

The former Foreign Minister, Roland Dumas, made explicit what Fabius had preferred merely to imply: 'None of the magistrates or the journalists are responsible, because they all are. They are the ones who have killed "Béré".'[9]

But the most excessive declarations came from François Léotard, the new Defence Minister. In hallucinatory tones, he wrote,

> In the beginning, there is a murder. This was not a suicide. This is not an electoral defeat. In the beginning, there is a murder. And the murder of Pierre Bérégovoy is special because it is not signed, nor will it ever be, for there is no need. It is furtive and without trace, thus escaping all sanction. A black aeroplane in a black sky ... Pierre Bérégovoy is the first victim of a new culture. In his way, he anticipates the future holocaust to come, a holocaust not of hatred, but more refined and more modest: a holocaust of derision.[10]

The virulence of all these remarks show how deeply entrenched is the idea that politicians are above the law, and that press criticism is impudence or worse.

Indeed, it is difficult to avoid the conclusion that the creation of the presidential regime in 1958 gave the *coup de grâce* to the independence of the judiciary, for that regime only made institu-

tionally easier certain practices which may have been current beforehand in France. The President of the Republic appoints all
the members of the High Council of the Magistrature. He chairs
its meetings, together with the Minister of Justice, who is the
Vice-Chairman. The Council is the body responsible for promot-
ing magistrates: extraordinary though it may seem, it is clear that
members of the judiciary are selected according to *political*
criteria.

The case of Thierry Jean-Pierre itself illustrates exactly how this
political pressure can work. In 1985 he asked to be transferred to
Le Mans, where he wanted to be appointed as an investigating
magistrate. He was refused, for the following (documented) reason:
'Judge Jean-Pierre is a man of great independence of mind. For this
reason, it is not suitable that he be appointed to the post of
investigating magistrate.'[11]

Because of the predominance of the President, substantial political
pressure can be exerted on the judicial process. Prosecutions are
ordered by the Ministry of Justice, and although the ministry does
not have the right to stop them, the Urba affair saw several
attempts to do just that. In theory, the prosecutor ought to act
independently of the wishes of the Minister of Justice of the day;
but promotions within the magistrature, and thus within the pro-
secuting service, are decided by the same High Council of the
Magistrature, under the control of the President and the minister.
As Inspector Gaudino puts it,

> To refuse to bend to the political will in the name of respect
> for the law is dangerous for a magistrate's personal interests.
> Unfortunately, there are very few magistrates who accept the
> risk of sacrificing their careers and refuse to bend the knee to
> partisan and illegal pressure exercised by their political super-
> iors. François Mitterrand had denounced this system when he
> was in opposition, calling it a grave attack on the independence
> of the judiciary. He promised to reform it. While he has been
> in power, however, nothing has been changed, and the Urba
> affair has proved that the occurrence of these immoral practices
> has only got worse.[12]

Indeed, Judge Jean-Pierre has said himself that 'The judicial process
is being manipulated, ridiculed and dishonoured every day'.[13] It is,

indeed, difficult to speak of democracy in a system where the head of the most powerful and least controlled executive in the Western world appoints, directly or indirectly, all the judges.[14]

Moreover, the French tradition of administrative law, whereby the organs of state are subject to a different jurisdiction from that of the common law, were used to their full in the Urba case. There are constant references to this practice and to its abuses in Antoine Gaudino's account of his pursuit of the truth in the Socialist Party's racketeering. For instance, as soon as the names of elected politicians appear in a judicial investigation, such as mayors and some of their deputies, who are officers of the judicial police, the case is immediately transferred to the Criminal Chamber of the Court of Cassation. This Chamber then designates a new magistrate to investigate the matter. Indeed, it was because of this procedure that the SORMAE affair was successfully buried.[15] At the moment when the Green Party MEP was trying to take the matter to court, for instance, his right to do so was decided upon by an administrative tribunal, the Council of State, which depends directly on the Ministry of the Interior. In the event, the case was won and the Green MEP was allowed to bring his prosecution; but Gaudino reflected at the time that 'This decision was due only to the courage of the judges'.[16]

It is small wonder that 82 per cent of French people think that judges are 'controlled by the government', while only 5 per cent think they are independent.[17] For the very existence and functions of institutions like the Council of State betray crucial differences between the constitutional structure of France on the one hand and Britain or the United States on the other. The Council of State is an *administrative court*, something which does not exist in England, because of the differences between the British and French understandings of the separation of powers and the rule of law. Indeed, it is because of the strange French attitude to the relationship between the state and the law that French politicians evoke the spectre of a 'government of judges' if ever there is any judicial investigation into their behaviour.

The doctrine of the separation of powers was originally based on a misinterpretation of the English constitution by Montesquieu in 1748. He thought that the executive, legislative and judicial powers in England were separate because the judiciary was indeed independent from political control, and that the executive (the Crown) was separate from the legislature (parliament). In fact, Britain is governed by the Crown-in-parliament, in other words by a fusion of the executive and legislative functions. While those roles are certainly distinct, this fusion is best illustrated by the fact that ministers (of the Crown) *must* be members of parliament, i.e. they must be members of the legislature in order to be able to be members of the executive. (In general they are members of the House of Commons, but they can occasionally be members of the House of Lords as well.) In France, by contrast, as in the United States, a minister need not ever have had a parliamentary career, and he is indeed forbidden from keeping his parliamentary seat once appointed to a ministry.

That there is no separation in Britain where the French constitution (like the American) insists that there must be, hides the deeper issue that it is part of Montesquieu's mistake in speaking of the judiciary as a 'power'. Certainly, the government ought not to interfere in the judicial process, and so therefore there should be a 'separation'; but the point is surely that if the judicial process were subject to control by the government then what judges would be administering would not be the law. Perhaps it is because of this confusion that French governments, in addition to abusing their power by interfering in the judicial process, have often sought to use the notion of the separation of powers in order to lay great stress on the reverse side of the coin as well: if the government may not interfere with judges, they have argued, judges ought to have no power to interfere in government. The latter, in short, ought to be above the law.

This abusive doctrine is basically Revolutionary in origin. Before then, the courts represented a significant brake on royal power. One of the Revolution's first acts was to pass a law that severely restricted the scope of judicial authority: 'Judicial functions are distinct and will always remain separate from administrative functions. Judges may not, on penalty of removal from office, disturb in any way whatever the operations of the administration or summon administrators before them on account of their official activities.'[18] This prohibition meant that the government was immune from legal suit by an aggrieved citizen, and that ordinary judges were forbidden from interfering in matters of public adminis-

tration. An aggrieved citizen could thus only ask the Head of State
or one of his ministers for relief as a matter of favour. Napoleon
found in the Council of State a means of filling this obvious judicial
void and he established within it a 'litigation committee' to hear
complaints and to recommend solutions, although it was only in
1872 that the Conseil d'État received a juridical status and that it
achieved a degree of independence from political power. A body of
law, called *droit administratif*, thus grew up, which governed the
relationship between 'the state' and the individual, and it was for
the Council of State to administer that law. The idea that there
should be a body of law governing the activities of the state, which
is different from the ordinary law that governs the citizen, is alien
to the traditional British and American concepts of law. The great
English Victorian constitutionalist, A. V. Dicey, wrote eagerly
about the essential difference between the French notion of *droit
administratif* and the English notion of common law:

> The government, and every servant of the government, pos-
> sesses, as representative of the nation, a whole body of special
> rights, privileges, or prerogatives as against private citizens,
> and that the extent of these rights, privileges, or prerogatives
> is to be determined on principles different from the considera-
> tions which fix the legal rights and duties of one citizen
> towards another. An individual in his dealing with the state
> does not, according to French ideas, stand on anything like
> the same footing as that on which he stands in his dealing
> with his neighbour.[19]

It is an added and even more unacceptable irony that, while the
Council of State derives its existence from the notion of the
separation of powers, it combines two apparently eminently separ-
able functions. Not only is it the judge of the administration, but it
is also the government's legal adviser! (It gives the government
advice on legislative drafts, since the constitution requires that all
legislation be submitted to the Council of State for possible modifica-
tions before being submitted to parliament.) This dual role is
underlined by the fact that the members of the Council of State
(who are appointed by the President of the Republic) customarily
spend time in other parts of the administration as well, and often
also in the government itself. Indeed, one close adviser of François

Mitterrand[20] retained an office at the Elysée Palace while serving as a member of the Council of State from 1983–6.

Another consequence of the French understanding of the separation of powers is that the French constitution, including the Declaration of the Rights of Man, has nothing like the role the American constitution has in US politics. Previously it was assumed that the 'representatives of the sovereign nation' were the 'sovereign representatives of the nation', and that nothing they could do could ever be subject to judicial review (although it is difficult to see how anyone could even pretend that this was in conformity with the doctrine of the separation of powers).[21] Until recently there has never been a supreme court which rules on the constitutionality of the government's actions in a way comparable to the American practice. Indeed, it was not until 1958, for the first time ever, that a body was set up, independent of the executive, to ensure respect for the constitution.

In most countries, a procedure of judicial and constitutional review is accepted as quite normal, but it is worth dwelling on the degree to which it was for long considered an unacceptable usurpation of the rights of the legislature in France. Indeed, the belief in the divine right of the National Assembly persists to this day, especially in Mitterrand's Socialist Party. In 1981, a Socialist deputy famously shouted down a right-wing member of the opposition, by saying, 'You are wrong in law because you are in a political minority!'[22] Similar nonsense is even propagated by left-wing judges themselves. In a publication entitled *The Clan*, a group of them declared, 'The law is an instrument of oppression. The decision of the judge is not neutral. It is a political act which we intend to politicize . . . against bourgeois justice, we must embrace the justice of the people.'[23] It is small wonder that it is has been a common right-wing complaint under Mitterrand that *la magistrature est rouge*.

It should be stressed that the supremacy of parliament was never the British view. Although it is often said that there are no limits on the power of the British parliament, this has never implied that the organs of state are above the common law. The existence of a very strong tradition of common law means that not all law is the result of legislation. Parliament intervenes (or should intervene) only in specific areas where necessary or desirable; otherwise it acts within the framework of the law. The mere fact that the English constitution has remained recognizably the same for over three centuries (undergoing gradual change all the time, but never being called into question in its entirety) should make it clear that there has been a very clear understanding about what may be changed and what may not.

In 1958, de Gaulle included in the constitution a body to ensure respect for it, the Constitutional Council (*Conseil Constitutionnel*). It hardly needs to be said that, Mitterrand having attacked the Council in 1964 as 'General de Gaulle's errand boy'[24] and having called for its abolition as late as 1978, proceeded when in power to exercise as much political influence over it as he claimed de Gaulle did. Once again, it is unfortunate that the institutions lend themselves easily to such abuse. The Council is composed of nine members, of which three are nominated by the President of the Republic, three by the President of the Senate and three by the President of the National Assembly. The fact that all three nominators are politically affiliated (neither the President of the National Assembly nor of the Senate make anything like the pretence at party-political independence which is demanded of the Speaker of the House of Commons in Britain) clearly encourages political influence, which is widely acknowledged.[25] Moreover, it is common practice for the judges on the Constitutional Council to continue to practise as public prosecutors, subject in that capacity to the authority of the Ministry of the Interior.[26] Under Mitterrand, the current President of the Council is Robert Badinter, an old ally of the President, who is a professional politician, having served as Minister of the Interior and Minister of Justice. The idea that a council should have a 'President' who leads from the front is itself strange; that the post should be occupied by a man who is an old friend of the President of the Republic, even stranger.

The Communists have traditionally been opposed to the role of the Constitutional Council, and traditional Gaullists also take a similar view. The attacks of these latter are not based on the Council's mere existence (it was, after all, created by de Gaulle himself), but on the powers which the Council voted itself in a seminal judgement of 16 July 1971. On that occasion, the Council was asked to review a law concerning the freedom of association, which is governed by a well known law of 1901. The proposal was to change it and to subject the freedom to create an association to prior judicial investigation on the instructions of the local Prefect.

The Council decided that the proposed new law was contrary to the Declarations of the Rights of Man of 1789. Thus, for the first time, nearly 200 years after the Declaration itself, a court used that text to overturn a legislative act. Prior to that, the Declaration of 1789 had never had a status comparable to that of the American constitution, and there had been no equivalent body to the US Supreme Court which would have had the authority so to rule.

The judgement of 1971 made a leap towards establishing an American-style process of constitutional review of legislation, although there are still important differences between the Constitutional Council and the US Supreme Court. Civil, penal and commercial matters are referred to the Court of Cassation; administrative affairs to the Council of State. Moreover, the Council's control is applicable only to laws before they are promulgated: once they have been promulgated they cannot be challenged. Therefore the control is abstract, and does not apply to the application of a law. Nonetheless, many recalcitrants still regard the Council's ruling as a judicial *coup d'état*, a point of view which is credible when the government's and the parliament's hand is tied over an issue which does not apparently affect fundamental rights. In January 1994, for instance, the right-wing government suggested removing the 10 per cent barrier to state financing of private schools: the bill was forbidden by the Council. Two lines of a ruling by judges are therefore worth more than a substantial parliamentary vote in France. It should be noted that the determination to maintain the secular nature of the republic is a deeply entrenched left-wing preoccupation, and that the Council's ruling was amenable to the Socialists who had been ejected from office nine months previously, but whose leader was still in power.

Because individual citizens cannot appeal directly to the Council,[27] French governmental habits are still predicated on being able to exercise power with almost no legal checks or balances. Government and administration, already deeply intertwined, can easily come to think of themselves as on a superior footing to the individual citizen. It is a curious fact that, despite the obvious abuses which occurred under Mitterrand, a deeply entrenched faith in 'independent' experts persists in France: it is often assumed that the institutionalized irresponsibility of decision-makers actually fosters the wisdom of their choices, because there is believed to be a contradiction between efficiency and democracy. It is a belief which is entirely misplaced, for as one analyst of the drift away from democracy under Mitterrand explains,

> The mistrust of the individual (considered to be potentially sinful or guilty) translates into numerous pettifogging procedural details which often end up completely blocking or at least slowing down the whole administration. The machine can work only if one takes liberties with the promulgated rules, the declared interdictions, and the established procedures . . . The civil servant, himself a prisoner within a legal-rational universe who is entangled within its rules, can achieve autonomy only by 'interpreting' those rules.[28]

In other words, the state can function only if it does so illegally. It is precisely because of the naïvely idealistic belief in the wisdom of experts that insufficient attention is given to the proclivities and failings of the human beings who will have to make the system work. As a result there is an underdeveloped reflection on such fundamental notions as 'conflict of interest'.

This is in turn linked to the dominant political culture in France, which sees politics as akin to management. This tendency infects all Western European countries, even if it is particularly strong in France. Politicians are expected to deliver results, especially at local level, and this puts great clientilist pressures on them. In a normally functioning democratic system, political parties, the media, parliament and the judiciary are the channels through which public control is exercised on those in power; in France all four institutions are unacceptably weak. Instead of being the media by which political accountability is ensured, political parties have themselves become the instruments of corruption and vehicles for the traffic of influence. Each deputy receives dozens of letters a day asking for favours: to help a son get out of military service, to help a grandfather get a bigger pension, to get a job, to get promoted, etc. Each request generates letters to the minister responsible in an attempt to intervene here and there in the administrative machine, an operation which itself requires the work of hundreds of officials.[29] Under such conditions, corruption tends to be the only oil which can make the wheels of the state machinery turn to produce such results. Politicians thus rely on their democratic legitimacy, and invoking their mission as 'company bosses' in the service of their town or region, are less and less worried about rules and procedures, which are considered useless and obstructive. They have been aided in this task by the contempt reserved by French people in general and the élites in particular for rules, which are indeed so numerous and complex that they would be the cause of total administrative paralysis if they were adhered to. The accumulation of offices has done the rest: the politician can choose the most effective structures and instruments to achieve what he wants. While the practise of accumulating posts may not itself be corrupt, it is one of the vectors by which corruption flows all too easily: in the Urba case, the corrupt financing of the Socialist Party took place mainly at local level, while funds were sent to the central organs of the party. As a result of the generalized accumulation of posts, indeed, no one knows in what capacity a certain man is acting. What counts in the politician's eyes, and, it seems, in the eyes of his voters, is the result and not the means by which it is achieved. The local worthy thus becomes a sort of *deus ex machina*, whose favours are solicited by everyone for everything, who cannot claim that he is juridically not responsible for something, but who has to make use of his capacities for intervention and of his network of friends. Thus, little by little, a whole counter-culture has developed in France which neglects, flouts or breaks the law.[30]

Because of the lack of overall reflection on the system, the laws against abuse within the normal penal code have been smothered under a patchwork of individual regulations which have often been cooked up in response to some scandal or other. For instance, a law was passed in 1972, in response to a financial scandal, which forbids deputies from being the directors of companies which win public contracts.[31] As a result, when the multimillionaire industrialist Marcel Dassault became a deputy in 1976, he asked the Constitutional Council to rule on whether his private activities as a defence contractor were compatible with his functions as a deputy. But because he was no longer the *titular* director of the company which bore his name, the Court ruled that there was no conflict of interest.[32] By the same token, someone like a press magnate who owns a substantial section of the French media would be ineligible for the post of deputy only if, say, he were to become the director of a catering company which supplied school meals, because only then would he be a supplier of public works. In a similar vein, a prominent minister, was able to take a lavish holiday abroad, which he claimed was paid for by a patron; but the favour was never investigated, and he was never even questioned by journalists about the propriety of a minister accepting such gifts.[33]

Mitterrand's long reign has shown that there is no efficiency without responsibility, and that, far from aiding efficiency, power without accountability simply atrophies. Not only this, but one macabre event for which his reign was to become notorious showed how puerile is the myth that the state does not itself have as many means and as much inclination to cheat and to traffic as any private enterprise.[34] This event, the contaminated-blood scandal, epitomized luridly just how, far from ensuring streamlined and morally superior decision-making, the bureaucratic mess which afflicts the French political system leads more often to 'authoritarian anarchy' – administrative muddle combined with an uncontrollable and irresponsible state machine – than to anything resembling either democracy or efficiency.[35]

The facts of this tragic story are easily recounted. The French National Blood Transfusion Centre has a state monopoly in the importing of blood. It also acts as adviser to the Ministry of Health. Centralized state control of the importation of blood was introduced in 1952 in order to 'rationalize' what had been a rather disparate system of decentralized blood distribution, and to forbid all commercial operations in the importing of blood: it was considered dangerous and immoral to allow the buying and selling of blood products.[36]

A grubby row blew up in the early 1980s between the French and American medical authorities, over who was the first to discover the HIV virus. It seems that the French were indeed the first to discover the virus. But the French medical authorities were slower to find a means of combating the problem, and in 1983 the Americans had already discovered that heating blood killed off the HIV virus. Thus pharmaceutical companies in the US were very rapidly producing safe blood products.

Meanwhile, France fell badly behind in its production of products for screening donated blood. In 1984, a competitor product, made by the American company Abbott, was banned, for fear that it would flood the market. It was later revealed that the primary consideration, explicitly dealt with in numerous letters between the National Centre for Blood Transfusion and the Ministry of Health, was that the Abbott test cost 15 francs, while the equivalent test produced by the French would cost 23 francs when ready.[37]

One doctor has described her attempts to persuade the medical authorities in the National Centre for Blood Transfusion to buy safe products from abroad.[38] In a manner which would be Kafkaesque were it not true, she was sent from pillar to post, unable to break out of the loop created by the refusal of the Head of Research at the Centre to authorize the necessary extra expenses involved in importing American products. She wrote in vain to the Director of the Centre at the time, who just sent her letter back down to the Head of Research. When she wrote to him a second time, he merely replied, 'The pasteurization of blood plasma is an effective way of killing off viruses . . . We could indeed treat some patients with such plasma, but certainly not all haemophiliacs, because these heated products are made by foreign firms who have only one aim, to conquer the French market.'[39]

Her attempts to get through to the Minister of Health, or even to his private office, were in vain. Nobody else she contacted was prepared to stick his neck out. She found herself a powerless victim of the French conception of authority, described thus by one analyst of the degradation of political life under Mitterrand:

> The traditional French conception of authority tends to concentrate powers in the hands of a single person: the monarch, the head of the family, the priest, the lord or the boss are at the summit of a hierarchical order which is rigid and subordinate. Even today, there are few countries where so much power is placed in the hands of a few officials. From top to bottom, power remains essentially monarchical in France: the Head of State, the Presidents of Regional and General Councils, in bygone days the Prefects, and mayors, are all emperors in their realm.[40]

The same principle seems to apply to senior doctors and health administrators, for the lone doctor finally had to use her meagre contacts to arrange the privilege of an interview with the Director-General of the Ministry of Health. In a ten-minute meeting with her, he said,

I have just signed an authorization for 2 million francs for immoglobulin imports because one doctor refuses to use immoglobulins from the National Blood Transfusion Centre. He says they are no good, because they have adverse effects on children with immunity deficiencies! So we are going to pay 2 million francs to import immoglobulins! Well, that will simply have to stop![41]

Well, it did stop. By early 1985, before France was able to make its own screening products, the National Centre was using up old stocks of blood, without having tested them for HIV. Blood given in France was customarily not tested (AIDS was thought mainly to come from the US), even though most of it came from prisoners in France, a high-risk donor category. The decision not to screen this blood was taken by the Director of the National Blood Transfusion Centre, Dr Michel Garetta, in full knowledge of the risks, as letters produced at his subsequent trial showed. His primary concerns were financial: facing criticism for lavish expense costs and for the Centre's huge debts, he was trying to make the country (and thus his National Centre) self-sufficient in blood donations. He would have incurred further costs of 7 million francs a month had blood been bought in from elsewhere.

The American screening product was finally registered by a ministerial decree, and its use authorized from 1 August 1985. This represented a delay of six months. During this time, thousands of haemophiliacs were contaminated with HIV, and hundreds of them died as a result. Far from removing all commercial logic from the transfusion of blood, the affair showed how small-minded bureaucratic stinginess, combined with the stagnancy which results from the general refusal within a big organization to take individual responsibility, sickens the very bloodstream of large statist organizations, with fatal results.

But the affair had very wide political ramifications as well. Four years after the events, when the whole scandal was well in the public domain, and Garetta's role was already under investigation (he had even had an eleven-hour interrogation) the head of the Decorations Department at the Elysée wrote to the Chief of Cabinet of the Minister of Health on 16 July 1989, 'The personal attention of the President of the Republic has been drawn to the case of Dr Michel Garetta. Having decided to award an exceptional honour to Dr Garetta, I would be grateful if you would make a suggestion in his favour.'[42] Garetta was awarded the Légion d'honneur by Mitterrand under exceptional circumstances. The award is usually given only to people who have performed twenty years of service: Garetta had been working for nineteen years, and so the decoration indeed occurred only with the express and personal intervention of the President. Mitterrand was never called on to explain why he had taken this extraordinary step.

Nor did the political fall-out stop there. Garetta was finally imprisoned for his criminal activities, but senior ministers were also implicated. In particular, the role of the Minister of Social Security, National Solidarity and Health, Georgina Dufoix, was critical. The Prime Minister, Laurent Fabius, had promised the National Assembly in June 1985 that all supplies of blood would be screened for AIDS. Later in the month, the Director of the Transfusion Centre in Toulouse wrote to Georgina Dufoix saying that they had received no instructions to screen blood, despite the Prime Minister's declarations, and that it was not taking place. He asked for a meeting with her to discuss the matter; she never replied to the letter.

Once again, while centralized state control was justified as a means of stopping abuse, the main decision-makers in the affair were able to occupy posts which made them interested parties. For instance, the man advising Laurent Fabius, the Prime Minister, on whether to import American screening products, François Gros, was none other than the Director of the Pasteur Institute, the direct competitor of the American company Abbott. Letters exchanged between Gros and Fabius which were published in 1994 led *Le Monde* to infer that protectionist considerations had prevented the importing of the product.[43]

And again, the practice of accumulating posts had proved unfortunate: at the same time as being a senior minister, Georgina Dufoix also occupied the positions of Government Spokesman and General Councillor in the Gard region; she also had a role in planning the Socialists' election campaign. It is absurd to pretend that an individual can be responsible for so many huge administrative machines. Thus, state organizations work on autopilot, until they crash. This explains why the ministers involved, from Laurent Fabius to Georgina Dufoix, repeatedly denied all knowledge of the contamination.[44]

Indeed, it soon became very clear that they did not even understand the very notion of ministerial responsibility. Laurent Fabius could not be prosecuted or even investigated under normal judicial procedures, because of his parliamentary immunity. The only solution was to call the High Court, a parliamentary instance intended for trials of high treason, which had not been called since the Oustric affair in 1930.[45] The decision to do this could only be taken by other parliamentarians, and so it became bogged down in politicking: Fabius found himself caught between the President of the Republic, who was prepared to throw his former Prime Minister to the wolves, and the Right, who were more determined to extract political capital from the affair than to get to the truth.

Meanwhile, politicians merely gave the impression of circling in a closed loop around old complexes and problems: Jacques Chirac huffed and puffed about the country demanding 'justice',[46] but at the same time betrayed the old French hostility towards the power of judges. 'Should the High Court be suppressed,' he asked rhetorically, 'and should we decide that politicians are justiciable before ordinary courts? Is it necessary that the executive be entirely subject to the judiciary in matters which concern politics?'[47] One would have thought that the answer was obvious. But, in a similar vein, when Bernard Kouchner put the following conundrum in a speech to the National Assembly at the end of October 1992, 'Are ministers responsible *although* they were ignorant of what was happening or *because* they were ignorant?', there was total silence. It was as if he had posed some insoluble philosophical riddle. But surely the answer to both him and Chirac is terrifyingly obvious: instead of speculating on abstractions, an investigation into the facts of the matter – which, because of the absurd tergiversations over the convocation of the High Court has not yet occurred – could *find out* whether the ministers were guilty of culpable ignorance. After all, common law and common sense recognize the concept of criminal negligence. It is astonishing that anyone, let alone the entire political and journalistic class, should be dumbfounded by Kouchner's question, because only an examination of the facts can decide, in this particular case, where guilt lies. A general, philosophical question on the issue is just bunk.

But it was a remark made by Georgina Dufoix which was to capture best the dehumanizing nature of the bureaucratic mind, and the haze of unaccountability which hangs over the entire system. In a phrase which became the gruesome epitaph of the whole affair, she defended her role within a system which, being out of the control of any individual, assumes a lethal life of its own, obscures all accountability, and slows down action when it is most needed, by saying that she and her officials were 'responsible, but not guilty'.

In general France seems to operate on the same principle as the Soviet Union used to, where good harvests were the responsibility of the General Secretary of the Communist Party, while bad ones were the responsibility of the Minister of Agriculture. Blaming officials for one's failures while taking the credit for their successes has become a full-time ministerial occupation. Steeped in French habits, Jacques Attali tried to blame his officials for the lavish overspending on the interior decoration at the European Bank for Reconstruction and Development in London, when the noose was closing around his neck. As one of France's foremost political commentators has remarked, this is a degradation which is particular to the Mitterrand era:

> The degree to which the political world has fallen into discredit is often astonishing. The discredit results mainly from the refusal to accept responsibilities. Ministers are there ... to appropriate for their own benefit the goods which result from the labour of the French people, and to congratulate themselves on their unparalleled genius, and on that of the king. They are not there to assume responsibility for their mistakes. Formerly, a minister would cover for his officials, and resign in the case of a mistake: he incarnated power in its good and bad aspects. Today ... the higher up in the hierarchy one is, the more one is exonerated for one's mistakes ... Resignation hardly ever occurs in today's France ... What we see in operation today is a sort of unwritten amnesty law: if you belong to the higher echelons of political power, you are above the common law. To have power in France today means to be no longer responsible: it is, on the contrary, to escape, in the most shameful way, from one's responsibilities.[48]

The truth of this was well illustrated by the short-lived Habache affair in February 1992, when the leader of the terrorist group, the Popular Front for the Liberation of Palestine, Georges Habache, was admitted to a Paris hospital for treatment. His arrival on French soil was scandalous for three reasons. First, he was wanted for questioning on his role in the bombing attack on the synagogue in the rue Copernic in Paris in October 1980, which killed four people and wounded twenty;[49] and also for his role in an arms cache which the police had discovered in Fontainebleau forest in 1986.

Second, his arrival revealed the untenable ambiguity of French foreign policy in the Middle East, which has for long tried to be simultaneously both pro-Palestinian and pro-Israeli. It underlined the foolishness of placing the control of foreign policy outside the parliamentary domain and in the hands of the supposedly omniscient President. Third, it also showed what happens when important decisions of this kind are taken by officials, and not by politicians, for structural irresponsibility thus accrues to French ministers, as the outcome of the scandal showed: the only people to resign over the affair were three officials.

Mitterrand's own reaction was classic. He did everything to exculpate everybody from blame, including, of course, himself. On the day he was confronted with the scandal, he declared, 'They are mad', a convenient way of offloading blame on to vague official-dom. He then made the following self-contradictory and self-justifi-catory declaration to the press:

> I telephoned Edith Cresson ... and we agreed that it was appropriate ... to punish those responsible. We did not know who that was, because we did not know anything about the affair ... The senior officials and Georgina Dufoix – who, in this affair, is in a very difficult position – are all remarkable people, and all have extreme nobility of character, but they made an error of judgement. They dealt with Habache's arrival as a routine matter ... It is an error of judgement which I have sanctioned ... There are three officials, people of great quality, who have admitted that they committed this error of judgement, and who immediately understood the reasons why they were asked to withdraw from their functions. I am thinking especially of Mr Scheer, the Secretary-General

of the Quai d'Orsay, a man for whom I have the highest
regard. He will not remain for long without a post, for he
would be sorely missed by a country such as France ... I say
that there was an error of judgement, this error of judgement
which I could not accept ... I have great respect for them,
and indeed affection as well ... but they did not make the
appropriate judgement.[50]

Apart from the sheer failure to register the degree of moral outrage
rightly felt by the public at this affair, the most curious aspect of
Mitterrand's declaration is this: in his eyes, it does not seem to be
among the essential qualities required for senior officials that they
have good judgement. Within three months all the officials were
reappointed to other important posts: François Scheer, for instance,
was appointed French Ambassador to the EEC within three months
(he later became the French Ambassador to Germany), while another was appointed Ambassador to Algeria.

Once again, the same lack of reflection on the notion of conflict
of interest was illustrated. The person who pressed for Habache to
be received in France was none other than Georgina Dufoix, the
same woman who had been the Minister of Health when hundreds
of haemophiliacs were given contaminated blood. It is odd that a
woman who, as one critic rudely contends, would not be deemed
capable of running a supermarket in the private sector, let alone the
Ministry of Health,[51] should have been appointed Director of the
French Red Cross – as she then was – after having served so
disastrously as a minister. But she was not only Director of the Red
Cross. It is illustrative of Mitterrand's clannish system of maintaining and controlling a network of friends in positions of power that
Dufoix also had an office at the Elysée Palace as an adviser to
President Mitterrand. Thus, when she requested that Habache be
received into France in her capacity as Director of the Red Cross, the
officials who agreed to the treatment, or failed to inform their
ministers that it was to occur, did so because they assumed that the
green light had come from the President himself.

Indeed, it is not impossible that this is exactly what happened,
but who knows? A fog of irresponsibility pervades the whole
system: like an anaesthetic ether, it seeps into all its nooks and
crannies, suffocating political life from the healthy invigoration of
open, clear public scrutiny. If the President had taken the decision,

all he had to do was to offload the blame on to his juniors, and there is no way of ever knowing the truth. As Jean-François Revel comments,

> It is in the logic of the Fifth Republic to make people irresponsible, since power is imparted within it by an omnipotent and irresponsible man to others who are mere emanations of his own essence, and who consequently participate in his privilege of irresponsibility ... The desire to protect the President from the daily oscillations of politicians' politics has led to conferring upon him the same irresponsibility which existed during the Absolutist period ... The delinquency of the parliamentary and judicial powers, aggravated to the point of catalepsy, completes the individualization of power, and the impunity of its protégés.[52]

Or, as another has put it, more succinctly, 'Corruption in France is not outside the system or parallel to it, but *inside* the system, like a gangrene.'[53]

8. The Cabinet Noir

There is no such thing as power. There is only the abuse of power.

Henry de Montherlant, The Cardinal of Spain

Many visitors to Paris – and many who know the city only from novels – are familiar with the Luxembourg Gardens. One of the largest parks in central Paris, the gardens offer a magnificent perspective of the Palace of Luxembourg, where the Senate sits: it is one of the great sights of Paris. Few tourists will be aware, however, that the Luxembourg Gardens were the site of one of the most extraordinary and farcical events in François Mitterrand's life, the 'Observatory affair'.

It occurred on the night of 15–16 October 1959. Mitterrand was a fairly well-known senator. He had been a minister eleven times, in a variety of governmental coalitions under the Fourth Republic. He had even served in the ministries of Justice and of the Interior, the two most senior ministries after the premiership. He had been driving along the side of the gardens when a gunman opened fire on him, riddling the car with bullets. He leapt out of the vehicle, and jumped over a hedge into the park. Because of his fame, and because the events were so extraordinary, the affair attracted huge media attention. Mitterrand explained to a magistrate, and to the assembled press, that he had been the victim of an assassination attempt. The French watched in amazement as the former Minister of Justice of France re-enacted his split-second leap over the hedge with the aid of a chair.[1] It was left to the public to draw the appropriate conclusions about who might have instigated this attack, from the fact that Mitterrand was the main opponent of General de Gaulle at the time.

Unfortunately for the hapless and hopeless opposition leader, Mitterrand was soon to be hoist by his own petard. For the whole thing was an elaborate hoax. Mitterrand had planned the attack himself, and had enlisted the help of an extreme right-wing deputy, Robert Pesquet. Pesquet belonged to the party led by Pierre Poujade, the extreme right-wing populist politician. (Jean-Marie Le Pen was also a deputy in the same parliamentary group at the time.) But Pesquet was no fool. Having been asked by Mitterrand to assist him in this grotesque montage, he sent himself two letters, poste restante, to his Paris address and to his home in the country, describing the plans for the hoax in detail. He allowed Mitterrand to make his declarations to the press and to the law, no doubt enjoying the four days during which the headlines were full of the affair. He then confronted Mitterrand face to face at the judicial hearings, allowed Mitterrand to dig himself further into a hole, and then explained to the judge the business about the letters poste restante.

Pesquet told the judge that he and Mitterrand had met for dinner at Brasserie Lipp, in front of which the 'hunt' was supposed to have started; that Mitterrand got into his blue Peugeot 403 and started to drive towards his home. He indicated the place where he was supposed to enter into action after a short chase, as well as the place where Mitterrand lay down on the grass, having parked his car and jumped over a gate. He said that Mitterrand had agreed to give the signal 'Ready!' when he was lying on the ground, so that the car would be full of bullets, and so that there would be a few marks here and there on the grass. Having heard these astonishing claims, the magistrate went in person to collect the letters poste restante, brought them back to the Palais de Justice, and opened them in Mitterrand's presence. The future President of the Republic apparently broke down in tears when their contents were read out. On 8 August 1966, the prosecution for attempted murder against Pesquet and Dahuron (the alleged gunman) was withdrawn. Mitterrand appealed on 7 November 1966; the appeal was rejected two weeks later, and Mitterrand had to pay costs. Although initially prosecuted for contempt of court, the case against him was never brought to trial.[2]

That Mitterrand had deliberately falsified evidence and committed perjury makes his frequent attacks against General de Gaulle for 'acts of state illegality' very ironic. Mitterrand pretended to be

especially outraged by de Gaulle's use of a private presidential
police force.

> De Gaulle has his *'cabinet noir'*. Above and outside the Ministry
> of the Interior and beyond the responsibility of the competent
> functionaries, he runs his own inquiries directly from the
> Elysée, he informs himself directly, and, occasionally, orders
> certain operations. Certain members of his entourage are en-
> tirely devoted to him; they are outside any other hierarchy,
> they inform him, pull the strings, and keep tabs on people.[3]

The expression *'cabinet noir'* refers to the name given to the secret
office of the kings of France – in so many respects the sources of
inspiration for Presidents of the Fifth Republic. They used it to
intercept letters and to monitor the state of public opinion. One
historian has remarked, 'This practice is as old as the postal
service.'[4]

In the minds of those of the Left, de Gaulle in particular and
the Right in general were (justifiably) associated with this kind
of behaviour. So when they came to power, Mitterrand's Socialists said that they were determined to change this aspect of life
as well. Like all Mitterrand's other promises, however, this one
evaporated like the morning mist after the revelries on the night
of 10 May 1981. One of the first actions of the new President
was to appoint a man in his private office to the post of phone-
tapper-in-chief.[5] The man in question, Gaston Deferre, published
an article in *Le Monde* on 3 June 1981, chirpily entitled, 'Let's
stop tapping phones once and for all.' Unfortunately, not much
came of the idea. Whatever their proclaimed convictions (in
1972, the common Socialist-Communist manifesto had declared,
'The parallel police forces will be dissolved'[6]) the Socialists soon
became converts to the practice of having secret police. On
the contrary, Mitterrand beefed up the secret forces of the
presidency.

On 2 September 1984, Charles Pasqua, then the head of the RPR
group in the Senate, in 1994 Minister of the Interior, attacked the
President for having created at the Elysée Palace a political police
force 'whose responsibility it is to draw up fake files on opposition
politicians'. The existence of this 'anti-terrorist cell' at the Elysée
has since become common knowledge, and many journalists and

politicians have had cause to protest about its activities. But the first on the trail was the investigative journalist, Jean Montaldo, an inveterate scourge of the President's corrupt and shady practices. He recounts the following extraordinary story. A journalist colleague of his at *Le Quotidien de Paris* had a talent for imitating people's voices. So he picked up the phone and, in Mitterrand's dulcet tones, asked to speak to Monsieur Coulerez, the man mentioned by Pasqua as being the head of the anti-terrorist cell. Coulerez, a policeman whom Mitterrand had brought back from retirement to run the cell, was not listed in the *Journal officiel*, and was not nominated officially in the Council of Ministers: his existence was entirely secret. Not surprisingly, he was an old friend of Mitterrand's from the Nièvre, his political fiefdom. His two subordinates, André Ferrand and Pierre Bergès, were former officers from the Renseignements Généraux, the secret services. The journalist was put through immediately to Coulerez's secretary. Dropping his pretended accent, he had the following extraordinary conversation.

Journalist:	Hello, I would like to speak to Mr Coulerez.
Secretary:	I am his secretary. Who's speaking please?
Journalist:	It's personal . . . and very important . . .
Secretary:	He is not here. But you can tell me.
Journalist:	I have got some information for him. Are you interested? It's about Pasqua . . .
Secretary:	Oh, absolutely!
Journalist:	Are you familiar with the stuff on him?
Secretary:	Yes, Monsieur Coulerez has told me about it.
Journalist:	Well, that's why I have to see Coulerez to give him some very important documents on Pasqua. It's urgent. Do you understand what I mean?
Secretary:	Yes, I see. Can you call him back in half an hour. He'll be back then. I do not know you. It is difficult to talk to you for much longer.
Journalist:	But of course you know me!
Secretary:	Oh really?
Journalist:	Yes, I was at the meeting with Commissioner Ferrand, the other day at the Elysée. Don't you remember? You have blonde hair, is that right?

Secretary:	Yes, that's me. Are you a friend of Monsieur Coulerez?
Journalist:	Heavens, I've known him for twenty years.
Secretary:	OK. Well, you can ring Commissioner Ferrand at the Ministry of the Interior if it's very urgent.

Delirious with their stroke of luck at guessing the colour of the secretary's hair, they telephoned the Ministry of the Interior as the secretary had suggested and asked for Police Commissioner Ferrand.

Journalist:	Hello, Commissioner Ferrand?
Ferrand:	Yes, speaking.
Journalist:	I have been asked to get in touch with you by a commissioner from the political police who works with Monsieur Coulerez and yourself at the Elysée ... I cannot remember his name, Berez, Beharez, Bergès, something like that ...
Ferrand:	Yes, I know who you mean. What is it?
Journalist:	I have to see you, Commissioner. I have important information to give you about Pasqua, you understand what I mean?
Ferrand:	Yes, very well. And who are you?
Journalist:	I worked with him in the past. Are you interested?
Ferrand:	Oh, yes, absolutely! I am extremely interested. Can you come and see me tomorrow at the Ministry of the Interior?
Journalist:	Well ...
Ferrand:	What is it?
Journalist:	Well, I worked at the Ministry of the Interior some time ago. I am afraid I might bump into people I know.
Ferrand:	OK, we can meet in a bistro if you like, but it's silly, come to the ministry, nothing will happen to you. No one will recognize you after such a long time! All you need to do is to come in by the small door at the back, rue Cambacérès, and come up to the fourth floor. Ask for me ...

Journalist: Commissioner, I will need money for this infor-
              mation about Pasqua. I need the cash, that's
              why I do this kind of thing.
Ferrand: Don't worry about that, we'll give you money.
Journalist: How much?
Ferrand: I don't know . . . quite a lot, depending on the
              nature of the information. Come and see me
              tomorrow, I'll be expecting you.

These conversations were reprinted in *Le Quotidien de Paris* and in
Le Monde on 13 September 1984. They caused an uproar, for they
proved that as early as then, there existed a presidential political
police force at the Elysée Palace. All knowledge of such a force was
denied by the President's office, even though two months previously, the same Elysian Inspector Clouseau had turned up at the
inventive journalist's flat, and asked the concierge and the neighbours questions about his private life.[7]

A journalist at *Le Monde*, Edwy Plenel, was also the object of
their kind attentions. His flat was surreptitiously broken into in
1990, documents were photographed and his work copied. Plenel, a
former extreme left-wing militant, had expected great things from
François Mitterrand as the first left-wing President in the history of
the Fifth Republic. He reacted all the more bitterly, therefore, when
he realized that this kind of intimidation, which he had always
associated with the Right, was also practised by his erstwhile
political friend. Indeed, according to a contact at the office of the
secret services in Place Saint-Thomas d'Aquin, France's internal
spies have never worked so hard as in the mid 1980s.[8]

The 'anti-terrorist cell', located within the presidential police
force at 2, rue de l'Elysée, next to the palace, was set up in 1982,
after a series of apparently meaningless terrorist attacks on a variety
of targets around Paris. As in any country under such conditions,
there was pressure for the government to 'do something'. Mitterrand therefore created a Secretariat of State for Public Security, to
whose head he appointed Joseph Francheschi, an old political
friend, who had been responsible for protecting him when he was
First Secretary of the Socialist Party. A 'co-ordinating committee
for information and action against terrorism' was created, directly
under the control of the President of the Republic. Its head was

Christian Prouteau, a commander in an élite section of the police. These choices express a very personal vision of the state, for the two men were promoted outside the usual hierarchies, exclusively because they enjoyed the personal confidence of the President. But they also represent an important innovation, because for the first time in the official history of the republic, a service of operations had been installed at the Elysée, without any control. Security thus became directly a matter for the Head of State, without any intermediary. To excuse this infringement of established practice, the Mitterrand faithful recall the heavy climate in that summer in 1982, and emphasize that there had to be a reaction to the terrorist threat. However, it would be to underestimate Mitterrand's clairvoyance not to think that the opportunity he seized reveals a very extensive understanding of the presidential 'reserved domain', with which a triumphant Gaullist would have felt quite at home.[9]

The choice of the third man in the cell, Paul Barril, is even stranger. At the time of his appointment, he was facing prosecution for alleged illegal traffic in weapons and for complicity in the illegal storage of explosives (the case was dropped in 1986). His presumed accomplice in these crimes was a Parisian perfume merchant who was also involved in arms dealing. The affair, which also involved figures from the extreme right, had ended enigmatically with the suicide in prison of the principal defendant.[10] None of this, it seems, was a bar to Barril's appointment.

On 28 August 1982, very soon after the creation of the cell, Barril went to the flat of three Irish people in Vincennes, a suburb just beyond the walls of Paris. He arrested them there, in classic cop-film fashion, pulling their jackets over their heads, and handcuffing their arms over their heads. The Secretary-General of the Elysée, Jean-Louis Bianco, issued a communiqué about 'important arrests of international terrorists', adding that 'documents and explosives' had been seized, even though the official Elysée spokesman, Michel Vauzelle, only heard of this on television.[11] At no stage in the arrest were the normal police or judicial authorities involved. The next day, the list of items seized was made public: 500 grammes of plastic explosive, two detonators, three guns, false passports, political documents, and a curious list of figures. The presidential police said they had been tipped off that the Irish had been preparing a terrorist attack for the following weekend.

First of all, the three Irish, Michael Plunkett, Stephen King and Mary Reid, were placed in solitary confinement, forbidden from receiving any visits or from having any communication with the outside world. After two months, they were classified as detainees under special surveillance. Mary Reid was separated from her young son all this time. They finally went on hunger strike. Five months after their arrest, the matter had still not come to trial; the case got into the press, notably as a result of the investigations of Edwy Plenel. After nine months, they were finally let out, and the case against them withdrawn. The whole thing had been a set-up, and the three Irish had been framed. The false documents and explosives had simply been planted in the apartment after their arrest.

The 'Vincennes Irish affair' was to achieve great notoriety. It was the first moment when Mitterrand's more intelligent left-wing supporters began to realize that the man they had elected was not what they had hoped. It was also ironic that sections of the right-wing press supported the Elysée cell. While Britain witnessed a number of cases of miscarriage of justice during the 1980s (the Birmingham six spent nearly twenty years in prison as the result of falsified evidence) the Vincennes Irish affair is interesting more for what it tells us about the way Mitterrand used his power.

For two policeman involved in the affair, Jean-Michel Beau and Pierre Caudan, were soon to spill the beans. Caudan's claims that the arms had been planted and the evidence falsified led to the release of the Irish and to the withdrawal of charges; in the ensuing internal inquiry, Beau alleged that 'they' told him that 'the powers that be want this affair to stick'. The 'they' in question was Christian Prouteau, the head of the cell, who reported directly to President Mitterrand. Beau was so disgusted with the way that the President was running the case that he published a book on the matter.[12] Prouteau had said to him, 'Don't worry. I have spoken to the President about it; there is no question of letting some little judge mess about policemen who are doing their duty, just for the sake of a few details' (October 1982); 'the public prosecutor is following the case closely and they have already intervened discreetly to get the message across. Just make sure you get all your men together, so that they know not to say anything stupid' (November 1982); 'The President wants everything to hold, and everything must hold!' (February 1983).[13]

Paul Barril had also claimed that the mission (i.e. the arrest) 'had been decided at the highest level of the state' and that 'was an affair of state'. This, he argued, justified – indeed demanded – the falsification of evidence. Despite these revelations in an internal inquiry, the case never came to court. The internal report was made 'a defence secret' and when Beau made an official request to see it in 1985, he was told, 'the document has never existed'. Before long, he was sacked from the police force, whence he became unemployed, drifting from one company to another in vain. Barril left the service a year later, on his own request, while Prouteau became a lieutenant-colonel, and was appointed a Prefect in 1985.

On 24 September 1991, nine years after these events, Jean-Michel Beau and Christian Prouteau were convicted of perverting the course of justice and complicity in the same, and each sentenced to fifteen months in prison. The judge found that Prouteau had been intimately involved in the execution of the operation, and not a mere bystander, as he had claimed in his trial. Even though he had lied in court, while Beau had admitted his crimes, they both received the same sentence. At the time of the trial, Prouteau, who was by then a Prefect of the Republic, was due to take up his functions as head of security at the Winter Olympics in Albertville within a few months. Both men appealed, and the case was heard, very briefly and very soon after the original hearing, on 15 January 1992. After a morning's hearing (the original trial had lasted three days), at which no new witnesses were called, Beau's conviction was upheld, while Prouteau's was overturned. Paul Barril was never even tried, nor even investigated by the magistrate responsible. Indeed, he even took Edwy Plenel to court for libel, and the case was heard on 17 September 1992. The judges' tribunal threw the case out, ruling that 'the truth of the allegedly defamatory facts has been proved'. They even took the trouble to criticize the 'inaction of the public prosecutor and the inertia of the investigating judge' over the affair.[14]

What is Mitterrand's role in all this? He was asked about the affair on television, on 17 September 1987, after Prouteau had been prosecuted. Mitterrand said he had warned the (right-wing) Minister of Justice in Chirac's government, Albin Chandalon, that he ought not to interfere with the course of justice, and that he should let the investigating magistrate do his job. If he did, he would be guilty of an abuse of his power. Then he said,

> Having said that, I must say to you that I have the greatest admiration for Colonel Prouteau, and that I like him a great deal; he works for me and will continue to do so, and I have full confidence in him. The French will learn to respect and to like Colonel Prouteau, who is the prototype of the kind of person our army can produce. I think he is not involved in this affair, and I have confidence in his courage and in his truthfulness.[15]

Quite how Mitterrand felt he could make a declaration of this kind without feeling he might be abusing his own power is not clear. Yet what did he really know? Quite apart from the fact that Prouteau reported directly to him, Mitterrand had been given proof that Barril's 'informers' and 'sources' were an invention. For the man who had told Barril of the existence of the Irish, Jean-François Jegat, had spent three years trying to get someone to listen to his explanation of why his tip-off had been misused. He had been to see policemen, a presidential adviser at the Elysée (Regis Debray, who had addressed a note to Mitterrand on the matter), journalists, a lawyer (George Kiejman, a famous lawyer, a close friend of Mitterrand, and future minister at the Ministry of Justice), and a deputy (Jacques Godfrain, RPR, who sent him to see another magistrate). Not one of them suggested that he go and see the magistrate investigating the affair. Thus, everybody who had anything to do with the case knew about Jegat; but once his story had been classified 'a state secret', the one man who should have heard his evidence, the judge, was successfully kept in the dark.

Jegat was a marginal political adventurer, who had befriended the three Irish in 1979. Following the machine-gun attack at the Restaurant Goldenberg in the rue des Rosiers, in the heart of the Jewish quarter of Paris on Monday 9 August 1982, at which six people sitting having lunch were massacred and twenty wounded, Jegat decided that the Identikit pictures of the suspected attackers published in the press were his Irish friends. He took his story to some journalists, who contacted the Ministry of the Interior. The Elysée was phoned, and the matter was handed over to Paul Barril,

whom Jegat went to see on 24 August. He brought him photos of
the two Irish to compare with the Identikit pictures. Barril said he
was convinced: he knew he was about to make a scoop. That
witnesses to the attack described the attackers as Arabs seemed not
to bother him, nor the fact that the Identikit picture showed them
to have black curly hair and dark skin, while the Irish, by contrast,
had untidy reddish-blond hair and pasty, broad faces. Plunkett,
moreover, had a copious beard before the attack, in Jegat's photo,
which he was still wearing when he was arrested a few days later,
whereas the Identikit men were clean-shaven!

A few days later, Barril went to Jegat's flat thinking that Plunkett
was about to arrive there. He intended to arrest him on his arrival.
In his bag he had two short-barrelled revolvers, a radio transmitter,
and some files on British personalities. When Jegat said, 'That
doesn't belong to Michael', Barril replied, 'Never mind, we'll
have to put something on them.' When Plunkett failed to turn
up, Barril took the bombs and guns Jegat had and stuffed them
in his bag. When Jegat read the newspaper reports of the objects
found in the Vincennes flat, a few days later, he realized that
they were the same weapons which had been in his own flat only
a few days previously; they had simply been taken there in Captain Barril's bag.

During the course of his attempt to make all this clear, Jegat
eventually telephoned the cell in September 1983. He evidently
thought that the framing of the Irish was a mistake. He introduced
himself on the phone as 'Frank', who had known Barril since
August 1982. The person on the other end understood immediately:
he fixed a meeting for him with one of his colleagues. The latter
saw him, took care to check his story, and asked Jegat to identify
the weapons he had given to Barril against photographs which he
had in his files. In other words, the Elysée cell had a dossier on the
affair in 1983, running in parallel with the one in the hands of the
judicial authorities, from whom they were deliberately withholding
information. The man who had put Jegat on to this associate was
none other than Christian Prouteau, the head of the cell, technical
adviser to the President of the Republic, and a future Prefect of the
Republic.[16] Prouteau was later to tell Régis Debray that Jegat
should not go to see the investigating magistrate.

Jegat finally went to see two officers from France's internal security police, in January 1985. He gave them a full account of what had happened, which took five and a half days to tell. He had told them he was prepared to be prosecuted himself for the role he had played in the affair; instead of which they offered to employ his services for 1,500 francs a month! He got no further than before. The full story did not get into the public domain until October 1985, when he met Edwy Plenel, the investigative journalist at *Le Monde*.[17]

This was not the last that the French were to hear of Christian Prouteau, nor of Edwy Plenel. On 4 March 1993, *Libération* published documentary evidence that the Elysée cell had been illegally tapping Plenel's telephone for at least two months during 1985. This was following what came to be known as the *Rainbow Warrior* affair. On this notorious occasion, 10 July 1985, the boat of that name belonging to the ecologist-pacifist group, Greenpeace, was bombed by the French secret services, the DGSE (Direction Générale des Services Extérieures) while it was moored in Auckland harbour. The attack resulted in the death of a Dutch photographer who had been on board. Although the two agents were caught and arrested, France insisted that they be given special dispensation, and insisted, by threatening New Zealand with an economic blockade, that instead of being tried for murder, they spend time on Muroroa Atoll. The New Zealanders eventually capitulated, but the French reneged even on this; before their time was up, they were spirited away back to Paris, on the false pretext that the woman agent was pregnant. Seldom can there have been such a brazen demonstration of a country looking after its own, at whatever moral cost. Two months after the event, Charles Hernu, the Minister of Defence, resigned, even though it has been suggested that the order for the sabotage may have come from higher up.[18] Indeed, the DGSE and its short-lived antecedent, the SDECE (Service de Documentation Extérieure et de Contre-Espionnage) was *de facto* controlled by François de Grossouvre, Mitterrand's close personal friend, who committed suicide in his office in the Elysée Palace in April 1994.[19]

Plenel had evidently taken what the Elysée considered to be an unhealthy interest in this and other affairs. His conversations were written up, and catalogued according to the subject he was discussing. Following publication of the documents in 1993, *Libération* contacted the men who had been the Prime Minister's and the President's *directeurs de cabinet* at the time: both of them denied any knowledge of the matter. They insisted that phone tapping, which had been authorized when the anti-terrorist cell was set up, was subject to strict rules, and they categorically denied any knowledge of Edwy Plenel's phone having been bugged. 'So who', asked *Libération* predictably enough, 'ordered the bugging?' At first neither the spokesman of the Elysée Palace nor the official government spokesman were prepared to comment. Then the Elysée and the Prime Minister's office said, respectively, 'This is a wild one-off, the act of an isolated individual who did this on his own initiative', and, 'They are fakes, which are being used to falsify the truth.'

Libération did not let go. The next week, on 12 March 1993, they published proof that there had been over 100 such incidents of phone tapping, of deputies, journalists – and even of an actress – during a period lasting at least three years between 1983 and 1986. Indeed, it was later to be revealed that the cell had tapped the telephones of the Superior Council of the Magistrature in 1987, in order to keep tabs on the activities of the judiciary.[20] The conversations recorded by these bugs were typed up on documents stamped with 'Source secret', and so it was not directly clear who had ordered the bugging. They all had an official reason for why the tapping had been authorized, such as 'close to terrorist circles', 'security of members of the Ministry of Defence', 'arms dealer', 'security of the President of the Republic', etc. However, an examination of the people in question makes a mockery of this pretence. One of the people bugged was a Christian Democrat MEP, François Froment-Meurice, who had founded an association called 'SOS Christians in Lebanon'; another was the girlfriend of the lawyer of the Vincennes Irish, Antoine Comte. Gilles Ménage, Mitterrand's *directeur de cabinet*, had written to Christian Prouteau, 'We must seriously start to deal with Antoine Comte'.

A similar thing happened to Jean-Edern Hallier, a radical writer and pamphleteer, whose phone was bugged between 1983 and 1985 because he wanted to publish a book, entitled *The Lost Honour of François Mitterrand* which dealt with Mitterrand's past as an official in the Vichy government during the war. Here the President's policemen were more subtle than usual. Instead of bugging his private line, they bugged five phones he used regularly: one in his favourite restaurant, La Closerie des Lilas; one in his favourite bistro, Le Vieux Comptoir (both from 24 January to 1 February 1985); and one used by his Ecuadorian cook, who lived in his apartment near the place des Vosges; finally, his phone at work (in the offices of a publishing company, L'Équerre) and the phone of his editor. Another journalist, the more moderate Alexis Liebaert, was also bugged from 12 September 1985, at the time when he started writing articles on the *Rainbow Warrior* affair in the weekly magazine VSD (Vendredi, Samedi, Dimanche). Most surprising of all was the discovery that an actress, Carole Bouquet, was also being bugged. It took some time for people to work out why, until they realized that she was a friend of Jacques Attali, himself working in the Elysée in the office next to Mitterrand at the time.

These revelations conclusively destroyed the claim that the shady activities of the cell were due merely to one individual, Paul Barril. He left in 1983, but the cell continued to function during the rest of Mitterrand's term in office. Prouteau would periodically announce the discovery of things like a new 'European Front of terrorism against Western Europe' in order to justify the cell's existence, but in 1985, it devoted much of its efforts to negotiating with Lebanese terrorists for the release of the French hostages they had taken.

A further escapade for which the President's private army was responsible was the dirty war in New Caledonia. In an uprising on 22 April 1988, hostages were taken by rebels in Ouvea. Four policemen were killed and two wounded. This occurred two days before the first round of the presidential election, and, as the war continued in the days after the hostage-taking, the flames were fanned by the heady political atmosphere in Paris. Three French hostages had been freed in the Lebanon on 3 May, and one of the agents involved in the operation against the *Rainbow Warrior* had been repatriated, in spite of international undertakings, on 6 May. Each side in the presidential campaign wanted to continue the run of triumphs. On 3 May, Mitterrand gave the green light to the operation to retrieve the hostages in Ouvea, against the advice of his political advisers, and on the advice of Christian Prouteau. In this way, the Elysée cell became a sort of army HQ. He despatched the head of the GIGN (Groupe d'Intervention de la Gendarmerie

Nationale), Captain Legorjus, at the head of fifty men composed of members of the GIGN, of the EPIGN (Escadron Parachutiste de la Gendarmerie Nationale), and of the presidential guard, the GSPR (Groupe de Sécurité de la Présidence de la République). Captain Legorjus' men tortured the rebel leaders with electric shocks to the face and neck with cattle truncheons; they were forced to crawl while carrying heavy stones; there were kickings, beatings with the butts of guns, and so on.[21] Children were tortured by the same methods. The operation caused twenty-one deaths, of which two were soldiers and nineteen natives. At least five of the latter were shot after being taken prisoner.

Le Monde gave their names, and the proof that they had been deliberately killed. Only the lawyer representing the GIGN denied the story.[22] There was no judicial or court-martial investigation. Nonetheless, two years later, Legorjus confirmed the reports in his own version of events, *La Morale et l'Action*, published in 1990. The man had undergone a moral crisis during his experience in New Caledonia: having refused to confirm the reports which came out at the time, he decided to reconcile himself with his conscience in the book. For, returning from New Caledonia at Charles de Gaulle airport two days after the assault, Legorjus had in his pocket a photograph taken back at the army camp a few moments after the attack. There were Alain Le Caro, the head of the presidential guard, Christian Prouteau, and Paul Barril (still!). The next day, 8 May, François Mitterrand was re-elected President of the Republic. Prouteau had by this time been responsible for the Vincennes Irish scandal, Barril's escapades, and the 'plumbers' who wired up the telephone bugs, who had been surprised one night by the ordinary police while breaking into a flat in Paris. The carnage in Ouvea was just another feather in his cap. While Mitterrand's other advisers protested, none of these things led Mitterrand to dismiss him. He left the Elysée discreetly in September 1988, it is true – but it was to take up his job in Albertville. On 14 July 1992, he was awarded the Légion d'honneur by the President, for services rendered.

As if all this were not enough, Mitterrand has also made strange use of the Renseignements Généraux, the official secret services. Their very existence has even been a matter of political dispute, and many have called for them to be dissolved. For, the Renseignements

Généraux are indeed a bizarre French exception. All democratic states have espionage and counter-espionage services, which correspond in France to the DGSE for external matters and the DST (Direction de la Sécurité Territoriale) for internal matters. Their role, as in any country, is to counter the intrigues of foreign countries or of internal subversives, including by illegal means. But other states have not set up a general service for police information such as the Renseignements Généraux, whose role it is to follow political parties and trades unions, politicians and elections, strikes and social movements, the press, foreign residents, and so forth.[23]

It is normal that the police should have the means to keep tabs on people who are criminals, or suspected of being such. But the operations of the Renseignements Généraux do not fall into that category. It is all the more surprising because they date from Vichy: although they grew out of previously existing police forces, their present statutes and title date from the law of 21 March 1942, which charges them with 'informing the government on all matters which might have an effect on public opinion and public morals, and on the actions of persons and groups which might have an effect on public morals and order'.[24]

When the Left came to power in 1981, they made vague noises about wanting to make the service more 'moral' and more open, limiting its action to 'political violence', by which they meant terrorism and the extreme right. Nothing came of these promises. Indeed, after Mitterrand's re-election in 1988, all pretence at reforming the service was abandoned with the appointment of a new head, Jacques Fournet, who wanted to reinvigorate the service as a whole. As is typical for Mitterrand, the new appointee belonged to the 'family': Fournet was a prefect from the Nièvre, Mitterrand's political power-base. He suggested increasing the domain of information for which the service would be competent; the development of new technological methods for obtaining that information; building up contacts within the worlds of business, science and communication; and an improvement in recruitment methods, making use of psychological studies. He also proposed increased resources. His suggestions were not in vain: by 1990, the Renseignements Généraux was composed of no fewer than 3,900 officials.

A year later, Fournet wrote a 'Plan of Action 1990'. He laid stress on the force's task of 'supplying high-quality information for preventive purposes'. He went on, 'The RG will go beyond the simple notion of information, and move towards that of intelligence, in order to aid the authorities to make decisions, and to aid the other sections of the police force in their work as well.' In addition to the 'fight against terrorism and financial circles involved in gambling and in drugs', the third area of activity in which they planned to interest themselves was 'penetrating circles of foreigners, especially Muslim fundamentalists, and ethnic minorities which pose a problem from the point of view of integration'. It is an interesting view of how to uphold democracy to assume that 'ethnic minorities' are rightly the object of such spying. Indeed, it was subsequently even published in the *Journal officiel* in March 1990 that the RG were keeping files on people with their 'ethnic origin, political, philosphical and religious opinions, and member- ship of unions' as part of the information regularly collected. With such a vague brief, it is perhaps not surprising that the methods the Renseignements Généraux used on journalists, pol- iticians, businessmen and even the rest of the police itself, often resembled ones which would have been better suited to tracking down terrorists: phone tapping, breaking into people's appart- ments, intercepting the mail, and so on. But unlike the rest of the police, the Renseignements Généraux are not subject to judicial authority.

It was not until a death occurred that the shady activity of the RG was publicized. The death was that of a priest, Joseph Doucé, a well-known militant homosexual. He ran a pro-gay pressure group called the Centre of Christ the Liberator; his partially decom- posed body was found in the forest of Rambouillet (which belongs to the President) on 18 October 1990. The Renseignements Génér- aux had picked up rumours that a paedophile ring was operating from the Centre of Christ the Liberator, and Inspector Jean-Marc Dufourg was put on the case. Already one can see what an extraordinary set-up the RG is: Why were the normal judicial police not called in? What possible responsibility could an internal political-security police – even if such a thing were to be deemed legitimate – have in such an affair? The only explanation is that the RG expected to pick up some compromising information in the process of their enquiries. Indeed, the RG set about secretly photographing the people who came and went, and a phone tap was set up under the heading 'administrative', which meant that it was directly under the control of the executive. An informer was violently forced to infiltrate the Centre. Dufourg must have realized that the game was up once Doucé's body was discovered, for he began to talk. It seems that a good deal of what he said was obscure, and that he was attempting to distract attention from the real truth. But some of what happened seems clear. He claimed that he had been ordered 'to recruit a young homosexual to offer his charms in order to compromise two public figures'.[25]

But this was only an appetizer. It also turned out that during 1990, a deputy and a former deputy, both Socialists, had been surprised to receive letters from young men proposing their charms: officers from the RG had replied to the gay advertisements in *Libération*, pretending to be the deputies. They then would intercept the post, hoping to find juicy details.[26] It was also revealed that magistrates who were intending to protest against the amnesty law for corruption were also under investigation, with files on their character, their political inclinations, and their membership of unions.[27] It was soon revealed that the RG had spied on the Gaullist party, the RPR, then in opposition, by means of a paid informer and a phone tap at the party's head offices; on the Front National, where another member of the party was paid monthly to provide information; and on the French Communist Party, whose mail was intercepted and photocopied between 1983 and 1985 by a postman recruited by the RG and paid 1,500 francs a month for his work.[28]

The death of Doucé – his killer has still not been found – provoked a considerable amount of public discussion on the role of the RG, whose involvement in the death nobody seemed to doubt. (It might be an indication of the extent to which violence sometimes seems to be viewed as a part of political life in France that the French Ambassador to Poland played down the similar killing of the Polish priest Father Popieluszko, reporting to the Elysée Palace that the death had been an awful mistake, and that the Polish secret police had not wanted to murder the priest but '*only* terrorize him and shut him up'! This version of events seems to have been

accepted as a valid excuse by the Elysée staff.[29]) A book was
written about the affair in 1994, and the author's theory is that
Doucé was kidnapped by special branch officers operating under
the instructions of the Elysée Palace, with orders to frighten the
priest off, but that the operation got out of hand and Doucé was
killed.[30]

In response to this public airing of their role, the then Minister
of the Interior, Pierre Joxe, announced on 30 October 1990 the
creation of a High Council for Police Activities, with an Information
Committee for the Activities of the Secret Police which would
report into it. Nothing came of the suggestion however, and
France is still waiting for her secret political police to come
under legislative, judicial, or any other form of non-executive
control.

However, there was a brief opening of part of the issue, under
Michel Rocard in the spring of 1991. He decided to pass a law
on phone tapping. Phone tapping had been legal when ordered
by a magistrate, but the law also allowed 'administrative' phone
tapping, which the government could order at its pleasure. The
new law required that reasons 'justifying' the bugging be given
in writing to the Prime Minister by the minister requesting the
bugging. A National Control Commission was to be set up,
which would check that the bugging was in conformity with the
law. Whatever the merits or demerits of this law, it allowed a
glimpse into the world of official phone tapping, because the
secret police were prepared to divulge the extent of activities
which had recently been legalized. An official at Matignon, in
charge of phone tapping, who was taking people around the
service, declared that during an average year, the service organized about 3,200 phone buggings, and that at that very moment
there were 1,092 buggings in operation.[31] The man, an army
colonel, was evidently quite relieved that, after thirty years of
illegality, the service was being put on to the statute book. This
did not prevent France from being condemned by the European
Court of Human Rights for the practice.

In early 1994, a report concluded that the 'anti-terrorist' cell at
the Elysée which had been responsible for ordering these phone
tappings, had shown 'grave malfunctioning'. With that discreet
use of euphemism for which such reports are famed, it concluded

that the cell's abuses were due to the absence of any meaningful control over its activities, and to the fact that its agents enjoyed 'the confidence of the highest authorities in the state'.[32] Everybody knows who the highest authorities of the state are.

9. The Architect of Socialism

In every town I go to, I feel myself Emperor or architect. I
decide, I judge, I arbitrate.

François Mitterrand[1]

The phenomenon of the court is well established in the behaviour
of French Presidents of the Fifth Republic: they have always
behaved rather like kings, because that is essentially what they are.
This has often been the occasion of caricature: *Le Canard Enchaîné*
used to have a weekly column in the 1960s on what had happened
in General de Gaulle's 'kingdom', while the final volume of Jean
Lacouture's magnificent biography of de Gaulle is simply entitled,
The Sovereign; in 1980, *Le Nouvel Observateur* showed Giscard dressed
as a monarch with a crown; *Le Point* repeated the same joke with
Mitterrand in the mid-1980s, and, quick off the mark as ever, the
Economist showed him as Louis XIV in 1992. Even Édouard
Balladur, for the time being a mere Prime Minister, is depicted
by the *Canard* as 'His Courteous Pomposity, Édouard Balladull
the First', a cross between a princeling and a Lord High Chamber-
lain.

But just as Mitterrand has outdone de Gaulle in the escapades of
his private court police, so he has seemed to outdo him in the
pursuit of other trappings of majesty as well. Like de Gaulle, he
found the Elysée Palace too small as a presidential residence. The
General used to dream of rebuilding the Tuileries Palace, burnt
down by the Communards in 1871, but for Mitterrand, even this
would not have been grand enough. He used to fantasize about
moving into Louis XIV's gigantic Hôtel des Invalides.[2] This would
have represented a decisive break with centuries of French tradition,
for the seat of political power has always been on the right bank,
but one wonders how he would have made do with the modesty of
10, Downing Street.

However, nowhere is his royal behaviour more apparent than in the *Grands Travaux*, the large prestige building projects with which he has occupied himself during his presidency. The tradition of undertaking large-scale prestige building projects dates in its recent form from Pompidou, although in a different age, Marshal Pétain and the Vichy government were proud of their *Grands Travaux* as well. Vichy France, like Nazi Germany, was run on the kind of Keynesian principles which Mitterrand used to justify the building projects. Like Pétain, who was no doubt inspired by the numerous Socialists in his own government, Pierre Laval being only the first of them, Mitterrand believes that such projects were essential to stimulate the economy and to reduce unemployment.[3] Indeed, he was already calling in 1981 for a relaunch of the European economy through large loans to finance European *Grands Travaux*, a theme to which French Socialists were often to return,[4] and which was eventually to be adopted.

But in the Fifth Republic, the purpose of the *Grands Travaux* has been mainly to entrench and enhance the glory of the Head of State who built them. General de Gaulle himself was not identified with any prestige projects of that kind; his successor, Georges Pompidou, began to make building a political issue when he campaigned for election partly on the basis that he would realize important works, such as the financially disastrous Anglo-French Concorde aeroplane. He also set about rebuilding the plateau Beaubourg, a project which resulted in the hideous and poorly built Centre Pompidou, whose closure for prematurely needed repairs was decided in 1994. In typical secretive French fashion, the true cost of the centre was kept a state secret, until it was revealed by François Giroud, the Minister of Culture, in 1976.[5] Giscard also undertook some projects, which came to fruition only after he had left office, the most famous of these being the conversion of the Gare d'Orsay into a museum.

Therefore, the frequency of the jokes about the monarchical behaviour of Presidents should not obscure the exceptional nature of François Mitterrand's behaviour. No President has devoted so much energy and money to building, turning so much of Paris into a permanent building site that it began to resemble Bucharest under Ceauşescu: the Grande Arche de la Défense, the renovation of the Louvre and the construction of a pyramid in front of it, the rebuilding of the Tuileries Gardens, the Opéra de la Bastille, the

Finance Ministry at Bercy, as well as various regional projects. Architecture, the most political of all arts, was always close to Mitterrand's heart, and he identified it with his own grandeur. Mitterrand even hired a court flatterer-in-chief to underline his own dominant role in the cultural life of the country, Jack Lang. The veteran Culture Minister could always be relied upon to bathe his master in glory, as during the 1988 election campaign when he declared, 'I worship François Mitterrand.'[6] Indeed, Mitterrand has so identified himself with these baubles which, combining vast expense with cheap appearance, now jut flimsily into the most sensitive corners of Paris, that many of his admirers accept that this will be his most important legacy. Roland Dumas, Mitterrand's faithful ally for decades, was once asked what people will remember of the Mitterrand years. He replied, 'The *Grands Travaux*, the Louvre pyramid and the Arche de la Défense, that's probably what will remain.'[7]

Under Mitterrand's reign, indeed, the famous 'reserved presidential domain' was extended even further than under de Gaulle, to include the preservation and stimulation of the nation's culture. With grandiose declarations, he justified *himself alone* spending 20 billion French francs (£2,300 million) of public money on glorifying his own term in office,[8] never understating the contribution he was making to French culture: 'A civilization is judged by the successes of its architecture. Will we succeed in inscribing in our space and in sculpting in material our cultural project? I shall devote myself to that with all my energy.'[9] Elsewhere he said, 'the *Grands Travaux* will allow our capital city to take its rightful place again amongst the great cultural metropolises';[10] 'to give back to our city a burst, a brilliance, an international fame, by investing in its architecture'[11] – as if Paris did not already have all of these things in abundance when he was elected. Indeed, the manner in which the biggest building programme of the Fifth Republic was announced reflects the monarchical nature of the project, and the contempt Mitterrand was to show for the Socialist Party whenever it ceased to serve his needs: at no stage while campaigning for election had he ever said anything about *Grands Travaux* to the Socialist Party. It makes little difference whether this shows that he wanted the projects to be associated with his own person, and not with the party, or whether his silence was due to fear of internal opposition from the party.

Moreover, as befits the profoundly centralized way France is governed, all the main *Grands Travaux* have taken place in Paris. The Channel Tunnel is the only main exception to this, but it is clearly in a different category from the others, because it is neither cultural (there was a pretence that even the Grande Arche de la Défense was partly cultural, although it finished up as just another glorified office block), nor funded by the state. Here, too, some justifications for the *Grands Travaux* have been contradictory: 'I am profoundly in favour of decentralization. However, where culture is concerned, there is a necessary centralism, for it is only from centralized elements that a genuine decentralized diffusion can operate.'[12]

With decentralizers like this, who needs Colbert? Not surprisingly, the President's wishes overruled all other considerations. The pyramid which now defaces the central courtyard of the Louvre, for instance, was fiercely opposed by no fewer than seven national cultural groups. A new one was even set up for the purpose, the Association pour le Renouveau du Louvre, but, unperturbed, Mitterrand suspended the usual jury channels by which such projects are decided, and simply imposed his own choice without any prior public competition.[13]

There were ostensibly ideological justifications for the building projects. Jack Lang said that Socialism had generally never been in power long enough anywhere to imprint its own architectural style.[14] Mitterrand also rather quaintly suggested that the works had preserved thousands of crafts, 'which otherwise would disappear, definitively interrupting artisan traditions, knowledge, science, a *savoir-faire* which is indispensable to a country like France'[15] – but he never quite specified which crafts he had in mind.

Indeed, claptrap ideology played a major role in the most hypocritical and wasteful story of them all, that of the Opéra de la Bastille. It is no coincidence that Roland Dumas did not mention this particular project in his little list of buildings which would be remembered. Part of the reason for the débâcle is Mitterrand's own lack of interest in music, even though he initiated the project himself. The aim of the Opéra Bastille has been accurately described as 'a bad answer to a question which did not exist.'[16]

The stated aim was to create a 'modern, popular opera'.[17] It was assumed that Paris needed a second opera house, like London,

Munich, Berlin and New York; but the thinking which went into the 'popular' aspect seems to have hardly gone beyond the simple equation, 'Bastille + 14 July = popular'.[18] Mitterrand had already inherited from Giscard the plan to build a city of music at La Villette. The state had built a huge complex of abbatoirs on the outskirts of Paris, but it turned out to be far too large for the needs of the market, and so the project was a total waste of money. Mitterrand decided to transform the buildings into a science park and city of music. But this did not satisfy his desire for a cathedral of music, one which would constitute a stunning incarnation of the 'presidential idea'. It is interesting to speculate on how he reconciled this desire with the stated desire that the opera be 'popular', and that it be the symbol of a 'democratic' cultural policy, accessible to all. Not surprisingly, therefore, the execution of the plan was bedevilled by what the Germans call *Konzeptlosigkeit*: a lack of direction and coherence. Indeed, the main preoccupation which united the partisans of the Opéra Bastille was a politically inspired disdain for the 'bourgeois' nineteenth-century Opéra Garnier; and thus the development plans of the former were propelled principally by a desire to discredit the viability of the latter.

President Mitterrand's own lack of interest in music itself only encouraged such incredible and unrealistic assessments: someone claimed that there would be three times as many opera places in Paris; another that the new opera would solve all the problems faced by the Palais Garnier; a third that the price of seats would drop spectacularly. The plan's specification thus lurched around spectacularly. Whereas at first there was talk of a theatre with 5,000 seats, the acoustic requirements meant that this figure had to be halved. The former producer who became the engineer of the whole project dreamt up a theatre with three times more rehearsal space than Garnier, and wanted to fill the theatre's 160,000 square metres with machines which turned out, for the most part, to be largely useless. Others talked about a 'modulable' hall to be added to the theatre itself, the adjective being of an imprecision which characterized the whole project from the start. The final result was a 423-page dossier of technical specifications dealing with 500 different parts of the opera. Faced with such an order, the architect, the Toronto-based Uruguayan, Carlos Ott, declared that 'it is a functional project which is not necessarily aesthetic',[19] a neat way of preparing the public and the authorities for the building's eventual grey, office-like interior and its bulky, brutalist façade. It seems that Mitterrand accepted the Ott plan with some reluctance, knowing that any further tergiversations in awarding the contract would only threaten the sacrosanct deadline for opening the theatre on 14 July 1989.

The original estimate for building the Opéra de la Bastille had been 300 million francs.[20] By the time the right-wing government led by the Mayor of Paris, Jacques Chirac, came to power in 1986, the project had already cost 800 million francs. The costs were thus already double what had been predicted, and none of the warnings about overshooting costs had been heeded between 1981 and 1986. Even when Chirac became Prime Minister, his attempt to impose some form of cost control were derisory: the UDF Culture Minister, François Léotard, made the maintenance of the project a political issue in the fight between his party and the dominant RPR. The total cost was eventually to rise to 3.1 billion francs, over ten times the original estimate. Moreover, the running costs require that the same sum be spent every seven years. This is massively in excess of the money spent on the Opéra Garnier, while the Opéra Comique gets no subsidy at all. At no time was any control ever exercised over the government which had spent these enormous sums.

The original pretence that it would be a 'popular' opera, making culture more 'accessible', vanished with the whole sad farce. Far from increasing the number of opera performances in Paris by 80 per cent, the original estimate, they have in fact fallen by 50 per cent. Both opera houses, Garnier and Bastille are dark half the time. The irony is particularly cruel when one compares what happened a century previously with the Opéra Garnier. The method of its financing, apparently so bourgeois, in fact enabled far greater public access. Then, the most expensive boxes (twenty boxes, 120 seats in all, out of 2,500), rented by the year, sufficed to pay for the construction of the whole theatre. In 1875, when the Opéra was opened, the tickets for the first night were addedly expensive, which helped to give the institution a comfortable profit. In 1989, by contrast, when the Bastille was opened, only politicians and their friends were present at the ceremony, at the exclusive expense, to be sure, of their long-suffering tax-payers.[21]

Indeed what the project shows is how the autocratic way the

project was directed spawned the totally chaotic manner of its execution. Far from being the streamlined, efficient mode of operation in which the French seem so resolutely to believe, autocracy is usually the bedfellow of confusion. For instance, a conflict erupted at one point over what colour the seats should be. The argument was made all the more bitter by the pretentious, yet sincerely held, belief that in choosing the colour of the seats, the protagonists were touching at the very nerve of the project's whole philosophy. Pierre Chéreau, the influential opera-producer, wanted red, because red and green were the only colours which did not disappear entirely in the darkness. Green was out, because it signified evil in ancient Roman theatres. But Michèle Audon, a key member of the 'Group of Four' in charge of the project, refused red, because 'Red corresponds to nineteenth-century theatres; blue to eighteenth-century ones. We need another colour for our century'.[22] François Léotard, then Minister of Culture, did not give an opinion, but Jack Lang agreed that red was out. Carlos Ott, the architect, was fanatically in favour of black, while Pierre Viot was violently opposed to it: as President of the opera, he thought it was his right to decide in favour of red. There was, at the same time, an auxiliary argument over whether the outside porch should be grey or white.

The solution to such existential dilemmas could only come from on high. An audience was thus duly arranged to solicit the opinion of the President of the Republic himself. For several days, one of the larger rooms in the Elysée Palace was given over to a display for the purpose. A large metal tent covering some twenty square metres was constructed, under which there were four seats. Everything was done to make the thing as realistic as possible: one side was covered with the blue-grey colour of the walls, another with photographs of the model of the room; on a third was a representation of the curtain. The four seats were placed on wooden steps, just like in the theatre itself. Light projectors had been subtly directed towards the black chair in order to encourage the presidential choice in that direction. Meanwhile, one of the management team, Gérard Charlet had tried to influence Mitterrand in favour of the white porch, which he thought would give it a suitably Hellenistic appearance.

When the great day came, the President visited the model solemnly, accompanied by Christian Sautter, the deputy Secretary-

General of the Elysée, and several other close colleagues. Each party pleaded its cause: Michèle Audon that of daring modernity, Carlos Ott the reasons for his sombre preference. Finally, the sphinx spoke. 'It is right, black is a real colour. It shall be black.' Even then, the battle was not over, for two members of the team continued to disagree as to whether Mitterrand had meant just the seats or the porch as well. In the end, the coalition between Viot, Audon and Ott carried the day in favour of black, and they defended their success in the memoir they wrote of the affair. Charlet wrote that he remembered that, as the President left, he turned to the group and said, 'The seat covers: black, black'.[23] Nobody knows, nor is likely ever to know, the cost of this little escapade.

There is a grubby little coda to this grubby tale. A long, learned and detailed book was written about the Opéra de la Bastille by Maryvonne de Saint-Pulgent, a journalist, conservationist and academic. She dealt not only with the Bastille affair, but also with the history of building operas in France and in the world. The book is unanswerable in its breadth and depth of knowledge about the art-form itself, about the policy imperatives involved in realizing such a project, and in its trenchant and often bitterly humorous account of the whole saga. However, few French people know even the details of the story, for *Le Monde*, *Libération*, and *Le Nouvel Observateur* never even reviewed the book. This is in striking contrast to the press attention devoted to the spendthrift activities of Jacques Attali at the European Bank for Reconstruction and Development in London, and it even contrasts unfavourably with the attention paid to the Opéra de la Bastille itself by the British press. The book was not merely ignored however: its author received several anonymous phone calls trying to frighten her by saying that her two daughters had been killed in an accident and that her husband had died of a heart attack.[24]

A similar confusion of roles and muddle have reigned – and are still reigning – in the project of the French Library. Here again one encounters the same combination of megalomania and incompetence which characterized the building of the Bastille Opéra. This classic piece of Mitterrandist modernist megalo-gigantism will symbolize the triviality of the Mitterrand era almost more than any other project. The President wanted a large project for his second term of office: evidently he considered that the others had not been lavish enough. Often compared to Cardinal Mazarin, the Florentine Prime Minister of Louis XIV, who is remembered for his scheming, as well as for having founded the Institut de France, it was perhaps with Mazarin in mind that, on 14 July 1988, Mitterrand announced his intention to devote his autumnal years to 'the construction of one of the largest or the largest and the most modern library in the world'. A month later he wrote to the Prime Minister, 'A very large library, of an entirely new type, which should cover all fields of knowledge, be at the disposal of everybody, which should be able to be consulted from afar, and which should be connected to other European libraries.'[25]

Considering that university and other libraries are chronically underdeveloped in France, compared to those in Britain or the United States, the plan is rather Utopian. Perhaps unsurprisingly, it was Jacques Attali who is said to be the author of the idea: such a project would fit the man's inflated sense of his own literary abilities. Given Attali's notorious failure at the European Bank in London, it is perhaps unsurprising that the scheme quickly became unworkable, beginning with its ludicrous brief. The person appointed to head the project was a journalist at the *Quotidien de Paris*: he was cultivated enough, but proved incapable of managing such a huge undertaking. Émile Biasini, the Secretary of State for the *Grands Travaux*, himself knew nothing about libraries.

This translated into a deep confusion over the project's purpose. One of the earlier briefs stated that 'The library should be organized around four main axes of documentation: a contemporary library, a library of sight and sound, a library for study, and a library for research'.[26] But suddenly, an announcement came which countermanded even this broad concept: the new library would also replace the National Library for all works published after 1945. This idea was launched without any prior consultation with the specialists at the National Library whatever. It provoked huge opposition from them as a result, especially from a former General Administrator of the National Library. He and others were convinced, as they still are, that one cannot cut the documentary memory of a nation into two parts. A national library, they kept repeating, is unlike any other library. But the powers-that-be were not sure whether they wanted a truly national library or a kind of

Disneyland for books. Worse, while the President was convinced that he was designing something entirely new (always guaranteed to titillate his modernist tendencies), he was in fact merely trying to combine two banal things which were in fact mutually incompatible.

The mix of the concept of a new central library for France with a kind of super-Pompidou Centre was to prove a major obstacle to the proper realization of the project. Protests were met with cheap political insults thrown at university researchers, who were portrayed by their opponents in government as being an élitist class concerned only with the protection of their 'privileges' – an interesting accusation coming from them! All this was decided without any thought being given to the difficulties of moving the books – specialists estimated that that would take four years – nor even to the cost of running the new library itself.

As if all this were not enough, the architectural plan for the library, for which the President was well known to have a special fondness, is supremely impractical. It comprises four L-shaped towers surrounding a central open space. The towers, it is said, were supposed to symbolize open books (standing upright). Mitterrand, no doubt recalling his own Jesuit upbringing, had been especially keen on the green space in the middle, describing it as a 'cloister', as if the purpose of visiting the library were to go for a walk in the garden. But the *coup de grâce* is that, however romantic that may sound, the books are supposed to be stored in the glass towers, while the reading rooms are supposed to be underground. Because the President was known to have taken the project to heart, architects and academics who made even technical criticisms about the project's evident impracticability[27] were treated with hostility by those who saw in them mere political attacks in disguise. Even those who pointed out that the library could be full within thirty or forty years were initially dismissed out of hand. It is an interesting reflection of the way that Mitterrand has encouraged a widespread sense of irresponsibility – because he himself never accepts the consequences of the policies which he pretends to support – that, without any convictions of his own, and interested only in glitzy appearance, he seems to have said, 'Build a library! It matters little whether one can put books in it or not.' The project, nonetheless, continues.

Perhaps the most intriguing aspect is this. In his determination
to transform Paris into a museum, Mitterrand has built perfect, but
unflattering, symbols of his own reign. All the buildings are made
of glass, and they play tricks with the light, refracting, changing
colour, glinting kitschily. Like that of their maker, their appeal is
thus ephemeral, intangible, rather simple, and deceptive. But these
vast trinkets symbolize Mitterrandism in a more sinister way too.
The most prominent are the Grande Arche de la Défense and the
Louvre pyramid, lying as they do along the central axis of Paris
which runs from the Louvre, through Place de la Concorde, up the
Champs-Élysées to the Arc de Triomphe, and now beyond. The
obelisk on the Place de la Concorde symbolizes the sun at noon:
one marches towards it under the Arc de Triomphe on ceremonial
occasions. But one reaches the Grande Arche by turning one's back
on it and walking towards the West and the setting sun. Mitterrand
has built in the Grande Arche nothing other than a symbol of the
decline and twilight years of France over which he has presided;
while the famous pyramid, is, of course, a tomb.

10. Not the Three Musketeers

When it tries to become systematic, conservative thought changes its nature: it becomes reactionary. On the contrary, the role of conservatism is to reconcile and to complement another kind of thinking. As a result, the modern Right, which insists on seeing in conservatism an extremist doctrine, turns away from it and devotes its energies to trying to wrest a reformist image from the Left. This prevents it from ever acquiring its own true identity. By rejecting its conservative heritage, the democratic Right has been reduced for more than a century to simply adopting an attitude of moderation in order to justify its existence and to maintain a certain kind of unity. This moderation can often appear simply opportunist.[1]

One of the most striking differences between French and British politics is the absence in France of a strong conservative party or tradition. It is partly for this reason that Mitterrand was able to achieve his own undoubted personal victory over the right wing. Indeed, it is remarkable that, although at the end of his second term, the Gaullist RPR party was without doubt the most powerful party in France, its pre-eminence had been bought at a very high price: the sacrifice of all the policies and character which marked it out as distinctively Gaullist. Now it is almost totally devoid of any political substance whatever.

Within a year of its election, and despite one of the largest parliamentary majorities ever recorded in French history, the government of Édouard Balladur showed itself incapable of implementing a single policy of which the previous Socialist government and the incumbent President did not approve. Nor was this simply because of the constraints of the cohabitation, or of the desire to do nothing too daring before the presidential election in 1995. The decision to revise the *Loi Falloux*, which limits the level of local authorities' grants to private schools, was abandoned after street demonstrations and a ruling from the Constitutional Court; the initial plan to restructure Air France was similarly abandoned after strikes and other protests; and the attempt to reduce the minimum wage for young people, a measure which might have reduced France's chronically high youth unemployment rate of some 25 per cent, was abandoned – again – after street demonstrations. It was even more extraordinary that, although the violence and the looting were organized by SOS Racisme, a left-wing front organization set up by Mitterrand, the Balladur government made no attempt to call the students' bluff by asking whether they were really the representatives of 'French youth' as they claimed, or merely a sectarian political force, nor indeed did it even to try to explain that over the last twenty years, the minimum wage has proved especially cruel for the young and unskilled, for every time it has been raised, youth unemployment has risen with it. All these climb-downs seemed only to confirm the impression that the new rulers themselves hardly believed in what they were doing.

It is hardly surprising that two out of three French voters now consider that the dichotomy between Right and Left has become irrelevant.[2] Moreover, while failing to pursue any particular policies whatever, the right-wing parties under Balladur soon became embroiled in their favourite pastime: fighting amongst themselves. It is small wonder that the French Right is often called 'the stupidest Right in the world', for the struggle for ascendancy in the opinion polls which soon broke out between Édouard Balladur and Jacques Chirac; the tergiversations of Charles Pasqua over whether to switch loyalty to the one or the other; the associated posturings of Philippe Séguin; and the parallel rivalry between Valéry Giscard d'Estaing's rainbow coalition, the UDF, and his Gaullist partners, all meant that the new right-wing leaders were pursuing the policies of the Left while concentrating on destroying each other.

The fundamental problem is that it is almost impossible to have a conservative party in a revolutionary country like France. Most French right-wing parties are not conservative at all, a fact which distinguishes France's political structures fundamentally from those of Britain and the United States, and to a lesser extent from Germany, where there is a solid body of right-wing philosophy supported by strong right-wing parties. In France, there is not one Right, but many, and it has become customary not to speak of '*la Droite*' but of '*les Droites*'.[3] This is because the French Revolution splintered the conservative movements into different mutually hostile factions and engendered important political movements of the Right, such as Gaullism, which do not necessarily think of themselves as right-wing at all. Indeed, it is partly a result of the French Revolution that the label 'conservative' is nearly always derogatory: no politician will proclaim himself '*conservateur*', because the word really only means 'reactionary'. One historian of political ideas has even coined the term 'sinistrism' to denote the historical phenomenon of right-wing parties refusing to sit on the right-hand side of the National Assembly, in order not to associate themselves with the 'Right'.[4] In 1958, the deputies of the Gaullist UNR group (Union pour la Nouvelle République) contrived to sit on the right, the left and the centre of the National Assembly; while right-wing parties of the Third Republic often had left-wing sounding names like 'Republican Left', 'Radical Left' or 'Democratic Left'. In general, they were none of these things.[5] The party of the authoritarian Colonel de la Roque, the 'Croix de Feu' (the Cross of Fire), for instance, was renamed the 'French Social Party'. This tendency continues today: the centrist party which governs in coalition with Balladur's Gaullists calls itself the Centre of Social Democrats, even though they identify most closely with the German Christian Democrats.

There are two reasons for this odd relationship to conservatism. First, it is nearly impossible in a revolutionary country to try to 'conserve' traditional political institutions which have been destroyed. France inevitably cannot have the same tradition of vesting authority in institutions as Britain. It is in keeping with France's revolutionary traditions that the (essentially English) notion of a process of slow, organic change, intended to preserve the established order, is a concept almost totally absent from French political thinking. Moreover, the French Revolution introduced a sharpness and an extremism into French politics which flowed precisely from the fact that whole swathes of the population did not even agree on the rules of the political game.

Second, the French Right has seldom developed along the same liberal lines as the British or American traditions. Whereas the French Enlightenment led to the overweening rationalism of Voltaire and Rousseau, carrying much 'conservative' thought along with it, the British (especially Scottish) Enlightenment was predi-

cated on philosophical empiricism. British Enlightenment philosophers denied the ability to predict what the world would be like in
advance of experience, and came to appropriately modest and
prudent conclusions about how the world *might* work on the basis
of available evidence. The father of British conservatism, Edmund
Burke, explicitly rejected the mentality of 'economists and calcu-
lators' in political life who thought that society could be omnis-
ciently and scientifically directed. He tried instead to replace that
mentality with a more humane, if partly mysterious, form of
reflection on the great political issues of the day. As a result, rather
than attacking left-wing dogma as intellectually fraudulent, and
instead of showing that society was not like a machine in the hands
of political engineers, the Right in France has often been merely
trying to catch up with the Left, a futile task, since it shares so
many of its rationalist assumptions. The eighteenth-century
counter-revolutionary philosopher, Joseph de Maistre, had an accurate slogan, 'Counter-revolution is not a contrary revolution but
the contrary of a revolution'; but it was a sentiment which the
Right have generally ignored, as it has often, like the Left, tried to
invent and impose a political order through overweening construc-
tivist state action, an attitude which in Britain is usually thought of
as left-wing. Indeed, the leading philosopher of modern liberal
conservatism, Friedrich von Hayek, saw France as the very incuba-
tor of that statist, bureaucratic, planning mentality which he identified as the essence of Socialism.[6]

Nor has economic liberalism ever been very dear to the French
heart, even though France has her fair share of good liberal
thinkers, such as Jean-Baptiste Say, Frédéric Bastiat and Turgot.
France has always been primarily an agricultural country, whose
great riches came overwhelmingly from the soil; she does not have
the same accumulated experience of several centuries of trade as
Britain. She is therefore traditionally less inclined to grasp the
power of commerce to generate wealth. The early roots of French
liberal economic thinking illustrate the problem: in the eighteenth-
century, a group of *laissez-faire* economists, the Physiocrats, opposed
the centralized, dirigiste, mercantilist policies inherited from Colbert
and Louis XIV, according to which the state oversaw agricultural
production and dedicated itself to increasing exports; yet even they
remained convinced that only agriculture created wealth, while

commerce was essentially parasitic on that activity. It is not difficult to see clear traces of this belief in present-day French attitudes to the GATT talks and the Common Agricultural Policy.

It may be because the French Right carries much ideological baggage from the French Revolution that one remarkable peculiarity in French politics is that throughout history a number of political causes have been espoused by both Right and Left: the 'nation' was originally a Revolutionary doctrine, while the nineteenth-century liberals, the predecessors of today's free-marketeers, used to be on the Left. The Mitterrand years even saw the revival under the aegis of the glitzy Minister for Humanitarian Affairs, of the notion of *le droit d'ingérence*, the right to intervene in the internal affairs of other countries for their own good, an idea which seems little different from the well-meaning British imperialism of the nineteenth century.[7] This confusion between Left and Right is only one phenomenon of the Right's lack of a solid identity.

The divisions of the French Right began as early as the date of the invention of the labels 'Right' and 'Left' themselves. These originate, as with so much in French history, in 1789, when the National Assembly debated the question as to whether the king could have a right of veto over legislation. Those deputies who were in favour of such a veto grouped themselves on the right, while those groups opposed to it sat on the left. But some members of the Right, the 'absolutists' or 'legitimists', rejected any subordination of royal power to that of the Assembly, and denied the Revolution any legitimacy whatever. Indeed, they believed it to be 'an appeal to all passions and all errors ... evil raised to the highest power'.[8] Those orators who supported the King's initial refusal to have any truck with such ideas, and who remained active in the constituent Assembly until its dissolution in 1791 when the new constitution was finally accepted by Louis XVI, were to evolve into the extreme right, a movement which remained a potent factor in French politics until well into the twentieth century.

Meanwhile, there were also those on the Right who were in favour of the royal veto. These were the liberal conservatives who subscribed to what they thought were the aims of the Revolution. One of their number, Mounier, had even written the first three articles of the *Déclarations des Droits de l'Homme et du Citoyen* of 1789.

Their aim was precisely to destroy the absolute power of the king, which made them the enemies of the royalists. Indeed, some of the latter were surprisingly in favour of a wider electoral base than the liberal-constitutionalists, because they saw in universal suffrage a way of stemming or overcoming the rising hegemony of the bourgeoisie, and preserving that of the monarchy. As a result, the legitimists even implicitly took on board the Revolutionary Rousseauist doctrine of the general will, which they thought only the king could embody. (Indeed, Rousseau himself may have been partly inspired by royal absolutism.) Nonetheless, the liberal Right was soon to abandon its initial support for the Revolution, especially after the humiliation of October 1789 when the King and Queen were forced to walk from Versailles to Paris, jeered by the populace, and obliged to live in the capital city.

The two Rights soon identified with different regimes: the absolutist, legitimist royalists with Charles X, and the constitutionalist-liberals with the July monarchy of Louis Philippe. The latter thus became known as Orléanist. Being mainly bourgeois, they tended to oppose universal suffrage, considering that the right to vote should be limited to the property-owning classes. Similarly, as Socialism became a rising force in the July monarchy, the liberals remained hostile to social reform, while the legitimists, whose incomes came mainly from their landholdings in the countryside, were able to manifest a more disinterested support for the demands of the urban working classes.

At the same time, a third Right was emerging, grouped around the memories of the Empire under Napoleon. This means that the three right-wing families which we know today had already constituted themselves by 1815.[9] After the Restoration, there was a large number of former soldiers, retired officers and other nostalgics for the Napoleonic era, who represented more a current of opinion than an actual political party. They were able to make people forget the Terror, the military defeats and Napoleon's tyranny. The Emperor became for them the 'little corporal' who had dared to stand up to the Great Powers, and who protected the peasants and other humble orders from the nobility. In novels by Balzac and Stendhal, in pamphlets, songs and poetry, a large and subtle work of rehabilitation of Napoleon took place. The revolution of 1848, which brought Napoleon's nephew Louis-Napoleon Bonaparte to power, crystallized these feelings into a real political force. Although initially supported by both the legitimists and the Orléanists (they thought they could control him), he trounced them both with a *coup d'état* by introducing universal suffrage at a stroke, and thereby profiting from the support on the Left of those who were disappointed with the bourgeois republic, in order to consolidate his power. Louis-Napoleon's actions and subsequent policies gave rise to a peculiarly French political doctrine: a combination of a strong state, with power in the hands of one man, often in a very personalized or even dictatorial way, but laced with a heavy dose of social policy, itself inherited from the Revolution. Popular sovereignty was welcomed, and the plebiscite became the instrument by which the President-prince-emperor legitimized his power. At different times in history, this Bonapartist Right has been with the Catholics or against them; with the workers, or against them; favourable or hostile to the rights of parliament; liberal or protectionist. But it has always dreamt of grand designs in foreign affairs, making itself into the champion of the nationalist Right. Indeed, in trying to reconcile authority and equality – two values very dear to the French heart – it sometimes seems that Bonapartism, of which Gaullism is usually thought to be the contemporary form, is the natural regime for the national passion for small properties as the economic and social ideal, defended by a strong central power which forbids the return to the privileges of the *Ancien Régime*. Political equality or pseudo-equality is recognized in the principle of universal suffrage, capped, above all, by a master who neutralizes divisions and revolutions.[10]

This crossover between Left and Right, and the divisions within the Right, continued with the rise of the authoritarian General Boulanger in the 1880s, who conspired to overthrow the republic by force. His movement gave rise to a current of right-wing politics which supported violence. Here, more than anywhere else, one sees how much some on the Right assimilated the Revolutionary traditions against which they ought to have been fighting. This subversive Right itself had two currents, the first being more a nebulous body of opinion, inspired by the writings of the Romantic nationalist Maurice Barrès and the anti-Semitic Édouard Drumont, who published *La France juive* in 1885. It became a sort of national-populist movement, but was never able to coalesce into a genuine political party. In time, though, that current of thought was to find its most ardent manifestation in the fascist leader, Jacques Doriot. A former Communist, Doriot dreamed one day of becoming the *Führer* of France.

The second current gave rise to one of the most brilliantly organized and powerful political organizations in twentieth-century French politics, the Action Française set up by Charles Maurras at the turn of the century. Maurras' success was partly due to the monarchist and nationalist resentment at the Dreyfus affair. He believed that French nationalism could never achieve fulfilment unless there were a restoration of the monarchy, although when Pétain came to power, Maurras famously declared it a 'divine surprise'. Like Pétain, Maurras held that France had been sabotaged by four enemies: individualist Protestants; anarchic liberals from Northern Europe and from Switzerland; the Jews, who defended their right to be different from everyone else while at the same time being destructively jealous of the strong national cohesion of others; and the anti-Catholic and pro-Enlightenment Freemasons. Much of the rampant suspicion and resentment of liberalism and internationalism which Maurras propagated is still very evident on both Left and Right in present-day France: the wild reaction against the signing of the GATT accord in December 1993, and the lurid denunciations of the 'speculators' against the franc on the foreign-exchange markets, are not much different from the kinds of sentiments the extreme right had been expressing fifty years previously.[11]

Indeed, in the protest movements of this extraordinary period, Left and Right cease to have much meaning. Drawing on the old French fascist and monarchist slogan, 'Neither Left nor Right', Maurras' criticism of liberalism and individualism led him to take positions similar to that of the Socialists. Even before 1914, the Action Française, which never hid its reactionary views, had been extremely interested in questions of social reform and in the possibility of attracting a working-class public. It vigorously wooed with posters, with meetings and with tracts, and Maurras declared, 'We are nationalistic and consequently social'.[12] Nor is the parallel with later left-wing movements fortuitous: as the proto-fascist Thierry Maulnier made quite clear, the enemy for him was democracy and capitalism, in other words the very bourgeois order which the moderate and traditional rights were determined to preserve.[13] Indeed, no other Communist Party in the world lost so many members to fascist groups as the Politburo of the French Communist Party.[14] In keeping with its revolutionary approach, the power of the Action Française reached its high point in the anti-parliamentary riots of 6 February 1934, when co-ordianted right-wing extremists very nearly succeeded in bringing about the violent death of the republic. The author has even met an elderly gentleman on the Place de la Concorde, on the occasion of the bicentenary of the execution of Louis XVI, who had taken part in those riots, and who was telling anyone who cared to listen about his involvement, with all the eagerness with which fifty years later his grandchildren's Communist-inspired generation was to boast of their participation in the 'events' of May 1968.

Vichy was to prove the apotheosis of this peculiarly French mixture of Left and Right.[15] Few ostensibly right-wing movements can have embraced nationalist and Socialist ideas as clearly as Marshal Pétain's government, except perhaps the Nazis themselves. Composed largely of Socialists, Vichy ignored De Maistre and prosecuted the doctrine of the 'National Revolution'. Indeed, it is a misleading myth to call sympathy for Pétain 'right-wing', and one which is propagated by those who wish to hide the fact that Vichy France, Nazi Germany and fascist Italy, were all overwhelmingly Socialist in their organization. *The Corporatist State* was, after all, the title of a book by Mussolini. Supporters of Vichy included Socialists like Pierre Laval, fascists like Jacques Doriot, radical Socialists like Marcel Déat, and technocrats like Alphonse de Châteaubriand.

But Vichy was also to prove the nadir of the traditionalist Right, for few spectacles can be more grotesquely self-contradictory than that of a nationalist, traditionalist leader like the Marshal-peasant Philippe Pétain pretending to defend France's honour and values, while in fact collaborating with the very victorious power which incarnated the nation's total humiliation. Nor was this collaboration with the enemy fortuitous: the extreme right hated their own (Revolutionary) country so much that they thought the invading Germans preferable to the left-wing Popular Front, 'the enemy within'. The legacy of the association of the Right with national defeat would have been insurmountable had it not been for de Gaulle.

It is ironic that 1940 should have reopened and entrenched the rupture between the traditionalist Right of the lugubrious 'National Revolution', and the vigorous and daring action of de Gaulle, because the latter clearly betrayed his strongly Maurrassian monarchical beliefs in his own political behaviour,[16] even if his nationalism differed from the more sectarian nationalism of Maurras, for whom true French history stopped after the Revolution. For the General, there was only one France.[17] Pétainism and Gaullism were also similar in that they were both based on a personality cult. This reflects the strongly personal nature behind a country better known for its love of ideology than men, but it also underlines how the Right has often sought to escape from its defensive position of intellectual incoherence by placing its faith in a providential man. Indeed, it is one of the most striking symptoms of the archaism of French politics that it should be the only country in Europe where a major political party, the Gaullist movement, is expressly founded to support the legacy of one man. To this day, the trappings of the General himself – the *'appel'* of 18 June 1940, the Cross of Lorraine, the Companions of the Liberation, the march down the Champs-Élysées in liberated Paris, Mount Valerien, Colombey-les-deux-églises – excite more admiration than any ideology. The speeches and broadcasts, the General's *Mémoires de guerre* and the *Mémoires d'espoir* are sacred texts, but de Gaulle's own definition of Gaullism, which he finally gave on 9 September 1968, is pretty vague: 'an enterprise of national renovation whose *raison d'être*, whose law and whose motive force is to serve France ... It is the contemporary form of the *élan* of our country ... towards a level of brilliance of power and of influence which correspond to our humane vocation amongst Humanity'.[18] Gaullism is a nationalism inspired by sentiment as much as by reason, cleansed of anything which might damage the rallying-around of the French on to France, something which is always necessary, and which always needs to be renewed in order to overcome the political divisions which have so often erupted into civil war in the past.

It is because of this rather nebulous attachment to ideology that there are some who reject the label 'right-wing' for Gaullism, notably Gaullists themselves. The General himself always insisted that his role as President was to remain above the party fray: when he was forced into a second round of voting for the presidential election in 1965 by François Mitterrand, the General was asked, 'How do you conceive the notions Left and Right?' He replied,

> France is everything at once, she is all the French. The Left is not France, the Right is not France. To presume that one can govern France with a faction is a grave error, and to presume to represent France in the name of a faction is an unforgivable national error. You will say to me: on the Right, people say that my politics are those of the Left; on the Left, as you well know, they say, 'De Gaulle is there for the Right, for monopolies, for I don't know what else.' The fact that the partisans of the Left and the Right declare that I belong to the other side proves precisely what I have said to you – that now, as always, I am not on one side, I am not on the other, I am for France.[19]

There were indeed several policy areas in which de Gaulle pursued policies which were welcomed by politicians on the Left and attacked by the Right. His policy of decolonization was agreeable to the Left, and detested by the Right, especially the extreme right; his dirigiste modernization of the French economy was also generally popular on the Left, as was the emphasis he laid on social policy, even though both were underpinned by the eminently conservative monetary policies of his great Finance Minister, Jacques Ruëff. He governed with the support of three million voters whom he had seduced from the Left, just as in his governments-in-exile both in London and in Algiers, he was often surrounded by men of the Left as much as of the Right; in his government immediately after the end of the war, the Communists were well represented. Indeed, his 1944 provisional government included the icon of the Left, Pierre Mendès-France, while André Malraux, his high-profile Culture Minister, was a former Communist. And yet at the same time, there is no doubt that he took from the Right his desire to ensure the grandeur and independence of the nation and his affirmation of the authority of the state.[20]

But a large part of Gaullism is simply style. Few people who listen to a de Gaulle press conference or broadcast from the 1960s can fail to be charmed by his determination and wit, in what can only be described as his literary or aesthetic approach to politics,

which one arch-Gaullist writer has called 'The Musketeer Right'.[21]
Who else but de Gaulle could have written the following passage?

> Faced with an event, it is to himself that the man of character
> turns ... He embraces action with the pride of the master,
> immersing himself in the action, for it is his ... A fighter who
> finds his ardour and his fulcrum within himself, a player who
> seeks gain less than success, and who pays his debts out of his
> own pocket, the man of character confers his own nobility on
> his action.[22]

It is clearly difficult for such a movement to continue after the
death of the man from whose personality it is inseparable.

The technocratic drift which has occurred to the Gaullist party
since his death was, then, inevitable. The party ceased to be the
mere emanation of the General's own political personality, and it
grew to be more like any other political party. Indeed, the whole
idea that there might be a political *party* – the very kind of
organization which de Gaulle hated the most – in the absence of a
charismatic leader, seems contradictory to the spirit of Gaullism.
After the death of Pompidou in 1974 – the General's former Prime
Minister and *directeur de cabinet*, and his nominated successor – the
Gaullists' fortunes began to wane. Valéry Giscard d'Estaing, a non-
Gaullist liberal, won the presidential election by just over 1 per cent
because Jacques Chirac withdrew his support from the Gaullist
candidate, Jacques Chaban-Delmas, and declared that he would
support Giscard. This enabled Giscard to win the presidency,
having received 11 per cent fewer votes in the first round than his
main rival, François Mitterrand, and Chirac was rewarded for his
support when Giscard appointed him Prime Minister.

There were fears at the time that this would lead to a 'Giscardiza-
tion' of the Gaullist party, and that they would be contaminated
with timid centrism by their close association with Giscard. Chirac
tried to avoid this by becoming leader of the Gaullist movement in
1974, and by finally breaking off relations with Giscard d'Estaing
by resigning in 1976 and re-founding the Gaullist movement,
dissolving the UDR (Union des démocrates pour la République)
and renaming it the RPR (Rassemblement pour la République). At
the same time, Giscard founded the Union pour la Démocratie
Française, a heteroclite coalition of political parties ranging from

the centrist Christian Democrats to Thatcherite free-marketeers –
neither persuasion having especially deep roots in French political
life – whose only point of agreement is the rather shaky one that
they are led by Giscard. This personal feud between the two men,
and between two very different right-wing traditions which they
incarnate, was to dominate and distort French right-wing politics
for the next twenty years.

Indeed, it is not impossible that Mitterrand gained his narrow
victory because of the votes of some disaffected Gaullists. Thus
began the Right's long period of opposition under a Socialist
President. During this time, Chirac's RPR has abandoned any
pretence that it can rally people on all sides of the political spectrum,
and now limits its ambitions to the right wing, declaring itself to be
the main and most resolute adversary of the Socialist-Communist
coalition with which Mitterrand has governed during the 1980s and
1990s – even if, as if to underline his own ideological promiscuity,
Chirac called in 1981 for the creation of a French version of the
British Labour Party!

During this period in opposition, he has led Gaullism away from
its original ideological roots, however difficult these may have been
to categorize in the first place. This is visible both in his party's
domestic and foreign-policy options. During the cohabitation government of 1986–8, when he was Prime Minister, he made the
economic policies of the RPR far more liberal and free-market than
they had been previously, so much so that the government undertook a privatization programme which was explicitly modelled on
the policies of the Thatcher government in Britain and on Reagan's
policies in the United States. The main architect of these policies
was the then Finance Minister, Édouard Balladur, and they were
supported by the Giscardian liberals, to whom Balladur often seems
closer than to the Gaullists: economic liberalism and privatization
had never been Gaullist dogmas beforehand; imitating Britain or
America, even less so.

That Chirac government lasted only two years, perverted as it
was by Chirac's main preoccupation, which was not to govern, but
to be elected President. For his part, Mitterrand managed, with
great political skill, to transform the Socialist Party's defeat in 1986
into his own victory, and into his own (and his party's) re-election
two years later. He achieved this political sleight of hand by a series

of traps laid at the door of the Chirac government, and was thus able to portray himself as a kind of counterweight to that government, preserving France's so-called 'social achievements' (which included record unemployment) against the government's so-called 'excesses'. Indeed, it was almost as if Mitterrand were according himself the royal veto which the constitution of 1791 had accorded to Louis XVI. Given that the notion of a President wrong-footing the government is clearly contrary to the logic of the constitution of the Gaullist Fifth Republic, which is based on the assumption of consistency within the executive, it is revealing that it was a supposed 'Gaullist', Édouard Balladur, who was the first to suggest the possibility of such a cohabitation between Left and Right in 1983.

During the electoral campaign in 1988, moreover, Mitterrand was able adroitly to trip Chirac up in several ways. Chirac was himself in an impossible position: he was standing for election for the post of President, while his prime ministership had been partly based on contesting the legitimacy of the President's right to rule against the wishes of the government. Just as it was an irony that Mitterrand portrayed himself as acting with exaggerated respect for the institutions, whose greatest critic had always been himself, it was also ironic that Chirac was portraying himself as the defender of the primacy of parliament and the government, in apparent contradiction to the spirit of the Gaullist republic which defended the primacy of the presidency. Thus Mitterrand was able to snatch from Chirac the Gaullist role of *rassembleur*, the one who unites the French. His election slogan was '*la France unie*', and, although obviously the leader of the Left, he was able to use the cohabitation period to revive the myth of the President who is above the political fray. In contrast to himself, he was able to make Chirac appear little more than a factional and sectarian upstart. From his Olympian heights, Mitterrand was able to dismiss Chirac – the deputy for Corrèze, the Mayor of Paris, the President of the RPR, and the Prime Minister who wanted to be President – simply as 'the man who wants everything'. It was a put-down whose supreme hypocrisy was equalled only by its stunningly successful effect.

Following this defeat, Chirac decided that he had to adopt and cultivate a more 'centrist' 'image'. Thus the decisive perversion of the original Gaullist message set in, induced by Mitterrand. While the General had denied that France could be governed by a faction, this clearly did not mean that she should be governed by a man with no identifiable political principles at all: rather the contrary. Yet Chirac, his lifetime spent in politics, could only think in terms of polls, not principles. Studying the electoral map, he concluded that he needed to attract wavering centrist voters to win. This decision had three results which were to prove decisive for French right-wing politics: it made the Gaullists indistinguishable from any other normal right-wing party; it played into the political hands of Giscard and his centrists and liberals, who, incarnating the 'centre', insisted on the adoption by the Gaullists of their policies; and it permitted the rise of the National Front.

This last phenomenon is probably the aspect of French politics which has attracted the greatest attention in recent years. France has a rich seam of extreme right-wing political action running through her history; indeed, Jean-Marie Le Pen himself is an old hand in French politics, having been a deputy under the Fourth Republic in the important extreme right-wing party led by Pierre Poujade, the Union de Défense des Commerçants et Artisans (UCDA). Le Pen even stood for the presidency in 1974, although he got only 0.74 per cent of the vote. But the definitive rise of the National Front into politics can be dated fairly precisely as 11 September 1983. Then, as the result of an alliance between the UDF-RPR and the National Front, a local councillor, Jean-Pierre Stirbois, was elected to the town council at Dreux, a town west of Paris. The following year, the National Front received 11.2 per cent of the vote in the European elections. In 1993, the Front may have lost its last parliamentary seat (it had been held by Stirbois' widow), but the party's showing in the legislative elections was stupendous: in the first round of voting, it won 3 million votes, compared to the RPR's 5 million. This meant that it was the fourth-strongest party in France, not far behind Giscard's UDF and the Socialists. Even without a parliamentary seat (because of the voting system), the Front is well represented at local level, with 3 councillors-general, 33 mayors, 239 regional councillors, 1,666 municipal councillors and 10 MEPs. Indeed, Le Pen is the leader of the Groupe des Droites Européennes in the European parliament. There are thousands of members, millions of FN voters, and the ideas of the

National Front are accepted by one voter in three: in an opinion poll in 1990, 32 per cent of those asked said that they were 'completely in agreement' or 'basically in agreement' with the ideas advanced by Le Pen.[23]

It is important to grasp that the party's rise would not have been possible without the encouragement of François Mitterrand. Just as Mitterrand's own political language is laced with references to the need for unity in France – under the umbrella of his own leadership, of course – he has devoted enormous energy to making sure that his enemies on the Right are constantly divided, a strategy which operates on fertile ground in France. His pincer movement on the Right included forcing it to move closer to the centre ground of politics which the Socialists dominated, and at the same time allowing the National Front to fill the void on the hard right.

He did this in various ways. The first was to intervene directly in the programming policy of France's television stations in order to insist that the National Front be given sufficient airtime to express its views.[24] The second was to introduce proportional representation for the legislative elections in 1986. The aim was to jig around with the voting system in order that the Right would have to seek an alliance with the National Front in order to be able to govern. He thought that this would put the Right in an impossible dilemma, between entering into an alliance with the National Front or languishing in political impotence. Playing with the race card in this way soon grew to a full-scale presidential strategy. It was outlined in Mitterrand's first term as a means of boosting the support and apparent legitimacy of the Socialist Party. During a meeting in February 1984, Laurent Fabius is reported as proposing a clear plan to reinforce Le Pen. 'We must change the electoral law before the end of April,' he said. 'The ideal result would be that the Right would not have a majority without Le Pen. We must create a vast extreme right-wing movement going from Pasqua to Le Pen.'[25] According to Jacques Attali's version of events, Mitterrand does not agree with the plan. However, it is clear that the idea was explicitly there in the heads of the President's immediate entourage. By 1985, Mitterrand was declaring that the fight against the National Front would be the main theme of the forthcoming elections.[26]

The extraordinary Carpentras affair illustrates this mentality at work. In May 1990, in the middle of the eruption of the Urba scandal, a Jewish cemetery was vandalized in the southern French town of Carpentras: a body was disinterred and impaled with an umbrella. Certainly it was a gruesome business, but the government's reaction was almost so cynical as to beggar belief. Without the merest hint of proof as to who the guilty were, the Socialist government immediately designated the National Front, the 'rise in racism', by implication the Right in general, as 'morally responsible' for the outrage, in virtue of their having made xenophobia banal. A march against racism was organized, with President Mitterrand at its head. Three years later, nobody has been charged with the violation of the cemetery – indication, if any were needed, that the culpability of any particular political party is far from proven. Was the whole thing set up by the government to distract attention from its own embarrassment over the unfolding corruption allegations?[27]

A similar and complementary strategy was the creation of the group, SOS Racisme, a left-wing front organization ostensibly devoted to 'the fight against racism'. As Attali once again makes clear, the group was created by the Elysée Palace. Far from being a genuine political movement, it had no autonomous existence of its own, and everything was organized by the President's men.[28] Whatever the obvious merits of such campaigns against racism, legislation and an independent body might have been thought a more effective and legitimate way of ensuring true justice. It should be added that France has a long tradition of assimilating immigrants into French culture, and that many on both Left and Right are very attached to what they call the 'republican' model, which is very close to the American model of cultural integration, the 'melting-pot'. However, the charismatic leader of the group, Harlem Désir, set about systematically trying to show that the racist threat came from the Right. Mitterrand himself used to say in private that the extreme right was within the RPR and the UDF.[29] The conclusion was unsurprisingly reached that only the Socialists can hold this threat at bay.

Unfortunately, the Socialist encouragement of Le Pen was only too successful, for it built upon a genuine electoral support which was itself encouraged by the duplicity and spinelessness of the main right-wing parties. If the Gaullists and the UDF resisted falling into the first trap, even though the electoral reform in 1986 meant that there were thirty-five National Front deputies, and that the centre-right had to govern with a very slender majority, and even though both parties undoubtedly contain people who are close to the Front, both formations seemed to abandon those solid right-wing policies which are proper to any democratic right-wing movement – such as the defence of the nation at home and abroad, and the maintenance of law and order – in favour of an emollient centrist discourse. This only exacerbated the original problem of allowing the National Front a *de facto* monopoly to speak on and to exploit certain policy issues.

Having lost in 1988, therefore, and having decided to 'recentre' his image, Chirac adopted a strategy which placed him in a position of supplicant for the support of the UDF, led by Giscard. He knew that he could not win the presidential election in 1995 without their support. This led to the decisive abandonment of classical Gaullism in September 1992, when Jacques Chirac and the other leading Gaullists joined ranks with the Socialists and the Giscardian liberals in supporting the campaign in favour of a 'yes' vote to the Maastricht treaty on European Union. They tried in vain to pretend that de Gaulle himself might have been pro-Maastricht, but their attempts to cover up the extent to which they had drifted from their original policies were in vain.

Everybody knew that de Gaulle had been famous for his defence of national sovereignty within Europe, best symbolized by his insistence on a national veto within the Council of Ministers. He had practised the famous 'empty-chair policy' for eight months in 1964–5, which ended in the so-called 'Luxembourg compromise' in 1965, a declaration which entrenched the right of individual countries to protect their vital national interests. However, the clearest difference between Chirac and true Gaullism lay in the fact that Chirac's decision to support Maastricht was nothing but a party-political calculation, inspired by the perceived paramount need to retain the fragile union between the RPR and the UDF. Far from speaking straight to the French people and incarnating their national sovereignty by direct means, the RPR had become just another political party, willing to do backroom deals with other parties simply in order to gain power.

To add injury to insult, Chirac's calculation backfired in political terms. Not politically courageous enough to embrace what he thought initially to be a lost cause, he failed to capitalize on the surprisingly high 'no' vote: despite huge pressure from the whole political class, over 49 per cent of the electorate voted 'no'. He put himself in the ludicrous position of leading a party which had no clear policy on Maastricht: the RPR's posters encouraged its supporters to vote either 'yes' or 'no' according to their own opinions! But had Chirac decided to lead the anti-Maastricht troops into battle, the 'no' cause would have lost its stigma of marginalization, and would probably have been victorious. Since François Mitterrand had staked his personal political credibility on the victory of the 'yes', it is likely that, under such conditions, he would have resigned, and Jacques Chirac would now be in the Elysée Palace.

After the elections in March 1993, the RPR became the most important political force in French politics. All the decisive personal rivalries were taking place within that party, even if political debate was not. Its coalition partner, the UDF, continues to exert influence, but has no role as an alternative to the Socialists because it explicitly agrees with the Socialists on the whole gamut of policies, both internal and external, and makes little pretence to the contrary. Yet the apparent supremacy of the Gaullist party has also occurred only after the systematic sacrifice of every single policy and character trait which made Gaullism a separate and recognizable force. The new Prime Minister, Édouard Balladur, whose imprimatur on the party is overwhelming, is hardly a Gaullist at all, and his government is full of centrist ministers, even though the centrists' share of the vote is a mere 6 per cent. Indeed, Balladur qualified for the job of Prime Minister only because Mitterrand insisted in 1993 on the absolute condition that the incoming Prime Minister support his policies on Europe, and, by extension, on domestic economic policy as well. With prominent ministries being given to centrist Gaullists like Nicolas Sarkozy and Alain Juppé, the party achieved its full metamorphosis under Balladur into nothing but another anodyne party of the technocratic Right. As poisoned in its political language as the Socialists, as calculating and manipulative as any political formation under the Fourth Republic, and with a leader who has been in place, and losing elections, for the last twenty years, the Gaullist movement may still contain some forceful characters who give the impression of having political convictions, but in the main, the party has gone the way of all the other French political parties: into decay.

Some commentators have welcomed the increasing centrism of French politics under Mitterrand, pointing out that it is preferable to the anarchy and extremism which used to characterize French history.[30] But if the era of the excessive domination of politics, the idea that 'everything is political', is merely succeeded by an unpolitical era, in which politics is limited to a consensual discourse on the notions of modernity and efficiency,[31] under such conditions, a truly political debate can no longer take place, because there are no real differences between the parties. But without real choice, there can be no real freedom.

11. *Past Imperfect*

Everything comes down to winning or losing. One should never remain stationary. Because not to move is to begin to lose.

François Mitterrand[1]

If Mitterrand's successful attack on the power of the Communist Party was based more on party politics than ideology, his victory over the Right has been more ideological than political. Mitterrand never seemed to mind very much about the Stalinism of the French Communist Party – he only cared about it as an electoral threat to him – but he had always hated both the personality and the politics of de Gaulle. It was a loathing which went back to his first uncomfortable encounter with the General in 1943, when he had first made contact with the Resistance in London. The General was doubtless suspicious and supercilious, not knowing quite what Mitterrand's true past was, and the coming-together of two such conceited personalities would doubtless never have been a success under any circumstances. One day at lunch in the Elysée Palace in 1985, one of the guests quoted André Malraux, de Gaulle's Minister of Culture, 'Everybody is, has been, or one day will be Gaullist.' Mitterrand's response was as swift as it was expected. 'Not me.'[2]

This hatred for de Gaulle has on occasions put Mitterrand into an alliance with the extreme right. Indeed one senior right-wing politician went as far as to maintain that the key to understanding Mitterrand's political personality is that he *is* really extreme right-wing underneath.[3] It is a charge which has recurred at different times during Mitterrand's long career. In the 1965 presidential election, for instance, he was supported in the second round of voting by the extreme right-wing Republican Alliance, led by Jean-Louis Tixier-Vignancour, a party which counted Jean-Marie Le Pen within its ranks. The extreme right so excoriated de Gaulle,

because of the withdrawal from Algeria, that they preferred anyone
to him. Mitterrand was happy to accept their support: in the week
between the two rounds, he changed the slogan on his election
posters from 'The united Left' to the more politically catholic 'The
united Republic'.

However, Tixier's support may have been more than merely
opportunistic. While Minister of Justice in 1956, Mitterrand had
actively defended France's continued colonial presence in Algeria, a
position now identified only with the extreme right. Indeed, so
determined was he that Algeria should remain French, that he
passed a special decree-law, that of 'flagrant crime'. A notion
hitherto foreign to French law, the law was little short of dictatorial.
It read: 'In Algeria, the competent authorities may order the
immediate prosecution by a permanent tribunal of the armed forces,
without prior investigation, of any person caught participating in
any action against persons or goods ... if these infractions are
liable to merit capital punishment.'[4] It is ironic that this law should
have been passed by a man who now presents himself to the French
public as a moral authority, and who devotes a large part of his
political rhetoric to denouncing the faults of others. It is also ironic
he now claims that his proudest achievement as President has been
to have abolished the death penalty, for as a direct result of this
law, sixty-one people were condemned to death in seventeen
months. Never *since 1831* has there been a Minister of Justice who
has presided over so many executions. Indeed, the guillotine was
used so often that it worked badly, and as a result the executions
were risky.[5] In the end Mitterrand had to ask the Ministry of
Defence to supply him with another one, which was duly constructed at the Arsenal in Toulon, and delivered free of charge to
the Ministry of Justice.[6]

Whether out of sympathy for the cause, or out of sheer spite for
the legacy of de Gaulle, when he assumed office in 1981, Mitterrand
immediately passed a law granting an amnesty to those in the army
who had resisted de Gaulle's drive for independence, and who had
plotted a military *putsch* against him. The decision to do this
surprised many, because the chief resistance to de Gaulle – as
during the war – had come from the extreme right, in the form of a
paramilitary organization, the OAS. Knowing how controversial
the matter was, Mitterrand had used the infamous 'confidence'

article, 49.3, in order to get the law passed.[7] It enabled the *putschist* generals to put their careers back together, start drawing their pensions again, and to escape from all other sanctions which had accrued to them.

Even more intriguing is Mitterrand's relationship to the Vichy government. For it is a little-known fact outside France that François Mitterrand worked for over a year as an official in the collaborationist Vichy government, and that he was decorated for his services with the highest personal honour awarded by Marshal Pétain.

François Mitterrand's background is rural, Catholic and bourgeois. He grew up in the country and, from 1934, studied at Sciences-Po, France's leading training ground for the political élite. At that time, the political atmosphere of France was feverish. Whole swathes of political opinion felt an immense disgust with capitalist democracy,[8] and with the anarchic parliamentary regime of the Third Republic which they identified with it. Fascinated by politics, and with eclectic tastes, the young Mitterrand went to listen to all the great political speakers of the day: to André Malraux, the left-wing anti-fascist who was later to be de Gaulle's Minister of Culture; to the Communist Maurice Thorez; and even to Jacques Doriot,[9] by whom he seems to have been fascinated.[10]

The traditionalist-monarchist movement led by Charles Maurras, Action Française, was especially influential. The time was agog for new ideas, and the impertinent, dynamic and iconoclastic royalists expressed them well.[11] There are persistent rumours that François Mitterrand had links with the Action Française in October 1934, though Mitterrand denies them. His name is to be found in the index of the classic reference work on the Action Française, written before Mitterrand became President, which says that Mitterrand 'briefly frequented the circle of the Action Française'.[12] Mitterrand's contemporaries, and the head of the student hostel in which he lodged, Father O'Reilly, testify to his interest in the movement's leader, Charles Maurras. There are indeed occasional favourable references to Maurras in Mitterrand's writings at this time. He was an active writer in the monthly review, *Combat*, in which a number of intellectuals from the young right were also prolific, such as Thierry Maulnier, Drieu La Rochelle, Robert Brasillach and Claude Roy, a friend of Mitterrand's from Angoulême. Indeed, to this day,

Mitterrand retains very right-wing literary tastes. He continues to read Drieu La Rochelle, who was an outright fascist, and has befriended the conservative German writer, Ernst Jünger.

But the rumours are of more than just a passing interest in the extreme right. A contemporary of Mitterrand's assures us that 'I was a member of the Students of Action Française, and I always considered François Mitterrand to have been of the same political persuasion as me. Indeed, all my friends from the Action Française thought that he was a member of "La Cagoule".'[13] La Cagoule ('The Hood') was a clandestine organization which reproached Maurras for not daring to use illegal means to destroy the republic. It supported violence in order to respond to the street demonstrations and the occupation of factories by the Communists. It possessed several arms caches, and the network was responsible for a number of violent attacks in Paris. The connections between Mitterrand and this group are circumstantial, but strong. Jean-Marie Bouyver was a good friend of Mitterrand: he was not only a member of La Cagoule (membership number 219) but also implicated in the assassination of Carlo and Nello Rosselli, two Italian brothers, both professors, who were known for their opposition to Mussolini. Bouyver was convicted of being an accessory to their murder in the spring of 1938. Mitterrand, always known for the value he attaches to friendship, whatever the circumstances, visited him regularly in the Prison de la Santé.

Other friends of Mitterrand were also connected with La Cagoule. One such was François Méténier, a member of the group who was resolutely pro-Mussolini and pro-Franco, as the head of Italian counter-intelligence testified at his trial. Méténier, who joined the Vichy government in 1940, had been involved in the bombing of the CGPF, the industrialists' association, in June 1937, a terrorist attack which killed two concierges. He was condemned to twenty years in prison and life-long 'degradation' for this in 1948. The Elysée claims that Mitterrand only met Méténier after the war, and that they hardly knew each other. However, Michel de Camaret, a National Front MEP and also a friend of Mitterrand's, claims that in 1950, Méténier said to him, 'Whatever you ask of Mitterrand [who was then a minister] in my name, you will have.'[14] Another character in the jigsaw puzzle is Eugène Deloncle, the leader of La Cagoule. Robert Mitterrand, the future President's brother and his *directeur de cabinet* after the war,[15] married one of Deloncle's nieces, Edith Cahier, even though she insists that François Mitterrand had never met her uncle. Apparently he was in prison on the day of her marriage to Robert.

Mitterrand himself has repeatedly stated that he has always been on the Left. He says, for instance, that before the war, 'Franco and his gang always horrified me,' even though he worked on a review, *L'Écho de Paris*, which was broadly favourable to Franco and hostile to the Left. He also claims that he went to demonstrations in favour of the Front Populaire, although none of his contemporaries recall his presence there. Indeed, they generally said he just watched the demonstrations if ever he came across them in the street.[16] A left-wing bias would hardly have suited either his family background nor the environment in which he found himself in Paris. The rise to power of the Popular Front was a trauma for the bourgeoisie, and one of the priests at the hostel recalls that, 'Our students were very conservative, and very hostile to the Popular Front. If some of them hoped for the victory of the Left, they were very few in number, and François Mitterrand was not among them'.[17]

To be sure, Mitterrand has always denied these rumours. In his autobiography, he writes,

> There is a tenacious legend that I belonged to the Action Française. Monsieur Debré, then Prime Minister, forgot himself so much as to reproach me with my past (and supposed) acquaintances on the extreme right. M. Debré often speaks fast and loose, but since he does it with conviction, it has a certain credibility ... What can the accused reply who is supposed to prove his innocence? Nothing. To deny the charge would be to demean oneself. And why should I reply? If it were true that I had been extreme right in my youth, I would judge it more favourable to be where I am now than to have followed the opposite path.[18]

He also recounts how he was once offered a cigar by a restauranteur. Mitterrand thanked the man warmly, but declined the cigar because he does not smoke. Thereupon the man whispered into his ear, 'I was in the Action Française.' And then added, 'Like you.' Mitterrand writes simply, 'I did not have the heart to deny it.'[19]

However, he reacts with less levity where the issue of his war record is concerned. In his memoirs he describes how he was captured by the German army in June 1940 and taken to Germany, where he was kept in Stalag IX A, near Kassel. He made three escape attempts, each more extraordinary than the other. The first time, in an extraordinary episode, he walked for twenty-two nights and days and 600 kilometres through the cold and the snow only to be stopped near the Swiss border, after making the fatal mistake of walking into a village before nightfall.[20] The second involved climbing over a four-metre-high fence with spotlights everywhere. He got out of the camp, but stayed at a hotel, where he was subsequently denounced by the receptionist. Recaptured, he was sent to a transit camp in Metz, whence he was supposed to be sent to Poland. But he managed to escape from this camp as well, where he disappeared under the noses of German soldiers, boarded a train which took him along the border until he jumped off it, at a point where it slowed down because of works (one wonders how he knew this in advance), was hidden by two old ladies in a *tabac*, and then taken by car to friends of his sister, Hélène.[21] Then he writes this: 'When I returned to France, I joined the Resistance.'[22]

However, the truth is more complex, for he omits to mention that from May 1942 until late 1943, he worked in the Vichy government, as an official in the Commissariat General for Prisoners of War. Moreover, he succeeded in frequenting the highest circles in the small world of Vichy, with especially good contacts in the immediate entourage of Marshal Pétain himself. He was friendly with Bernard de Chalvron, a member of the Marshal's *cabinet*, and he got his job in the Vichy government through the offices of Raphael Alibert, who had been an influential member of La Cagoule.

Another link was with Gabriel Jeantet, a former President of the Students of the Action Française, who was later responsible for La Cagoule's arms supply. During the war, Jeantet was a senior adviser in Marshal Pétain's *cabinet*, and later its *directeur*. Jacques Laurent, the pro-Vichy novelist and Academician, who to this day can still be found boozing quietly in the corner of the Brasserie Lipp, affirms that Mitterrand and Jeantet were 'very close'. Laurent adds, 'Jeantet, however, was a great Resistant.'[23] Indeed, Jeantet was one of the people who well illustrates the surprisingly heterogeneous nature of Vichy. Although his politics were clearly Pétainist – he was virulently anti-capitalist, anti-democratic, anti-Semitic, anti-Gaullist, and anti-Communist – he was also very anti-German and, as such, anti-Nazi. He claims in his book *Hitler contre Pétain* that he was the contact point between Pétain and the German army officers who plotted against Hitler, and that he was working with emissaries from de Gaulle to prepare a reconciliation between Pétain and the Gaullists after the Liberation.

In June 1942, when already Pétain's *directeur de cabinet*, Jeantet founded a review, *France, Revue de l'État Nouveau*. In the first edition, he railed against the fact that France had been pushed into the war on the side of the capitalist democracies by 'a gang of international financiers, Talmudic prophets, Communists in the pay of Stalin, and inept politicians who were badly prepared for the shock because of years of anarchic delinquence beforehand'.[24] In December 1942, Mitterrand himself published an article in this magazine. Above his name on the list of contents stands that of Philippe Pétain himself, as a speech by him is reprinted in the same number. There is also an article on the eugenics of the French race, entitled 'The Science of Man';[25] and an anti-Semitic tract entitled 'The Jews in Rome under the Papacy'.[26]

Mitterrand's own article, entitled 'Pilgrimage to Thuringia', is an account of his journey to Germany as a prisoner of war. In it, he describes the beauty of the countryside and the historic grandeur of the towns through which he passes:

> Our convoy seemed symbolic to me. In its tragic reality, it marked the consequences of our progressive abandonment of reality. France, by nourishing Europe with her fraternal ambitions, by imposing her warlike ardour, by spreading her blood beyond her frontiers – and for impossible frontiers – had exhausted herself, and I thought that we, the inheritors of these 150 years of errors, were responsible. I hated that triumphalist history which ineluctably preceded this long march of a generation in animal trucks. I could discern the logic of events and I asked myself whether it was just that our misery was the payment for little-understood glories. More precisely, I wondered whether it was just that our fall was blamed on us because, although we had abandoned our arms,

everything else had been taken away from us beforehand anyway. I thought of the judgements which would condemn our débâcle. The collapsed regime, the useless men in charge, the institutions emptied of all their substance – and those judgements would be right. Will the glorious mistakes also be condemned?[27]

The reference to '150 years of errors' is an anti-Revolutionary remark usually only found on the extreme right. The Pétainist regime certainly had little time for the ideals of the Revolution, and the heavy emphasis laid on his sense of guilt was also a constant Pétainist preoccupation. (One of Pétain's most famous slogans was '*Français*, remember your sins.') It is perhaps not surprising that Mitterrand shared these views. There were 1,800,000 French prisoners of war in Germany at the time, a third of the active male population. Fifty-one thousand of them were never to return. Clearly, there was huge resentment at the officer class and at the political system of France for having allowed such a catastrophe to occur. In June, General Weygand declared at Bordeaux, 'France has deserved her defeat, she has been beaten because for the last fifty years, successive governments have chased God out of our schools!' That France was paying for her pre-war sins was to become an important plank of Pétainist propaganda.[28]

In such conditions, it is not surprising that Marshal Pétain was so successful. His themes – the cult of the nation, glorification and protection of the family, community spirit, regionalism, the return to the earth – all responded to the emotional needs of a traumatized country. The strong presence within his government of Socialists and technocrats, under the overall control of a Field Marshal, gave out the right number of different signals to different sectors of the population. That Pétain was the victor of Verdun was a way of allowing the French the illusion of thinking that they were reminding the Germans that they had been defeated twenty years previously. Pétain's appeal was thus above all personal. With his slogan, 'I was with you in the days of glory, I shall remain with you in the days of darkness', the unexpressed message was 'Trust me, and I will protect you'. It was a regime of somnolence, illusion and forgetting.

Moreover, for most French, the dichotomy between de Gaulle and Pétain was not as clearly visible as it is nowadays. De Gaulle's famous 'appeal' to the French, broadcast on the BBC on 18 June

1940, was heard by hardly anybody. The socially distinguished French General in London, who had been sent there by Pétain himself, hardly seemed to be the incarnation of the notion of resistance. Indeed, de Gaulle and Pétain had been personally very close. Pétain had taught de Gaulle at the military school at Saint-Cyr, and thought very highly of him. De Gaulle, who ghost-wrote books on military strategy for Pétain, reciprocated with a very high regard for the Victor of Verdun: Charles de Gaulle's son Philippe, the future Admiral and Senator, was named 'Philippe' after Pétain himself, who was his secular godfather.[29] Thus, there developed the idea that Pétain was the 'shield' of France while de Gaulle was the 'sword'. Although this subsequently became an extreme right-wing theory to defend Pétain, it is fairly easy to see why people believed it then. It is also clear that Mitterrand held a similar view at the beginning of the war. 'We had very little information,' he wrote. 'Seen from the camps, Pétain and de Gaulle appeared the same. They were both representatives of official France engaged in battle. Pétain was for me, as for the majority of my companions, an old marshal who was there to bandage up the wounds ... Seen from Germany, Pétain and de Gaulle did not represent contradictory policies.'[30]

His experience as a prisoner of war may have marked him in other ways. In his own autobiography, he writes,

> Cut off from the world, we set about building our own society. In the first months, the social order depended on the knife and on the law of the jungle. This was rapidly swept away, and the knife, which came to be used to cut bread, soon became an instrument of justice ... I think that I learned much more from this commando closed in upon itself, than from the teachers of my adolescence. I will not claim that we built Utopia, but I have never known a more balanced community.[31]

As someone commented jokingly afterwards, 'François thought that the Stalag model could be transposed, and that French society could draw inspiration from it.'[32] However sarcastically meant, it implies that Mitterrand shared the view that society needed to be re-founded, a sentiment nourished by the cataclysmic collapse of an old world. In that period, such views were common on both Right and Left, for both sides spoke of renewal, Pétain's 'National Revolution' being only the most obvious example of this.

But many contemporaries of Mitterrand do testify to his apparent sympathy for Pétain at the time. One described the future President as 'completely right-wing'. 'Monarchist,' says another. 'He went on and on about the monarchy.'[33] Paul Delouvrier, a friend of Robert Mitterrand, recalls that 'I often heard news of François from his letters to Robert, and I remember that their tone was always very Pétainist. For a *petit bourgeois* like him, Pétain was the great defender of family values.'[34] Another contemporary recalls him saying in 1943 that he found the corporatist structures of Vichy very interesting.[35]

Mitterrand has said that he was a Resistance infiltrator. There were some politicians who, in virtue of having been successful Resistance infiltrators, were able to pursue prominent political careers under de Gaulle afterwards: Maurice Couve de Murville is the best example of this. Having been Director of Foreign Trade in the Finance Ministry until early 1943, he became Prime Minister under de Gaulle.[36] (Indeed, there are some, like Maurice Papon, a minister under Giscard in the 1970s, who had been fairly committed Pétainists: Papon was Prefect for Jewish Affairs in Bordeaux from 1942–4.) But few Resistants succeeded in publishing articles in the main official anti-Semitic magazine of the Vichy government, in the company of Marshal Pétain himself.

However, the strangest aspect of Mitterrand's career in Vichy is that he was decorated in late 1943 with the Francisque Gallique, a medal bestowed by Pétain as a mark of personal favour for services rendered to him and to France. Although at first Pétain awarded the medal on a personal basis, its attribution was regulated in August 1942, when a council was created which met every month in order to decide to whom to award it. There were two conditions: 'Before the war, to have accomplished national and social deeds which are in conformity with the National Revolution'; and 'Since the war to have a strong attachment to the work and personality of Marshal Pétain'.[37] To obtain the medal one had to swear an oath of allegeance to Philippe Pétain: 'I give my person to Marshal Pétain, as he has given his to France. I undertake to respect his discipline and to rest faithful to his person and to his work.'[38] Mitterrand received the award, number 2202, listed in the official journal of the

Francisque. Despite the fact that this has inevitably become a political football, he has never deigned to clear up the issue with a clear statement on the matter, preferring to try to bury the issue by refusing to give clear details. Even some of those who do not doubt his Resistance record have attacked his imprecision.[39]

He and his defenders have thus given various explanations: either that the medal was the ideal cover for Resistance agents like himself secretly working against Vichy;[40] or that it was awarded to all members of the Commissariat Général pour les Prisonniers de Guerre, and that it would have been highly impolitic to refuse it;[41] or that he never asked for the medal in the first place (one wonders which medals one *does* ask for!);[42] or that many other members of the Resistance received the medal as well.[43] Some say that it was not awarded for his activities in the Commissariat Général, but that it was for having been a prisoner of war.[44] Indeed, in Jacques Attali's account of Mitterrand's explanation of what he did in Vichy ('He recalled ... Vichy, where he created the Prisoners' Association'),[45] it seems that Mitterrand is even trying to justify what he did do, by intimating that it was a positive action which contributed to the overall effort.

Some of these explanations are simply overblown. One journalist has even said that wearing the Francisque was practically proof that one was in the Resistance,[46] and Mitterrand has himself used this tactic. The only problem is that it is not correct. There are very few great members of the Resistance who figure on the list of holders of the Francisque.[47] Moreover, when using this defence, Mitterrand mentioned 'my friend, Marshal de Lattre de Tassigny' as having been in the same category as himself.[48] But, as the specialist on Vichy France, Robert Paxton, points out, the Marshal de Lattre, who was later to command the army of the Resistance, had himself been a sincere supporter of Pétain.[49] Moreover, those members of the Resistance who did receive the medal were decorated before January 1943. Mitterrand, by contrast, obtained it well after that, towards the end of the year, and long after the Southern Zone of France had been occupied by the Germans.

There is also a curious imprecision which surrounds the exact date on which he received the honour. He has said that it was in December 1943, by which time he was already in London, having left France in November.[50] Thus, he says that he never actually

physically received the medal. In this he has generally been believed.[51] But some authors who defend him say that he received the
medal in 'Autumn 1943'.[52] But why the imprecision of 'Autumn'?
Indeed, even the manner of his departure to London has been
questioned. He claims to have come on a British aircraft, but the
captain of that flight denies ever having had him on board.[53] Alain
Griotteray, a true veteran of the Resistance, comments:

> Nobody knows exactly under what conditions he got to
> London. It does not matter much whether he went on a
> Lysander aircraft or not – the Lysander of which not a single
> mention is made in the very elaborate British archives. Wit-
> nesses were found later on to confirm that they had seen him
> take off from an aerodrome, obviously secret, near Angers.
> For my own part, I tend to think that he left via Spain, maybe
> even in a sleeping-car, like Couve de Murville, under one
> identity or another. When one has a taste for the secret and
> when one has been excelling in things like that since even
> before the war, everything is easy, all the more so because
> one's Spanish and (even more so) Portuguese friends are
> numerous when one is an official admirer of Marshal Pétain
> and therefore also of Salazar.[54]

One theory is that the medal was awarded to Mitterrand in August,
not December.[55] If this is so, and if the pro-Mitterrand authors
know that he did indeed receive the medal, it might explain their
ambiguous use of 'autumn', which could just about mean November, but which might just about mean August. There are indeed
unconfirmed rumours that a photograph exists of Mitterrand at the
award ceremony.[56] In any case, this author can reveal something of
which, to his knowledge, no other treatment of the subject has
been able to confirm. A former supporter of Vichy, Henri Guitton,
used to claim in private that he had received the medal at the same
ceremony as François Mitterrand.[57] Unfortunately, Guitton died in
the summer of 1993.

In any case, even if it is true that Mitterrand was no longer in his
post in Vichy when the medal was awarded, and that he was
spending the majority of his time in his Resistance activities, he did
not blush after the war to preserve his friendships and other
contacts with people in the entourage of Marshal Pétain. In June

1946, he was appointed Director-General of the Editions du Rond-Pont, a publishing-house which belonged to *L'Oréal*, and which had been founded by Eugene Schueller, a well-known Nazi supporter and member of the La Cagoule. Mitterrand ran the magazine *Votre Beauté* for a few months. Indeed, as late as the 1970s, he gave his very favourable biographer, Franz-Olivier Giesbert, the names of his two sponsors for the Francisque, Gabriel Jeantet and Simon Arbellot. Yet both these men were convinced Pétainists. Jeantet, as we have seen, was heavily involved in La Cagoule, while Arbellot, a pro-Pétain journalist and a former prisoner himself, who describes Mitterrand as 'a great Resistant', says of Mitterrand,

> He was familiar with the patriotism, the sense of near sacrifice, which animated the Marshal and his friends. He knew the daily inner struggle of Pierre Laval, and the resistance of these two men – so different but so constant. One day he asked me and Gabriel Jeantet, who ran the youth movements, to present his candidature for the Francisque. He was admitted unanimously by the council under the approving monocled eye of Admiral Platon.[58]

A man who could still claim in 1966 that Pierre Laval was a Resistant is hardly very politically correct, yet Mitterrand was happy to admit his friendship with him. Moreover, the remarks appear to contradict Mitterrand's own claim that he never asked for the award.[59]

The issue has continued to dog him throughout his political life. The first occasion was in April 1945, when the Communist Pierre Verrier attacked him over the issue in the National Assembly, and demanded when the National Federation of Prisoners of War was being set up, that Mitterrand, its proposed head, should appear before a committee of inquiry to ascertain the truth about his Francisque. Mitterrand at first just denied everything ('All that is false').[60] He then added that de Gaulle accepted him into the Resistance without qualms, and that this proved that he cannot have been a collaborator.[61]

De Gaulle himself never exploited Mitterrand's Vichyite past for political reasons, not even during the presidential election campaign of 1965 when Mitterrand forced him into a second round. According to one of his close collaborators at the time, de Gaulle would have been incapable of entering into such grubby politicking, since he believed himself to be way above such matters, thinking of himself as nothing less than the saviour of France.[62] But de Gaulle's followers did not have the same scruples. In 1972, deputies of the Gaullist movement, the UDR, published a communiqué in which they reproached Mitterrand for 'having been associated during the Nazi occupation with the actions of the Vichy government. Honoured to the point of receiving the Francisque, the highest honour awarded for services rendered'.[63]

Jacques Attali reports that Mitterrand was 'deeply hurt' by an attack made just before he was elected President in 1981.[64] General Alain de Boissieu, a brother-in-law of General de Gaulle, publicly attacked Mitterrand for having worked in Vichy during the war, clearly hoping to influence the election result by so doing. Boissieu declared, two days after the televized debate between Giscard and Mitterrand,

> People are trying ... to make a great Resistant of Monsieur François Mitterrand. Well, I can read you the judgement which General de Gaulle passed on Monsieur Mitterrand's career. He said this to me, in front of witnesses, 'Having worked for the Vichy government, for which he was decorated with the Francisque, he made contact with the Resistance, then with the Allied services, and finally with our Free French forces, before placing himself in the hands of the British services.' De Gaulle said that Mitterrand had had his snout in every trough, and that he had behaved all this time of his career like an *arriviste* and an intriguer.[65]

Another famous occasion was when two right-wing politicians, Alain Madelin and Jacques Toubon (who in 1993 became respectively Industry Minister and Culture Minister in the Balladur government) were censured under parliamentary procedure for the infraction of 'insulting the President' because, during the course of a furious exchange between Socialists, Communists and the Right, each party had accused the other of having members within their ranks with shady pasts.[66] It is certainly difficult to imagine a British or American leader being so well cushioned by the prestige of his office, and thereby so successfully avoiding a proper investigation into the matter.

Perhaps the most interesting aspect of the affair is the way in which his supporters excuse his involvement with the Vichy regime when, if it concerned anyone else, they would rightly treat it as totally unacceptable. Franz-Olivier Giesbert makes a mild reprimand which amounts to little more than a call to let sleeping dogs lie.

> It is possible that Mitterrand may have found some merit in the 'French state' of Vichy. This would be proof of an ambivalent spirit which always tends to accord virtue to one's adversaries – in private at least. But to go from that to saying Mitterrand was a 'collaborator' . . . many have done it. However, the legend of Mitterrand backing two horses (playing up his Resistance activity and playing down his Vichy decorations) has proved to be long-lived. All the more so because he has never thought it necessary to elucidate the obscure question-marks which hang over his behaviour under Vichy, even though this would have been easy.[67]

A less charitable interpretation is offered by Stéphane Denis: 'He forgot the war because he had the faculty, so common with children, of believing in his own stories, rather as one forgets a bad deed, the manner in which one behaved towards a girl, or a bad evening which leaves a bitter taste.'[68]

Edwy Plenel, a bitter left-wing critic of Mitterrand, makes an even-handed judgement:

> Like the majority of French people, he was in search of himself, humiliated by the defeat and disappointed by the regime which had allowed it. [In his job in the Vichy government] he came across civil servants and politicians who were far from all being dedicated collaborators, but who believed that they could reconstruct France in the shadow of the occupier. Men who ensured the continuity of the state, who had their doubts about de Gaulle . . . [69]

But the feelings Mitterrand may or may not have entertained about Vichy at the time are perhaps less relevant than the feelings about the regime which he still has today. In this regard, his practice of sending a wreath to be laid on Marshal Pétain's tomb on the Île d'Yeu every 11 November, on the anniversary of the Armistice in 1918, is remarkable. Mitterrand is not the first President to have honoured France's First World War hero in this way, but he has shown an uncanny enthusiasm for the practice.[70] Indeed, he is the instigator of the regular exercise of what he regards as 'this republican tradition'. Whereas de Gaulle had had a wreath laid only once, on the fiftieth anniversary of the Armistice in 1968; whereas Georges Pompidou did the same once, in 1973 after the reburial of Pétain's remains following the coffin's exhumation by Pétainist supporters; and whereas Valéry Giscard d'Estaing (whose uncle and father were both senior Pétainist politicians) laid a wreath in 1978 on the occasion of the sixtieth anniversary of the end of the Great War, François Mitterrand has had wreaths laid on 22 September 1984 (to mark his famous hand-holding ceremony with Chancellor Helmut Kohl at Verdun), on 15 June 1986 for the seventieth anniversary of the Battle of Verdun, and, from 1987 to 1991, every 11 November. This is a total of eight times.[71]

When pressured to desist from this practice, and for France to take more responsibility for sins committed by Vichy, Mitterrand is given to saying that the republic cannot be held to account for a regime which was itself explicitly anti-republican. The France of Vichy was not the present France.[72] Unfortunately, this argument misses the central point, no doubt deliberately, for what is special about Vichy is that the very notion of collaboration was specific to France, having been proposed, on his own initiative, by Philippe Pétain. Moreover, Mitterrand's own career is the perfect case of continuity between Vichy and the subsequent republics.

Perhaps even more arresting is the Bousquet affair. René Bousquet, the former Vichy police chief, and the man primarily responsible for the deportation of thousands of French Jews to the German extermination camps,[73] was shot dead in his apartment by an apparently mad assassin in June 1993, Christian Didier, two days before he was due to go on trial for crimes against humanity. What the French press failed to mention was that Bousquet was an old friend and political ally of François Mitterrand. Mitterrand and Bousquet used to see each other until at least the early 1980s. When Bousquet was received at the Elysée in 1981, Mitterrand declared to one of his officials, surprised at the company the President was keeping, 'Don't worry. He's an old friend: he has done a lot for me.'

Mitterrand was probably referring to the support which Bousquet gave him during his election contest against de Gaulle in 1965, when he controlled the influential provincial newspaper, *La Dépêche du Midi*. Bousquet was a radical Socialist during the war, and had stood as an anti-Gaullist candidate at the legislative elections in 1958 – with the support of Mitterrand's small UDSR party.

Yet the extraordinary circumstances of Bousquet's death were met with hardly any comment or investigation by the French media. It was extraordinary that, Bousquet's case having taken years to come to court, he should have been killed immediately before he was due to stand trial. As such, the death was reminiscent of Pierre Bérégovoy's suicide a month before the start of the Péchiney insider-trading trial, at which his *chef de cabinet*, Alain Boublil, was one of the main defendants, and to which he may have been called as a witness. Nor was there any questioning of the claim that Didier just rang Bousquet's doorbell and walked into his apartment with a gun in his bag. Professional photographers testified that a contemporary photograph of Bousquet was worth 100,000 francs, yet if it was so difficult to shoot him with a telephoto lens, it is strange that he could so easily be shot with a Remington 38.[74]

While the French authorities were happy to try the German Klaus Barbie, French collaborators have generally not been brought to trial for crimes against humanity. The well-known Nazi-hunter, Serge Klarsfeld, went so far as to claim in 1990 that Mitterrand was deliberately trying to ensure that Bousquet never came to trial.[75] Georges Kiejman, an old political ally of Mitterrand's who was a Justice Minister at the time, argued that there were other ways of denouncing Vichy than in a court of law. 'It is more important to preserve civil peace in France,' he declared.[76] Indeed after Bousquet's murder, even Klarsfeld rather surprisingly rushed to close the dossier, saying that everything was known about Bousquet already, and that the trial would have revealed nothing new – as if a prosecution were nothing but an exercise in historical research.

Mitterrand's position has always been that Bousquet stood trial in 1949 and was sentenced to 'five years of national indignity', a sentence which was suspended immediately afterwards, on the basis that he had only been doing his job. However, this simple affirmation leaves out an important detail. When Bousquet stood trial in 1949, the Gaullists were no longer in power, a relevant fact considering that, in France, judicial procedures are not infrequently the object of political manipulation. Bousquet was one of the last people to be tried by the High Court for collaboration: four years after the end of the war, the parliamentary world thought only of forgetting what had gone before, and of granting amnesties.[77]

Moreover, the government at the time, composed of a rag-tag of different coalition parties, included none other than François Mitterrand, the leader of the little UDSR party which was to make and unmake so many governmental coalitions during the Fourth Republic. Indeed, it was Mitterrand who, in his capacity as Secretary of State for Information, presented to the Council of Ministers (the Cabinet) on 22 June 1949, the second day of Bousquet's trial, the first major proposal for granting an amnesty to those guilty of collaboration. Furthermore, a number of those who testified in favour of Bousquet – that he had really been defending France all along, that if he had resigned, then his post would simply have been filled by someone else – were former prisoners of war who belonged to the Rassemblement National des Prisonniers de Guerre, the prisoners-of-war movement created by ... François Mitterrand.[78]

Mitterrand's first contacts with the Free French in London date from November 1943. This was nine months after the defeat of the Germans at Stalingrad (in February) and a few months after the King of Italy had changed sides and Mussolini was overthrown (in October). One did not have to be a political soothsayer to know which way the war was turning. Moreover, if his Resistant activities are undoubted, one of his enemies poignantly remarks, 'He never himself talks about what he did during those years which his friends say were heroic ones.'[79] Franz-Olivier Giesbert's laudatory biography devotes eight pages (out of 400) to the Resistance, of which nearly three deal with trivial details – what cigarettes he then smoked, what clothes he wore, and which girls he was going out with.

It seems that the bulk of his activity was devoted to 'making contacts' and 'exchanging information'. There have been tentative claims that some of this information came from behind German lines, and that they may, 'perhaps', even have included information about the existence of concentration camps at Auschwitz and Buchenwald.[80] Networking has since become his *forte*: Mitterrand was always to use a cohort of people close to him upon which to build his authority. As another contemporary has written, 'François had the tendency to give responsibility to people according to their fidelity towards himself, instead of according to their real capacities.'[81]

Certainly, he got into the swing of politics then. One of his colleagues at the time has remarked on how Mitterrand soon became top dog in the group:

> Today it is difficult for me to analyse how François Mitterrand became the first among us within a few months. He was never referred to as President, but it was from him that I received information, instructions, and, later, money . . . He showed far too much assurance, irony, and he was sometimes offhand . . . We found him individualist and cold, but it was above all his frequent lateness for meetings which annoyed and worried his friends.[82]

It is a portrait which is still imediately recognizable today, even the famous habit of lateness. Another contemporary commented in the same vein, 'He was already a professional politician when the rest of us had no real designs.'[83] This may explain the bad odour which was immediately generated between him and de Gaulle at their first meeting at the end of 1943. The encounter of two such power-driven personalities was bound to be explosive. De Gaulle treated him as a 'suspect nonentity',[84] and merely gave him a few orders about how he should arrange his network, an evident intrusion into the little circle in which Mitterrand had made himself king. No doubt he resented it.

But there is a more important reason why de Gaulle treated Mitterrand so briskly. It was not so much the fact that he was employed by Vichy – a number of his most faithful lieutenants were to be too – but more that he was connected with prisoners of war. Quite simply, De Gaulle considered that they were a suspect and lily-livered lot. In his day, unwounded prisoners of war were interrogated on their release by a War Council. When the Resistance of the prisoners of war was mentioned, de Gaulle simply replied, 'But there is no insurrection from sheep!' According to Maurice Pinot, the former head of the Commissariat General for Prisoners of War in which Mitterrand worked, 'the General had an open contempt for us, and regarded the German camps as just despicable little islands of Vichy.'[85] One Gaullist confirms this:

> Between François Mitterrand's groups and ours there was a fundamental difference of mentality. For us Gaullists, captivity represented a failure, and in order to cleanse ourselves of that stain, we wanted to engage ourselves in military action. By contrast, the people in the Rassemblement National des Prisoniers de Guerre, whom we thought of as Pétainists, considered that the defeat constituted the judgement of God; they believed that since they, the unfortunate prisoners, had done penance for the others, they were there to bring a purification push to the country, which would enable it to redress itself. We thought they were a load of cry-babies and we found their 'prisoners' mystique' pretty boring.[86]

The mixture of guilt at defeat and moral superiority as a result of it is reminiscent of the sentiments expressed in Mitterrand's 1942 article. If so, it underlines the fact that Mitterrand's wartime experience was one of defeat and compromise, whereas that of de Gaulle was one of courage and victory. Forty years on, a man was to be elected to the presidency of France who was not at all sure that France won the war. That may have been a refreshing attitude after so many years of Gaullist triumphalism,[87] but, like all men who return in their old age to the habits and thought-patterns of their formative years, Mitterrand's wartime experience was to be a decisive factor in his European and German policy. A constant and visceral anti-Gaullist, Mitterrand has believed from his earliest days in the virtues of political slipperiness, and in the weakness of France.

12. *In Search of Times Past*

He did not see in front, he only saw behind.

Chateaubriand on Talleyrand.[1]

'Monsieur, since you have said something incorrect, I do not need to reply to you. When you have verified your information, you can come back and see me.'[2] Mitterrand's dismissal of the question was icy and haughty. It displayed all the childish petulance of a man who cannot bear being put on the spot, especially on an issue where he been so spectacularly proved wrong. The question which had elicited this put-down had come from a German journalist, and it was brief, to the point, and entirely justified: *'Monsieur le Président*, why did you oppose German reunification after the fall of the Berlin wall?'[3]

To this day, anything or anyone who suggests that Mitterrand may not have been up to the challenge of history in 1989 attracts the fury of the Elysée. Indeed, so obsessed is he with his record on the matter that he devoted an entire press conference in Karachi (of all places!) to the matter.[4] For though he speaks no foreign languages, Mitterrand is convinced of his own pre-eminence in foreign policy. 'Foreign policy is my affair,' he once declared. 'I define it, and I am going to keep it for myself.'[5] One of his ministers confirmed this. 'Make no mistake,' he said. 'The only subject he is really interested in, the one to which he devotes the main part of his time, is foreign policy.'[6]

Mitterrand is indeed occasionally credited with the status of a 'statesman', because as President he incarnates the foreign visage of France, and the public seem to like hearing his language of protection. His calm, his reflection, his patience are always underlined. But the leading role which he plays in foreign policy, and the success which has been attributed to him, have been equalled only by the lack of any serious content or substance to those policies whatever.

Perhaps this is because of the strange French attitude to 'abroad'. It often seems that they regard foreign countries as a threat, for theories of international conspiracy against France are legion. The political class often panders to this view, and even encourages it: no doubt its members hope thereby to gain some shreds of legitimacy for their huge domestic powers over French civil society. Indeed, if as Hannah Arendt suggests, foreign affairs are the last domain of modern government where activity is still truly political in the ancient Greek sense, for only on the international stage do statesmen meet in the same conditions of publicity and mutual equality as the citizens of Athens used to, and if in foreign affairs, there is a freedom of action and a premium on personality and symbolism which is absent from a modern political world increasingly dominated by the necessities of economics, then it is on that stage that politicians reveal their innermost political character.[7]

Charles de Gaulle had laid a huge premium on foreign policy because his whole political career, from 1940 onwards, was devoted to ensuring France's rank in the world. The search for French glory was itself inseparable from her national independence, of which de Gaulle was the very embodiment. As Maurice Couve de Murville, de Gaulle's Foreign Minister, once remarked, 'For eleven years, the Fifth Republic was primarily, indeed essentially, a foreign policy.'[8] If de Gaulle succeeded in foreign policy, it was precisely because he was inspired by 'a certain idea of France', and because his political personality was strong enough to bear the burden of singular, courageous action. As a result, and because of accumulated constitutional practice, foreign and defence policy have become unofficially to be considered a 'reserved domain' in which the President has exclusive competence. It is inevitable, therefore, that the foreign policy of France should tell us a great deal about the character of the man who occupies the highest position in the land.

After his resignation in 1969, de Gaulle wrote to the Comte de Paris, the pretender to the French throne, to say that throughout his whole career he had been always been trying to follow the politics of the French kings, for whom it had been axiomatic that no sovereign could have legitimacy within France if he were subject to a superior, foreign power.[9] This is a very old notion, and one which is almost indissoluble from the idea of France according to which it is the French *nation* which stands as the last rampart against the (German) *Empire* to the East. Indeed, according to Alexandre Sanguinetti, one of the 'barons' of Gaullism, the relationship between France and Germany is the key to the history of Europe. He distinguishes the two countries thus: 'Germany is an ethnic group ('une éthnie'), France is an idea.' France, after all, is ethnically and culturally very mixed: there is Latin, Celtic, Gallo-Roman and German blood, and groups as different as the Basques, the Flemish, the Catalans and Alsatians, the Bretons and the *Provençaux*. It is only because France is built on the Roman conception of *jus soli*, the right of soil, that these disparate people have been able to be united.

> It is [writes Sanguinetti] the basis of our idea of Nation. Consciously or unconsciously, for the different dynasties, powers and regimes who have succeeded one another in our country for the last eleven centuries, there is the fundamental idea that wherever the land is French, there is the Frenchman. The history of France is the history of gathering together French land, whatever may be the ethnic groups which are on that land. They are given a constructed language, which for many was an imposition, a formidable instrument of unity and of civilization: the French language![10]

The German, by contrast, has not inherited this concept from Rome. He is determined by his customs and by *jus sanguinis*, the right of blood. 'He thinks and says: Wherever the blood is German, there shall be German land. He knows no other geographical limits than those marked by the advance or retreat of men who call themselves German and speak German.'[11] 'France', he concludes, 'is a nation, created by a state. Like the Spaniards, our history is one of reconquest.'[12]

For this reason, there is a geopolitical imperative that France's foreign policy be European. Unlike Britain between 1815 and 1914, France cannot turn her back on the Continent and devote herself to the sea. Perhaps this is why geopolitics remains alive and well in French political thinking, for the French know that the intimate link between their geography, national character, and foreign policy must be preserved consciously and with determination, or else

France will not be France. The sense of this link seems lost in Britain: the constant references to the British as an 'island race', of the kind which one finds in Sir Winston Churchill's *History of the Second World War*, have now been banished from the modern lexicon of political correctness. And if France has a geopolitical role, then it is easily defined by her situation on the edge of the European continent. De Gaulle and Churchill agreed on this as soon as they met in 1940: 'Mr Churchill and I modestly agreed on the following banal but definitive explanation of why the West had been smashed: in the final analysis, England is an island, France is the cape of a continent, and America is another world.'[13] To return to Sanguinetti:

> Napoleon said that a nation's politics is determined by its geography. Ours is determined by our *finis terrae*, at the end of the huge Asiatic continent and of the European peninsula. For thousands of years, the Asiatic races have been pushing the Slavs, who have been pushing the Germanic races, who have been pushing on to us, in the eternal march of peoples to the West.
>
> We are at the end of the journey, we cannot push on to anyone else, because we have our backs to the sea. So we devote ourselves to the battle to stop the advance, which is the present purpose of our nuclear capability.
>
> If we fail in our defence, our enemy spreads himself out like a fan over the whole of France, down to the Alps and the Pyrenees. We repeated that fact on the Somme in 1940. It is one of the reasons why we have always wanted to push our limits further east.
>
> In 1815, one of the preoccupations of the treaties of Vienna was to leave a wide door open on to us, via the plain of Flanders. It resulted in this creation of the kingdom of the Netherlands and then of Belgium at our gates.
>
> Both of them fulfilled their role perfectly in 1914 and 1940.[14]

France's inevitable preoccupation, then, is with Germany. Here, the event which looms over the Franco-German relationship is inevitably the defeat of 1940. This is not only because France was reduced to suing for peace after only six weeks of terrifyingly efficient

German invasion. It is rather because Vichy has something quintessentially French and home-grown about it. For

> France was the only occupied country whose legally established and widely supported government had worked actively and openly for a German victory. Far from practising covert resistance to shield France, Vichy had offered more than the Germans asked in both blood (including Jewish blood) and treasure. In the vain hope of ingratiating themselves with Hitler and playing a privileged role in his new Europe, the men of Vichy had merely facilitated their country's enslavement.[15]

The most reactionary elements of Vichy, especially Pétain himself, had become so disgusted with the France of the interwar years – and with the whole of post-Revolutionary France – that they arrived at a conclusion which was as horrendous as it was paradoxical for nationalists. Their hatred of their own country convinced them that it was doomed to defeat, and that it would be forced to change for the better only by being under the tutelage of the victorious Nazis. In other words, their behaviour during the Occupation was only another episode in the struggle between the forces of Revolution and counter-Revolution which had dictated French politics since 1789.

But the consciousness of defeat also impregnates France's relations with other countries, including that with the maritime powers, Britain and America, with whom France has occasionally allied herself in order to face up to the German threat. (The alternative alliance for the same purpose is with Russia.) From Louis XIV's failure to re-install James II, to Napoleon's defeat at Waterloo, the sense of inferiority towards England is well entrenched.[16] A common view along similar lines is that while post-war Britain may now be weaker, she has escaped the sense of humiliating decline to which France is prey because she can take vicarious enjoyment in the power of the United States, a power which in France is perceived as a threat.[17] This sense of decline no doubt explains a good deal of French anti-Americanism.

The single most surprising aspect about Mitterrand's foreign policy is that it has seemed far more pro-American than that of any of his predecessors. The Americans certainly did not expect to find him such a co-operative partner, especially after his nomination of four Communists in the first Mauroy government. Indeed, if he surprised people by this aspect of his foreign policy, it was part of a broader surprise at his anti-pacifism. Perhaps because he was alive at the time of Munich, Mitterrand showed himself to be at odds with those younger Socialists whose politics had been formed primarily under the period of decolonization, and for whom all war was abhorrent.

The clearest and most striking illustration of this came in the unconditional support Mitterrand gave to Margaret Thatcher over the Falklands War. Indeed, French support for Britain came more swiftly than even that of the United States. Nor was this without internal opposition: Claude Cheysson, Mitterrand's Foreign Minister at the time, was determined to support Argentina. 'This is an anti-colonial liberation military operation,' he said, 'even if it is being run by dictators.'[18] Mitterrand unconditionally overruled him, and rang up Mrs Thatcher immediately to offer his support. Jacques Attali reports listening to the conversation thus:

> 'Naturally, we are with you in this affair. France will support you in the United Nations . . . No, we will not break off diplomatic relations with Argentina, that is too much to ask. But keep me in touch daily with what is happening, I will see what I can do to help you . . . I am thinking of you . . . Not at all, you're most welcome.'
>
> He put down the phone, and said, 'She thought I was going to support Argentina. She said I was the first to call her, that she was going to pursue the matter all the way, and that she is prepared to send the Royal Navy. I believe her. In her place I would do the same thing.'
>
> Later, Mrs Thatcher often used to talk to me (i.e. Attali) about that telephone conversation.[19]

There are two reasons for his robust attitude. The first was self-interest. Mitterrand knew that if Argentina were able to take the Falkland Islands with impunity, then France's numerous island colonies around the world would also be at risk. But the second reason is more interesting: Mitterrand was determined to bring Britain further into the European family. As he stressed to Cheysson, 'European solidarity takes precedence over everything.'[20] He recognized that Britain's traditional reticence over excessive European integration would jeopardize his own plans for it, and was thus determined to help her. It is interesting to speculate on why this initiative was not the occasion for a durable warming in Franco-British relations, and whether European politics in the 1980s might have followed a different path if it had been.

However, the most obvious area in which Mitterrand surprised a suspicious Atlantic alliance was in his apparently anti-Soviet attitudes. This represented a departure from previous Gaullist and Giscardian policies. De Gaulle not only gave precedence to national or regional interests over the priorities dictated by the division of the world into two ideological blocs; he exploited it. The recognition of Communist China in 1964; the condemnation of the American intervention in Santo Domingo in 1965; the speech at Phnom-Penh denouncing American policy in Vietnam in 1966; the support for Biafran independence in 1967; the condemnation of Israel in 1969; the 'Long live free Quebec!' speech in Montreal in the same year, in which he compared the sensation he had among the Québécois to his experiences during the Liberation; his vetoes of British membership of the European Community in 1962 and 1968 – all these were inspired by his obsession with resisting American 'hegemony' in Europe. Like many Frenchmen, he still resented the fact that at the treaty of Versailles in 1918 it was the United States which dominated the negotiations, although, if the victory was anybody's, it was France's; and like Giscard after him, de Gaulle used France's semi-detached membership of NATO to balance between the two blocs, augmenting France's importance by pretending to act as 'honest broker' between East and West. As one of Chirac's foreign-policy advisers emphasizes, 'From 1945 to 1989, the great glaciation of the Cold War was beneficial for France. That fixed order allowed her to deploy her diplomatic talents to the full . . . In the Cold War, France found comfort and flourished.'[21] One might recall the famous remark made to Bismarck by his banker, Bleichröder, when the Iron Chancellor used the same phrase to describe the position he wanted Germany to have in Europe: 'Sir, there is no such thing as an honest broker.'[22]

However, the intimacy of Giscard's relationship with the Soviet Union soon passed beyond the level of friendship required for a political manipulator, and had begun to look more like full-blooded

fraternization. He was well known to have presented Brezhnev, a
keen car collector, with a red Porsche – although it is difficult to
image that Mogadon behind the wheel of such a zippy little
number. Moreover, although commentators readily recall that
the General Secretary of the French Communist Party, Georges
Marchais, publicly supported the Soviet invasion of Afghanistan,[23]
they recall less frequently that Valéry Giscard d'Estaing himself
travelled to Warsaw on 19 May 1980, where he declared,
Chamberlain-like, that Soviet troops would soon withdraw from
that escapade. The next year France refused to boycott the Moscow
Olympics. When confronted with objections about human rights,
Giscard would merely make repeated references to the imperatives
of geopolitics, which he said were dictated by the Yalta rules of
zones of influence – a mistaken line of reasoning, for Yalta had
specified that the Soviet zone of influence remain democratic.

Giscard's behaviour in 1980 totally undermined Western solidarity, and it elicited from Mitterrand the insult that he was 'the little
messenger boy of Warsaw' ('*le petit télégraphiste de Varsovie*').[24]
Mitterrand conveniently did not refer to the fact that, at the
beginning of December 1979, a few weeks before the invasion of
Afghanistan, he too had given Brezhnev an accolade, saying, 'A man
like Brezhnev is a man of peace, that is what I believe';[25] but the jibe
against Giscard struck home. His campaign against the latter's
excessive fraternization with Brezhnev probably won him numerous
right-wing votes, and he repeated this criticism to numerous
American interlocutors, including Henry Kissinger in August 1981.[26]
Indeed, it was partly because of Giscard's excessively pro-Soviet
orientation that Marie-France Garaud, the veteran Gaullist anti-
Soviet campaigner, former adviser to Georges Pompidou, and candidate for the presidency in 1981, announced that she would not choose
between Mitterrand and Giscard in the second round of voting.

Thus Mitterrand built up an Atlanticist reputation. In 1986, he
wrote,

My support for the Atlantic alliance, which dates from thirty
years ago, still satisfies me. Untouched by any anti-Soviet
obsessions, I continue to believe that the greatest danger for
us, as for our neighbours in Western Europe, would be
precisely if America were to leave the shores of our continent

... The Rights of Man, with the capital letters which they have in official speeches, are at the centre of everything. No foreign policy should define itself otherwise than by them, and according to whether it serves liberty or imprisons it, helps people to live or kills.[27]

This reference to human rights, a constant theme in his speeches, was always reassuring to the Americans. He even tried to build something of a reputation for his interest in this area. The programme for government in 1981 had promised to 'defend human rights wherever they are denied, undermined or threatened'.[28]

But the first concrete sign that Mitterrand's policy would be more Atlanticist than that of his predecessors came when Germany began to wobble on the issue of stationing Pershing missiles on her soil. The problem had begun well before, in December 1979, when Germany very nearly refused to allow Pershings to be stationed, so frightened were her leaders of the peace movement. At that stage, Giscard's France had said absolutely nothing, and the strong complicity between the French President and the German Chancellor, Helmut Schmidt, only strengthened their resolve to do nothing. Mitterrand, however, spoke out. On 5 December 1979, he declared (with a charming use of the royal 'we', and an equally disarming faith in the words of 'experts'), 'We do not want there to be an imbalance between East and West. If the experts agree that there must be Pershing missiles in order to ensure a balance, then we are favourable to it.'[29]

At his very first meeting with Margaret Thatcher, Mitterrand spoke freely of his fears of German pacifism. 'The slogan "Better red than dead" is employed nowadays in certain milieux of the German Left. It is essential to take account of this situation. Germany is a country stuffed with explosives which refuses to be the battleground for other people's wars.'[30] No doubt his lack of trust in the German Left on this matter is one reason why his relations with Chancellor Kohl turned out to be so warm. It was partly in order to demonstrate the strength of that relationship that Mitterrand addressed the German Bundestag on 20 January 1983, when he encouraged Germany to accept the stationing of Pershing missiles. He summed up his attitude to the integrity of the Western alliance, neatly defending his beliefs against the attacks of lefty pacifists at home, by saying repeatedly, 'I am against Euromissiles as well. It's just that I observe that the Euromissiles are in the East while the pacifists are in the West.'[31] Ronald Reagan was also later to confide that 'François' had been among the most reliable and the most convincing of his allies. Despite the Communists in his government, therefore, Mitterrand's action arguably helped to undermine the Kremlin, and, ultimately to facilitate the revolutions in Eastern Europe. At this stage, his *Ostpolitik* was faultless.

He earned his laurels again in 1984, when, addressing the Supreme Soviet in 1984, he spoke of Sakharov, of human rights, and of the Helsinki commitments. These were matters for which Giscard had hardly seemed to care: as far as he was concerned, there was liberty in the West and Communism in the East, and that was that. Later, in December 1988, Mitterrand was to demand to see Vaclav Havel in Prague, an action which the future Czech President was often to recall fondly. (Unfortunately for Mitterrand, Havel was neither so grateful nor so stupid as to accept the French President's plan for a 'pan-European confederation' – without an American presence – when he announced the idea in Prague in 1991.)

Perhaps the most obvious apparent demonstration of Mitterrand's supposedly Atlantic tendencies was France's involvement in the Gulf War in 1991. Like his support for Britain over the Falklands, his decision to support the American-led United Nations campaign was not without internal political costs: it provoked the resignation of his Defence Minister, Jean-Pierre Chevènement, who had been Chairman of the Franco-Iraqi Friendship Society, a position he preferred to retain rather than the ministerial portfolio with which it was in conflict.

However, it is worth dwelling on Mitterrand's motives for that involvement. As with the Falklands, a good deal of self-interest was involved. He was determined that France would be in the Gulf War mainly because he thought that it was essential for France's standing in the world in the 'new world order'. Throughout the war, Mitterrand spoke constantly of France's 'rank' in the world. France herself has few interests in that part of the Middle East, a fact which was well illustrated by President Mitterrand's tendency to mispronounce 'Kuwait' and call it 'Koveit'. Instead, the purpose of France's involvement was not any commitment to the liberation of Kuwait, nor even to ensuring stability in the Middle East and the continued supply of oil. It was purely and simply that – as Roland Dumas claimed in print[32] – France wanted to have a role in the overall peace process in the Middle East when the negotiations restarted.

It was doubtless because of this ulterior motive that French policy in the Gulf was a typical Mitterrand failure. In order to understand why, it is important to recall that Mitterrand had also been innovative in French foreign policy in his unprecedented support for Israel, something which has been called 'without any doubt the most original aspect of Mitterrand's foreign policy'.[33] He was the first French Head of State to pay a state visit to Israel: prior to that, France had had hardly any dialogue with the Jewish state, and certainly no pretensions to be an intermediary between Arabs and Jews. In contrast to Mitterrand, de Gaulle's anti-Israeli stance was part and parcel of his overall anti-American obsessions: he famously denounced Israel for being the aggressor in the Six Day War in 1969, angrily referring to the Jews as 'this people who thinks of itself as an élite, sure of itself, domineering'.[34] Valéry Giscard d'Estaing's Middle Eastern policy was similarly pro-Arab.

The Israelis, for their part, generally returned the compliment and have been very pro-Mitterrand: Shimon Peres even managed to persuade the then Prime Minister, Menachem Begin, to delay an air attack on the Iraqi nuclear installation at Tamuz, planned for 10 May 1981, in order not to put the election of Mitterrand into jeopardy. He presumably feared that the pro-Israeli vote, which Mitterrand was seeking to attract, might have been thrown off course if Israel had seemed to be too aggressive.[35] Doubtless it was for this reason that Mitterrand wanted his first state visit abroad to be to Israel.[36] However, within the framework of his overall strong support for Israel, Mitterrand always tried to keep a door open to the PLO. In 1982, he gave a seminal and now famous speech to the Knesset, in which he called for a solution to the Palestinian question. He helped Yasser Arafat to obtain safe passage out of Lebanon, and later received him at the Elysée Palace, despite strong protestations. By keeping several doors open at once – as he was to become famous for doing in all areas of policy – he hoped that France would be an intermediary between the two sides.[37]

But as ye sow, so shall ye reap. Here as elsewhere his ambiguity

proved fatal, for his Palestinian connections were severely undermined, with no apparent profit to France, by French support for
the US in the Gulf War. By the time of the 'historic handshake'
between Arafat and Shamir in Washington in September 1993,
France was completely absent from the negotiations which began in
Madrid in November 1991. (Britain was too, but then she had
never pretended that things would be otherwise.) What with the
absurd Georges Habache affair, France's Arab policy was left in
ruins. As one wit jibed, 'What is left of France's Arab policy?
Nothing but Barbès-Rochechouart [a well known Arab quarter in
Paris]'. Mitterrand was reduced to appearing on a chaotic television
discussion with Yasser Arafat and Shimon Peres – at which the
former seemed to hardly have time to come to the telephone – in an
attempt to prove to the French that their country had had a role. It
was a classic example of how Mitterrand substitutes hollow publicity
gestures for the substance of true politics.

Indeed, it underlined how counter-productive in foreign policy
are the wheeler-dealing tactics so common to French domestic
politics, for, because he operated with no reference to principles, he
only confused his allies and aroused distrust. Divided between
rhetoric and reality as ever, and evidently feeling that he is never
bound by his words, Mitterrand declared at the beginning of the
war that French troops would not be under American command;
then he did place them under US command. And just before the
ultimatum expired, he sprung a last-minute 'peace plan' on the
world, just as John Major was leaving the Elysée Palace, not
having said a word about it during their two-hour discussion.
The world was simply left with an impression of schizophrenic
incoherence. As one critic remarks,

> These presidential volte-faces are not surprising. Or rather,
> they are no longer surprising. François Mitterrand has made
> us get so used to his changes of mind and opinion, to his
> mental meanderings which follow a clever and complex stra-
> tegic path. This practice has become so common that the
> President does not even need to explain why, finally, all things
> considered, he has decided to do the opposite of what he had
> said he would do. Because he is not judged on the logic of his
> actions, but on his capacities to navigate between obstacles, to

indicate false wrong paths in order better to choose the right one, to reconcile that which seems contradictory.[38]

What this story suggests is that Mitterrand's apparent pro-Americanism and anti-Sovietism were inspired by different motives from the ideological commitment of someone like Mrs Thatcher. Throughout the early 1980s, her strategy was to seek out young apparatchiks in the Soviet Communist Party who would be more 'reform-minded' than their predecessors. She devoted a huge amount of effort to this task, eliciting from Jacques Attali, Mitterrand's chief foreign-policy adviser at the time, the snide and snobbish remark that her search had become an 'obsession'.[39] But it is sad that, publishing the book in 1991, and now that the Cold War has been definitively won as a result of the Thatcher-Reagan stance, Attali seems unable to accept the moral enormity of their effort and success, especially since her strategy had already paid off triumphantly in 1984, when Mihail Gorbachev visited London before he became General Secretary, and then again with her own subsequent triumphant visit to Moscow in 1987.

For the success in ending the Cold War was certainly not France's. Instead of taking sides unambiguously against the Soviet Union with Britain and the United States, France was consistently trying to obstruct what it saw as American influence in (Western) European affairs. This even extended to an extremely conciliatory attitude to things like the shooting-down of the South Korean Boeing 747 at the end of August 1983.[40] Eight days after that event, Mitterrand was in Moscow reminding Foreign Minister Gromyko that France had hardly raised a finger in protest. Rather than bandying about accusations, said Mitterrand, 'France has opted for a positive attitude, preferring to ensure that such things do not happen again.' He then reassured Gromyko that 'France and the Soviet Union are not enemies'.[41] Similarly, France did everything to wreck American Soviet policy, and was, as usual, the odd-man-out in Europe on the matter. Attali even ponders once in his memoirs why France is always alone in resisting the American 'threat' to 'European autonomy',[42] even though it should be clear to any reader of his memoirs that he and Mitterrand treated everything that came out of Washington, however sane and sound, with suspicion.

The area of greatest tension between the US and France was

over Ronald Reagan's rigorous economic and technological blockade of the Soviet Union through COCOM. While Reagan and
Thatcher were fighting the Evil Empire, Mitterrand, apparently less
convinced of its evil nature, was still trying to act the 'honest
broker'. With a mixture of the political old hand's attachment to
round-table discussions and flabby consensus, and an overestimation
of his own country's importance, Mitterrand would declare rather
ludicrously that 'Harmony in Europe will come about only through
the Franco-Soviet dialogue'.[43] The remark was not only silly, but
incredible, because there seems to have been so little effective
Franco-Soviet dialogue. Mitterrand, who had just sat passively and
waited for things to change in the Soviet Union, was honoured in
1985 when Gorbachev chose to make his first foreign trip abroad as
General Secretary to France. But instead of exploiting the opportunity to see whether Mr Gorbachev was a man he could (in Mrs
Thatcher's famous phrase) 'do business with', he refused, against
Gorbachev's wishes, to sign a joint communiqué at the end of their
meeting. It was later leaked that Gorbachev had been extremely
disappointed by his visit to Paris.[44]

This meant that France isolated herself from the subsequent
momentous events in the Soviet Union during the latter half of the
decade. While German-Soviet relations became almost indecently
warm, and while Mrs Thatcher was almost equally indecently being
swept off her feet by dark-eyed Misha in the Kremlin, Franco-
Soviet relations, although punctuated by frequent state visits, never
really took off in the same way. France was partly incapacitated by
the semi-permanent electoral campaign in which she was immersed
from autumn 1985 to spring 1988, and thus one might argue that
French eyes were not on the foreign-policy ball. But Mitterrand's
rather stand-offish declarations, denying the need to help Gorbachev, seemed to betray more indifference than an understanding
of the political seismic shift which was under way in that country.
Thus, as she was celebrating the bicentennial of her own Revolution, France was only looking backwards when Eastern Europe
began liberating itself in 1989. The kitschy displays produced to
order and minutely prepared in advance encouraged Mitterrand to
forget that real revolutions not only change the framework of
societies, but also mess around with people's diaries.

Mitterrand's re-election to the presidency in 1988 encouraged him to believe that he could manipulate and surf on world events in the same way that he did in domestic politics. In the view of some commentators, de Gaulle became victim to a similar megalomania towards the end of his reign too, as the ludicrous 'Vive le Québec libre!' speech showed.[45] No doubt it is an occupational hazard for the holders of such an immensely powerful and irresponsible office. Mitterrand had believed since 1981 that he could accurately predict not only the break-up of the Soviet Union, but also the exact date when it would occur: 1996.[46] It seems that he was not prepared to let anything get in the way of his timetable. After all, if one had believed that one could manage a national economy, why could one not manage international politics too? So when the two most important events of the end of the twentieth century – the fall of the Berlin Wall in 1989, and the dislocation of the Soviet Union following the Moscow *putsch* in 1991 – occurred unexpectedly early for him, Mitterrand's behaviour could only be reactionary.

Indeed, as the European cauldron began to boil over in the summer of 1989, Mitterrand's preference for 'managed' politics was already clear. He intoned,

> The Germans' undeniable right to self-determination cannot force itself on to the facts. The two governments would first have to be in agreement. Neither of the two German states can impose its point of view on the other. This aspect of intra-German relations is fundamental. The West German leaders, the ones I have met, have never pretended that they would try to obtain reunification in a way that would increase the tensions in Europe ... *Observers say that there has been a real shift in public opinion. But nothing suggests that elected politicians, the government or the Chancellor have changed their position.*[47]

In preferring the opinions of the 'elected' German politicians – only an approximate truth, for in reality, they are nominated from party lists – to those of the citizens of Germany, Mitterrand was, indeed, in agreement with those politicians. They too preferred the company of other politicians, whether 'elected' or not, to the pressures of public opinion. The very aim of the *Ostpolitik* begun under Willy Brandt, and continued ever since, was to accept the legitimacy of East Germany and to try (or to pretend to try) to obtain concessions from the Communist authorities in order to improve the well-being of the sorry inhabitants of that country. In fact what happened was that the huge financial support given to East Germany merely eased the pressure for change on the Honecker dictatorship, and thus increased the length of suffering of the East German population.[48] It also led to much unpleasantly close fraternization between West German politicians of all political persuasions and their East German counterparts.

Nonetheless, there was an important difference between France and Germany. Mitterrand firmly believed that the Soviet Union would never accept the reunification of Germany. Chancellor Kohl had also thought this until Gorbachev gave him to understand otherwise at a meeting in Bonn in 1989. After dinner, Gorbachev and Kohl went for a walk in the park of the Chancellery, and, at the bottom of the garden, they sat on a wall, watching the Rhine flow by in the moonlight. Kohl looked at the river, and the two men spoke of German-Soviet relations. Gorbachev suggested that the two countries start to put their relations on a new footing, and he suggested that they sign a treaty. Kohl agreed in principle, but added, 'We cannot enjoy good relations unless you accept the unification of Germany. For as a long as you prevent it, the division of the country will remain an open wound between us.' Gorbachev simply remained silent. Kohl was later to say, 'For the first time, Gorbachev did not contradict me. I am not making anything up. It is exactly how it happened: that night, sitting on a wall in the Chancellery garden, watching the Rhine flow by, I understood that the Soviet Union would not oppose German reunification.' In order to press his advantage with Gorbachev, Kohl added, 'You cannot stop the Rhine. You can put all the obstacles you like in its way, the water will always continue to flow. In the same way, you cannot stop the reunification of our country.'[49]

Mitterrand, by contrast, remembered Gorbachev saying the opposite to him, 'The day that the reunification of Germany occurs, there will be a two-line communiqué announcing that a Soviet marshal is sitting in my chair.'[50] However, there was more to their difference than a mere lack of information on Mitterrand's part. Because he believes that stability can come only from governmental decisions, Mitterrand was convinced that reform in Eastern Europe was conceivable only within the framework of continuing Soviet hegemony there. Roland Dumas, Mitterrand's mouthpiece, argued on the day after the Berlin Wall fell that, while Gorbachev deserved the credit for the changes, the Soviet Union would continue to set limits to what happened in Eastern Europe, principally via the Warsaw Pact. Gorbachev had to be preserved, or else there would be chaos.

When the Berlin Wall did finally fall on the night of 9 November 1989, Mitterrand was in Copenhagen. His first reaction was a very limpid, if unwitting, revelation of his thoughts and worries. He said, 'This happy event shows how liberty is progressing in Europe. It is likely that this great popular movement will be contagious and that it will continue elsewhere and go further.'[51]

His use of the word 'contagious' showed that, for all the *langue de bois* in his speeches about human rights, freedom and democracy, Mitterrand was terrified of the instability which he believed the liberty of Eastern Europe would cause. Having spent all his life in the corridors of power, his sympathies lie more with governments than with the governed. Indeed, so terrified was he that he simply did not know what to do. Two days later, on 12 November 1989, he addressed the European parliament at Strasbourg. He welcomed the popular liberation movements which were springing up all over Eastern Europe, but referred only to Hungary and Poland, and *omitted any mention of Germany whatever*! Three days later, on 15 November 1989, the pretence was still continuing: Roland Dumas, the Foreign Minister, declared at the tribune of the National Assembly, 'German reunification is not on the agenda.'[52]

In fact, Paris' thinking on the matter was exactly the same as that of the East German Communists. Two days after Dumas' declaration, the East German Prime Minister, Hans Modrow, reaffirmed 'the legitimacy of the German Democratic Republic as a Socialist and sovereign state'.[53] As events progressed, the gap between Paris and Bonn grew wider, and Mitterrand began explicitly to stress his differences with Bonn:

> That we should have different points of view, different interests, and different instinctive reactions is perfectly normal . . . History is there: I take it as it is . . . The Germans simply have to understand that history just is not made like that. My own view comes from an evident observation, that things are going

quickly, very quickly. Things will not go as quickly as may be
desired by those who are speaking of reunification as something for today . . . I am not making a definite prediction, but
reunification poses many problems of which I shall warn as
the events unfold.[54]

Mitterrand wanted the EC to be the main instrument with which to
slow down this process. On 9 December 1989 he declared that
European unification actually took priority over German.[55] Dumas
had expressed the same thought on 7 December: 'The evolution of
the German question will depend on the evolution of Europe
herself; when I say "Europe", I am thinking above all of the
EEC';[56] and later: 'The German question will find its solution with
a process of maturation which we will neither oppose nor precipi-
tate. This solution will be what Europe makes of it.'[57]

But for all the talk about 'Europe', Mitterrand's policy in fact
made the EC a total irrelevance. France held the presidency of the
European Community in the latter half of 1989. The regular six-
monthly meeting of the EC heads of state and government was due
to be held on 8–9 December; when the Berlin Wall fell, most EC
countries expected it to be brought forward to discuss the unfolding
events. But Mitterrand did nothing. Dumas explained that the
summit had more important things on the agenda, such as the
desire to save the Social Charter, the television and film industry,
relations with third countries, and economic and monetary union![58]
The most important political event since the end of the war had
just occurred, and France proposed publicly to ignore it.

So while he wanted to devote two days of discussions to pan-
European workers' councils and relations with Switzerland, Mitterrand felt that a little dinner party at the Elysée Palace would be
sufficient to deal with the momentous events happening in Germany. But at this point, political surrealism took over. After the
dinner, François Mitterrand held a press conference. He spoke of
the reasons for calling the meeting – solidarity and cohesion among
Europeans, the project of creating a bank for the development of
Eastern Europe, the urgency of advancing in the construction of
Europe – but not a single word on Germany. One had to wait for
the journalists' first questions to hear the astonishing reply, 'We did
not talk about that.'[59]

Not only is this reply the height of absurdity; not only does it show that the Europe of committees was putting its head in the sand when the Europe of peoples was exploding; not only did it show Mitterrand being deliberately obstructive; it also showed how hollow is the justification for the omnipotence and irresponsibility of the French President, who is traditionally thought omniscient in foreign policy. Instead of providing France with a statesman able to fulfil her high ambitions and able to respond swiftly and with daring to world events, Mitterrand incarnated nothing so much as obtuse narrow-mindedness and obstinate meanness of spirit. A few days later, Chancellor Kohl announced his ten-point plan for German reunification, without even having consulted the European partners with whom he had dined only a day or two previously. The EC had been relegated to the margins of history indeed.

There is an important distinction to be made between the attitude of Margaret Thatcher and that of Mitterrand, even if the German press, with its characteristic hysteria against the former, was still attacking her three years later for having been opposed to German reunification.[60] Thatcher certainly had her reservations, but she did nothing to stop the process. She took expert academic advice on the German question, by holding a special seminar at Chequers, which concluded that there was nothing to worry about. However, her objection was not to the reunification of Germany as such, it was to the reunification of Germany *within a European federation*.[61] She recognized that within a single political entity, such as that which Delors and Mitterrand envisaged the European Community becoming, the most powerful country would dominate. She has never varied from this view since.[62]

In any case, she soon accepted German unification, while continuing to oppose European integration. The day after Kohl announced the ten-point plan, the Americans gave it their basic approval. In a little three-point declaration of their own, they insisted that self-determination must take place 'without prejudice to its outcome' (the opposite of the French position), and that Germany should remain in NATO. Thatcher immediately agreed with both these points – which were eventually what happened – and thus showed herself to be closer to the position of the German government than Mitterrand was.[63] Unlike Thatcher, he was determined to take

concrete steps to frustrate the East Germans' desire for self-determination. It is no exaggeration to say that twenty-five years of
Franco-German co-operation – and especially the seven years since
1982, when relations had been especially warm – were put in
jeopardy by Mitterrand's cussed opposition to the ten-point plan.

First, he sent Roland Dumas to see Gorbachev in Moscow on 14
November 1989. Dumas assured Gorbachev and Shevardnadze, the
Soviet Foreign Minister, that 'The right of peoples to self-determination cannot be allowed to be the cause of instability, and that
France would not support anything which seemed in danger of
causing such an instability'.[64] Dumas also gave implicit support to
the preservation of the Warsaw Pact, underlining his and Mitterrand's preference for the 'stability' of Communism to the 'instability'
of popular democratic revolution.

Second, not content with this, Mitterrand himself decided to go
and see Gorbachev in Kiev on 6 December 1993, a week or so after
the announcement of the German ten-point plan. The exact content
of their discussions was not revealed, but it must be assumed that
he was trying to prevent German reunification. There are rumours
that Mitterrand had previously asked Thatcher to intercede with
Gorbachev to prevent it.

But the best was yet to come. On 20 December 1989, Mitterrand
undertook an official visit to East Germany itself. It is worth
dwelling on the magnitude of this. The whole country was in open
revolt, the state's existence was explicitly under threat, forty years
of dictatorship were crashing to an end, and the President of France
undertook a state visit in order to express his support for the
regime there. All the Communist leaders, from Hans Modrow, the
Prime Minister, to Gregor Gysi, the head of the Communist Party,
thanked France for her gesture of support for the German Democratic Republic. The East German press saluted Mitterrand's act:
the Communist organ *Junge Welt* emphasized that the central point
of the French position was 'to maintain the sovereignty of the two
Germanies'. On television, Mitterrand spoke of the 'German people
of the GDR' just as the crowds were chanting 'We are one people'
in the streets of Dresden.[65] At the official dinner on the day of his
arrival, Mitterrand spoke of the 'contribution which your country
has made to world civilization' and referred to 'the debt which the
philosophy of the Enlightenment owes to Berlin, to Prussia, to

Frederick the Great', thereby repeating almost word for word the standard elements of East German politico-cultural propaganda.[66] On and on he went: 'The dramatic events ... are making us think about the future, and about how the identity of the GDR has transformed itself, thanks to the determination and the initiative of certain people, into a vast movement of liberation, which has been maturing for a long time in the work of writers and artists.'[67] He was referring to a group of bearded left-wing intellectuals in East Germany, which had constituted itself into a rather drippy group, the 'New Forum', whose manifesto, published two weeks previously, had taken a clear position in favour of the maintenance of the GDR as a separate state. Mitterrand had no difficulty recognizing in Communist practice the role of 'intellectuals' within his own country, an essentially supporting role which his own coterie of pseuds was only too happy to play. (During the campaign in favour of the ratification of the Maastricht treaty, he saw to it that Jack Lang produced a bevvy of self-appointed 'intellectuals' to campaign for a 'yes' vote.)[68] In case there was the merest shadow of doubt, Mitterrand made his position clear: 'In this difficult quest, *you may count on the solidarity of France with the German Democratic Republic*.'[69]

To cap it all, he left Germany an hour or so before a ceremony formally to open the Brandenburg gate. Could he not have waited for a few hours to be present at this extraordinary moment? 'I did not think of it,' he said later, 'but if I had done, I would not have stayed.' He explained that the events in Romania prohibited it. As such, France was absent from the most important ceremonial moment in the history of post-war Germany, as a result of Mitterrand's sheer underestimation of the will of the East Germans for reunification, and of the abilities of Kohl. The result, as in the Gulf, was that he had completely marginalized France. In trying to put a brake on change, the French President, the declared defender of the rights of peoples to choose their fate, preferred to support states which already existed, or rather the heads of those states, to the people themselves. 'He preferred the reassurance of what is established to the adventure of new freedoms, immobility rather than movement ... Instead of taking action, he manoeuvred, as he likes to do, and the manoeuvre was a piece of nonsense.'[70]

13. The Strange Defeat

We cannot unite the states of Western Europe and at the same
time encourage the breakaway of Soviet republics.

Jacques Delors[1]

Given Mitterrand's behaviour, it was hardly surprising that in early
1991 the liberal German weekly, *Die Zeit*, argued that France had
become the problem country of Europe. For the last hundred
years or so, of course, it has usually been Germany which is
graced with that epithet: too small to dominate the whole of the
Continent with ease, but too big to have a normal relationship
with her neighbours, Germany had been a loose cannon as a
result of her national neuroses following the foundation of the
German Reich in 1871. France, for her part, had often tried to
offset German power, either by alliances with Britain and
America, or with Russia. Seen in this light, Mitterrand's renewal
of the Franco-Russian alliance in order to put a brake on German
reunification might have been thought a classic French reaction
to the renascent German question, and therefore nothing new.
However, the circumstances were very different from those of
the late nineteenth century, and certainly very different from the
1930s: Mitterrand's behaviour was hardly appropriate when millions
of people were on the verge of being liberated from forty years of
Communist dictatorship.

De Gaulle initiated the idea that France should balance between
the two superpowers, a rather perverse way of exploiting the Cold
War division of Europe, and a luxury which he might not have
awarded himself if there had not been an American defence of the
Western half of the Continent. However, his policy was predicated
on his constant desire to affirm France's difference from other
countries – *la spécificité française*. Mitterrand's, by contrast, flowed
from other considerations, even if his behaviour did contain some
elements of more classical geopolitical manoeuvring. As an un-

named source close to Mitterrand commented at the time of the Moscow *putsch* in 1991, 'His instinct is always to support public order instead of the movement of the masses. Faced with a historical event, he is always reactionary.'[2]

For, despite all his talk about supporting human rights, there have been constant indications that Mitterrand prefers authority and stability to liberty. The first of these came in December 1985 when he decided to receive General Jaruzelski in Paris. Even the imperious manner in which his decision was announced befitted the typically Mitterrandian motives which inspired it. Jaruzelski was the man whose very name was synonymous with the brutal suppression of dissent in Poland, followed by mass arrests and tortures, which culminated in the beating and murder of Lech Walesa's confessor, Father Jerzy Popieluszko in 1984. But when the news broke that Mitterrand was to receive him, neither the Prime Minister, Laurent Fabius, nor the Minister of the Interior, Lionel Jospin, had been informed.[3] In vain did Fabius commit presidential *lèse-majesté* by protesting that he had been kept ignorant of the visit.[4] As with the German question, the contrast between François Mitterrand and Margaret Thatcher is illuminating. When she travelled to Poland three years later, she deliberately embarrassed her hosts by going to see Lech Walesa in Gdansk, where she publicly attended mass with him.

Mitterrand had two justifications for receiving the Polish dictator. The first was that many other leading politicians had done the same: Helmut Kohl, Hans-Dietrich Genscher, Bettino Craxi, Willy Brandt and even the Pope. Indeed, Willy Brandt, the President of the International Socialist, even refused to meet Lech Walesa on an official visit to Poland in 1985. Brandt had seen Mitterrand just after the declaration of martial law in 1981, and was 'very moderate' in his criticism of the events in Poland: he was evidently prepared to accept what had happened without much protest.[5] Nor did Brandt's views change much later on: he still refused to ask Lech Walesa to his seventieth birthday in 1989, attended by the great and the good of International Socialism, because he thought it might be an insult to the Polish government. He preferred the company of Communist thugs like Mieczeslaw Rakowski at his birthday celebrations instead.

Perhaps this merely shows just how compromised the European

political class is, especially as details seep out about the extent of the Kohl-Genscher collaboration with the East German Communists, and now that Bettino Craxi is under investigation for alleged corruption, along with the majority of the old Italian political class. But Mitterrand's second justification was more interesting. It was that he believed that Jaruzelski's decision to introduce martial law into Poland in 1981 was necessary in order to preserve civil peace, and to prevent the Soviet Union from invading Poland to impose order itself. He may even have held that Jaruzelski's actions had actually facilitated Poland's early transition to democracy. Nor was Poland the only country where Mitterrand thought dictatorship was appropriate: in 1983 he had argued that Portugal, too, was politically unstable except under dictatorship.[6] Indeed, Mitterrand went further: even when Jaruzelski had been appointed, i.e. even before the introduction of martial law, Mitterrand considered him a bulwark against the Russians.[7]

He was far from alone in holding this opinion, which is still current in some circles,[8] and it is certainly the image which Jaruzelski likes to give of himself. The Polish primate, Monsignor Glemp, even told Pierre Mauroy that he thought Jaruzelski was a Polish patriot.[9] It is difficult to decide whether this attitude betrays an authoritarian sympathy for those in power, or simply the belief that politics is always a dirty business which is not subject to moral criteria. Whatever the truth, quite apart from the sheer unpleasantness of consorting with dictators, Mitterrand's interpretation of Jaruzelski is simply wrong. As files released by Russia in August 1993 show, the General's claim that he had acted in order to forestall an impending Soviet invasion was pure invention. Far from having been the last bastion against such an eventuality, Jaruzelski had in fact implored the Russians to intervene in his country to suppress the growing dissent. It was only when they made it quite clear that they had no intention of doing so that he decided to impose martial law himself. It was significant that Mitterrand's instinctive sympathies should have been with him and not with the long-suffering Polish people.

Mitterrand's high opinion of Jaruzelski is further evidence of his conviction that change in politics can be managed. This view, which in fact stems from a fear of change itself, became more and more visible as the liberty which Jaruzelski had tried to quash began to erupt all over Eastern Europe during 1989. As the drama unfolded, with East German refugees fleeing to the West in ever greater numbers via the Austro-Hungarian border and from the German embassy in Prague, Mitterrand-Metternich saw the spring-time of nations as a dangerous factor for destabilization. He thus sought to 'stabilize' it with a reinforcement of the strength of the European Community, just as he placed his faith in the same panacea for the German problem as well. On 3 November 1989, less than a week before the fall of the Berlin Wall, he declared, 'The quicker the events in Eastern Europe go, the quicker we must accelerate and reinforce the European Community.'[10]

However, in early 1990 Mitterrand realized that his attempts to slow down German unification were doomed to failure. Although he then changed his approach, he retained his profound assumption that stability can come only from more government: the new approach was motivated by the same desire to counterbalance Germany as the first one had been. Having initially hoped to be able to squash the German *risorgimento*, he then decided to squeeze his newly bulky neighbour in a heavy embrace. In parallel with Chancellor Kohl, Mitterrand proposed that the national govern-ments of the European Community be liquidated into a European Union with one currency managed by a single European central bank. This project was to become the Maastricht treaty on European Union.

The central part of the Maastricht treaty, monetary union, was drawn up by a committee headed by his close political ally, Jacques Delors. The Delors committee had reported in April 1989, and had sketched out three stages leading to monetary union. In the April following the fall of the Iron Curtain, Mitterrand and Kohl issued a joint letter calling for the creation of an economic, monetary and political union of the member states of the European Community, based on the Delors report. Intergovernmental conferences were called in December 1990 to draw up the treaty, and the final text was eventually signed a year later, in December 1991.

Although the governments of the majority of member states enthusiastically supported Maastricht, it is not difficult to identify a mainly Franco-German influence on the text. The predominance of 'independent' (i.e. unaccountable) institutions in the EC was already strong: Maastricht proposed to strengthen that predominance by the creation of an extra independent body, the central bank, and the reinforcement of the others, the Council of Ministers and the Commission. Although each of the two countries exerted its own influence on different parts of the treaty, the lowest common denominator was the predilection which both share for bureaucratic government. This can perhaps be explained by Germany's (albeit diluted) Prussian legacy, itself partly a product of French influence. Because of the fiscal and other budgetary controls needed to maintain price stability within a monetary area, this project amounted to one in favour of a single government for Europe. It is an amusing, if unsurprising, irony of history that a previous French Socialist had come up with an almost identical plan in the nineteenth century. Henri de Saint-Simon, the arch-planner of society, who once proposed that the entire planet be ruled by scientific 'Councils of Newton', who would also propagate the 'Cult of Newton' and worship at the temple of that great man, had similarly placed his faith in 'one single governing bank' (*'une banque unitaire, directrice'*) as the most 'rational' way of administering the whole of society and the whole economy. Karl Marx and the Bolsheviks were mere copycats from Saint-Simon when it came to trying to plan economies.[11]

The plan had two main advantages to Mitterrand's mind. First, it was supposed to reinforce the Franco-German alliance upon which the European Community had rested since the reconciliation between de Gaulle and Adenauer in 1962, and thereby to provide France with control over Germany in an area which had for long been a source of tension between the two countries, monetary policy. He hoped that this would counterbalance what Mitterrand thought was the unified Germany's new weight. Second, the European project would allow him to distract attention from the vacuity and failure of his domestic policies. He wanted 'Europe' to be the theme by which his second seven-year term was to be remembered. As one critic has remarked, 'Having failed to govern France, he raised himself up above France, putting his image above that which he was supposed to serve.'[12]

Mitterrand tried to pretend that his Maastricht policy was the continuation of de Gaulle's European policy, a curious invocation of the man whose policies he had always fought. But while de Gaulle may have been the author of the Franco-German reconciliation, he never sought to confine France to Europe, for he knew that her foreign-policy presence had to be worldwide. Mitterrand, by contrast, was incapable of inventing anything new and merely sought to make the entirety of his foreign policy dependent on the axis with Germany.

Moreover, it was striking that all of Mitterrand's arguments in favour of Maastricht were predicated on a conviction that France was inevitably the weaker of the two countries, an assumption which was to prove self-fulfilling. No doubt his youthful experience of French defeat by Germany in war, and his subsequent involvement in Vichy, had entrenched that conviction in his mind. During the referendum campaign on the treaty in September 1992, Mitterrand addressed the French in a two-hour-long televized debate from the Sorbonne. In reply to one question, he used the word '*menace*' no fewer than nine times. He dwelt luridly on all the threats which beset Europe and France – unnamed 'external agression', crime ('the Mafia is international, you know'), drugs, disease, AIDS ('viruses, like murderers, know no frontiers'), Yugoslavia, Eastern Europe, economic competition from Japan, political domination by America, even, astonishingly, by the European single market: 'The key to the Maastricht treaty is that it protects Europe from the dangers of its own development.' He concluded, 'The European Union means protection: a common response to common threats!'[13] The assumption was explicit and profound: France herself was incapable of facing up to these challenges on her own. (It was also remarkable that Mitterrand's tactics directly imitated those of Jean-Marie Le Pen, who had also evoked all the same dangers, only claiming that Maastricht would make them worse.) Few occasions have illustrated Mitterrand's Pétainist appeal better than that one: he wanted to present himself as a wise old professor, a slightly inscrutable protector of France in difficult times, and not as a politician on the hustings. Having left the scare tactics to his cohorts – politicians like Michel Rocard and Roland Dumas dwelt especially on the so-called neo-Nazi threat from Germany if Maastricht was not ratified – the paralysing boredom of the broadcast befitted his somnolent message, which was 'Trust me, and I will protect you'.

For their part, the Germans also had an interest in pushing for the treaty. With the overdependence of the German export economy on the EC market, Germany needs a stable economic environment within which to flood her exports. At the same time, she has a deep geopolitical need for stability on her frontiers, which are numerous in virtue of her central position in Europe. German advocates of the treaty, who claimed that they wanted to prevent their country from returning to the so-called 'special path' she had pursued in the past, were making a very inaccurate diagnosis of Germany's use of diplomacy during her periods of aggression in two world wars. Far from being alone at the beginning of those conflicts, she had had allies grouped around her (Austria-Hungary in the First War, Italy and the Soviet Union in the Second) and she was strong as a result. Indeed, it was only when she lost those allies that she began to weaken, and thus eventually to lose the war. Thus, the contemporary German desire for allies *as a means to augment her strength* was merely the twentieth-century manifestation of a geopolitical conundrum which Prussia had faced since the eighteenth century: a country which lies in the middle of Europe is very vulnerable to pressure from her neighbours.[14]

Mitterrand never gave any sign of understanding this German need. Rather than extracting concessions from the Germans by threatening to walk away from the Franco-German alliance, an action which would have underlined to the Germans the reasons why they need France, Mitterrand preferred to adopt a strategy which was predicated on the assumption that France needed the alliance more than Germany. It was hardly surprising that his assumptions of French weakness proved to be self-fulfilling. This was especially clear in the negotiations over the centre-piece of Maastricht, monetary union. Germany is a traditional stickler for price stability, and the Germans were determined not to give up the Deutschmark in favour of the ecu unless they felt sure that the latter would be as 'stable' as the former. Thus, through sheer economic and political weight, Germany was able to insist on her own conditions for monetary union, especially in the crucial area of the structure and tasks of the proposed central bank, which was deliberately modelled on the Bundesbank.

This represented an important initial victory for the Germans, and it perhaps explained their enthusiasm for a plan which the French thought was mainly in their own favour. After all, it took a sea-change in French centralist thinking to accept that monetary policy might be conducted by an 'independent' central bank not under the tutelage of the Ministry of Finance. France gave ground on other issues too. Previous French thinking on European monetary union had had a distinctly dirigiste flavour: they had argued that monetary union should come first and economic convergence later. The Germans took the opposite view, insisting that certain convergence criteria be respected before a monetary union could be created, a position which carried the day in the treaty negotiations.

Because Mitterrand was determined to get the German Chancellor's signature on a piece of paper at any price, the Germans got all they wanted in all these areas. Meanwhile, Mitterrand treated the text of the treaty in a rather cavalier fashion. As he revealed during the referendum campaign, he seemed to care little for the provisions of the treaty stipulating the central bank's independence, for he confidently asserted on television that control of monetary policy would be in the hands of the European Council of Ministers. This declaration elicited considerable protest and denial in Germany, for it was the opposite of the truth, and contrary to the Germans' greatest preoccupations. Meanwhile, various prominent Socialists, including Michel Rocard, insisted that the advantage of Maastricht was that it would allow monetary policy to be relaxed, in favour of other priorities which concerned the French, notably unemployment. All this was anathema to Bonn.

The fear that monetary union was a trap laid by the perfidious French to steal the virtuous Germans' hard-won monetary stability soon caused a backlash in Germany, led by sections of the press, including the mass-circulation tabloid, *Bild*, and a few politicians. One of these, a former official at the European Commission, was so disillusioned with the bureaucracy, dirigisme and authoritarianism of the European Community in general and of the Maastricht treaty in particular, that he took the treaty to Germany's constitutional court in Karslruhe, claiming that it violated Germany's independent statehood and its constitution. This court case was to be decisive, for although the court rejected his claim in October 1993, and allowed the treaty's ratification, it did so in such a way that changed fundamentally the terms on which the French (and the other member states) thought that they had signed the text. By saying that Maastricht did not violate German sovereignty, the court was obliged (and probably happy) to reassert its and Germany's own ultimate authority over the applicability of the treaty in Germany. Had the court not claimed this right, and had it not reminded the European Community that its existence flowed only from the continuing consent and will of the member states, then it would have been obliged to accept the claim and reject the treaty.

Few commentators noticed at the time, however, that the ruling overturned the basis on which the European Community had been run for thirty years, because it rejected the doctrine of the primacy of Community law. According to this principle of European jurisprudence, European legislation operates with direct effect and direct applicability over and above the national law of member states. While the German court said that it would continue to act in a spirit of co-operation with the European Court of Justice in Luxemburg, it retained the ultimate right to rule on the German constitution, and insisted that the German parliament and government have a continuing say over the process towards monetary union. In particular, it insisted that the criterion of 'price stability' be respected, and that the convergence criteria laid down in the treaty remain unchanged. It also denied that the dates in the treaty represented an irrevocable commitment, despite the text's clear statement to the contrary.

Moreover, at the time of ratification, the German constitution itself had been amended, with, among other things, the addition of a new article, 88.2. This new article allows the transfer of the Bundesbank's competences to the European central bank, 'whose goal is price stability'. The court thus obtained *for Germany* the right to say whether it thought that price stability was realizable *in Europe*, and to withdraw from the whole agreement if she considered that it was not. Germany thus gave herself a sovereign constitutional right to make or break European monetary union exclusively on her own terms. The binding force of Maastricht on Germany was shattered, and, by a succession of moves, the country's institutions had turned it around from being a French designed strait-jacket into an instrument for the imposition of her own economic and monetary priorities on the whole of Europe.[15]

Finally, the Germans successfully insisted that the new central bank be sited in Frankfurt, the home of the Bundesbank. According to them, that city was the only one with a sufficient 'culture of price stability', which sounded like a euphemism for saying that they could control it better there. Indeed, Chancellor Kohl welcomed the choice of Frankfurt by saying that 'it shows that European monetary policy will be henceforth be German monetary policy.'[16] This publicly unadmitted outcome must be deeply embarrassing for Mitterrand and for France, because it shows that the German Gulliver cannot be bound down after all. On the contrary, smaller countries who try to bind her down only get dragged along with her.

Throughout 1989, and especially at the CSCE conference which he organized in Versailles in November 1990, Mitterrand had made the call to 'get out of Yalta' ('*sortir de Yalta*') one of his favourite slogans. Like many, he wanted to overcome the post-war division of Europe. What was worrying was that, however grandiose his plans for Western Europe, they fitted into an even more grandiose plan for the whole Continent. These plans became clear at a conference organized in February 1992 by a group of his favourite intellectuals and politicians, including Bernard-Henri Lévy and Jacques Delors. Indeed, it was probably initiated under his own influence, for he himself made a 'surprise appearance' at it and talked for over an hour. The title of the conference was 'Europe or Tribalism?',[17] and his message was simple: 'I want a permanent structure for the whole of Europe'.[18]

With very little sympathy for the concept of free nationhood, Mitterrand and his ilk seemed to be suggesting with their unfortunate choice of title that demands for national independence were akin to 'tribalism', and thus a threat to peace and stability. He played on the old canard that the Yugoslav war was somehow the result of 'an eruption of ancestral ethnic hatreds' which no longer had the 'discipline' of Communism to contain them – when the instigator of the war was the hysterical nationalist-Communist, Slobodan Milosevic of Serbia – and he and his friends argued that similar 'nationalism' both in Western and Eastern Europe must be countered by the establishment of ever greater layers of statist or super-statist control.

The project to create a pan-European structure, therefore, was complementary to the project to transform the European Economic Community into a political union. Indeed, it was to be one half in the overarching structures which he envisaged for the whole Continent. As Roland Dumas said at the beginning of the Yugoslav conflict, when commenting on whether there should be a military intervention to support Bosnian or Croatian independence, 'It is not the role of the EC to promote the independence of peoples.'[19]

The idea of a politico-security structure for the whole of Europe dated at least from the previous year, when he had travelled to Prague to try to peddle it there. When he launched the idea of a 'European Confederation' on 25–6 April 1991, he got short shrift from the Czechs, including from Vaclav Havel, for (as if by chance!) Mitterrand had omitted to include the Americans. The badges distributed at the conference depicted a map with a huge USSR on it, while Czechoslovakia was invisible, an accurate indication of Mitterrand's own priorities.

At the same time, it became increasingly clear that Mitterrand wanted to exclude the countries of Eastern Europe from ever joining the European Community itself. The 'European Federation', rather like the 'Partnership for Peace' arrangements dreamed up by NATO in early 1994, was not intended to be a stepping-stone to full EC membership, but rather a way of obviating its necessity and thus putting it off until the Greek kalends. During the campaign in favour of the Maastricht treaty, Mitterrand argued that it would take 'decades' for the newly liberated countries of Eastern Europe to be able to join. The irony – and, once again, failure – was that his obvious hostility to the Czechs and to Eastern Central Europe generally only succeeded in driving them further into the German orbit, thus augmenting the influence and political weight of the country, instead of reducing it as he was trying to do.

Indeed, judging by his reluctance to see the break-up of the Soviet Union, it may be affirmed that his desire to see a reinforced European Community in Western Europe would emulate and complement the hegemony of the Soviet Union in the East. This apparent preference for the hegemony of Communism over the springtime of peoples was nowhere clearer than in his reaction to the Moscow *putsch* in August 1991. Eighteen months after the fall of the Berlin Wall, Mitterrand was still convinced that the unification of Germany had occurred too quickly. He continued to fear the danger of the knock-on effect in Moscow of which Gorbachev had warned him. Thus, when the news of the *putsch* broke, Mitterrand assumed that it was the concrete confirmation of the destabilization which he, in his infinite wisdom, had predicted.

On the day of the *putsch*, Mitterrand appeared on French television. His broadcast will probably be remembered for some time as the veritable nadir of his presidency, because he not only failed to condemn the *putsch* until prompted to do so by a journalist, but also accorded the *putschists* considerable legitimacy, among other things by declaring that 'The *putsch* has succeeded in its first phase'.[20] Referring to the *putschists* as 'the new Soviet authorities', he expressed the desire that they should continue along the path of 'reform' – which merely underlined his readiness to accept that they should stay in power – and said that he would ask for guarantees from them to that effect.

Worse, his tardy condemnation of their actions came only after he had announced that he had received a letter from their leader, Gennadi Yannaev. The British government had also received the same letter – it was evidently a circular sent to all the main world capitals – but they had immediately treated it with the contempt it deserved. John Major had condemned the coup from the very beginning, an immediate and unequivocal condemnation which seemed to Mitterrand, with his constant desire always to weave and twist, to slam a door shut which he would rather have kept open. Bush also seems to have been initially more conciliatory, but he had changed his mind by the time he spoke to the nation the same evening, six hours after Mitterrand.

Not only did Mitterrand boast of having received the letter, he also read it out in full. The weight which he thereby lent to its contents – a litany of platitudes about 'reform', 'democracy', 'glasnost and perestroika' – and his apparent desire to show off his international contacts, even with *putschists*, provided yet further evidence that he was prepared to collaborate with the regime. He ruled out sanctions against it, saying that it was too early to think of such measures. Instead of rejecting what had happened as simply unacceptable, he returned to his theme of monitoring promises, ensuring respect for the Helsinki process and the CSCE agreement signed in Paris the previous year, and other such trivia.[21] Referring to the 'new direction' which the Soviet Union had taken (a charming euphemism!), he even expressed the view that the 'new government' might be 'sincere' and that extraneous things like the Middle East peace process might continue unimpeded.

Mitterrand's final error was a series of omissions. He failed to mention the people of Moscow; he failed to recall that Yeltsin was the first democratically elected President in Russian history; and he forgot to remind French television watchers that Gorbachev was the only legitimate Soviet interlocutor for the international community. There can have been few clearer displays of the classic Mitterrand instinctive reaction – deeply ingrained in him after fifty years of sucking-up to the powers that be – always to sail with the political wind. It was hardly surprising that *Le Monde* should publish a cartoon after the coup had failed which perfectly summed up the absurdity of Mitterrand's behaviour.[22] It simply showed Mitterrand sitting at his desk, pen in hand, writing a reply, 'Dear Mr Yannaev . . .'

But his initial support for the *putsch* was very revealing of Mitterrand's overall view of the world. The *putsch* occurred because Gorbachev was trying to prevent the break-up of the Soviet Union. It took place on the day that a conference was opened which was supposed to lead to the signature of a treaty establishing looser links between the Soviet republics. The hard-line elements in the Communist Party thought that even this half-way house was giving the republics too much ground.

Mitterrand seemed to agree with the *putschist* view. In contrast to what he perceives as dangerous anarchy, Mitterrand is attached to what he calls 'the theory of *grands ensembles*'.[23] According to this so-called doctrine, the world is best governed by large overarching geopolitical structures based around geographical zones. He has used the theory as much to try to preserve the existence of the Soviet Union, as to attack the small separatist movement in Corsica. He sees the democratically elected national leaders in Eastern Europe, whether they be principled anti-Communists like Vyautatas Landsbergis in Lithuania or brash populists like Yeltsin, as threats to this overarching order.

Thus, Mitterrand had been convinced that Gorbachev would never succeed in getting the new treaty of Union signed. He reasoned that the country would be put under huge internal stress. According to his bureaucratico-Jacobin thinking – raised here to a continental scale – the USSR should not be allowed to break up as a political entity, a view shared by other European politicians.[24] Thus, when the *putsch* occurred, he thought it was the Polish experience all over again. Yannaev was Jaruzelski; the territorial integrity of the country had to be maintained, and stability should be preserved. '*Comme ça, on sera tranquille.*'

Once the outcome of the *putsch* was known, however, Mitterrand immediately jumped on a new bandwagon. He went on television for the second time in two days, on 21 August, and sent Michel Vauzelle, then President of the Foreign Affairs Committee of the National Assembly, as his personal representative to Moscow. (This shows an interesting interpretation of the separation of powers!) Vauzelle somehow managed to get himself on to the balcony of the Russian parliament in Moscow, the only foreigner among the Yeltsin supporters. He made a short speech in which he said that France had supported Yeltsin all along. Mitterrand also sent his old friend Elie Wiesel to Moscow, while his chief courtier, Jack Lang, came up with an instant 'International Committee for Democracy in the USSR', a gathering of the usual band of tinny intellectuals for whom he and his boss have such a penchant. Mitterrand held fast to his obsession with mediatic kitsch as a substitute for substantial policy.

During the second broadcast, he said he knew all along that the coup would fail, having announced on Monday night that it had succeeded. He listed the names of all the world politicians with whom he had been in contact – Bush, Major, Kohl, Andreotti, Mulroney and several others – in a kind of game of international political name-dropping, as if to emphasize that he was there at the top. He added grandly, 'I have communicated my thoughts to them.' But as always in French politics, politicking soon took over. Valéry Giscard d'Estaing, who has never forgiven Mitterrand for beating him at the presidential elections in 1981, decided to get his own back on Mitterrand for having called him a messenger boy in 1980. He rebuked Mitterrand for his emollient attitude, and referred to him as 'the author of the *coup d'état*', a wickedly cruel pun on Mitterrand's book of that title in 1964. The day of his second broadcast, the ever faithful Jack Lang replied with an attack on Giscard for going and hunting bears with Messrs Gierek and Ceauşescu. Mitterrand could not resist having a go as well. He declaimed pompously, 'I do not see how we could ever confide the government of a country like France to certain politicians who evidently cannot keep their cool. In any case, it is not a fate I would wish on my country.'[25] But the degree to which he had been politically wounded was already evident: when he informed the television channels that he was going to make a second declaration, they made him wait until after the news from Moscow itself before letting him on: normally a presidential address replaces the news.

As with the mistake over German unification, Mitterrand's behaviour over the Moscow *putsch* is more than just a silly error. In the second broadcast, Mitterrand said that he had always believed in Boris Yeltsin. He pointed out that he had rung Yeltsin, but omitted to mention that Major and Bush had rung him first, even before the outcome was clear. In fact, this served only to underline the inadequacy of his policy to date, for, as most observers knew, the treatment which Mitterrand and other Socialists meted out to Yeltsin varied between an hauteur bordering on the frigid and a quite astonishing rudeness. When Yeltsin visited the European parliament in 1990, the leader of the Socialist group, Jean-Pierre Cot, called him a populist and a peasant. (Cot's father had been a very senior Communist.) Mitterrand, while less publicly rude, then refused to receive Yeltsin as a Head of State when the latter was in Paris. He was afraid of upsetting Gorbachev, and lacked the courage to base his decisions on anything other than short-term political calculation. While all other Western leaders were pro-Gorbachev, few of them went to the same ludicrous lengths to be anti-Yeltsin as the French. After much pressure from Yeltsin, Mitterrand reluctantly agreed that he would be received by the Secretary-General of the Elysée Palace (the equivalent of the Chief of Staff at the White House). Afterwards it was made known that the French President had seen Yeltsin, as if by accident, in the corridor. Mitterrand was reduced to saying on television that, contrary to what had been officially announced, he had received Yeltsin in his own office and not in that of the Secretary-General next door!

However, despite his declared support for Yeltsin in the second television broadcast, Mitterrand continued to insist that the failure of the *putsch* had proved that Gorbachev was right, and that perestroika was there to stay. The reality, of course, was the opposite. There was no more talk of 'restructuring' either the Soviet Union or the Communist Party, and within a short while both of them had been dissolved. Gorbachev was proved so hugely wrong and Yeltsin so hugely right that the *putsch*'s failure, and Yeltsin's success, led directly to Gorbachev's fall from power. Once again, Mitterrand's error of judgement reflected his own political tastes: for him, Gorbachev, perestroika, the Common European Home, Maastricht, managed change, Socialism with a human face – all these are just his cup of tea. And the result of this error of judgement was that Franco-Russian relations subsequent to the *putsch* simply evaporated into thin air.

It came as no surprise, therefore, that Mitterrand should have been one of the most fervent supporters of the maintenance of the Yugoslav federation under Serb hegemony. It would be wrong to blame France more than most other European countries for their incessant and ham-fisted interference in Yugoslavia – Britain, for instance, must share a huge burden of responsibility. But Mitterrand's support for the hegemonial power, and his belief that the federation could be maintained, are interesting because they do at least betray a certain consistency of thought, whereas British policy, run by Mr Douglas Hurd, was inspired by mere appeasement.

Mitterrand's policy was also driven by a desire to counter what he considered to be excessive British influence in Yugoslavia (Lords Carrington and then Owen had been the EC 'peace negotiators'). He appointed his old friend, Robert Badinter, to run a committee in early 1992 which stipulated the conditions which the secessionist states had to fulfil if they were to be recognized by the EC. It was also striking that, as in Britain, the French élite reverted almost instinctively to an anti-Hun stance, reproaching the Germans for their premature recognition of Croatia and Slovenia, and almost explicitly basing their support for Serbia on a desire to contain Germany. It was a stupid stance, not least because the German recognition in December 1991 occurred some six months after Serbia first attacked Croatia, and after several Croatian towns, including Dubrovnik, had been subjected to shelling. Mitterrand even made a stupid (but subsequently very common) reference to the Nazi-Croat alliance during the Second World War. It was curious to see the champion of post-war Franco-German reconciliation reverting not only to Second World War propaganda, but to First World War reactions too.

France, like Britain, sent troops to the former Yugoslavia to protect the humanitarian effort. In Britain, this tactic was used to pretend that Yugoslavs were being killed by starvation when in fact they were being killed by bullets. Their real purpose was to ensure diplomatic and military stagnation, for every time the Americans or anyone else suggested air strikes, Douglas Hurd would reply that they would endanger the humanitarian effort, while never pausing to think whether the arms embargo against Bosnia and the refusal to take action against Serbia might be increasing the number of deaths by prolonging the war and supporting the aggressor.

In France, however, the notion of humanitarian involvement had become something of an ideological fad. Mitterrand even had a Minister for Humanitarian Aid, who was later also to become the Minister of Health, Bernard Kouchner. Like many leading Socialists a former *soixante-huitard* (he had been the Leader of the Union of Communist Students in 1968), Kouchner was the epitome of Mitterrand-style spray-on Socialism. He was famous for his photo-calls carrying sacks of rice on his back to starving Somalis, for bursting into tears over the contaminated-blood scandal, and for other such authentic television appearances. Kouchner was a particularly fervent supporter of the ideology of humanitarian aid, saying that the 'right to intervene' ('*le droit d'ingérence*') which it implied was the first step on the way to a world government. One would be hard pushed to find a better statement of modern left-wing imperialism.

But this was not the only glossy sheen with which Mitterrand sought to cover the vacuity of his policy. After the Lisbon summit in June 1992, Mitterrand mounted a *coup de théâtre*, of the kind which had long become his hallmark: in the absence of any real ideas in foreign policy, he frequently uses such gestures as a substitute for any real policy. Without informing his European partners (who in any case seemed more preoccupied with the European soccer championships, the German Chancellor, the Danish Prime Minister and the Danish Foreign Minister having all taken mini-TVs into the summit meeting to watch the football match in which Denmark had replaced Yugoslavia)[26], Mitterrand flew directly and secretly to Sarajevo from Lisbon. But the gesture was intended only to obscure his role as one of the chief proponents of doing nothing. He knew that by coming to do nothing in person, and avoiding saying anything of substance, his tarnished image would be smartened up.[27] Thus, in foreign affairs as in domestic, Mitterrand's policies have increasingly resembled the Louvre pyramid: a haven of eternal sleep covered with a cheap and glossy patina. Glinting and shining on the outside, the flimsy structure of the pyramid is in fact empty within and devoid of substance.

As Mitterrand grew old, his foreign policies came increasingly to resemble those which had excited him in his youth, the illusions of Vichy. Many writers testify to Mitterrand's predilection for bucolic idylls. Jacques Attali describes how the old man prefers countries which one can reach by land rather than by sea[28] – which makes it clear that his famous 'European' sympathies are only Continental, including Russia but excluding Britain and the United States of America. In Carl Schmitt's essay on the geopolitical difference between the Land and the Sea, and between the continental powers and the maritime ones, the former stand for immobilism and authoritarianism, while the latter represent freedom and movement. Schmitt describes the extraordinary courage and sense of adventure which led to the growth of maritime power, and he grasps the intimate connection between the sea and free trade: the maritime powers are liberal and commercial while the terrestrial powers are agricultural and economically closed.[29]

The immobilism of the land is a central theme in Mitterrand's own writings, especially the youthful ones. In the 1942 essay in *France, revue de l'état nouveau*, there are a number of the themes which were dear to Vichy. Pétain encapsulated his idyllic evocation of the peasantry and the countryside in all its eternal goodness in the slogan '*La terre, elle ne ment pas*' ('The soil does not tell lies'). Forty years later, in his autobiography, Mitterrand indicated that his name means '*milieu des terres*',[30] even saying that there is a field, geographically in the middle of France, called *Le champ de Mitterrand*. Describing his return to France from captivity, he says:

Birds were flitting through the air, flying to the ground and standing there with their heads high; a dog, panting through its muzzle, loped from one side of the road to the other. The fields were laid out before me, rich and empty, incubating secret births beneath the winter winds. White and grey villages separated the paths and men nonchalantly sawed wood outside their doors, called to each other for last night's news, pushed gently on the pedals of their bicycles.

I was content to find her thus once again, my nearly forgotten France. I had imagined I know not what storms, and even that the colour of the clouds would have changed. But the smoke, the roofs, the crossroads, the patchwork of the land, the rectangular hedges and the pure horizons, the uncurious and cold people, it was indeed this that I had left behind . . . Thus I returned to my cramped vineyard, among simple and uncultivated men . . . I had become a free man by placing my liberty in the bosom of the earth from which I came.[31]

Just as his *Grands Travaux* encapsulate symbols of decline and death, so in his foreign policy, he has attempted to reassure himself and the more cowardly elements in French society by seeking refuge in immobile solutions for a rapidly changing Continent, solutions which grew out of his own limited, exclusively Continental vision. His faith in the Maastricht treaty was little but the mentality of the Maginot line erected into a foreign policy, a useless rampart. Having understood, after several years at the Elysée, that ordinary government is thankless, disappointing and laborious, he decided to reassure the French by making a little reassuring history.[32] It was thus by listening to the voices of the past – the voices of Yalta and Versailles and Westphalia – that he tried to preserve the Cold War Europe like some soggy fruit in a bottle of eau-de-vie. In mistaking the *putsch*, in mistaking the fall of the Berlin Wall, and in continuing to believe that the events in Eastern Europe could be retarded and that the cosy Western European Community can be preserved, he respected one principle alone: order before change.

His mentality is perhaps best encapsulated in his annual habit of walking up the hill at Solutré with his 'friends from the Resistance' on the feast of Pentecost. This little ceremony, which has passed into Mitterrand folklore, symbolizes the man to a tee. In his book, *La Paille et le Grain (The Straw and the Grain* – even the title is bucolic), he describes the ceremony: 'I remain for a long time contemplating the spectacle to which I devoted myself twenty-eight years ago. From there, I can see better what has come, what has gone, and, above all, what has not changed.'[33]

'Above all, what has not changed.' This is Mitterrand's epitaph: the old man of the provinces with his dog and his epigones, undertaking a television stunt, looks out at the world from his modest high point and concentrates on the unchanging aspect of eternal France. Mrs Thatcher used to credit Mitterrand with having a good sense of history; but what he really has is a strong sense of the more changeless science, geography. As a boy, he declared geography to be 'my passion, my poetry'.

> I live France. I have an instinctive and profound consciousness of France, of physical France. I have a passion for her geography, for her living body. There, where my roots grew. I have no need to seek the soul of France, for it dwells within me just as it dwells within the whole French people. A people which sticks to its land can no longer be separated from it.[34]

Geography and history; land and sea. These are the categories by which politicians and nations can be judged. One might even invent a new political typology, a distinction between the geographer and historian politicians. The former may occasionally encourage the dictatorship of the real, while the latter are known for their invention of the virtual.

> Historian politicians can certainly become public dangers, subjecting their peoples to their creative madness. But geographer politicians, in their pusillanimity and their prudent respect for contours and hills, often lack foresight ... Geographer politicians do not invent. They take note, they conserve, they survey and measure. They wait, even if it means that they are overtaken. They contemplate, even if it means they are surprised. Nothing is more disagreable to them than chance, the unexpected or the novel, anything which blurs their maps, and muddles up their scales and their co-ordinates.[35]

One of Mitterrand's favourite sayings is, 'you must give time time' ('*il faut qu'on laisse le temps au temps*').[36] But time and tide wait for no man, not even for a king.

Conclusion

The last few years have seen an explosion of British interest in European politics. Not long ago, Britain compared herself principally with the United States, and her attention was directed more across the Atlantic than across the Channel. The introduction of the Single European Market and the furious debate in Britain over the Maastricht treaty have no doubt been causes and symptoms of this change.

The Maastricht debate, which split the Conservative Party down the middle, was furious because it was about far more than Britain's foreign policy. Indeed, it attained an intensity comparable to that between the Westernisers and the Slavophiles in nineteenth-century Russia, since it touched the very heart of national identity, democracy and the constitution. Because monetary union, the core proposal of the treaty, means a single economic government, and because the orientation and execution of those economic policies will be placed in the hands of an unaccountable institution, the proposed independent European Central Bank, the Maastricht treaty represents a clear attack on the principle and practice of parliamentary democracy itself.

Indeed, none of the institutions of the European Community are democratic. The Commission, which is responsible for initiating all legislation and for executing some of it, is composed of unelected and unaccountable civil servants. Its power and arrogance, is, indeed, in direct proportion to its status as a body which is above the control of ordinary citizens. The same is true of the Council of Ministers, which is the sovereign legislative body of the EC. When they meet in the Council, ministers, i.e. members of national executives, have the extraordinary privilege for ministers of sitting as legislators, i.e. as parliamentarians. No doubt this explains the great popularity of the European Community among the governments of the member states, for it is a very attractive way of bypassing parliamentary control. The Council itself is accountable to no one, neither to national parliaments, nor to the European parliament, nor to any electorate; and when votes are taken by majority rather than unanimity, no individual member of the Council is accountable to his national parliament either, because, if taken to task over a piece of EC legislation, he can always claim that he was in a minority and that the vote went against him. As a result of the well-entrenched principle that EC law overrides national law, there is no possibility of recourse against legislation voted in this way.

As for the European Parliament, those who suggest that it may one day become the parliament for the whole continent are only displaying an embarrassing ignorance of what a parliament should be. It is no exaggeration to say that Britain has the most dynamic parliament among the major world powers. Even those Scandinavian parliaments, such as the Danish one, which exercise a good degree of control over their governments, are probably less strong than Westminster where the vitality of debate is concerned. The role which the British parliament plays in constituting the political life of the country is simply without parallel. Prime Minister's questions, the daily questions to other ministers, debates, the Select Committees: it is easy for the British to overlook all this by taking it for granted. It is similarly easy for them not to grasp the constitutional problems faced by other countries in Europe which do not have Britain's parliamentary heritage.

France assumes a dual role in this British debate, both as subject and object of the argument. She is the European country which the British know best, and the one which epitomises Europe for them. She is also the European country which, until recently, has dominated the European Community, and which has placed her imprimatur on it more than any other. Even if the future will see an increase in the political weight of Germany, this will occur within the overall framework of the Franco-German axis. Above all, further European integration will only deepen the unacceptably undemocratic elements of the EC, on the basis of that bureaucracy which is the lowest common denominator between two such superficially different countries.

Much of the impetus behind the so-called 'pro-European' arguments in Britain comes from a hatred for Britain's parliamentary system, and a desire to see it re-modelled along more 'Continental' or administrative lines. This motive is itself a consequence of the modern economist trend, and it feeds off the British capacity — which is one shared by the French — for excessive self-deprecation. Even the most redoubtable conservative can sometimes melt before the supposed superiority of the planning capacities of the French administration. It is curious that this sentiment very often attaches to public transport, and, in the case of France, especially to the TGV high-speed train. The image of 'Europe' has often been confused with this myth of excellent public transport.

The grass is always greener on the other side. However successful the TGV may be, its advocates in Britain forget that its tickets cost far more than those of normal trains, and thus represents a 'luxury' form of transport, built at the state's expense. One wonders whether they would welcome a similar division of British Rail or the National Health Service into two tiers. They also tend to ignore the huge losses incurred by SNCF, as well as its notoriously chaotic reservations and passenger-information systems. However, the point is not to argue about trains. People simply use the trains as a means of arguing the deeper political point that government by administration is better than government by parliament.

It is, therefore, a defect of the British argument about Europe that it is often used as a surrogate for discussion of other, deeper issues. This is reflected in the false dichotomy between being 'in' or 'out' of Europe, one which is usually exploited by the 'pro-Europeans'. They counter all criticism of the way the European Community functions with the platitudinous reply that we had better be in it than outside of it. This false dichotomy is bad for Britain because it encourages us to mortgage our parliamentary democracy for the price of EC membership. However, it is also bad for Europe because it assumes — ironically for the pro-European argument — that Britain is a political island, and that the only question facing her is whether or not to join the Continent. As such, there is little sense that Britain might one day insist on her own standards and encourage the development of Europe towards her model of government which has, after all, stood the test of time.

Moreover, the prevailing tendency throughout the world is to confuse politics with economics, and to see governments more as managers of the national economy rather than in a political capacity. This downgrading of politics means that democracy is overlooked, because it ignores the fact that the open society is possible only within a properly structured *political* order, of which the government of the day is the chief trustee. The free-marketeers of the 1980s may have committed a partial mistake by speaking only of 'reducing the power of the state', for the real issue is what the qualitative role of the state should be: to uphold and to incarnate political legitimacy. Political legitimacy does not come from providing the public with the maximum of goods or wealth: it comes from acting justly and in accordance with the law. Much of the economist discourse of modern politics encourages people to turn a blind eye to government corruption and criminality, as much as to the more gradual undermining of political legitimacy which occurs in any country where its spirit is not kept properly alive. The case of Italy, where it took forty-five years to throw off the yoke of a criminal political system, shows that economic wealth alone is not a sufficient criterion for acceptable government. Similar problems of opacity, corruption, sclerosis and excessive bureaucracy are also faced by Germany, Belgium, Spain, Greece, and others. Even Britain has already drifted too far in that direction. It has been the purpose of this book to take a critical look at the kind of administrative political system which the pro-Europeans advocate. France has not prospered politically or morally under it; Continental Europe has not; and nor shall we.

Notes

Introduction

1. Alain Duhamel, *De Gaulle et Mitterrand: la marque et la trace*, Flammarion, Paris, 1991, p. 19.

2. Patrice Higonnet, *The darkened legacy*, in *Times Literary Supplement*, 6 August 1993, p. 5.

3. Jean-Jacques Rousseau, *Le Contrat Social*, I, vii.

4. See Michel Troper, *La séparation des pouvoirs et l'Histoire constitutionnelle française*, Librairie générale de droit et de jurisprudence, 1980.

5. Bruno Boccara, *L'insurrection démocratique*, Democratica, Paris, 1993, p. 174, p. 176.

6. Edmund Burke, *Reflections on the revolution in France*, Penguin, ed. Conor Cruise O'Brien, 1986, p. 151.

7. Francois Furet, *Penser la révolution française*, Gallimard, 1983, p. 203.

8. See Yves Mény, *La corruption de la République*, Fayard, Paris, 1992, p. 29.

9. *The Federalist or The New Constitution*, Papers by Alexander Hamilton, James Madison, John Jay, 1787–1788; New York, Heritage Press, 1945, pp. 54–62.

10. Raoul Girardet, *Mythes et mythologies politiques*, p. 143 and p. 158. He is very interesting about the place of the revolution in this process, and shows how it completed the centralising work done by the kings of France. See also Eugen Weber's essay, 'Who sang the Marseillaise?', in which he writes,

    > In 1792, by all accounts, French was as foreign to most *provençaux* as to Senegalese a century later. As a matter of fact, it was unfamiliar to most people within the borders of France. The Abbé Gregoire, who undertook a vast official survey of the question in 1790, concluded rather hopefully that three-quarters of the people of France knew *some* French. On the other hand, he admitted that only a portion of these could actually sustain a conversation in it, and he estimated that only about three million could speak it properly – while fewer, of course, could put their French into writing ... In 1824, a third of a century after the *Marseillaise* was born, the official *Statistique des Bouches-du Rhone* recognized that the normal speech of the middle and lower classes was Provençal, and added, 'it will take a good many years, perhaps centuries, before the French language becomes commonplace.'

11. Quoted by Sue Collard, *Mission impossible: les chantiers du président*, French Cultural Studies, No. 8, June 1992, p. 100.

12. Speech at Gueret, 3 May 1982.

13. *Le Monde*, 24 May 1988.

14. *Le Monde*, 4 May 1992.

15. *François Mitterrand ou le pouvoir vain*, by Nicolas Tenzer, *Le Débat*, Sept–Oct 1993.

16. Philippe Meyer, *François Mitterrand ou le masque de cire*, in *Le Débat* Sept–Oct 1993, p. 136.

17. Nicolas Tenzer, op. cit., p. 123.

18. Jacques Attali, *Verbatim, Tome 1, 1981–1986*, Fayard, Paris, 1993, p. 9.

19. Jean-Marie Colombani, *La France sans Mitterrand*, Flammarion, Paris, 1992, p. 12.

20. *L'Heure de Verité*, 25 October 1993.

21. Alain-Gérard Slama, *L'angélisme exterminateur: essai sur l'ordre moral contemporain*, Bernard Grasset, Paris, 1993.

22. Nicolas Tenzer, op. cit., p. 130.

23. Edmund Burke, op. cit., p. 185.

Chapter One: The Amazing Technocratic Turncoat

1. Gaston Deferre, *Si demain la gauche*, Preface, quoted by Catherine Nay, *Les Sept Mitterrand, ou les metamorphoses d'un septennat*, Grasset, Paris, 1988, epigraph.

2. Jacques Attali, *Verbatim, Tome 1, 1981–1986*, Fayard, Paris, 1993, p. 9.

3. Before the foundation of the PS, the SFIO (Section Française de l'International Ouvrier) was notorious for its lack of interest in questions of Socialist dogma. Despite the obviously Socialist legacy of the French Revolution, French Socialism does not have a 'great theoretician' to rival Labriola, Kautsky, Bernstein, Lenin, Trotsky, Rosa Luxemburg or Otto Bauer. See Hugues Portelli, *Le Socialisme français tel qu'il est*, Presses Universitaires de France, Paris, 1980.

4. Andrew Appleton, 'Maastricht and the French Party System: Domestic Implications of the Treaty Referendum,' *French Politics and Society*, Vol. 10, No. 4, Fall 1992, p. 16.

5. The Gaullist movement has passed through various incarnations: the Union Gaulliste of René Capitant in 1946; the Rassemblement du Peuple Français (RPF), founded by de Gaulle in 1947; the Union pour la Nouvelle République (UNR), created to support de Gaulle's new constitution in 1958; the Union des Démocrates pour la République (UDR), founded in 1967; and now the RPR.

6. Yves Meny, *La Corruption de la République*, Fayard, Paris, 1992, p. 316.

7. François Borella, *Les Partis politiques dans la France d'aujourd'hui*, new edn., Editions du Seuil, Paris, 1990. Georges Marchais was replaced as General

Secretary of the French Communist Party at the end of January 1994, after twenty years in the job.

8. Eric Dupin, *L'après-Mitterrand: le parti socialiste à la dérive*, Calmann-Lévy, Paris, 1991, p. 172.

9. Hugues Portelli, 'Le Parti socialiste', *La Vie politique en France* ed. Dominique Chagnollard, Editions du Seuil, Paris, June 1993, p. 273.

10. Dupin, op. cit., p. 112.

11. Portelli, 'Le Parti socialiste', p. 272.

12. See Chapter 8, 'The Cabinet Noir'.

13. Michel Winock, *'L'Irrésistible Ascension de François Mitterrand'* in 'Les Années Mitterrand', *L'Histoire*, No. 143, April 1991, p. 12.

14. Franz-Olivier Giesbert, *François Mitterrand, ou la tentation de l'histoire*, Seuil, Paris, 1977, p. 118.

15. Alain Bergounioux and Gerard Grunberg, *Le Long Remords du pouvoir*, Fayard, Paris, 1992, p. 266.

16. Dupin, op. cit., p. 66.

17. Quoted by Winock, op. cit., p. 12.

18. Borella, op. cit., p. 159.

19. Attali, op. cit., p. 106.

20. Bergounioux and Grunberg, op. cit., p. 269.

21. François Mitterrand, *Politique 2, 1977–1982*, Fayard, Paris, 1981.

22. Jean-Marie Vincent, *Le Quotidien de Paris*, 20 March 1981.

23. Dupin, op. cit., p. 84.

24. According to Winock, op. cit., p. 16.

25. Patrick Wajsman, *Le Figaro*, 27 March 1981.

26. Louis Pauwels, *Le Figaro*, 17 April 1981.

27. Attali, op. cit., p. 46.

28. Dupin, op. cit., p. 85, emphasis added.

29. Nay, op. cit., p. 14.

30. Attali, op. cit., p. 75.

31. Nay, op. cit., p. 20.

32. Attali, op. cit., p. 310.

33. Ibid., pp. 312–13, 390.

34. Ibid., p. 412.

35. Ibid., pp. 403–8.

36. Ibid., p. 410.

37. Ibid., p. 413.

38. Ibid., pp. 414–16.

39. Michel Noblecourt, *'Les Differents Visages du president'*, introduction to *Le Bilan économique des années Mitterrand* ed. Alain Gélédan, Éditions Le Monde, Paris, 1993, p. 3.

40. See my article, 'Où sont les neiges de soixante-huit?', *Spectator*, 8 May 1993.

41. *Le Point*, 29 January 1994, p. 13.

42. See my article 'The Vichy Syndrome', *Spectator*, 5 December 1992.

43. The theory of Claud Nicolet. See Robert Tombs, 'The Dark Years', *Times Literary Supplement*, 28 January 1994, p. 10.

44. 5 November 1991.

45. 28 November 1992.

46. See Maurice Allais, 'Non au libre-échangisme mondial', *Le Figaro*, 16 June 1992; 'Les Perversions du libre-échangisme mondial', *Le Figaro*, 24 November 1992; 'L'Intolérable Diktat américain', *Le Figaro*, 25 November 1992.

47. Interview with the *Financial Times*, quoted (without reference) by *Courier international*, No. 174, 3–9 March 1994, p. 11.

48. Alain Gomez, 'Le Gatt doit mourir', *Le Monde*, 28 November 1992.

49. For an excellent refutation of this ludicrous thesis, see Patrick Messerlin, 'La Communauté, la France et l'Uruguay Round', *Commentaire*, No. 63, Autumn 1993.

50. François Mitterrand, *Un socialisme du possible*, Seuil, Paris, 1970, p. 13.

51. François Mitterrand, *Politique 1*, Fayard, Paris, 1977 (quoted from Bergounioux and Grunberg, p. 262).

52. Dupin, op. cit., p. 67.

53. Ibid.

54. Francis Delaisi, *La Révolution européenne*, Editions de la Toison d'Or, Paris, 1942.

55. Ibid., p. 7.

56. John Hellmann, *The Knight-Monks of Vichy France, Uriage, 1940–1945*, McGill-Queen's University, Montreal, 1994. See also chapter 11.

57. Jean-Jacques Roche, 'La politique étrangère de François Mitterrand', *Politiques*, No. 3, Summer 1992, p. 49.

58. See Michel Winock, *Nationalisme, antisémitisme et fascisme en France*, Editions du Seuil, Paris, 1990, the chapter entitled 'L'Antiaméricanisme français' (chapter 3).

59. See Tombs, op. cit., p. 10.

60. Nay, op. cit., p. 130.

61. Quoted by Nay, op. cit., p. 130.

62. Quoted in ed. Gélédan, op. cit., p. 3.

63. Jean Bothorel, 'Une décennie sans grandeur', *Revue des deux mondes*, May 1991, p. 46.

64. See François Mitterrand, *Lettre à tous les français*, 1988.

65. Zeev Sternhell, *Ni droite, ni gauche: l'idéologie fasciste en France*, Editions Complexe, Paris, 1987.

66. Nay, op. cit., p. 117.

67. Ibid., pp. 117, 119.

68. Attali, op. cit., p. 452.

69. Nay, op. cit., p. 119.

70. At a lecture given at St Antony's College, Oxford. See Mark Almond, *The Rise and Fall of Nicolae and Elena Ceauşescu*, Chapman, London, 1988, p. 200.

71. Dupin, op. cit., p. 67.
72. Nay, op. cit., p. 120.
73. Ibid., p. 144.
74. Quoted by Noblecourt, op. cit., p. 4.
75. See *Le Point*, Saturday 29 January 1994.
76. Alain Peyrefitte, *La France en désarroi*, Editions de Fallois, Paris, 1993, p. 139. His figures are taken from *La Criminalité en France en 1983*, published by La Documentation Française. The Parisian murder rate is twice that of Hamburg, Munich, Frankfurt and Brussels; ten times that of Copenhagen or Tokyo.
77. Thierry Pfister, *La République des fonctionnaires*, Albin Michel, Paris, 1988, p. 117.
78. Jean Mottin, 'Chomage: les effectifs réels', *Le Figaro*, 25 January 1993.
79. Philippe Durupt, 'Sous les pavés, le franc', *Valeurs actuelles*, 21 March 1994, p. 20.
80. See the graph in 'Down and out in Paris', *Wall Street Journal Europe*, 11–12 March 1994, p. 6; see also Bruce Bartlett, 'Illusions about Wages', same edition.
81. 'Down and out in Paris', p. 6.
82. Quoted by the *Wall Street Journal Europe*, ibid.
83. 'Galilee' (pseud.), 'La tragédie du franc fort', *Revue des deux Mondes*, September 1993, p. 17.
84. Attali, op. cit., p. 350.
85. *Le Figaro*, 5 August 1993.
86. See Guillaume de Truchis, 'Plan de vol à l'anglaise', *Valeurs actuelles*, 21 March 1994, pp. 40–2.
87. 'L'Exception britannique', *Valeurs actuelles*, 21 March 1994, p. 22.
88. *Le Monde*, 28 March 1994.

Chapter Two: The Republican Monarchy

1. François Mitterrand, *Le Coup d'état permanent*, Julliard, Paris, 1964.
2. Quote by Attali, op. cit., p. 436.
3. Tristan Doelnitz, *La France hantée par sa puissance*, Belfond, Paris, 1993, p. 55.
4. See George Steiner, 'Aspects of Counter-Revolution', *The Permanent Revolution: the French Revolution and its Legacy 1789–1989* ed. Geoffrey Best, 2nd edn., Fontana, London, 1989, p. 135.
5. See Michel Winock, *La Fièvre hexagonale*, Calmann-Lévy, Paris, 1987, p. 134.
6. René Rémond, quoted by Charles Zorgbibe, *De Gaulle, Mitterrand et l'esprit de la constitution*, Hachette, Paris, p. 71. Jean-Louis Quermonne also said that the change would enable France to test the legitimacy of the Fifth Republic.
7. I owe this *aperçu* to Marc Ferro, *La Grande Guerre 1914–1918*, Gallimard, Paris; quoted by Doelnitz, op. cit., p. 118.

8.   Speech at Bayeux, 16 June 1946.

9.   See Steiner, op. cit., p. 135.

10. S. E. Finer, *Comparative Government*, Penguin, London, 1970, p. 273.

11. In 1962, the election of the President by universal suffrage was introduced; in 1969 de Gaulle tried to introduce a measure of decentralization, which was rejected in a referendum; in 1973 Pompidou tried to reduce the presidential term to five years, but failed; in 1974 Giscard enlarged the conditions under which appeals can be made to the constitutional court, allowing sixty deputies or senators to make such an appeal; in 1984, Mitterrand tried to enlarge the use of the referendum, a project which also came to nothing; in 1990 he allowed appeals to the constitutional council by any justiciable person; in 1992, the constitution was amended to allow the ratification of the treaty of Maastricht; while in 1993 constitutional changes were made to include the provisions of the Schengen agreement into the constitution.

12. Winock, *La Fièvre hexagonale*.

13. Attali, op. cit., p. 668.

14. Edmund Burke, 'Letter to a noble Lord' (1796), *Further Reflections on the Revolution in France* ed. Daniel E. Ritchie, Liberty Fund, Indianapolis, p. 316. It is hard to resist quoting the passage in full:

> Abbé Sieyes has whole nests full of constitutions, ready sorted, ticketed and numbered; suited to every season and every fancy; some with the pattern at the top; some plain, some flowered; some distinguished for their simplicity; others for their complexity; some of blood colour, some of *boue de Paris*; some with directories, others without a direction; some with councils of elders, and council of youngsters; some without any council at all. Some where the electors choose the representatives; others where the representatives choose the electors. Some in long coats, some in short cloaks; some with pantaloons; some without breeches. Some with five shilling qualifications, some totally unqualified. So that no constitution-fancier may go unsuited from his shop, provided he loves a pattern of pillage, oppression, arbitrary imprisonment, confiscation, exile, revolutionary judgement, and legalized premeditated murder.

15. Benjamin Disraeli, *A Vindication of the English Constitution in a letter to a learned and noble lord*, Farnborough, Gregg International, 1969, reprint from original facsimile edition, London, 1835, pp. 32, 68:

> This innocent monarch seems to have supposed that the English constitution consists merely of two rooms full of gentlemen, who discuss public questions and make laws in the metropolis at a stated season of the year. The King of France had no idea that political institutions, to be effective, must be founded on the habits and opinions of the people whom they pretend to govern ... The French chambers represented none – they were only fitted to be the tools of a

faction, and the tools of a faction they became ... The political institutions of England have sprung from its legal institutions. They have their origin in our laws and customs. These have been the profound and perennial sources of their unexampled vigour and beneficence, and unless it had been fed by these clear and wholesome fountains, our boasted Parliament, like so many of its artificial brethren, would soon have dwindled and dried up, and, like some vast canal, filled merely with epidemic filth, only to be looked upon as the fatal folly of a nation.

16. Charles de Gaulle, *Discours et messages*, Plon, Paris, 1970, Vol. III, pp. 179–80, quoted by Jean Lacouture, *De Gaulle, 3. Le Souverain, 1959–1970*, Editions du Seuil, Paris, 1986, p. 328.

17. 'Rédaction de la constitution française du 4 octobre 1958', Jean Foyer, *Théorie et pratique du gouvernement constitutionnel: La France et les États-Unis*, ed. Terence Marshall, Editions de l'Espace Européen, La Garenne-Colombes, 1992.

18. Zorgbibe, op. cit., p. 18.

19. Aristotle, *Politics*, Book IV, Chapter 4, 1292 a 26–7.

20. Zorgbibe, op. cit., p. 19, quoting from Malberg, *Revue du droit public*, 1931.

21. Marshal Pétain was also convinced that the defeat of 1940, the seminal event which founds modern France, and without reference to which nothing in post-war French politics can be properly understood, was due in great measure to the weakness of her political institutions. He shared de Gaulle's anti-parliamentarianism, and much Vichy propaganda caricatured deputies as gross animals. Needless to say, unlike de Gaulle, he did not compensate this with an attachment to a real form of popular sovereignty.

22. Zorgbibe, op. cit., p. 27:

> Le levier de l'action de René Capitant n'est pas une nostalgie du parlementarisme classique à la Michel Debré, mais, au contraire, un 'anti-parlementarisme démocratique', né de Rousseau. Pour le disciple de Carré de Malberg, la pensée de Rousseau n'a jamais cessé de provoquer, dans notre pays, de façon plus ou moins consciente, une protestation démocratique contre ce transfert abusif de la souveraineté du peuple au Parlement – et plus largement à toute sorte de représentant.

23. The distinction between '*pays réel*' and '*pays légal*' was originally drawn by the liberal philosopher, Guizot, but popularized by the traditionalist, monarchist philosopher and founder of the Action Française, Charles Maurras.

24. As René Char, the Resistance poet and writer, was to say of his time in the Resistance, 'At every meal that we eat together, freedom is invited to sit down. The chair remains vacant, but the place is set.' Hannah Arendt

comments, 'After a few short years they were liberated from what they originally had thought to be a "burden" and thrown back into what they now knew to be the weightless irrelevance of their personal affairs, once more separated from "the world of reality" by an *épaisseur triste*, the sad opaqueness of private life.' René Char, *Feuillets d'Hypnos*, Paris, 1946; in English, *Hypnos Waking; Poems and Prose*, New York, 1956; quoted by Hannah Arendt, *Between Past and Future*, Penguin, London, 1968, p. 4.

25.   '... la vraie France, la France éternelle ...' Paris, 25 August 1944.

26.   In 1960 he was to speak of 'the national legitimacy which I have incarnated for the last twenty years'. See de Gaulle, op. cit., p. 166, television and radio broadcast, 29 January 1960.

27.   '*Moi, j'étais la France, l'État, le gouvernement. Moi, je parlais au nom de la France. Moi, j'étais l'indépendance et la souveraineté de la France.*' Ibid., Vol. II, press conference, 7 April 1954.

28.   Emmanuel d'Astier de la Vigerie, the founder of the Resistance movement, Liberation, wrote of him thus in April 1942. See his *Sept fois, sept jours*, Paris, Editions de Minuit, 1947, pp. 80–1; quoted by Jean Lacouture, *De Gaulle, The Rebel, 1890–1944*, translated by Patrick O'Brien, Collins Harvill, London, 1990, p. 486. D'Astier goes on: 'He so thoroughly embodied the nation, he so wholly felt himself to be the nation that he forgot the people in it and the immediate present and the incoherence and the necessary Utopia that remote future which is called mankind. How could one tell him of it? There is no arguing with a Symbol about that which he symbolizes.'

29.   The exchange is reported in Adrien Dansette, *Histoire de la Libération de Paris*, Fayard, Paris, p. 313; reference taken from Giesbert, op. cit., p. 106.

30.   Article 6 of the Declaration of the Rights of Man and of the Citizen of 1789 says, 'the law is the expression of the general will.'

31.   See, for instance, his words at the press conference on 31 January 1964. Op. cit., Vol. IV, p. 164.

32.   Emile Combes had said that, 'In a truly republican regime, it is not the government which should lead the parliamentary majority, but for the majority which represents the country to guide the government.' Quoted in Lucien Jaume, 'L'État républicain selon de Gaulle', *Commentaire*, No. 51, Autumn 1991; Jaume's reference is C. Nicolet, *L'idée républicaine en France*, Paris, Gallimard, 1982, p. 429.

33.   Edmund Burke, in his famous speech to the electors of Bristol had denied that parliament was a mere congress of ambassadors, claiming that it was instead the deliberative assembly of the whole nation. Similarly, one revolutionary, Barnave, had realized that parliamentarians had a more active role than to be mere delegates from their electors. They were supposed 'to propose things, to listen, to discuss, to modify their views,

and finally form in common a common will' (quoted by Lucien Jaume, 'L'État républicain selon de Gaulle', in *Commentaire*, No. 51, Autumn 1991, p. 529); but this was not a common view.

34. René Capitant, *L'Aménagement du pouvoir exécutif et la question du chef de l'état*, Vol. X ('*L'État*') of *L'Encyclopédie française*, published by the Société de gestion de la nouvelle encyclopédie française, Paris, 1964, pp. 145–9, his italics.

35. A fascinating explanation of the sacred character of Gaullism is to be found in Fabrice Bouthillon, 'Les Schèmes qu'on abat: à propos du Gaullisme', *Commentaire*, Autumn 1993, pp. 467 ff.

36. Lady Spears (Mary Borden), *Journey Down a Blind Alley*, Hutchinson, pp. 113–15; quoted by Lacouture, *De Gaulle, The Rebel*, p. 265, emphasis added.

37. Raymond Aron, 'La République Gaulliste', *Le Figaro*, 9–10 January 1961.

38. De Gaulle, op. cit., Vol. I, Plon, Paris, 1970, p. 664.

39. De Gaulle, *Mémoires de Guerre*, Vol. III, Plon, Paris, 1959, p. 239.

40. 'A danger of dictatorship exists when the credit of our laws, the cohesion of governments, the efficiency of the administration, and the prestige and authority of the state fall victim to the citizens' disaffection with their political institutions.' Speech, Bayeux, 16 June 1946.

41. Dominique Chagnollaud, 'Droit et politique sous la Ve République', Chapter 1 of op. cit. ed. Chagnollaud, p. 16.

42. De Gaulle, *Mémoires de guerre*, Vol. III, p. 240.

43. De Gaulle, *Mémoires d'espoir, Volume I, Le Renouveau, 1958–1962*, Plon, Paris, 1990, p. 37.

44. De Gaulle, *Mémoires de guerre*, Vol. III, p. 240.

45. A sharp attack on these and other aspects of the constitution of the Fifth Republic can be found in Finer, op. cit., p. 318 f.

46. 'The President of the Republic ensures respect for the constitution. He ensures, by his judgement, the regular functioning of the public authorities and the continuity of the State. He is the guarantor of national independence, of the integrity of the territory, and of the respect of accords of the Community and treaties.'

47. Speech to the Conseil d'État, 27 August 1958, quoted by Olivier Duhamel in 'Réformes électorales et fins de la République Gaullienne', op. cit., ed. Marshall, p. 195.

48. Zorgbibe, op. cit., p. 24.

49. See Foyer, op. cit.

50. Quoted without reference by Alain Duhamel, *De Gaulle–Mitterrand: la marque et la trace*, Flammarion, Paris, 1991, p. 45. This is an interesting parallel with the medieval understanding of kingship, itself derived from the bishop's relation to the Church, according to which the king 'married' his realm just as a bishop married the Church. Both sorts of 'marriage' were symbolised by the wearing of a ring, episcopal or royal. See Ernst

Kantorowicz, *The King's Two Bodies, A Study in Medieval Political Theology*, Princeton, 1957, p. 212.

51. See Finer, op. cit., pp. 304–5.
52. Press conference, 11 April 1966; see Jean-François Revel, *L'Absolutisme inefficace: contre le présidentialisme à la fran*çaise, Plon, Paris, 1992, p. 36.
53. Zorgbibe, op. cit., p. 52, emphasis added.
54. Duhamel, op. cit., pp. 190–91.
55. Ibid.
56. Ibid.
57. Referendum on the constitution in September 1958; legislative elections in November 1958; referendum on the self-determination of Algeria in January 1961; referendum on the agreements ending the Algerian war in April 1962; referendum on the constitution in October 1962; legislative elections in November 1962; presidential elections in December 1965; legislative elections in March 1967; legislative elections in June 1968; referendum on decentralisation of the constitution in April 1969.
58. De Gaulle, *Mémoires d'espoir, Volume II, L'Effort, 1962-*, Plon, Paris, 1971, p. 13.

Chapter Three: The Permanent Coup d'état

1. *Paris-Match*, March 1984.
2. Remark made during his annual climb up the rock of Solutré, May 1986, quoted by Nay, op. cit., p. 170.
3. In March 1981. Quoted by Edmond Dantes, *Mitterrand par lui-même: Critique et analyse d'une vie politique*, Jacques Grancher, Paris, 1992, p. 48.
4. See Dantes, op. cit., p. 183.
5. Zorgbibe, op. cit., p. 11.
6. Attali, op. cit., entry for 11 May 1981, p. 17.
7. Ibid., 22 May 1981, p. 23.
8. Franz-Olivier Giesbert, *La Fin d'une époque*, Fayard Seuil, Paris, 1993, p. 19.
9. Zorgbibe, op. cit., pp. 60, 62.
10. Ibid., p. 59.
11. On 17 August 1967. See op. cit. ed. Chagnollaud.
12. Zorgbibe, op. cit., p. 64.
13. During thirty-five years of the Fifth Republic there have been only thirteen.
14. Zorgbibe, op. cit., p. 122, emphasis added.
15. Nay, op. cit., p. 142.
16. Attali, op. cit., p. 579; in the event, the letter is not sent until eight months later, in July 1984, when he appoints Fabius. The letter, six dense pages long in Attali's book, is reprinted on pp. 672–8.
17. 'Un premier ministre est-il encore utile?', *Le Quotidien de Paris*, Wednesday 6 November 1991.

18. Zorgbibe, op. cit., p. 121.
19. Beregovoy, Vauzelle, Charasse, Bianco, Glavany, Royal, Bredin and Guigou.
20. Dumas, Joxe, Mermaz, Le Pensec, Mexandeau, Malvy, Laignel, Josselin and Neiertz.
21. Lang and Keijman.
22. The Minister of the Budget, Michel Charasse, an old Mitterrand ally. See Edwy Plenel, *La Part d'ombre*, Stock, Paris, 1992, p. 176.
23. Revel, op. cit., p. 46, emphasis added.
24. Thierry Brehier, 'Hésitations et lenteurs', *Le Monde*, Saturday, 9 May 1992, emphasis added.
25. Zorgbibe, op. cit., p. 123.
26. Attali, op. cit., p. 668.
27. Revel, op. cit., p. 44.
28. Recounted by Giesbert, *La Fin d'une époque*, p. 50.
29. Revel, op. cit., pp. 26–7.
30. Ibid., p. 33.
31. Attali, op. cit., entry for 27 May 1981, p. 26.
32. Ibid.
33. Ibid., entry for 9 June 1981, p. 35.
34. Revel, op. cit., p. 18.
35. Jean-Michel Bélorgey, *Le Parlement à refaire*, Gallimard, Paris, 1991, p. 10.
36. Bruno Boccara, *L'Insurrection démocratique: manifeste pour la Ve République*, Democratica, Paris, 1993, p. 129.
37. Press conference, 31 January 1964. See Zorgbibe, op. cit., p. 83.
38. Quoted by Zorgbibe, op. cit., p. 93.
39. Zorgbibe, op. cit., p. 111.
40. Ibid., p. 74.
41. Ibid., p. 107.
42. Revel, op. cit., p. 58.
43. Zorgbibe, op. cit., p. 44. A lucid statement of the Gaullist position can also be found in the writings of Georges Vedel, who is a veteran opponent of the institutions of the Fifth Republic. In his report, submitted to the President on 15 February 1993, he wrote,

> Étant donne les pouvoirs du chef de l'état selon les textes et la pratique, une investiture de sept ans est vraiment excessive. Il n'existe, dans une démocratie contemporaine, aucune comparaison possible s'agissant d'organes dotés de compétences réelles. Si le général de Gaulle a choisi la durée de sept ans, il a accompagné ce choix d'un recours systématique au référendum de responsabilité en cours de mandat . . . En démocratie, il n'y a pas d'autorité sans responsabilité. On ne peut à la fois reconnaître au président de la République française des pouvoirs qui cumulent ceux d'un chef d'État présidentiel

        et ceux d'un chef de gouvernement parlementaire pour sept ans un
        statut d'irresponsabilité.

44.   Jean Lacouture, *De Gaulle, 3. Le Souverain, 1959–1970*, Chapter 24, p. 657.

45.   Such as in President Mitterrand's television debate with Philippe Séguin
       in September 1992; also de Gaulle in 1965.

46.   Press conference, 4 April 1984, quoted by Bergounioux and Grunberg,
       op. cit., p. 285.

47.   Zorgbibe, op. cit., pp. 115, 117.

48.   Ibid., p. 51.

49.   Dantes, op. cit., p. 64.

50.   He declared recently, 'There is no reserved domain. I have been saying so
       for the last twelve years,' on 'L'Heure de Vérité', France 2, Monday 25
       October 1993.

51.   *Le Monde*, 24 February 1990.

52.   The remark was made in 1985. See Zorgbibe, op. cit., p. 87.

53.   Robert Elgie and Howard Machin., 'France: the Limits to Prime-
       ministerial Government in a Semi-Presidential System', *West European
       Politics*, Vol. 14, No. 2, April 1991, p. 75; and Samy Cohen, *Politique
       étrangère*, No. 3/89 (Autumn 1989) for the relationship between President
       and Prime Minister during cohabitation.

54.   Attali, op. cit., entry for 6 October 1981, p. 101.

55.   See Chapter 9, 'The Architect of Socialism'.

56.   Quoted by Zorgbibe, op. cit., p. 125.

57.   Baruch Spinoza, *Tractatus politicus*, I, 6 (translated by R. M. Elwes).

58.   Revel, op. cit., p. 11.

Chapter Four: The House of Mitterrand

 1.   Alexis de Tocqueville, *L'Ancien Régime et la révolution*, Book 2, Chapter
       VI, in *Oeuvres Choisis*, Penguin, London, 1946, pp. 108–9; translated as
       The Ancien Regime by John Bonner, Everyman, London, 1988, pp. 50–1.

 2.   Mitterrand, *Le Coup d'état permanent*.

 3.   Quote by Jean Montaldo, *Lettre ouverte d'un 'chien' à François Mitterrand au
       nom de la liberté d'aboyer*, Albin Michel, Paris, 1993, p. 161.

 4.   See de Tocqueville, *The Ancien Regime*, Book 2, Chapter II.

 5.   Attali can hardly believe it, for example; op. cit., p. 196.

 6.   Ibid., p. 169.

 7.   'La Famille Tonton', *Les Dossiers du canard*, *Le Canard Enchaîné*, Paris,
       1991, p. 5.

 8.   See Charles Villeneuve, *Les Liaisons dangereuses de Pierre Beregovoy, enquête
       sur la mort d'un premier ministre*, Plon, Paris, 1993, p. 29.

 9.   Quoted by Nay, op. cit., pp. 32–3.

10.   Quoted ibid., p. 33.

11.   Quoted ibid.

12. Interview with *Globe-Hebdo* magazine, March 1986.
13. 'L'Effet dévastateur de l'irrésponsabilité', *Libération*, 3 February 1992.
14. 'Le Parrain converti', *Le Débat*, No. 20, May 1982, p. 16.
15. Revel, op. cit., p. 87.
16. Thierry Pfister, *Le Point*, 21 November 1988.
17. Revel, op. cit., pp. 28, 30–1, 47.
18. See Appendix 3 in ibid.
19. *Le Figaro*, 17 October 1992.
20. Revel, op. cit., pp. 28, 30–1, 47, 87.
21. 'La Famille Tonton', op. cit., p. 6.
22. *Journal Officiel*, 125e année, No. 75, Monday 29 March and Tuesday 30 March 1993, pp. 5727–40.
23. Attali, op. cit., p. 723.
24. France Inter, 10 February 1993.
25. Attali, op. cit., p. 25.
26. 'La Famille Tonton', op. cit., p. 33.
27. People who fall into this category are Jean-Louis Bianco, Michel Charasse, René Teulade, Jacques Attali, Georgina Dufoix (who was made president of the Red Cross after having lost her parliamentary seat in 1988, and also kept an office at the Elysée), and the officials sacked after the Habache affair (see below).
28. Jacques Jessel, *La Double Défaite de Mitterrand*, Albin Michel, Paris, 1992, p. 171.
29. Ibid., p. 179.
30. Ibid., p. 173.
31. E.g. by Alain Touraine, *Le Monde*, 6 July 1987.
32. There is a good chapter, 'The Source of the Scientist Hubris: the École Polytechnique', in F. A. Hayek, *The Counter-Revolution of Science: Studies in the Abuse of Reason*, Liberty Press, Indianapolis, 1979 (1st edn., The Free Press, Glencoe, Illinois, 1952), pp. 185 ff.
33. Odon Vallet, *L'École, ou la vanité considerée comme un mode de gouvernement*, Albin Michel, Paris, 1991, p. 33.
34. Jean-Luc Bodiguel, *Le Monde*, 1–2 August 1976.
35. For an analysis of the parlous state of the French education system, see Philippe Némo, *Le Chaos pédagogique*, Albin Michel, Paris, 1993.
36. Pfister, *La République des fonctionnaires*, p. 78.
37. An excellently cutting account of the hierarchical system of castes within the civil service, written from the inside, is given by Vallet, op. cit.
38. Yves Cannac, '*Les Élites diregeantes françaises en question*', *Le Debat*, No. 53, January–February 1989, p. 60.
39. *La République des ducs* is the title of the second volume of Daniel Halevy's *La Fin des notables*, Sauret, Paris, 1944; *La République des camarades* (by Robert de Jouvenel, Grasset, Paris, 1914); *La République des professeurs* (by Albert Thibaudet, Grasset, Paris, 1927).

40. Pfister, *La République des fonctionnaires*, p. 14.

41. Ibid., p. 46.

42. 'Jacques Attali: un ami qui se veut du bien' in 'La Famille de Tonton', op. cit., p. 20.

43. Friedrich Engels, '*Herrn Eugen Dühring's Umwalzung der Wissenschaft, (Anti-Dühring)*, 3rd ed., 1894, p. 302; see also Friedrich Engels *Gesamtausgabe*, published by the *Institut für Marxismus-Leninismus der Zentralkommittee der Kommunistischen Partei der Sowjetunion und vom Institut für Marxismus-Leninismus beim Zentralkommittee der Sozialistischen Einheitspartei Deutschlands*, Berlin, 1975, Volume 27; see also Hayek, op. cit., p. 252.

44. Alexandre Wickham and Sophie Coignard, *La Nomenklatura française, pouvoirs et privileges des élites*, Pierre Belfond, Paris, 1988, p. 19.

45. Alain Etchegoyen, *La Démocratie malade du mensonge*, Editions François Bourin, Paris, 1993, pp. 40, 45.

46. See Jessel, op. cit., pp. 179–80.

47. Quoted by Attali, op. cit., p. 626.

48. Michel Bauer and Benedicte Bertin-Mourot, *Les 200. Comment devient-on grand patron?* Seuil, Paris, 1987.

49. See Pfister, *La République des fonctionnaires*, pp. 54–7.

50. Wickham and Coignard, op. cit., pp. 28–9.

51. Vincent Wright, preface to Guy Thuillier, *Regards sur la haute administration en France*, Economica, Paris, 1979. It is ironic that this view should have been influential in Britain, and that it has contributed to the creation of the Civil Service College, which was partly inspired by ENA, because ENA itself was inspired by the British civil service in the first place.

52. Jean-Marie Colombani notes approvingly that 'For thirty years, the European Community was built by the impulsion of enlightened despotism'. See Jean-Marie Colombani, *La France sans Mitterrand*, Flammarion, Paris, 1992. In a similar vein, Raymond Barre, the former Prime Minister, speaks with enthusiasm of 'A multinational group of independent personalities working to elaborate common conceptions on the great questions which the Community faces'. See Alain Prate, *Quelle Europe?*, Julliard, Paris, 1991, p. 10.

53. Pfister, *La République des fonctionnaires*, pp. 49–50.

54. Yves Mény, op. cit., p. 107.

55. Ezra Suleiman, *Les Hauts Fonctionnaires et la politique*, Seuil, Paris, 1976 and *Les Élites en France, grands corps et grandes écoles*, Seuil, Paris, 1979; Pierre Birnbaum, *Les Sommets de l'état*, Seuil, Paris, 1977.

56. Michel Schiffrès, *L'Enaklatura*, Lattes, Paris, 1987.

57. Pfister, *La République des fonctionnaires*, p. 37.

58. Donald Cameron Watt refers to 'that bureaucratic élitist conspiracy which led to the establishment, first of the European Coal and Steel Community and then of the European Community' in *How War Came*, Mandarin, 1990, p. 132.

59. Quoted by Schiffres, op. cit.
60. Bruno Boccara, op. cit., p. 22.
61. Finer, op. cit., pp. 295–6. Finer goes on (writing about the Fourth Republic),

> The fragility of the Cabinet in the face of the obstinacy or opposition of the Assembly prevented it from ever constraining political pressures. It had to give way to them or abdicate: and Cabinets did both. While they changed, the pressures in the Assembly were continuous. Hence, not very long after the adoption of the 1946 Constitution, a position of deadlock between these pressures resulted. This deadlock is what in France is called *immobilisme*. Meanwhile, by the same token, bold planning or orientation of society and its economy was beyond the reach of ministers. Instead they lived out their short lives by trimming to every sectional interest in turn.
>
> Each powerful pressure group tried to 'colonize' the bureaucracy, either by planting spokesmen in the appropriate ministries or conversely by employing ex-civil servants (a practice known as *pantouflage*). These exercises were, on the whole, very successful. But the weakness of ministers worked against the pressure groups as well as for them. For though all pressure groups were successful up to a point – that point was where they were met by the determined resistance of another pressure group. A sort of balance of power established itself: in short, the *immobilisme* of which we have been speaking.

62. Mény, op. cit., pp. 109–10.

Chapter Five: The Death of Politics

1. De Gaulle, *Mémoires d'Éspoir, L'Effort, 1962–*, Plon, Paris, 1971, p. 23.
2. Georges Vedel, *Le Monde*, 5 December 1991. There is much other literature besides on the decline of the parliament. See, for instance, 'La Pauperisation politique de l'Assemblée Nationale', by François Hollande, a deputy from the Corrèze, in 'Misère du parlementarisme', *Autrement: Serie 'Mutations'* No. 122, May 1991; also Bélorgey, op. cit.
3. 'One can already speak of totalitarianism when one adds together absolute despotism, generalized corruption, the shame of a country without justice, the indignity of a cretinous level of political dialogue, technical bankruptcy, and the destruction of all citizenship other than electoral.' Boccara, op. cit., p. 130.
4. René Rémond. Quoted, without reference, by Colombani, op. cit., p. 42.
5. Dantes, op. cit., p. 26.
6. See Jean-Pierre Camby, 'Le Parlement', *État politique de la France, Année 1991*, ed. Dominique Chagnollaud, Quai Voltaire, Paris, 1992, p. 30.
7. The British Prime Minister, John Major, was able to obtain final parliamentary approval for the Maastricht treaty only because he used an

invented version of this on 23 July 1993: he obtained ratification of the treaty even though a majority of the House of Commons was against the treaty in the form he had signed it. Contrary to what was reported at the time, the Tory Euro-rebels were not joining Labour in voting for a motion to include the Social Chapter. The motion for which they voted, defeating the government on 22 July 1993, was for the removal of the special protocol on social policy. Had this occurred in a renegotiation of the treaty, the British government would have still been able to veto the Social Chapter for Europe as a whole. But the comparison with John Major's subversion of the British constitution (seldom, if ever, had such a measure been used before) risks hiding the enormity of Article 49.3. The House of Commons had, at least, spent several hundred hours debating Maastricht: this is not possible under 49.3.

8. Bélorgey, op. cit., p. 7.

9. Ibid., p. 8.

10. Sylvie Pierre-Brossolette, 'Le Dernier des Mohicains' (a reference to Mitterrand), *L'Express*, 14 November 1991. The article is reprinted in *Les Cahiers de L'Express*, September 1992, p. 96, which is a collection of articles about the constitution published in *L'Express*, from 1958 to the present day.

11. Boccara, op. cit., p. 123.

12. See especially Christopher Booker and Richard North, *The Mad Officials*, Constable, London, 1994, reviewed in the *Spectator* by Alasdair Palmer, 12 February 1994. Booker and North find that 3,359 'statutory instruments' were passed in 1992, or roughly ten new sets of regulations a day. These instruments are applied at the executive's discretion, without proper parliamentary scrutiny.

13. Georges Burdeau, *Droit constitutionnel et institutions politiques*, 16e edn., Librairie Générale de Droit et de Jurisprudence, Paris, 1974, pp. 577–8.

14. Gilbert and Sullivan, *Iolanthe*, Act I.

15. See Philippe Ardant, *Institutions politiques et droit constitutionnel*, 1991, LGDJ, Paris, p. 555.

16. Daniel Amson, 'Parlement: contre le monopole de l'ordre du jour', *Le Quotidien de Paris*, 27 January 1992.

17. *Le Figaro*, 10 December 1990.

18. Reported ibid., 21 June 1990.

19. Xavier de Villepin, 'Le Contenu des accords de Schengen', *Études*, September 1992.

20. 'L'application des accords de Schengen est reportée "sine die"', *Le Monde*, 27 January 1994.

21. See Eric Branca, 'A quoi sert le parlement?', *Valeurs actuelles*, 24 January 1994.

22. Philippe Séguin, *Le Figaro*, 3 December 1991.

23. André Laurens, 'Pour un retour à la vie civile', *Le Monde*, 13–14 October 1991, a review of Bélorgey, op. cit.

24. Quoted by Nay, op. cit., p. 210.

25. Pfister, *La République des fonctionnaires*, p. 144.

26. Mény, op. cit., p. 42.

27. Boccara, op. cit., p. 99; quoted from his *L'impot truqué*, Encre, 1985, Chapter XV.

28. Jean Foyer and Guy Lardeyret, *Le Monde*, 18 April 1991.

29. *Le Monde*, 6 September 1991.

30. Bélorgey, op. cit., draws on the British parliament for inspiration.

31. Ibid., p. 9.

32. A cartoonist for *Minute*, a magazine close to the National Front, was recently cleared of this crime following the publication of a caricature of Laurent Fabius, the former Prime Minister. See *Le Monde*, 30 March 1994.

33. Attali, op. cit., pp. 29, 43, 48.

34. See 'Le PS dénonce le "verrouillage des médias par le gouvernement"', *Le Monde*, 18 February 1994.

35. See Chapter 6, 'An Inspector Calls.'.

36. Antoine Gaudino, *Le Procès impossible*, Albin Michel, Paris, 1993, pp. 145, 184.

37. Revel, op. cit., p. 48; Attali, op. cit., p. 704.

38. Pfister, *La République des fonctionnaires*, p. 60.

39. See Jean Massot, 'Président de la République et Premier Ministre', *L'État politique de la France, Année 1991* ed. Dominique Chagnollaud, Quai Voltaire, Paris, 1992, p. 21.

40. Giesbert, *François Mitterrand*, p. 138–40.

41. Bélorgey, op. cit., p. 8.

42. Revel, op. cit., p. 115.

43. Especially Nicolas Tenzer and Rodolphe Delacroix, *Les Élites et la fin de la démocratie fran*çaise, Presses Universitaires de France, Paris, 1992, p. 95.

44. Pfister, *La République des fonctionnaires*, p. 162.

45. Boccara, op. cit., p. 150.

46. France Inter, 10 February 1993.

47. 26 October 1993.

48. See also 'Une majorité des français met en cause le manque d'indépendance des journalistes', *Le Monde*, 16 January 1992.

49. 'Le Téléphone Sonne', France Inter, 20 January 1993.

50. Ivan Levai, France Inter, 11 February 1993.

51. Colombani, op. cit., pp. 87–8.

52. Revel, op. cit., pp. 121–2.

53. Etchegoyen, op. cit., p. 39.

54. Jacques Delors, 'L'Heure de Vérité', 17 May 1992.

55. Nicolas Tenzer, 'François Mitterrand ou le pouvoir vain', *Le Débat*, September–October 1993, p. 122.

56. Villeneuve, op. cit., p. 163.
57. Revel, op. cit., p. 63.
58. Zorgbibe, op. cit., p. 124.
59. Revel, op. cit., p. 116.
60. Pfister, *La République des fonctionnaires*, p. 189.

Chapter Six: An Inspector Calls

1. Ed. Pierre Manent, Editions Complèxe, Paris, 1988, chapter IV, p. 65.
2. Laurent Fabius, the future Prime Minister, was to say that the difference between the Right and the Left was 'morality'. See Lupin, op. cit., p. 155.
3. See Dantes, op. cit., p. 183.
4. Attali, op. cit., p. 16.
5. Montaldo, op. cit., p. 130.
6. William Shakespeare, *Richard III*, Act I, Scene I, lines 1–2. Later in the same speech, Richard declares,

> And therefore, since I cannot prove a lover,
> To entertain these fair well-spoken days,
> I am determined to prove a villain,
> And hate the idle pleasures of these days.

7. Attali, op. cit., p. 16.
8. The problem is widely recognized, and there has recently been a spate of books on the subject: Sophie Coignard and Jean-Francois Lacan, *La République bananière: de la démocratie en France*, Belfond, Paris, 1989; Thierry Wolton, *Les Écuries de la Ve*, Grasset, Paris, 1989; Stephane Denis, *Le Roman de l'argent*, Albin Michel, Paris, 1988; Airy Routier, *La République des loups: le pouvoir et les affaires*, Calmann-Levy, Paris, 1989; Alain Minc, *L'Argent fou*, Grasset, Paris, 1990; Wickham and Coignard, op. cit.; Pfister, *La République des fonctionnaires*; Pierre Pean, *Secret d'État: La France du secret et les secrets de la France*, Fayard, Paris, 1986; Gaudino, op. cit.; Josua Giustiniani, *Le Raquet politique*, Albin Michel, Paris, 1990; and most recently, Gilles Gaetner, *L'Argent facile: dictionnaire de la corruption en France*, Editions Stock, Paris, 1992; Plenel, op. cit.; Caroline Bettati, *Responsables et coupables: une affaire de sang*, Editions du Seuil, Paris, 1993; Montaldo, op. cit.
9. Calmann-Lévy, Paris, 1989.
10. Robert de Jouvenel, *La République des camarades*, Paris, 1914; Daniel Halévy, *La République des comités*, Paris, 1934; Albert Thibaudet, *La République des professeurs*, Grasset, Paris, 1927. *La République des ducs* is the title of the second volume of Daniel Halévy's *La fin des notables*, Sauret, Paris, 1944.
11. Mairi Maclean, 'Dirty Dealing: Business and Scandal in Contemporary France', *Modern and Contemporary France*, Vol. NS1, No. 2, 1993, p. 161.

12. Gaudino, quoting Gilles Boulouque, op. cit., p. 233.

13. *L'Express* 20 April 1990; see also Boccara, op. cit., p. 19.

14. *Ma part de vérité*, quoted by Catherine Nay, *Le Noir et le Rouge*, p. 29, and by Giesbert, *François Mitterrand ou la tentation de l'histoire*, p. 24, and by Plenel, op. cit., p. 320.

15. 'My dear ancestors, one must not think the Revolution finished just because you have cut off a few heads. In order to conquer liberty, you must be more vigilant than that which has you in its grasp. You have chased away kings ... but you have not understood that the most powerful king of all continues to taunt you. *Money, the money-king.* He has built castles, drawbridges and palaces! But no one sees them, because everyone believes he can profit from it. And little by little, stitch by stitch, the net is closing, the net of gold, the net of blood ... We shall write in vain the words democracy and tolerance, solidarity and fraternity, all this shall fall to ashes unless we discern under these words the enemy who is lying in wait for us, international money.' 26 October 1944 in *Libres*, the review which succeeded *L'Homme libre*, a clandestine journal for prisoners and deportees. Quoted by François Mitterrand, *Politique 1*, p. 26, and by Edwy Plenel, op. cit., p. 335.

16. At the foundation of the Socialist Party at Epinay in 1971. See Mitterrand, *Politique 1*, p. 536.

17. In 1978. See Mitterrand, *Politique 2, 1977–1981*, Paris, p. 201.

18. He reacted angrily to this suggestion, made by a student on the hard left (a supporter of Jean-Pierre Chevenement), during a long talk at the Institute of Political Science in Paris in July 1992.

19. In his television broadcast to the nation on 14 July 1993, he was asked whether he had subscribed to the Balladur loan; he said that he had not, because he had no investment portfolio, just his presidential salary; therefore he never made such investments.

20. It also gave the first formulation to the corporatist-fascist doctrine of 'subsidiarity'.

21. See, for instance, Delaisi, op. cit., *passim*. Delaisi especially attacks the gold standard as an instrument of Anglo-Saxon hegemony, recalling the words of Dr Walther Funk, the Nazi Reichsminister for Economics and President of the Reichsbank, who wrote in 1942 that 'If Europe wants to be modern, then she must abandon the gold standard'. See the conference Europäische Wirtschaftsgemeinschaft (European Economic Community), held in Berlin in 1942 under the aegis of the Nazi government and the Berlin Union of Businessmen and Industrialists, the lectures of which were printed up in 1942 by Haude & Spenersche Verlagsbuchhandlung Max Paschke, Berlin. The conference is described in my article, 'The Thousand Year Reich', *Spectator*, 22 June 1991, and extracts from it have been translated into English by the *International Currency Review*,

Occasional Paper No. 4, published by World Reports Ltd, 108 Horseferry Road, London SW1P 2EF, September 1993.

22. Broadcast to the nation on 12 August 1940, quoted by Léon Liebmann in 'Entre le mythe et la légende: l'anti-capitalisme de Vichy', *Revue de l'Institut de Sociologie*, 1964, p. 110.

23. 'Money is the arbiter of democratic power because, without it, that power falls into nothingness or chaos. No money, no newspapers. No money, no voters. No money, no expression of public opinion ... Corrupt, corrupting, money was the vice of princes.' Charles Maurras, *Mes idées politiques*, Fayard, Paris, 1968, pp. 206–8; see also p. 187.

24. See Jean Daniel, *Les Religions d'un président*, Grasset, Paris, 1988, pp. 165–95.

25. A splendid description of the almost unbearable ructions caused by political scandals during the Third Republic can be found in Sir Winston Churchill's essay on Clémenceau in his collection, *Great Contemporaries*, Thornton Butterworth, London, 1937.

26. These are very funnily described by Brian Jenkins and Peter Morris in 'Political Scandal in France', *Modern and Contemporary France*, Vol. NS1, No. 2, 1993, p. 128.

27. See ibid.

28. See Villeneuve, op. cit., p. 35; see also the full version of the report by Judge Thierry Jean-Pierre in *Le Point*, 7 January 1994, p. XII.

29. Ezra N. Suleiman, 'The Politics of Corruption and the Corruption of Politics', *French Politics and Society*, Vol. 9, No. 1, Winter 1991.

30. Yves Chalier, *La République corrompue*, Robert Laffont, Paris, 1991.

31. *Le Nouvel Observateur*, 5–11 September 1986.

32. Boccara, op. cit., p. 47.

33. Quoted from Coignard and Lacan, op. cit., p. 77.

34. Revel, op. cit., p. 99.

35. Montaldo, op. cit., pp. 119–20.

36. See Mény, op. cit., p. 258.

37. The Treasurer of the Socialist Party claims that the figure was 173.3 million in 1991, although Claude Popis, who ran the SORMAE slush fund, and was imprisoned as a result for several months, claims that 'year in, year out, Urba brought the Socialist Party between 38 and 58 million francs annually. This is relatively little when one considers that the real budget of this party exceeds 250 million francs a year, *excluding the cost of electoral campaigns*.' See Claude Popis, *L'Argent, le bâtiment, la politique sous la Ve République*, Albin Michel, Paris, 1992, p. 130.

38. *Libération*, 16 March 1989.

39. According to the head of a large supermarket chain. See *L'Expansion*, 20 January–2 February 1989, p. 42.

40. Louis-Marie Horeau, 'Les Châteaux en Espagne d'un bureau d'études socialiste', *Le Canard Enchaîné*, 8 December 1982; Jean-Louis Remilleux,

'Comment a fonctionné le piège des bureaux d'études du parti socialiste'. See also Gaetner, op. cit., p. 372.

41. Quoted from Delcroix papers by Plenel, op. cit., p. 360–1.

42. The Gaullist RPR party's expenses rose from 67 million francs in 1987 to 129.6 million francs in 1991. (See *Rapport de la commission d'enquête sur le financement des partis et des campagnes électorales sous la Ve République*, published by the Assemblée Nationale, 9th legislature, No. 2348, 15 November 1991 (quoted by Plenel, op. cit., pp. 361–2).) The British Conservative Party spent £15.6 million (135 million francs) in 1991. (See Income and Expenditure Account, Year Ended 31 March 1992, Conservative Central Office, audited 25 September 1992.)

43. His name was first published on 20 November 1990 in *Le Figaro*. See Gaudino, op. cit., p. 63.

44. Villeneuve, op. cit., p. 42.

45. See Montaldo, op. cit., pp. 125–7; and Gaudino, op. cit., p. 12.

46. 'Attention, corruption!', *Projet*, No. 232, Winter 1992–3, p. 11.

47. Gaudino, op. cit., p. 11.

48. Ibid., p. 123.

49. See Chapter 8, 'The Cabinet Noir'.

50. Gaudino, op. cit., p. 56.

51. Ibid., pp. 64–5.

52. Ibid., p. 66.

53. Ibid., p. 67.

54. Ibid., p. 68.

55. Ibid., p. 156.

56. Ibid., pp. 156–8.

57. *Le Monde*, 6 December 1989.

58. Ibid., 19 October 1990.

59. Gaetner, op. cit., p. 374; Gaudino, op. cit., p. 144.

60. Gaudino, op. cit., p. 162. The lawyer, Pierre-François Divier also published his own account of the affair, *Lettre raccommandée à François Mitterrand sur l'affaire Urba-Gracco*, Editions du Rocher, Monaco, 1992.

61. Gaudino, op. cit., p. 179.

62. One of the best experts on the subject, Mény, op. cit., p. 309 and *passim*, hovers very close to this suggestion.

63. Colombani is one of the editors of *Le Monde*. See his 'La Politique et l'argent: toujours plus!', *Le Monde*, 18 January 1992.

64. *Le Monde*, 13 April 1991.

65. Mény, op. cit., p. 31.

66. *Le Quotidien de Paris*, 30 November 1990, my italics.

67. Gaudino, op. cit., p. 112.

68. See Gaetner, op. cit., pp. 60 ff.

69. See Chapter 7.

70. Suleiman, 'The Politics of Corruption and the Corruption of Politics', p. 64.

71. Quoted by Boccara, op. cit., p. 44.

72. *Le Monde*, 6 October 1989.

73. *Le Nouvel Observateur*, 29 October 1992.

74. Interview on France 3, Friday 19 February 1993, printed in *Le Monde*, 21–2 February 1993.

75. Mény, op. op. cit., p. 256; N. Fournier and E. Legrand, *C . . . comme combines*, A. Moreau, Paris, 1975, p. 49.

76. Interview on France 3, Friday 19 February 1993, printed in *Le Monde*, 21–2 February 1993.

77. Quoted in *Le Matin*, 4 December 1987.

78. See 'Les Comptes occultes du parti républicain', *Le Monde*, 29 March 1994.

79. *Le Monde*, 29 January 1992.

80. L'Heure de Verité, Antenne 2, Monday 25 October 1993.

81. Interview on France 3, Friday 19 February 1993, printed in *Le Monde*, 21–2 February 1993.

82. Quoted by Nicolas Tenzer, 'François Mitterrand ou le pouvoir vain', *Le Débat*, September – October 1993, pp. 123.

83. As some day it may happen that a victim must be found,
    I've got a little list – I've got a little list,
    Of society offenders who might well be underground,
    And who never would be missed – who never would be missed!
    There's the pestilential nuisances who write for autographs–
    All people who have flabby hands and irritating laughs . . .
                                            Ko-Ko, *The Mikado*, Act I

84. Dupin, op. cit., p. 153.

85. Villeneuve, op. cit., *passim*.

86. Attali, op. cit., p. 411.

87. Villeneuve, op. cit., pp. 175–6.

88. '*Cette fumisterie de Maastricht*'; quoted by Villeneuve, op. cit., p. 168.

89. 'Dans le box, les amis de la famille' *Le Quotidien de Paris*, Wednesday 2 June 1993.

90. Montaldo, op. cit., p. 31.

91. See 'Affaire Pelat: le rapport du juge', *Le Point*, 8 January 1994, p. VI.

92. See Jean Montaldo and François Labrouillère, *Le Quotidien de Paris*, 8 February 1993.

93. Jean Miot reported them in *Le Figaro*, 3 May 1993.

94. Montaldo, op. cit., p. 32.

95. Plenel, op. cit., p. 292.

96. See Montaldo, op. cit., pp. 83–4.

97. Gaetner, op. cit., p. 308 note 3.

98. Plenel, op. cit., p. 293.

99. Montaldo, op. cit., p. 83.

100. Jean-François Lacan, Georges Marion and Edwy Plenel, 'L'Énigme Experta et Pelat', *Le Monde*, 27 January 1989.

101. Plenel, op. cit., p. 294.

102. Montaldo, op. cit., p. 87.

103. Gilles Senges and François Labrouillère, *Le Piège de Wall Street*, Albin Michel, Paris, 1989, pp. 249–75, Chapter entitled 'Le Banquet final'; Montaldo, op. cit., p. 86.

104. He did so twice in a week: on '7 sur 7', the famous television interview programme with Anne Sinclair, on 12 February 1989, and again on France 3, on Friday 19 February 1989, reported in *Le Monde* of 21–2 February 1993.

105. Plenel, op. cit., quoting from Christine Clerc, a friend of the Pelat family, in *Le Figaro*, 8 March 1989.

106. Montaldo, op. cit., p. 76.

107. Plenel, op. cit., p. 310.

108. Gaetner, op. cit., p. 355.

109. See Plenel, op. cit., p. 313.

110. Montaldo, op. cit., pp. 80–81.

111. Ibid., p. 77.

112. Gaetner, op. cit., p. 305.

113. Plenel, op. cit., p. 315.

114. Gaetner, op. cit., pp. 305–8.

115. *Le Figaro*, 23 September 1991.

116. Giesbert, *La Fin d'une époque*, pp. 201 ff.

117. See Montaldo, op. cit., p. 36.

118. Attali, op. cit., p. 437.

119. Thierry Jean-Pierre, 'Affaire Pelat: le rapport du juge', *Le Point*, 8 January 1994, p. V.

120. 'Le Trafic d'armes passait par le siège du PS', *Le Figaro*, 17 January 1992.

121. *Le Quotidien de Paris*, 17 February 1993.

122. 'Affaire Pelat: le rapport explosif', *Le Point*, 24 December 1993, p. IV

123. Jean-Pierre, op. cit., p. VII.

124. Letter from Philippe Séguin to Philippe de Villiers, Paris, 18 January 1994.

125. Plenel quotes this exchange, op. cit., p. 303.

126. Stephane Denis, op. cit., p. 51.

127. Giorgio Bocca, author of *Hell, an Enquiry into the Land of the Mafia*. Interview in *Le Point*, 15–21 May 1993.

128. 'L'homme de confiance de Mitterrand s'est suicidé', in *France Soir*, 8 April 1994, p. 7.

129. Edwy Plenel, 'François de Grossouvre, l'ami blessé', *Le Monde*, 9 April 1994.

130. Ibid.

131. Jean Montaldo, *Mitterrand et les 40 voleurs*, Albin Michel, Paris, 1994, p. 13.

Chapter Seven: Cry 'Havoc' and Leash the Dogs

1. Speech, Palais des Congrès, Versailles, 7 April 1994.

2. L'Éloge trés politique signé Mitterrand, *Le Quotidien de Paris*, Wednesday 5 May 1993, emphasis added.

3. *Le Nouvel Observateur*, 28 May 1992. The event took place on 12 July 1985.

4. *Le Quotidien de Paris*. The letter itself was dated 5 February 1983.

5. 'Ils l'ont tué', *Le Monde*, Tuesday 4 May 1993, p. 7.

6. *Le Monde*, Friday 7 May 1993, p. 8.

7. 'M. Vauzelle: l'injustice du système médiatique' *Le Monde*, Tuesday 4 March 1993, p. 6.

8. 'Le Suicide d'un juste', *Le Monde*, Tuesday 4 May 1993, p. 6; emphasis added.

9. Article in *Journal de la Dordogne*, Friday 7 May 1993, reported in *Le Monde*, Friday 7 May 1993, p. 8.

10. 'Le premier victime d'une nouvelle culture', *Le Monde*, Tuesday 4 May 1993, p. 7.

11. Quoted by Villeneuve, op. cit., p. 46.

12. Gaudino, op. cit., p. 49.

13. Speech at Le Mans, 30 November 1990, quoted ibid., p. 74.

14. Revel, op. cit., p. 126.

15. Gaudino, op. cit., p. 138.

16. Ibid., p. 168.

17. Seven per cent think they are 'just'; 20 per cent, 'honest'; and 23 per cent, 'competent'. See Peyrefitte, op. cit., p. 131.

18. Quoted by George A. Bermann in his *The Conseil d'État: Structure and Role*, published by the *Bureau d'Information du Public*, June 1984, p. 1.

19. A. V. Dicey, *Introduction to the Study of the Law of the Constitution*, 1st edn., Macmillan, London, 1885; 8th edn., Macmillan, London, 1915; quoted from reprint of 8th edn. by Liberty Classics, Indianapolis, 1982, pp. 219–20.

20. Paul Legatte, *Le Principe d'équité: defendre le citoyen face à l'administration*, Presses de la Renaissance, Paris, 1992.

21. France's leading constitutionalist, Georges Vedel, argues that the doctrine never implied the supremacy of the law as voted by parliament: 'On the contrary, the principle of representative government and the separation of powers were intended to prevent any branch of public authority, even the legislative branch, from claiming to be the sole repository of national sovereignty. By restoring the prerogatives of the executive, the 1958

constitution began to realize this objective.' Georges Vedel, 'Abrégé de l'histoire des droits de l'homme en France depuis 1789', *Commentaire*, No. 59, p. 925.

22. Dominique Rousseau, 'Le Conseil constitutionnel', op. cit., ed. Chagnollaud, p. 109.

23. Peyrefitte, op. cit., p. 132. See also a review of this book by François de Closets, *Le Figaro*, 22 January 1993.

24. Quoted, without page reference, by Dominique Rousseau, op. cit., p. 131.

25. Ibid., pp. 112–13.

26. Meny, op. cit., p. 38.

27. The 1958 constitution allowed for appeals to the Court to be made only by the President of the Republic, the Prime Minister, the President of the National Assembly or the President of the Senate. In 1974, Valéry Giscard d'Estaing introduced a change in the constitution which permitted appeals to the Court to be made by sixty senators or deputies. Whatever the motive for this change – the Left did not welcome it, no doubt because their Jacobin traditions accorded ill with this essentially liberal concept of the state – it predictably increased the number of appeals to the Court. Whereas between 1958 and 1974, it had only pronounced on nine laws, since 1974 it has ruled on over 300. In 1989, Robert Badinter suggested that the Court should be able to hear appeals from ordinary citizens, but for the time being there has been no agreement on such a change.

28. Mény, op. cit., p. 16.

29. Pfister, *La République des fonctionnaires*, p. 147.

30. Mény, op. cit., p. 303.

31. Ibid., p. 35. The scandal in question was the *Garantie foncière* affair.

32. Ibid., p. 37.

33. Revel, op. cit., p. 100.

34. Ibid., p. 70.

35. Ibid., p. 128.

36. Michel Garetta claimed at his trial that 'The system of transfusion benefits from a position of monopoly which is intended to prevent all commercial approaches and all trade in blood.' See Bettati, op. cit., p. 29.

37. Ibid., p. 59.

38. Professor Yvette Sultan in Eric Favereau, *Le Silence des médecins*, Calmann-Lévy, Paris, 1994.

39. Quoted in 'Sang, un médecin raconte tout', *Valeurs actuelles*, 7 February 1994, p. 6.

40. Mény, op., cit.

41. Quoted in 'Sang, un médecin raconte tout', op. cit., p. 7.

42. Bettati, op. cit., p. 93.

43. Franck Nouchi, 'De nouveaux documents précisent le degré d'information

des services du premier ministré en 1985', *Le Monde*, Wednesday 9 February 1994, p. 11.

44. E.g. Laurent Fabius in *Le Monde*, 29 October 1991.
45. Maclean, op. cit., p. 163.
46. *Le Monde*, 25 November 1992.
47. Ibid.
48. Jean d'Ormesson, quoted by Colombani (without reference), op. cit., pp. 57–8.
49. Henry Rousso, *Le Syndrome de Vichy de 1944 à nos jours*, Editions du Seuil, Paris, 1990, pp. 192–4; extreme right-wing groups were suspected as well, but one theory is that they were fingered or even manipulated by the Palestinians. This is the theory advanced by the inquiry published by Annette Levy-Willard in *Libération*, 3 October 1984.
50. Jessel, op. cit., p. 169.
51. Boccara, op. cit., p. 23.
52. Revel, op. cit., pp. 77, 83, 86.
53. Mény, op. cit., p. 316.

Chapter Eight: The Cabinet Noir

1. The newsreel showing this can be consulted in the archives of Pathé-Cinema.
2. Montaldo, op. cit., pp. 42–50.
3. Plenel quotes this passage, op. cit., pp. 98–9.
4. A. Corvisier, quoted by François Bluche, *L'Ancien Régime, institutions et société*, Livre de Poche, Paris, 1993, p. 177.
5. Attali records (without comment), 'Gaston Deferre sets up a committee to regulate phone tapping.' See op. cit., p. 27.
6. Patricia Tourancheau, '*Un homme de services secrets et d'influence*', *Libération*, 9–10 April 1994, p. 4.
7. Montaldo, op. cit., pp. 60–1.
8. Plenel, op. cit., p. 19.
9. Ibid., p. 37.
10. Ibid., p. 43.
11. Attali, op. cit., p. 304.
12. Jean-Michel Beau, *L'Honneur d'un gendarme*, Sand, Paris, 1989, Livre de Poche, Paris, 1990.
13. Quoted by Plenel, op. cit., p. 60.
14. Ibid., pp. 85–6.
15. Ibid., pp. 86–7.
16. Ibid., pp. 77–80.
17. Ibid., pp. 65–9.
18. Revel, op. cit., p. 65.
19. Tourancheau, op. cit., p. 4.

20. Villeneuve, op. cit., p. 51.
21. See Plenel, op. cit., p. 128.
22. Ibid., p. 133.
23. Ibid., p. 169.
24. Ibid., p. 170.
25. Ibid., pp. 178–9.
26. *Le Canard Enchaîné*, 31 October 1990, quoted ibid., p. 183.
27. *Le Point*, 29 October 1990, quoted by Plenel, op. cit., p. 183.
28. *Le Figaro*, 5 and 7 November 1990.
29. Attali, op. cit., p. 710.
30. The book is *Mort d'un pasteur* by Bernard Violet. Its imminent publication was reported in *The European*, 6–12 May 1994. See *Murdered priest is latest ghost to haunt Mitterrand* by Roger Faliot and Anne-Elisabeth Moutet, p. 1.
31. Plenel, op. cit., p. 197.
32. Erich Inciyan, 'La Cellule antiterroriste de l'Elysée a écouté des particuliers au prix de graves dysfonctionnements', *Le Monde*, 27 January 1994, p. 11.

Chapter Nine: The Architect of Socialism

1. In *La Paille et le grain: chronique*, Flammarion, Paris, 1975, quoted by Nay, *Le Noir et le rouge*, p. 50. Mitterrand also wrote a book called *L'Abeille et l'architecte: chronique*, Flammarion, Paris, 1978.
2. Attali, op. cit.p.22.
3. Internal document of mission: l'impact économique des Grands projets, 8 October 1985.
4. E.g. Michel Rocard in October 1993, and François Mitterrand at the Brussels European Summit in December 1993.
5. Revel, op. cit., p. 96.
6. '*Je suis Mitterrandolâtre.*'
7. Giesbert, *La Fin d'une époque*, p. 17.
8. Mény, op. cit., p. 271.
9. Quoted by Francois Chaslin, *Les Paris de François Mitterrand*, Gallimard, Paris, 1985.
10. Official communiqué of the Council of Ministers, 24 January 1990.
11. Quoted by Chaslin, op. cit., p. 18, note 5.
12. Emile Biasini (Secretary of State for the *Grands Travaux*), 'La nouvelle programmation', interview in *Le Moniteur*, 20 January 1989.
13. Sue Collard, 'Mission, impossible: les chantiers du président', French Cultural Studies, No. 2, 1992, p. 107; see also the attack published by the Association pour le Renouveau du Louvre, by B. Foucart, S. Loste, A. Schnapper, *Paris mystifié: la grande illusion du grand Louvre*, Paris, Julliard, 1985.

14. Marc Emery, 'Une interview de Jack Lang, Ministre de la Culture', *Architecture d'aujourd'hui*, No. 222, September 1982, ix–xi.

15. Speech by Mitterrand at the Centre de Formation des Apprentis at Troyes, 11 June 1991.

16. Hugues Gall, director of the Grand Theatre in Geneva, March 1990, quoted by Maryvonne de Saint-Pulgent in *Le Syndrome de l'opéra*, Accords, Robert Laffont, Paris, 1991, p. 9.

17. Elysée communiqué of 8 March 1983.

18. Philippe Meyer, 'L'Opéra de l'Opéra de la Bastille', *Le Débat*, May – August 1992, No. 70.

19. De Saint-Pulgent, op. cit., p. 252.

20. Revel, op. cit., p. 98.

21. Ibid.

22. De Saint-Pulgent, op. cit., p. 256.

23. Gerard Charlet in Philippe Urfalino, *Quatre voix pour une opéra: une histoire de l'Opéra-Bastille raconté par Michele Audon, François Bloch-Laine, Gerard Charlet, Michael Dittmann*, Editions Metaille, Paris, 1990, p. 264.

24. Meyer, op. cit., p. 111.

25. Quoted by Pierre Nora, 'Bibliothèque de France: d'où venons-nous, où allons-nous?' *Le Débat*, No. 70, May – August 1992, p. 113.

26. *Note d'orientation* given to the architects on 11 April 1989; quoted by Nora, op. cit., pp. 113–14.

27. Phillipe Leighton, *Le Débat*, No. 65, May – August 1991; Patrice Higonnet, 'Scandal on the Seine', *New York Review of Books*, 15 August 1991.

Chapter Ten: Not the Three Musketeers

1. André Chevalier, *L'Éloge du conservatisme*, Plon, Paris 1992, p. 8.

2. See Eugen Weber, 'Fascism, Religion and the French Right' *Times Literary Supplement*, 9 July 1993, p. 10.

3. Especially since the publication of René Rémond, *Les Droites en France*, Aubier, Paris, 1982. See also the three-volume reference book, a collection of essays ed. Jean-Francois Sirinelli, *Histoire des Droites en France*, Gallimard, Paris, 1993.

4. Alfred Thibaudet, *Les Idées politiques en France*, Stock, Paris, 1932, p. 23.

5. The composition of French politics at this time is well dealt with by Finer, op. cit.

6. See especially Hayek, op. cit.

7. Alain-Gérard Slama, 'Bonald, Tocqueville, Maurras et les autres', *L'Histoire*, No. 162, January 1993; for the soft-liberal British imperialist tradition, see Corelli Barnet, *The Collapse of British Power*, *passim*, Alan Sutton, London, 1972.

8. Quoted by Michel Winock (without attribution) in 'Voyage à l'intérieur de la droite', *L'Histoire*, No. 162, January 1993.

9. Rémond, op. cit., is the author of the view that there are three right-wing tendencies in France.

10. Winock, 'Voyage à l'intérieur de la droite'.

11. See my article, 'The Vichy Syndrome', *Spectator*, 5 December 1992.

12. In the third number of the daily *Action fran*çaise, 23 March 1908. See Eugen Weber: 'Nationalism, Socialism and National Socialism', *My France: Politics, Culture, Myth*, Belknap Press of Harvard University Press, Cambridge, Massachussetts, 1991, p. 263.

13. Thierry Maulnier, 'Le seul combat possible', *Combat*, July 1936.

14. Sternhell, op. cit., especially chapters 4, 5 and 6, 'Le révisionisme idéaliste du marxisme: le socialisme éthique, d'Henri de Man'; 'Un socialisme pour toute la nation'; and 'Le Planisme ou le socialisme sans proletariat'.

15. The classic work on Vichy is Robert Paxton, *La France de Vichy, 1940–1944*, available in paperback, *Editions du Seuil*, Paris, 1973. Sternhell, op. cit., also makes the link clear between fascism and Socialism.

16. For a monarchist interpretation of de Gaulle, see Bouthillon, op. cit., pp. 467 ff.

17. See Jean Charlot, *'Le Gaullisme'*, op. cit., Vol. I. ed. Jean-Francois Sirinelli, p. 657.

18. Quoted by Jean Charlot, 'Le Rassemblement pour la République', *La Vie politique en France*, Editions du Seuil, Paris, June 1993, p. 243.

19. Televized interview with Michel Droit, 15 December 1965.

20. Jean Charbonnel, 'Les derniers Gaullistes', *L'Histoire*, No. 162, January 1993; see also Charlot, *'Le Gaullisme'* op. cit., p. 663, for the importance of notions like 'association' and 'participation' and pp. 666–7 for his repudiation of capitalism. Charlot argues that despite the attraction to him of the notion of a 'third way', de Gaulle never repudiated capitalism with the same force with which he repudiated Communism.

21. Denis Tillinac, *Le Retour de d'Artagnan*, La Table Ronde, Paris, 1992.

22. Charles de Gaulle, *Le Fil d'Épée*, quoted by Jean-Pierre Rioux, 'Le Cas de Gaulle', *L'Histoire*, No. 162, January 1993.

23. SOFRES/RTL/*Le Monde*, 22–6 September 1990 and 15–17 October 1991.

24. See Giesbert, *La fin d'une époque*, p. 166.

25. Attali, op. cit., p. 775.

26. Ibid., p. 867.

27. Gaudino, op. cit., pp. 81–2.

28. Attali, op. cit., p. 793; see also Tony Judt, 'Chauvin and his Heirs', *Times Literary Supplement*, 9 July 1993, p. 11.

29. Attali, op. cit., p. 777.

30. See François Fejtö, *La République du centre*, Editions Pluriel, Paris 1986, *passim*.

31. Chevalier, op. cit., p. 49.

Chapter Eleven: Past Imperfect

1. Letter to his sister, Geneviève, 5 March 1938, quoted by Franz-Olivier Giesbert, *François Mitterrand: Histoire d'une ambition*, Seuil, Paris, 1990, p. 29.

2. Quoted by André Fontaine, 'Diplomatie française: un modèle gaullien?' *Politique internationale*, No. 52, Summer 1991, p. 57.

3. Alain Griotteray, *Trois portraits cavaliers: de Gaulle, Giscard d'Estaing, Mitterrand*, Editions de Fallois, Paris, 1990, p. 122 f.

4. The decree-law can be found in the *Journal Officiel*, 19 March 1956, p. 2656.

5. See Alain Peyrefitte, *Quand la rose se fânera: du malentendu à l'espoir*, Paris, Plon, 1983.

6. Quoted by Montaldo, op. cit., p. 164.

7. See Attali, op. cit., p. 361.

8. Weber, 'Nationalism, Socialism and National Socialism', in *My France: politics, culture, myth*, Belknap Press, Cambridge Mass, 1991, Introduction, p. 7.

9. See Chapter 10.

10. Giesbert, *François Mitterrand ou la tentation de l'histoire*, p. 33.

11. See Weber, *My France: Politics, Culture, Myth op. cit., introduction*, p. 7.

12. Eugen Weber, *Action Francaise*, Fayard, Paris, 1962 (translated from English, *Action Française*, Stanford University Press, California, 1962) p. 569.

13. Jean-Baptiste Biaggi. Quotation taken from Giesbert, *François Mitterrand*, p. 34. Giesbert also quotes François Dalle who recalls only arguments between Mitterrand and Biaggi.

14. Nay, *Le Noir et le rouge*, p. 66.

15. According to the hard-right magazine, *Le Choc du mois*, at least, 'Mitterrand et La Cagoule', July – August 1991, p. 11.

16. Giesbert, *François Mitterrand ou la tentation de l'histoire*, p. 35.

17. Father O'Reilly, the head of the hostel, quoted by Nay, *Le Noir et le rouge*, pp. 62–3.

18. Mitterrand, *Ma part de vérité*, p. 18.

19. Ibid., p. 19.

20. Giesbert, *François Mitterrand ou la tentation de l'histoire*, p. 49.

21. Ibid., pp. 50–1.

22. Mitterrand, *Ma part de Vérité*, pp. 20–21. Even the title is dishonest.

23. Nay, *Le Noir et le rouge*, p. 68.

24. *France, Revue de l'État Nouveau*, June 1942, quoted by Nay, *Le Noir et le rouge*, p. 102.

25. By Dr Alexis Carel.

26. By Louis de Gérin-Ricard. He writes, 'There are few historical examples which give a better idea of the Semitic peril than the way in which Rome

dealt with the Jews, who encouraged prostitution, gambling, theft, and pederasty.'

27. *François Mitterrand, 'Pèlerinage en Thuringe', France, Revue de l'État Nouveau,* No. 5, December 1942.

28. In 1941, Felix Gaillard, the future President of the radical-socialist Council of Ministers (Prime Minister), who was then a young officer in the Vichy version of the Hitler Youth, the Chantiers de Jeunesse, declared, 'We lost the war because we wanted to undertake a national struggle with a government of political parties. In a democratic government [something he obviously rejected], a man must be a man of his party before being a man of his country.' See Nay, *Le Noir et le rouge*, p. 86.

29. Jean-François Tournoux, *Pétain et de Gaulle*, Plon, Paris, 1964, p. 101.

30. Interview with Franz-Olivier Giesbert, October 1973, quoted in *François Mitterrand*, p. 45.

31. Mitterrand, *La Paille et le grain*, quoted by Nay, *Le Noir, et le rouge*, p. 90.

32. Nay, *Le Noir et le rouge*, p. 90.

33. Ibid., p. 92.

34. Ibid., p. 93.

35. Ibid.

36. Giesbert, *François Mitterrand ou la tentation de l'histoire*, p. 54.

37. Ibid., p. 60

38. Quoted by most people who discuss the issue, e.g. in Dantes, op. cit., p. 12.

39. Pierre Viannson-Ponte, *Lettre ouverte aux hommes politiques*, Albin Michel, Paris, 1976, pp. 52–3.

40. Interview with Roger Priouret in *L'Expansion*, July – August, 1972.

41. Giesbert, *François Mitterrand ou la tentation de l'histoire*, p. 61.

42. Rousso, op. cit., p. 211.

43. Pierre Jouve and Ali Magoudi, *François Mitterrand, portrait total*, Carrère, Paris, 1986, p. 163.

44. Winock, *'L'irresistible Ascension de François Mitterrand'* p. 11.

45. Attali, op. cit., p. 14.

46. Simon Arbellot, *Ecrits de Paris*, January 1966.

47. Françoise Gaspard and Gerard Grunberg, 'Les Titulaires de la Francisque Gallique', *Le Gouvernement de Vichy*, Fondation Nationale des Sciences Politiques, Arnmand Colin, Paris, 1972, pp. 71–85.

48. Jouve and Magoudi, op. cit., p. 163.

49. Paxton, op. cit., p. 353.

50. Nay, *Le Noir et le rouge*, pp. 107–8.

51. Jouve and Magoudi, op. cit., p. 163; Viansson-Ponté, op. cit., pp. 52–3; Winock, 'L'Irresistible Ascension de François Mitterrand', p. 11.

52. Rousso, op. cit., p. 211; Giesbert, *François Mitterrand ou la tentation de l'histoire*, p. 61.

53. 'Mitterrand et La Cagoule' quotes the captain, Hugh Verity, *We Landed by Moonlight*.

54. Griotteray, op. cit., p. 126.

55. 'Mitterrand et La Cagoule'.

56. Edith Calvier claims to have one. See *L'Idiot international*, 16 May 1991.

57. Personal remarks communicated to the author.

58. *Écrits de Paris*, 1966, quoted by Nay, *Le Noir et le rouge*, p. 107.

59. Rousso, op. cit., p. 211; Giesbert, *François Mitterrand ou la tentation de l'histoire*, p. 60.

60. Nay, *Le Noir et le rouge*, pp. 108–9.

61. See Tombs, op. cit., p. 10.

62. I am grateful to Gilbert Pérol for this explanation.

63. Giesbert, *François Mitterrand ou la tentation de l'histoire*, p. 62.

64. Attali, op. cit., pp. 14–15.

65. *Le Monde*, 9 May 1981.

66. Rousso, op. cit., pp. 214–15.

67. Giesbert, *François Mitterrand ou la tentation de l'histoire*, p. 57.

68. Stephane Denis, *L'Amoraliste*, pp. 23–4.

69. Plenel, op. cit., p. 376.

70. Eric Conan, 'Enquête sur le retour d'une idéologie', *L'Express*, 9 July 1992.

71. Plenel, op. cit., p. 408.

72. Broadcast to the nation, 14 July 1992.

73. See *Le Dossier Bousquet*, supplement to *Libération*, 13 July 1993.

74. See my article, 'Past Imperfect', *Spectator*, 26 June 1994.

75. *Libération*, 21 October 1990. See also Plenel, op. cit., p. 374.

76. Quoted by Plenel, op. cit., p. 375.

77. See Ibid., p. 379.

78. Stephane Denis, 'Quand René Bousquet financait les amis politiques de Mitterrand', interview with Pascal Krop, *L'Événement du jeudi*, 18–24 April 1991.

79. Stephane Denis, *L'Amoraliste*, p. 24.

80. Giesbert, *François Mitterrand ou la tentation de l'histoire*, p. 70.

81. Quoted by ibid., p. 71.

82. Quoted Nay, *Le Noir et le rouge*, p. 111.

83. Quoted ibid.

84. Griotteray, op. cit., p. 127.

85. Quoted by Nay, *Le Noir et le rouge*, p. 114.

86. Philippe Dechartre, quoted by Nay, ibid.

87. Stephane Denis, *L'Amoraliste*, p. 39.

Chapter Twelve: In Search of Times Past

1. Quoted by Giesbert, *La Fin d'une époque*, p. 102.

2. At a press conference on 20 September 1991 in Weimar. See Jessel, op. cit., p. 107.

3. Ibid.

4. Alain Généstar, *Les Péchés du prince*, Grasset, Paris, 1992, p. 88.

5. Quoted by Fontaine, op. cit., p. 57. Also quoted by Pierre Favier and Michel Martin-Roland, *La Décennie Mitterrand*, Vol. I. *Les Ruptures*, Seuil, Paris, 1990.

6. Quoted by Fontaine, op. cit., p. 58.

7. The classic view that that old postulate of political science, the state of nature, can still be found in the relations between sovereign states, is part of the thesis of Anthony de Jasay's brilliant book, *The State*, Blackwell, Oxford, 1985.

8. Maurice Couve de Murville, *Une politque étrangère 1958–1969*, Plon, Paris; quoted by Doelnitz, op. cit.

9. Quoted by Fontaine, op. cit., p. 60.

10. Alexandre Sanguinetti, *L'Histoire du soldat, de la violence et des pouvoirs*, Editions Ramsay, Paris, 1979, p. 93.

11. Ibid.

12. Ibid., p. 95.

13. De Gaulle, *Memoires de Guerre, L'appel, 1940–1942*, Vol. I, Plon, Paris, 1954, p. 88.

14. Sanguinetti op. cit., p. 96.

15. Tombs, op. cit., p. 9. The book which advances this argument is, of course, the classic *Vichy France: Old Guard and New Order, 1940–1944* by Robert Paxton, 1972, available in French translation, *La France de Vichy, 1940–1944*, Editions du Seuil, Paris, 1973.

16. François Crouzet, *De la supériorite de l'Angleterre sur la France*, Perrin, Paris, 1985.

17. Doelnitz, op. cit., pp. 134–5.

18. Attali, op. cit., p. 200, entry for 2 April 1982.

19. Ibid., p. 201.

20. Ibid.

21. François Bujon de l'Estang, *Politique Internationale*, Winter 1992–3, p. 178.

22. Quoted by Georges Vallance, *France – Allemagne, le retour de Bismarck*, Flammarion, Paris, 1990, p. 93.

23. On television, 11 January 1980. See *Le Nouvel Observateur*, No. 1509, 7–13 October 1993, p. 51.

24. Généstar, op. cit., p. 137.

25. Dantes, op. cit., p. 104.

26. Attali, op. cit., p. 70.

27. François Mitterrand, *Reflexions sur la politique étrangère de la France*, Fayard, Paris, 1986, Introduction.

28. Roche, op. cit., p. 51.

29. Généstar, op. cit., p. 99.

30. Attali, op. cit., p. 88.

31. Ibid., p. 515.

32. Interview with *Le Journal du dimanche*, 10 February 1991.

33. Interview with Samy Cohen, 'François le gaullien et Mitterrand l'européen', L'Histoire, No. 143, April 1991, p. 34.

34. Doelnitz, op. cit., p. 116.

35. Attali, op. cit., p. 15.

36. Ibid, p. 32.

37. Alain Duhamel, op. cit., p. 84.

38. Génestar, op. cit., p. 47.

39. Attali, op. cit., p. 577.

40. Ibid., p. 493.

41. Ibid., p. 496.

42. Ibid., p. 427.

43. Ibid., p. 554.

44. Jessel, op. cit., pp. 36–7.

45. Revel, op. cit., p.139. The Quebec episode is described by Lacouture, *De Gaulle, 3, Le Souverain, 1959–1970*, p. 521.

46. Attali, op. cit., p. 107.

47. Interview, *Le Nouvel Observateur*, 27 July 1989.

48. This is the thesis of Timothy Garton Ash's book, *In Europe's Name*, Cape, London, 1993.

49. Kohl told this story during an interview with journalists, including Franz-Olivier Giesbert, who recounts it in *La Fin d'une époque*, pp. 102–3.

50. Génestar, op. cit., p. 110.

51. Ibid., p. 107.

52. Revel, op. cit., p. 139.

53. Jessel, op. cit., p. 65.

54. Ibid., p. 67.

55. Ibid., p. 68.

56. Ibid., p. 69.

57. Before the Senate, 20 December 1989. See Jessel, op. cit., p. 72.

58. Génestar, op.cit., p. 113.

59. Ibid., p. 114.

60. *Der Spiegel*, No. 41, 11 October 1993, published extracts from Lady Thatcher's memoirs, with the explanation 'She wanted to prevent reunification', even though there is nothing in the memoirs to suggest that. Chancellor Kohl also had a little outburst, saying that Mrs Thatcher was 'pre-Churchillian' and out of date. See *The Times*, 12 October 1993.

61. Margaret Thatcher, *The Downing Street Years*, Harper Collins, London, 1993, p. 791.

62. See, for instance, her speech at the Hague, given in May 1992. It is reprinted in an edited form in *Visions of Europe* ed. Stephen Hill, Duckworth, London, 1993.

63. Thatcher, op. cit., p. 795.
64. Généstar, op. cit., p. 116.
65. Ibid., p. 118–19.
66. Jessel, op. cit., p. 75.
67. Ibid., p. 75–6.
68. Colombani, op. cit., p. 226.
69. Revel, op. cit., p. 139.
70. Généstar, op. cit., p. 105–23.

Chapter Thirteen: The Strange Defeat

1. Speech to the European parliament, 23 August 1991. Reported in *The Times* the next day. Quoted from *The Cost of Europe* ed. Patrick Minford, Manchester University Press, Manchester, 1992, p. 107.
2. *Le Point*, 31 August 1991.
3. Serge July, 'Les Années Mitterrand', p. 266.
4. Attali, op. cit., p. 896.
5. Ibid., p. 147.
6. Remark to George Schulz, quoted by Attali, op. cit., p. 465.
7. Attali, op. cit., p. 117.
8. Alain Généstar shares it. See op. cit., p. 103.
9. Attali, op.cit., p. 143.
10. See Jessel, op. cit., p. 66.
11. See Hayek, p. 279. In general, see Chapter 14, 'The Religion of the Engineers: Enfantin and the Saint-Simonians'. It is only sad that Saint-Simon's theories are universally practised at national level in all modern so-called capitalist economies.
12. Paul Thibaud, 'Pour une Europe politique', *Le Monde*, 23–4 August 1992.
13. See my article, 'They Are All Gaullists Now', *Spectator*, 12 September 1992.
14. Gregor Schoellgen, *Die Macht in der Mitte Europas, Stationen deutscher Außenpolitik von Friedrich dem Großen bis zur Gegenwart*, C. H. Beck, Munich, 1992, *passim*.
15. See my article on this, 'The Court Turned the EC upside down', *Wall Street Journal Europe*, 14 October 1993.
16. 'Maastricht attérit a Francfort', Eric Branca in *Valeurs actuelles*, 8 November 1993, p. 28.
17. 'Les Tribus et l'Europe', Palais Chaillot, 29 February 1992.
18. See 'Je plaide pour une structure de l'Europe toute entière', *Le Monde*, 3 March 1992, p. 4.
19. On 'The World at One', BBC Radio 4, 1.00 p.m. 7 July 1991. I am obliged for this quotation, and for a huge amount besides to Mark Almond and his book *Europe's Backyard War: the War in Yugoslavia*, Heinemann, London, 1994, of which he kindly allowed me to see an early version.

20. The broadcast, like the *putsch*, occurred on 19 August 1991. See Jessel, op. cit., p. 127.

21. Dantes, op. cit., p. 106.

22. *Le Monde*, 23 August 1991.

23. He refers to it constantly, e.g. 'L'Heure de Vérité', Antenne 2, Monday 24 October 1993.

24. Such as, for instance, Sir Leon Brittan.

25. Genestar, op. cit., p. 142.

26. I am grateful to Mark Almond, op. cit., for this grotesque anecdote.

27. Ibid., Chapter 11.

28. Attali, op. cit., p. 10.

29. Carl Schmitt, *Land und Meer: eine weltgeschichtliche Betrachtung*, 1943.

30. Mitterrand, *Ma part de vérité*, p. 13.

31. Quoted, without reference, by Giesbert, *François Mitterrand ou la tentation de l'histoire*, p. 59.

32. Stephane Denis, op. cit., pp. 56–7.

33. Mitterrand, *La Paille et le grain*, p. 182.

34. François Mitterrand, interview in *Le Quotidien de Paris*, 26 October 1977; reprinted in Mitterrand, *Politique 2, 1977–1981*, p. 13.

35. Plenel, op. cit., pp. 430–31.

36. It is often quoted, but the full passage, from a speech he gave on 2 May 1981, eight days before his election, is worth knowing: 'Ideas mature like fruit and like men. One has to give time time. No one passes from one day to the next from sowing to reaping, and the scale of history is not that of gazelles. But after patience, there comes the springtime. We are there, I believe.' See Griotteray, op. cit., p. 143.

Bibliography

Ardant, Philippe, *Les institutions de la Ve République*, Hachette, Paris, 1993.

Askolovitch, Claude & Attal, Sylvain, *La France du piston*, Robert Laffont, Paris, 1992

Attali, Jacques, *Verbatim, Tome 1, 1981–1986*, Fayard, Paris, 1993.

Avril, Pierre, *La Ve République, histoire politique et constitutionelle*, PUF, 1987

Appleton, Andrew, 'Maastricht and the French Party System: Domestic implications of the Treaty referendum' in *French Politics and Society*, Volume 10, Number 4, autumn 1992.

Bélorgey, Jean-Michel, *Le parlement à refaire*, Gallimard, Paris, 1991.

Bellier, Irène, *L'ENA, comme si vous y etiez*, Seuil, Paris, 1993.

Bergounioux, Alain, *Le long remords du pouvoir: le parti socialiste français, 1905–1992*, Fayard, Paris, 1992.

Best, Geoffrey, ed., *The Permanent Revolution: the French Revolution and its Legacy 1789–1989*, 2nd ed., Fontana, 1989.

Bettati, Caroline, *Responsables et coupables: une affaire de sang*, Seuil, Paris, 1993.

Birnbaum, Pierre, *Les sommets de l'Etat*, Seuil, Paris, 1977.

Bloch, Marc, 'L'étrange defaite', Folio Histoire, Editions Gallimard, 1990 (written in 1940).

Boccara, Bruno, 'L'insurrection démocratique: manifeste pour la Ve Republique', Democratica, Paris, 1993.

Bothorel, Jean, 'Une décennie sans grandeur', in *Revue des deux mondes*, Mai 1991.

Brizay, Bernard, *Le patronnat: histoire, structure, stratégie du CNPF*, Seuil, Paris, 1975.

Burdeau, Georges, *Droit constitutionnel et institutions politiques* by Georges Burdeau, 16e edition, Librairie Generale de Droit et de Jurisprudence, Paris, 1974.

Cayrol, Roland & Perrineau, Pascal, *Le guide du pouvoir, Présidentielles 88*, Paris, ed. Francois Doumic, 1988.

Cennac, Yves, 'Les élites dirigeantes françaises en question', in *Le Débat*, No. 53, Janvier-Fevrier 1989.

Chagnollaud, Dominique, *Le premier des ordres: les hauts fonctionnaires, XVIIIe–XXe siècles*, Fayard, Paris, 1991.

Chagnollaud, Dominique ed., *La vie politique en France*, Editions du Seuil, Paris, June 1993.

Chalier, Yves, *La République corrompue*, Paris, Robert Laffont, 1991.

Chantebout, Bernard, *La nation*, in Krisis, Numéro 5, Avril 1990.

Chazal, Claire, *Balladur*, Flammarion, Paris, 1993.

Chevalier, Alain, *Éloge du conservatisme*, Plon, Paris 1992.

de Closets, François, *Tant et plus! Comment l'Etat gaspille notre argent*, Grasset-Seuil, 1992.

Coignard, Sophie & Lacan, Jean-François, *La République bananiere*, Belfond, Paris, 1989.

Coignard, Sophie & Wickham, Alexandre, *La nomenklatura française, pouvoirs et privileges des élites*, Pierre Belfond, Paris, 1988.

Collard, Sue, *Mission impossible: les chantiers du president*, French Cultural Studies, No. 8, June 1992.

Colombani, Jean-Marie, *La France sans Mitterrand*, Flammarion, Paris, 1992.

Crouzet, François, *De la supériorité de l'Angleterre sur la France*, Perrin, Paris, 1985.

Crozier, Michel, *The Bureaucratic Phenomenon*, Chicago University Press, 1964.

Dantes, Edmond, *Mitterrand par lui-meme: Critique et analyse d'une vie politique*, Jacques Grancher, Paris, 1992.

Delaisi, Francis, *La révolution européenne*, Paris, 1942.

De La Gorce, Paul-Marie; Schor, Armand-Denis, *La politique étrangère de la Ve République*, PUF 1992.

Delacroix, Rodolphe & Tenzer, Nicolas, *Les élites et la fin de la démocratie française*, Presses Universitaires de France, Paris, 1992.

Denis, Stéphane, *L'Amoraliste*, Fayard, Paris, 1992.

Divier, Pierre-François, *Lettre raccommandée à Francois Mitterrand sur l'affaire Urba-Gracco*, Editions du Rocher, Paris, 1992.

Documentation Française, *La criminalité en France en 1983*

Doelnitz, Tristan, *La France hantée par sa puissance*, Belfond, Paris, 1993.

Duhamel, Alain, *La république de M. Mitterrand*, Grasset, Paris, 1982.

Duhamel, Alain, *De Gaulle-Mitterrand: la marque et la trace*, Flammarion, Paris, 1991.

Dupin, Eric, *L'après Mitterrand: le parti socialiste à la dérive*, Calmann-Levy, Paris, 1991.

Duverger, Maurice, *La Monarchie républicaine*, Robert Laffont, 1974.

'L'Évènement du jeudi', *La France du piston*, 6 fevrier 1992.

Etchegoyen, Alain, *La démocratie malade du mensonge*, Bourin, Paris, 1993.

Faligot, Roger & Kauffer, Rémi, *Eminences Grises*, Fayot, Paris, 1992.

Favier, Pierre & Martin-Roland, Michel, *La décennie Mitterrand*, Seuil Paris, 1991, 2 vols.

Favereau, Eric, *Le silence des médecins*, Calmann-Levy, Paris, 1994.

Frossard, André, *Excusez-moi d'être français*, Fayard, Paris, 1992.

Furet, François, *Penser la révolution française*, Gallimard, Paris, 1983.

Gaetner, Gilles, *L'argent facile: dictionnaire de la corruption en France*, Stock, Paris, 1992.

Gallot, Didier, *Les graces de Dieu*, Albin Michel, Paris, 1993.

Gaspard, François & Grunberg, Gérard, 'Les Titulaires de la Francisque

Gallique' in *Le Gouvernment de Vichy*, Fondation nationale des sciences politiques, Armand Colin, Paris, 1972

De Gaulle, Charles, *Mémoires d'espoir*, Plon, Paris, 1971.

De Gaulle, Charles, *Mémoires de guerre*, Plon, Paris, 1954.

Gaudino, Antoine, *L'enquête imossible*, Albin Michel, Paris, 1990.

Gaudino, Antoine, *Le procès impossible*, Albin Michel, Paris, 1992.

Gélédan, Alain, ed., *Le bilan économique des années Mitterrand, 1981–1993*, Editions Le Monde, Paris, 1993.

Généstar, Alain, *Les péchés du prince*, Grasset, Paris, 1992.

Giesbert, Franz-Olivier, *François Mitterrand ou la tentation de l'histoire*, Seuil, Paris, 1977.

Giesbert, Franz-Olivier, *Le Président*, Seuil, Paris, 1990.

Giesbert, Franz-Olivier, *La fin d'une époque*, Seuil, Paris, 1993.

Giustiniani, Josua, *Le racket politique: aministie et fausses factures*, Albin Michel, Paris, 1990.

Griotteray, Alain, *Trois portraits cavaliers*, Editions de Fallois, Paris, 1990.

Goldsmith, Jimmy, *Le piège: entretiens avec Yves Messarovitch sur quelques idées reçues*, Fixot, Paris, 1993.

Goodman, John, 'Monetary Policy and Financial Deregulation in France' in *French Politics and Society*, Volume 10, Number 4, autumn 1992.

Grosser, Alfred, 'La politique extérieure de la France', in *Politiques*, No. 3, 1992.

Guillauma, Yves, *La presse en France*, Editions la Decouverte, Paris, 1988.

Guyomarch, Alain & Machin, Howard, 'A History of Hesitations on the Road to Maastricht', in *French Politics and Society*, Volume 10, Number 4, autumn 1992.

Halimi, Serge, 'Le parti socialiste à bout de souffle', in *French Politics and Society*, Vol. 10, Number 4, Fall 1992.

Hall, Peter A.; Hayward, Jack; Machin, Howard, *L'évolution de la politique française*, PUF, Paris 1992.

Hallier, Jean-Edern, *La force d'âme, suivi de, L'honneur perdu de François Mitterrand*, Belles Lettres, Paris, 1992.

Hellman, John, *The Knight-Monks of Vichy France, Uriage, 1940–1945*, McGill-Queen's University, Montreal, 1994.

Hervieu, Bernard, 'Un impossible deuil: à propos de l'agriculture et du monde rural en France', in *French Politics and Society*, Vol. 10, No. 4, autumn 1992.

Hude, Henri, *Éthique et politique*, ed. Universitaires, Paris, 1992.

Imbert, Claude, 'France-Allemagne, le coup de pompe du pouvoir', in *Le Point*, 26 March 1990.

J'allais vous dire: Journal apocryphe d'un président, Editions Jean-Claude Lattes, Paris, 1993.

Jenkins, Brian & Morris, Peter, 'Political Scandal in France', in *Modern & Contemporary France*, No. 2, 1993.

Jessel, Jacques, *La double défaite de Mitterrand: de Berlin à Moscou, les faillites d'une diplomatie*, Albin Michel, Paris 1992.

Joffrin, Laurent, *La regression française*, Seuil, Paris, 1992.

Jouve, Pierre Magoudi, Ali, *François Mitterrand, portrait total*, Carrère, Paris, 1986.

Krauthammer, Elmar, *Vichy – Alger 1940–1942: Le Chemin de la France au tournant de la guerre*, Economica, Paris, 1992.

Lacroix, Bernard, ed., & Lagroye, Jacques, ed., *Le président de la République: usages et genèses d'une institution*, Presses de la FNSP, Paris 1992.

Lacouture, Jean, *De Gaulle*, 3 vos, Editions du Seuil, Paris, 1986.

Lefort, François, 'La France et son droit: la constitution de la liberté', Collection Laissez Faire, dirigée par Francois Guillaumat, Les belles lettres, 1991.

Marshall, Terence, ed., *Théorie et pratique du government constitutionnel: La France et les Etats-Unis*, Editions de l'Espace Européen, La Garenne-Colombes, 1992.

Masset, Jean-Pierre, 'The Foreign Policy of France in the contemporary world', in *Pakistan Horizon*, No. 4, October 1991.

Menière, Laurent, *Bilan de la France, 1981–1993*, Pluriel, Paris, 1993.

Mény, Yves, *La corruption de la République*, Fayard, 1992.

Mény, Yves, 'Corruption et politique', in *Esprit*, Novembre 1992.

Messerlin, Patrick, 'La Communauté, la France et l'Uruguay Round' in *Commentaire*, No. 63, autumn 1993.

Mitterrand, François, 'Pélerinage en Thuringe', in *France, Revue de l'Etat nouveau*, No. 5, Decembre 1942.

Mitterrand, François, *Ma part de Verité*, Fayard, Paris, 1969.

Mitterrand, François, *La paille et le grain: chronique*, Flammarion, Paris, 1975.

Mitterrand, François, *Le coup d'état permanent*, Plon, Paris, 1964.

Montaldo, Jean, *Lettre ouverte d'un 'chien' à François Mitterrand au nom de la liberté d'aboyer*, Albin Michel, Paris, 1993.

Nay, Catherine, *Le Noir et le Rouge*, Grasset, Paris, 1984.

Nay, Catherine, *Les sept Mitterrand, ou les metamorphoses d'un septennat*, Grasset, Paris, 1988.

Némo, Philippe, *Le chaos pédagogique*, Albin Michel, Paris 1993.

Olivennes, Denis, *L'Affaire du sang contaminé, analyse d'un scandale*, Notes de la Fondation Saint-Simon, avril 1992.

Paxton, Robert, *Vichy France, Old Guard and New Order, 1940–1944*, 1972; available in French translation as *La France de Vichy, 1940–1944*, Editions du Seuil, Paris, 1973.

Peyrefitte, Alain, *La France en désarroi: entre la peur et l'espoir*, Fallois, Paris, 1993.

Plenel, Edwy, *La Part d'Ombre*, Stock, Paris, 1992.

Pfister, Thierry, *La Vie quotidienne à Matignon au temps de l'Union de la gauche*, Hachette, Paris, 1985.

Pfister, Thierry, *Lettre ouverte à la generation Mitterrand qui marche à côté de ses pompes*, Albin Michel, Paris, 1988.

Pfister, Thierry, *La République des fonctionnaires*, Albin Michel, Paris, 1988.

Le Point No. 844, 21 November 88, *Mitterrand: Le Roi et sa Cour.*

Popis, Claude, *L'argent, le batiment, la politique sous la Ve République*, Albin Michel, Paris, 1992.

Portelli, Hugues, *Le Socialisme français tel qu'il est*, Presses Universitaires de France, 1980.

Projet, Hiver 1992–1993, *Attention, corruption!*

Rémond, René, *Les droites en France*, Paris, Aubier, 1982.

Revel, Jean-François, *L'absolutisme inefficace, ou contre le présidentialisme à la française*, Plon, Paris, 1992.

Robert, Jacques, 'Le giscardisme et les libertés', revue *Pouvoirs* No. 9, 1979.

Roche, Jean-Jacques, 'La politique étrangère de François Mitterrand', Politiques, No. 3, Été 1992.

de Rose, François, 'La diplomatie au fessier', in *Le Quotidien de Paris*, 10 April 1992.

Routier, Airy, *La République des Loups: Le Pouvoir et les Affaires*, Calmann-Lévy, Paris, 1989.

Sadoun, Marc, *De la démocratie française*, Gallimard, Paris, 1993.

de Saint-Pulgent, Maryvonne, *Le Syndrome de l'Opéra*, Robert Laffont, Accords, Paris, 1991.

Schneider, Robert, *La haine tranquille*, Seuil, Paris, 1992.

Schweisguth, Etienne, 'Les avatars de la dimension gauche-droite', in *Mars 1986, La Drôle de Défaite de la Gauche*, dir. Elisabeth Dupoirer et Gérard Grunberg, Paris PUF, 1986.

Sirinelli, Jean-François, *Histoire des droites en France*, 3 vols, Gallimard, Paris, 1993.

Slama, Alain-Gérard, *L'angélisme exterminateur, essai sur l'ordre moral contemporain*, Grasset, Paris, 1993.

Steiner, George, 'Aspects of Counter-Revolution', in Best, Geoffrey, ed., *The Permanent Revolution: the French Revolution and its Legacy 1789–1989*, 2nd ed., Fontana, 1989.

Sternhell, Zéev, *Ni droite, ni gauche, l'idéologie fasciste en France*, Editions Complexe, Paris, 1987.

Sternhell, Zéev, *La droite révolutionnaire, les origines françaises du fascisme*, Editions du Seuil, Paris, 1978.

Suleiman, Ezra, *Les Hauts Fonctionnaires et la politique*, Seuil, Paris, 1976.

Suleiman, Ezra, *Les Élites en France, grands corps et grandes ecoles*, Seuil, Paris, 1979.

Tenzer, Nicolas, 'François Mitterrand ou le pouvoir vain' in *Le Débat*, September–October 1993.

Thatcher, Margaret, *The Downing Street Years*, Harper Collins, London, 1993.

Tombs, Robert, 'The Dark Years', in *Times Literary Supplement*, 28 January 1994.

Tournoux, J.-R., *Pétain et de Gaulle*, Plon, Paris, 1964.

Vallance, Georges, *France-Allemagne, Le Retour de Bismarck*, Flammarion, Paris, 1990.

Vallet, Odon, *L'École ou la vanité considerée comme un mode de gouvernement*, Albin Michel, Paris, 1991.

Vernet, Daniel, *La renaissance allemande*, Flammarion, Paris, 1992.

Viansson-Ponté, Pierre, *Lettre ouverte aux hommes politiques*, Albin Michel, Paris, 1976.

Villeneuve, Charles *Les liaisons dangereuses de Pierre Bérégovoy: enquête sur la mort d'un premier ministre*, Plon, Paris, 1993.

Wacquandt, Loic, 'Banlieues françaises et ghetto noir américain: de l'amalgame à la comparaison', in *French Politics and Society*, Vol. 10, Number 4, autumn 1992.

Weber, Eugen, *My France: Politics, Culture, Myth*, Cambridge, Massachusetts, 1991.

Weber, Eugen, *L'Action Française*, Fayard, Paris, 1962.

Winock, Michel, *Nationalisme, antisémitisme et fascisme en France*, Editions du Seuil, Paris, 1990.

Young, Arthur, *Travels in France and Italy during the years 1787, 1788 and 1789*, J. M. Dent (Everyman), London, originally published 1792.

Zarka, Jean-Claude, *Fonction présidentielle et problématique majorité presidentielle-majorité parlementaire sous la 5e République, 1986–1992*, Paris, 1992.

Zorgbibe, Charles, *De Gaulle, Mitterrand, et l'esprit de la constitution*, Hachette, Paris, 1993.

Index